Owning Ideas

Owning Ideas is a comprehensive account of the emergence of the concept of intellectual property in the United States during the long nineteenth century. In the modern information era, intellectual property has become a central economic and cultural phenomenon and an important lever for allocating wealth and power. This book uncovers the intellectual origins of this modern concept of private property in ideas through a close study of its emergence within the two most important areas of this field: patent and copyright. By placing the development of legal concepts within their social context, this study reconstructs the radical transformation of the idea. Our modern notion of owning ideas, it argues, came into being when the ideals of eighteenth-century possessive individualism at the heart of early patent and copyright were subjected to the forces and ideology of late nineteenth-century corporate liberalism.

OREN BRACHA is a professor of law at the University of Texas School of Law. He is one of the leading scholars of the history of Anglo-American intellectual property. He has published extensively in the fields of intellectual property law and legal history.

Cambridge Historical Studies in American Law and Society

Recognizing legal history's growing importance and influence, the goal of this series is to chart legal history's continuing development by publishing innovative scholarship across the discipline's broadening range of perspectives and subjects. It encourages empirically creative works that take legal history into unexplored subject areas, or that fundamentally revise our thinking about familiar topics; it also encourages methodologically innovative works that bring new disciplinary perspectives and techniques to the historical analysis of legal subjects.

Series Editor

Christopher Tomlins, *University of California, Berkeley*

Previously Published in the Series:

Anna Leah Fidelis T. Castañeda Anastacio, *The Foundations of the Modern Philippine State: Imperial Rule and the American Constitutional Tradition in the Philippine Islands, 1898–1935*

Anne Twitty, *Before Dred Scott: Slavery and Legal Culture in the American Confluence, 1787–1857*

Robert Deal, *The Law of the Whale Hunt: Dispute Resolution, Property Law, and American Whalers, 1780–1880*

Sandra F. Vanburkleo, *Gender Remade: Citizenship, Suffrage, and Public Power in the New Northwest, 1879–1912*

Reuel Schiller, *Forging Rivals: Race, Class, Law, and the Collapse of Postwar Liberalism*

Ely Aaronson, *From Slave Abuse to Hate Crime: The Criminalization of Racial Violence in American History*

Stuart Chinn, *Recalibrating Reform: The Limits of Political Change*

Ajay K. Mehrotra, *Making the Modern American Fiscal State*

Yvonne Pitts, *Family, Law, and Inheritance in America: A Social and Legal History of Nineteenth-Century Kentucky*

David M. Rabban, *Law's History*

Kunal M. Parker, *Common Law, History, and Democracy in America, 1790–1900*

Steven Wilf, *Law's Imagined Republic*

James D. Schmidt, *Industrial Violence and the Legal Origins of Child Labor*

Rebecca M. McLennan, *The Crisis of Imprisonment: Protest, Politics, and the Making of the American Penal State, 1776–1941*

Tony A. Freyer, *Antitrust and Global Capitalism, 1930–2004*

Davison Douglas, *Jim Crow Moves North*

Andrew Wender Cohen, *The Racketeer's Progress*

Michael Willrich, City of Courts, *Socializing Justice in Progressive Era Chicago*

Barbara Young Welke, *Recasting American Liberty: Gender, Law and the Railroad Revolution, 1865–1920*

Michael Vorenberg, *Final Freedom: The Civil War, the Abolition of Slavery, and the Thirteenth Amendment*

Robert J. Steinfeld, *Coercion, Contract, and Free Labor in Nineteenth Century America*

David M. Rabban, *Free Speech in Its Forgotten Years*

Jenny Wahl, *The Bondsman's Burden: An Economic Analysis of the Common Law of Southern Slavery*

Michael Grossberg, *A Judgment for Solomon: The d'Hauteville Case and Legal Experience in the Antebellum South*

Owning Ideas

The Intellectual Origins of American Intellectual Property, 1790–1909

OREN BRACHA

University of Texas, Austin

CAMBRIDGE
UNIVERSITY PRESS

CAMBRIDGE
UNIVERSITY PRESS

University Printing House, Cambridge CB2 8BS, United Kingdom

One Liberty Plaza, 20th Floor, New York, NY 10006, USA

477 Williamstown Road, Port Melbourne, VIC 3207, Australia

314-321, 3rd Floor, Plot 3, Splendor Forum, Jasola District Centre, New Delhi - 110025, India

79 Anson Road, #06-04/06, Singapore 079906

Cambridge University Press is part of the University of Cambridge.

It furthers the University's mission by disseminating knowledge in the pursuit of education, learning and research at the highest international levels of excellence.

www.cambridge.org
Information on this title: www.cambridge.org/9781108790697

© Oren Bracha 2016

First published 2016
First paperback edition 2019

A catalogue record for this publication is available from the British Library

Library of Congress Cataloging in Publication data
Names: Bracha, Oren, author.
Title: Owning ideas : the intellectual origins of American intellectual property, 1790-1909 / Oren Bracha.
Description: New York : Cambridge University Press, 2016. | Series: Cambridge historical studies in american law and society | Includes bibliographical references and index.
Identifiers: LCCN 2016039094 | ISBN 9780521877664 (hardback)
Subjects: LCSH: Intellectual property–United States–History. | Copyright–United States–History.
Classification: LCC KF2979 .B66 2016 | DDC 346.7304/809034–dc23 LC record available at https://lccn.loc.gov/2016039094

ISBN 978-0-521-87766-4 Hardback
ISBN 978-1-108-79069-7 Paperback

Contents

Acknowledgments

When a book has been in the making for as long as this one, its author accumulates many debts. It is a pleasure to acknowledge some of them here. My greatest debt, intellectual and otherwise, is to Morton Horwitz, Terry Fisher, and Duncan Kennedy. Each of them helped shape my intellectual agenda and persona in ways that pervade this project and go well beyond it. The marks left by their influence, guidance, and example are evident in this book. Ron Harris has been another major source of formative influence and support. I am grateful to him for setting me on the path that led to this work and for his early encouragement and guidance.

I was able to engage in the demanding and lengthy research underlying this work thanks to the unwavering and generous support of the University of Texas School of Law. Even more important than the institution were the people making it. I have benefited greatly from interaction and conversations with many of my colleagues. The most sustained and material contributions to this project were made by Willy Forbath, David Rabban, and John Golden, who devoted their effort, time, knowledge, and wisdom to reading this work and suggesting ways of improving it. I have also benefited from the work and insight of many other scholars, too numerous to mention. Although they may not be aware of it, Lionel Bently, Ronan Deazley, Catherine Fisk, Mark Rose, and Talha Syed were particularly influential in shaping my thought about the themes discussed in this book.

I am grateful to the helpful and knowledgeable staff of the National Archives and to the devoted librarians of the University of Texas School of Law Library, who valiantly assisted my efforts to locate many obscure sources. Claire Gherini and Megan Wren supplied devoted and diligent research assistance. Chris Tomlins deserves special thanks for his guidance and encouragement as editor and for not losing faith.

The largest share of my gratitude is given to Tammy Sheffer-Bracha. This project has been our constant companion for many years, from well before our daughter was born. Without her patience, sacrifice, and support it would have not seen the light of day. This work is dedicated to her.

Introduction

Intellectual property is all around us. We have grown so accustomed to the idea that it is easy to forget how strange it is. But it is strange. Glossy brochures of the World Intellectual Property Organization may tell us that intellectual property rights are like any other property right. Learned law professors may patiently explain that there is no reason why property rights should not apply to intangible resources. No matter. When one thinks about it, the concept of owning an intangible product of the mind is strange and exotic. What does it mean to own an idea? How did we come to think and speak this way about this increasingly important part of our economic, cultural, and social life? This is what this book is about.

One starting point for answering these questions is the notion of expansion. In 1918 Justice Louis Brandeis wrote: "The general rule of law is, that the noblest of human productions – knowledge, truths ascertained, conceptions, and ideas – become, after voluntary communication to others, free as the air to common use."[1] When Brandeis wrote those words, intellectual property rights had already grown in coverage and strength beyond what anyone could have imagined a century earlier. Today intellectual property rights have expanded further, most likely well beyond what Brandeis could have imagined. Exclusive legal rights have been asserted (with a varying degree of success) in an astonishing range of intangibles, including yoga sequences, methods of playing golf, a system for hedging investment risk, genetic sequences, and the appearance of a street performer dressed as a mostly naked cowboy, to name just a few

---

[1] *International News Service v. Associated Press*, 248 U.S. 215, 250 (1918).

recent examples. One is tempted to wonder whether we have crossed the line where Brandeis's rule flips and the freedom to use ideas becomes the exception. James Boyle has dubbed this process the second enclosure movement, the intellectual resources equivalent of the eighteenth-century English process in which open land used in common was converted into tightly controlled private property.[2]

If we are in the midst of a second enclosure movement – whether it started in recent decades as some seem to think or has been unfolding for centuries – what could explain it? The immediate suspects are technology and economics. Much of the wealth in our society is in the form of informational resources of the kind covered by intellectual property rights, rather than land or other tangibles. This raises the stakes of private control of these intangible sources of wealth through intellectual property rights. Historically, technological development fueled this process. New technology gave rise to new valuable intellectual resources – anything from an innovative industrial process to motion pictures – and helped create markets for their exploitation. For better or worse, this resulted in increased private demand and public interest in the legal mechanisms for controlling and allocating the value of these resources. This narrative explains much. But it leaves out another powerful factor, namely ideas. The expansion of intellectual property rights is the result not only of technological development and economic demand but also of a specific set of ideas. Over the last three centuries our culture has developed a unique ideology that gives meaning to the notion of owning ideas. While deeply influenced by technology and economics, this ideology was not merely their intellectual reflection. Ideas about ownership of intangibles have exerted their own semi-autonomous force in interaction with those other factors. They form the intellectual origins of the second enclosure movement.

Some of the history of the modern ideology of owning intangibles in England and the Continent has been thoroughly explored, especially in the context of copyright. In a nutshell, the practices and regulations out of which intellectual property grew existed at least since the fifteenth century. They were not seen, however, as either "intellectual" or "property." While certain entitlements existed in regard to technology-related economic activities and later book publishing, they were not understood as ownership of an intangible object. New ideas of ownership

---

[2] James Boyle, "The Second Enclosure Movement and the Construction of the Public Domain," 66 *Law Contemp. Probs.* 33 (2003).

of property rights in the intellectual product of one's mind began to appear around the early eighteenth century. By the end of the century, the ideological foundations of both patents and copyright had been transformed. Both fields came to be dominated by a version of possessive individualism applied to intellectual creation. At the heart of this new construct stood the individual – either author or inventor – who through his mental labor creates new ideas. This individual was now seen as the owner of his intellectual creation.

When the American copyright and patent regimes were created in the last two decades of the century, this new framework was already well established. It is tempting, therefore, to think about the modern authorship-ownership framework as embedded in the DNA of the American intellectual property system. Following this assumption one may envision the tremendous growth of American intellectual property since the modest beginnings of the 1780s as a natural and necessary unfolding of this inceptive genetic code. To be sure, technology developed, new markets opened up, and vast new opportunities for commercializing information appeared. But the process was one of extending the original authorship-based model of intellectual property to new domains, perfecting its tenets and adapting it to new circumstances. It was nothing of the sort. The nineteenth century was a crucial formative era for intellectual property. New elements that were anything but natural extensions of the original authorship ideology developed and became central within intellectual property law and its underlying conceptual foundation. And yet the constitutive image of the authorial owner refused to depart. Even as individual authorship disappeared from the law (or failed to appear in the first place), its Cheshire cat smile kept hovering over it. Sometimes it exerted real force, at other times it elicited mere lip service, and in yet others it took perverse forms. What emerged early in the twentieth century, after a gradual but profound process of change, was a thoroughly new intellectual framework. This book examines the development of this modern framework of intellectual property in the context of the two oldest and most important branches of the field: patent and copyright.

At the end of the eighteenth century the fields of patent and copyright were in a state of deep transition. To an extent, each of the fields reflected its new official understanding as a universal regime of creators' property rights in the product of their minds. In important respects, however, they retained many of their former features. In essence, the traditional privileges of publishers and entrepreneurs were universalized and bestowed on authors and inventors. In the following century this basic framework was subjected to various pressures: the claims of economic interests, competing ideological commitments, and new social conditions. The end result of this process was a new conceptual synthesis of ownership of ideas.

Was there a general pattern? Recent accounts suggest that a major theme of nineteenth-century American intellectual property was "the democratization of invention."[3] According to these accounts invention was democratized in the sense that hard-to-obtain privileges, bestowed sparingly on a small elite, were supplanted by generally accessible, universal rights. Procedural and substantive barriers to entry were lowered. Patents and copyrights became available to all on satisfaction of standardized general criteria designed to maximize the public benefits of the regime. The result was the harnessing of the creative energy of a broad swath of technological and cultural innovators who could enjoy some of the social value of their innovation through property rights. There is much truth to this account. Around the middle of the nineteenth century invention was indeed democratized in America. So was incorporation. The structural similarity between the democratization of invention and the rise of incorporation as a generally available form of doing business is striking. The latter story, however, has familiar later chapters. By the end of the nineteenth century the "democratization" of incorporation brought about the incorporation of America. Numerous individuals and small firms continued to rely on the useful mechanism of the corporation, but the period's most important and enduring phenomenon was the rise of big business. Democratization was followed by enormous concentration of wealth and power in a new market dominated by large, hierarchical private organizations. Something similar happened with the democratization of invention. In the late nineteenth century, "democratized" intellectual property rights became important tools for big business, and their form was adapted to the new corporate environment. The eighteenth-century individualism of authorial ownership met corporate liberalism. What emerged was a new synthesis. Authorship became authorship incorporated.

As happened in other contexts, the official individualist image of the field was not discarded by the new framework of authorship incorporated. Even as important aspects of intellectual property rights came to rest

---

[3] B. Zorina Khan, *The Democratization of Invention: Patents and Copyrights in American Economic Development, 1790–1920* (Cambridge: Cambridge University Press, 2005).

on other premises, the constitutive myth of the field remained that of the individual author or inventor who owns the product of his or her mind. This resulted in a variety of curious legal and conceptual forms. Some elements of the intellectual framework of owning ideas were simply underdetermined or open to a wide range of interpretations under the abstract authorial ownership construct. For example, the premise that authors and inventors own their intellectual creation left ample room for maneuver on the questions of what it was exactly that was owned and what it meant to own it. Here it was a variety of other ideological and economic forces that shaped the concrete meaning of owning ideas. In other contexts official authorship ideology came into direct conflict with other powerful influences. The assumption of strong originality as the hallmark of the genius creator, for example, clashed both with economic demands for broad availability of intellectual property rights and with a new prevalent image of intellectual commodities whose value is determined by the market alone. The result of such conflict was intricate ideological concepts embodying contradictory assumptions as well as mechanisms for mediating these contradictions.

What emerged at the dawn of the twentieth century was a new ideological scheme for giving meaning to the idea of intellectual property. Its anatomy was roughly as follows. One set of concepts constituted the creator-owner entitled to property rights by defining the essential qualities of this figure. Another cluster of ideas applied to what was being owned. It created a concept of an intangible object to which legal rights applied. A third and related group of ideas gave meaning to the notion of owning an intellectual object. These ideas defined the relationship between the owner and others in regard to the postulated intangible object.

The book is organized around this structure of meaning in its copyright and patent variants. Chapter 1 lays down the foundation for understanding the legal and conceptual transformations of the nineteenth century by explaining the background of the English, colonial, and state origins of American intellectual property law. It shows how at the eve of creating the federal regimes the practices of copyright and patent were already grounded in a new abstract ideology of authorship and yet lacked a well-developed framework of owning ideas along the three dimensions described above.

Chapters 2 and 4 focus on the concept of the genius creator in its copyright and patent iterations: the author and the inventor. In each of these fields the abstract defining feature of authors – intellectual creation – was instantiated in specific institutional arrangements. These arrangements revolved around a focal organizing notion: originality in copyright and the inventive faculty in patent. In this way each field developed its own version of the image of the individual creator and placed it at its ideological center. At the same time, each field radically limited the practical significance of the ideological image, often containing concrete rules at direct odds with it. In this way by the end of the nineteenth century intellectual property law became caught in a paradox. It was all about original authorship and had little to do with it. One aspect of elaborating the concept of authorship related to the nature of the claim of the individual author on the state. In both patent and copyright there emerged a particular understanding of these claims as "rights" rather than "privileges." Whether intellectual property rights were philosophically grounded in natural rights or public utility, they acquired the institutional form of universal entitlements open to all and accompanied by a duty of the state to grant and enforce them on a formally equal basis.

Chapters 3 and 5 follow the development of the idea of an intangible object of property and of the meaning of ownership in such an object in the fields of copyright and patent respectively. A preliminary question about the ownership of intangibles pertains to the identity of the owner. The answer seems to follow inevitably from the grounding of the field in individual authorship: the owner is the author who created the intangible through his or her mental powers. In the second half of the nineteenth century, however, the principle of authorial ownership came under increasing pressure from economic interests who trumpeted the "necessity" of shifting ownership away from individual creators. The result was a complex array of rules that in some contexts – most importantly that of employment – deprived creators of the status of owners. There also emerged a set of techniques for managing the tension between these rules and the ideological principle of authorial authorship.

Another aspect of owning intangibles related to the object being owned. In traditional property law one could point at a concrete physical object of property – a plot of land or a piece of jewelry. The physicality of property grounded ownership in a graspable phenomenon: a seemingly natural connection between the owner and the owned based on physical possession. It also endowed the object of property with clear physical boundaries that supposedly defined the scope of the legal right in an objective manner. The lack of physicality thus posed a serious challenge once the idea of intellectual property was taken seriously and had to be translated into concrete rules and practices. The initial response was to create a construct of a semi-materialist object of ownership, at once intangible and endowed with qualities equivalent to those of owned physical objects. This construct was embodied in the concept of the "copy" in copyright and that of the mechanical design in patent. Each of those presented the object of ownership as an intellectual template capable of producing an endless series of identical material embodiments. Gradually, however, both fields developed a very different notion of the intangible owned object that relied on a distinction between essential essence and ephemeral form. The "work" in copyright and the "invention" in patent were reimagined as elusive intellectual essences capable of manifestation in numerous concrete forms.

This was exactly the point where the concept of the object of property interfaced with that of ownership. If the traditional idea of ownership was based on being able to exclude others from physical intrusion on the object of property, what did it mean to own an intangible? At first, it meant having the power to prevent others from making and selling exact physical reproductions of the original. Gradually, however, ownership came to mean something very different. Intellectual works or inventions came to be seen as intellectual commodities with potential value in numerous possible markets. Ownership became the right to internalize this market value by controlling the markets for all the concrete embodiments of the intellectual essence. Potential markets defined the broad scope of the intellectual object of ownership, which in turn defined relevant markets. A corollary set of new principles, such as copyright's distinction between ideas and expressions or the rule against patents in natural principles, defined the outer boundaries of ownership. These principles managed the rising tension between the broadening sweep of the new concept of ownership and a widespread anxiety over private ownership of knowledge.

All of this sounds very metaphysical, but the new ideological framework of owning ideas had very concrete implications. It is this underlying framework that explains the intellectual stakes in the central jurisprudential debates of nineteenth-century intellectual property law such as the American common law copyright debate or patent's battle over the ownership of principles. These debates were fueled by competing economic claims on the developing intellectual property system. What gave them concrete meaning and shaped their form, however, was the emerging ideology of owning intangibles. Even more important, this ideology helped shape actual legal institutions with specific real-world implications. Whether it was invoked explicitly or, as happened more often, was simply latent in legal rules and reasoning, it gave meaning and coherence to a particular way of thinking about intellectual property rights and implementing them. It was this intellectual framework, for example, that explains why in the late nineteenth century it became self-evident that a translation was copyright infringement, while half a century earlier the prevalent view was that it was not because it was not a "copy." It also sheds light, to take another example, on how late-nineteenth-century jurists could define the patent scope on increasing levels of abstraction, insisting all along that all "knowledge" remained free. Last but not least, the new intellectual framework of intellectual property played an important role in reshaping the general understanding of property. Early in the nineteenth century the intellectual challenge faced by jurists was fitting the new strange creature of owning intangibles into a familiar framework of property. By the dawn of the twentieth century the new legal constructs developed in this effort came to shed new light on the general idea of property itself. They helped abstract the concept of property and detach it from a necessary connection to any physical relationship. To modern eyes property came to be seen as an abstract legal relationship among people allocating control over the value of any possible resource. Property, in other words, assumed its modern meaning within which intellectual property seems unremarkable.

How does one go about thinking about the profound change of intellectual property during the long nineteenth century? There are many ways. This book is an intellectual history. It is premised on the assumption that ideas are important as a motivating force in human history, rather than being just echoes of economic or social developments. Accordingly the focus of the book is the development of ideas about intellectual property. To be sure, such ideas did not develop in a closed intellectual sphere. Systems of ideas are shaped in interaction with social and economic practices. In this work discussions of social, economic and technological developments are limited. They appear at the background as the necessary context for understanding the development of ideas.

Furthermore, this is an intellectual history written, so to speak, from the top down rather than from below. It is concerned with the official, public ideology of owning ideas. While this work locates this ideology in institutional and social context, it is not a close study of the social practices through which it was implemented and given meaning in the lives and actions of specific individuals. This means that the primary sources on which this work draws are mainly of the formal and highly intellectualized sort: legal treatises, appellate court opinions, Supreme Court briefs, and newspaper articles. The dangers of this sort of approach are known. It risks producing a stylized version of ideas far removed from social reality that has little to do with the concrete experiences of actual historical actors. There are also advantages, however. Concentrating on these sources allows widening the lens and capturing a broad image of the framework of owning ideas. This framework played an important role in constructing specific, practical experiences of intellectual property. It is painfully obvious that intellectual property is a constructed human concept. Treatise writers, judges writing opinions, and lawyers crafting legal arguments were those who most directly and explicitly wrestled with the conceptual challenges of owning ideas. There is a good reason to assume, however, that the concepts they manufactured diffused beyond the limited sphere of professional, abstract writing, not because most inventors or authors spent their time reading legal treatises, but owing to various agents of transmission. The new ideology of owning ideas was embedded in operative legal rules and concepts. Intellectual property is an area where the rules matter a great deal in shaping everyday practices. Patent agents drafting patents, lawyers counseling clients and later holding top positions in corporations, and even the semi-professional and general press all acted as intermediaries. These agents were in the business of going back and forth between the intellectualized sources of law and ideology and the messy work of building and maintaining the plumbing of commercial, technological, and political life. In doing so they converted the abstract ideology of owning ideas into concrete practices and arguments, thereby spreading it beyond the small mandarin circle where it was created. Specific studies of these intermediaries and the social practices of intellectual property, both existing and future ones, are sure to refine, enrich, and correct the sort of bird's-eye image of intellectual property ideology offered here. Hopefully they will also benefit from it.

Studying the history of intellectual property as intellectual history gives rise to another question not explored closely here but worth commenting on briefly. Social and economic forces shape ideas. Specifically, this work makes frequent references to the influence of economic interests on legal rules and the concepts underlying them. But what was the causal mechanism? How were laws and ideas embedded in them shaped by economic interests? In many cases there was no mystery involved. Large parts of intellectual property law, especially copyright, were reshaped through legislation. Here the familiar dynamics of interest group politics was at work. Lobbying is woven into the history of American intellectual property from the travels of Noah Webster designed to spur state legislatures and later Congress into action to late-nineteenth-century campaigns orchestrated by trade associations. Other crucial aspects of the transformation of intellectual property unfolded mainly through litigation. Adjudication works differently from legislation. But it has its own mechanisms that allow influence, sometimes disproportionate influence, of economic power on the outcome of the process. These include superior legal representation and other systemic advantages of repeat players such as the ability to strategize and play for the rules. In some areas changing social circumstances made the demands of dominant economic interests, whether pursued through lobbying or litigation, seem natural or even necessary. For example, the shift to production of many technological and expressive innovations in centralized, corporate settings made employee–creators seem as subordinate wage-laborers rather than genius authors. This made employers' claim for ownership of their employees' intellectual product both natural and easier to accept. Similarly, the increasingly sophisticated ways in which publishers developed and exploited secondary markets for books, such as the ones for translations, created a sense that it was "necessary" for copyright to cover these secondary markets. And then there was also the feedback loop of ideas. Once certain ways of thinking about intellectual property got a foothold they tended to have a cumulative effect, paving the way for the next wave of claims. The photography industry, for instance, had to overcome many obstacles before its product was fully accepted as a standard area within the coverage of copyright. Motion pictures had a much easier time. It was both because clever lawyers managed to squeeze film into the technical legal category of photographs and, more important, because photography's struggle for recognition already established the conceptual foundation for unshackling copyright from its traditional print-bound orientation. Causation, in other words, ran both ways. Economic interests and their demands shaped ideas. But it was also the case that ideas shaped economic interests and their interaction with making and manipulating the law. While the primary focus of this work is ideas, I also hope to highlight this dynamic and how it produced the modern intellectual framework of intellectual property.

One other theme that runs through this work is the dialectic of change through constancy. Two methodological concepts from two intellectual traditions usually seen as being a world apart capture the premise of this theme. The first is path dependence. Path dependence refers to the phenomenon of past actions constraining subsequent ones even when the circumstances that motivated them are no longer relevant. A classic example is the persistence of the QWERTY layout in computer keyboards even when the need to minimize the mechanical jamming of frequently used typewriter keys had perished. The second is the often misunderstood concept of bricolage. Social systems of meaning, Claude Levi-Strauss argued, often retain traces of their former logic even after social circumstances forced them to change.[4] In this sense they are much like the bricoleur who builds new things from preexisting objects whose purposes and shapes constrain the design of the new apparatus. The ideological framework of owning ideas was created by path-dependent bricoleurs. As it developed the framework was changed to accommodate new ideas and social demands. The adaptation was done, however, by reconfiguring and rearranging preexisting ideas and institutional forms. Over a long period the changes were significant, even radical. But at each point in time the law and ideology of intellectual property incorporated much of the ideas and institutions forged earlier under different circumstances. This is why elements of the earlier printer and entrepreneur trade privileges are clearly visible in the 1790 authorship-based copyright and patent regimes. It is also why many important late-nineteenth-century legal concepts in the field seem to have deep roots extending all the way back to eighteenth-century English law.

It is for the same reason that understanding the early intellectual framework of owning ideas as it crystallized by the beginning of the twentieth century is crucial for understanding the present dynamics of intellectual property. It is this framework of authorship incorporated, this mélange of eighteenth-century possessive individualism and late-nineteenth-century corporate liberalism that forms the intellectual origins of the second enclosure movement. Much has changed in the law of intellectual property and the socioeconomic circumstances surrounding it since the ending point of the survey offered here. And yet the fundamental and constitutive assumptions of contemporary intellectual property thought are still rooted, to a large extent, in these century-old origins, even if some of the circumstances that produced them have changed. It is my hope that exploring these origins can shed some light on our present understanding of intellectual property and the forces that shaped it.

---

[4] Claud Lévi-Strauss, *The Savage Mind* (Chicago, IL: University of Chicago Press, 1966).

I

The Origins of the American Intellectual
Property Regime

When Americans created their first national patent and copyright regimes
in 1790 they were not writing on a clean slate. They were immersed in two
rich intellectual and institutional traditions. The first tradition was English:
the centuries-old practice of royal patent privileges and the copyright
regime under the 1710 statute of Anne.[1] The other was closer to home.
It consisted of an amalgam of legislative practices and limited statutory
arrangements used in various times in some of the North American British
colonies and later in the states. Uncovering the meaning of the early
American patent and copyright framework requires understanding its
relation to these two sources of influence. The new American regime was
at once innovative and deeply rooted in the past. It relied heavily on
familiar forms and institutions, while introducing some innovations. Even
the novel elements, however, were mostly rearrangements of traditional
practices or continuations of institutional development processes that had
begun earlier. Thus, before looking more closely at the synthesis of 1790,
some elaboration of its English, colonial, and state origins is needed.

   The brief survey of centuries of institutional development offered here
reveals two dominant patterns of change. The first is a gradual transition
from ad hoc discretionary privileges to general regimes of universal rights.
The second involves reconceptualization of the substance of the relevant
entitlements. It consists of a shift from an understanding of patents and
copyrights as exclusive entitlements of exercising certain economic activities
to a conception of ownership of intangible objects. Both of those processes

[1] 8 Ann. c. 19.

were incomplete at the end of the eighteenth century. The 1790 American patent and copyright regimes were created at a historical moment of flux and ambiguity in regard to these two crucial dimensions. The arrangements created by these regimes and the concepts employed by them reflected their transitory character as links between the old intellectual universe of trade privileges and the modern conceptual world of intellectual property.

INTELLECTUAL PROPERTY: RIGHTS IN INTANGIBLES

"[I]ntellectual property, the labors of the mind, productions and interests," wrote Justice Levi Woodbury in 1845, is "as much a man's own, and as much the fruit of his honest industry, as the wheat he cultivates, or the flocks he rears."[2] This captures the essence of the modern concept of "intellectual property," the overarching category whose two most pedigreed members are patent and copyright. Woodbury conveyed the two distinguishing features of this concept: the sense of a universal entitlement as a matter of right and the attachment of this entitlement to an abstract intellectual "object" – ideas, information, or the product of the mind. Both of these features require some elaboration.

Under the modern intellectual property scheme patents and copyrights are viewed and practiced as universal rights. This is a basic feature shared by the various modern strands of thought about intellectual property rights. Whether patents and copyrights are seen as natural rights or as positivist entitlements, whether they are justified on the basis of utilitarian reasons, notions of moral desert or some other ground, all modern observers implicitly assume a common institutional model: that of universal rights. Under this scheme patents and copyrights are governed by universal legal norms of general applicability. These norms define a standard set of formal and substantive criteria for legal protection and identify the persons entitled for such protection. The norms also create a uniform set of entitlements and powers enjoyed by the owners of the entitlements. Finally and most important, the relation between the criteria for protection and the protected entitlements is automatic. Whenever the standard criteria are met, the person identified by the legal norms as the owner is entitled to enjoy the uniform entitlements as *a matter of right*. This means that relevant governmental organs, the U.S. Patent and Trademark Office, or the courts, for example, must recognize and enforce

---

[2] *Davoll v. Brown*, 7 F. Cas. 197, 199 (C.C.D. Mass. 1845).

the entitlements as defined by the general legal norms. These government organs may have some discretion in the process of interpreting the norms and determining their application to specific fact situations, but the moment it is determined that the general requirements for protection apply to a specific case, the owner has a right to demand enforcement and the state organ has a duty to comply.[3]

Just as important, modern patents and copyrights are seen as rights in intangible objects. In other words, observers and practitioners postulate an abstraction, an intangible entity that forms the point of reference for legal protection. Modern lawyers use two terms of art to designate this abstraction: the "work" and the "invention." Within intellectual property discourse, unlike colloquial usage, these terms refer to an intangible intellectual entity that is distinct from any physical object. In this sense, copyright protects rights in creative works of authorship, and patents apply to inventions. Various conceptual and legal mechanisms are employed to define these elusive abstractions and to demarcate their "borders." The specifics of these mechanisms may be contested, but all participants in the modern discourse of intellectual property share the general postulation of an intangible, informational entity that stands at the heart of the legal entitlements.[4]

The sixteenth-century origins of Anglo-American patent and copyright had neither of these two features. They were not seen and practiced as universal rights or as entitlements in intangible objects. In this sense, early patents and copyrights were neither "intellectual" nor "property." By the end of the eighteenth century, after two centuries of evolution, some of the elements of the modern intellectual and institutional framework began to appear. There occurred a conceptual shift toward regarding patents and copyrights as entitlements in intangible objects. To a lesser extent, the universal right form began to displace the ad hoc privilege. Circa 1800, however, these new features were still embryonic. In many respects Americans had not yet created a firm, well-developed conceptual and institutional framework of patents and copyrights as general rights in intangible objects. Much of the invention of "intellectual property" was to unfold during the following century.

---

[3] See Oren Bracha, "The Commodification of Patents 1600–1836: How Patents Became Rights and Why We Should Care," 38 *Loy. L.A. L. Rev.* 177, 181–83 (2004).

[4] Oren Bracha, "Owning Ideas: A History of Anglo-American Intellectual Property," S.J.D. diss., Harvard University (2005), 1–2. For a similar, though not identical argument, see Brad Sherman and Lionel Bently, *The Making of Modern Intellectual Property Law: The British Experience, 1760–1911* (New York: Cambridge University Press, 1999), 47–50.

PATENTS: ENGLISH ORIGINS

Modern patents originated in administrative practices of granting exclusive economic privileges, which probably first appeared in some of the Italian republics during the fifteenth century,[5] and later spread to other parts of Europe.[6] The direct source of American patents was the English version of these practices. Although there were antecedents in England,[7] the rise of extensive and systematic use of patents for invention there occurred in the late sixteenth century[8] during the reign of Elizabeth I and

---

[5] See Max Frumkin, "The Origin of Patents," 27 *J. Pat Off. Soc'y* 143 (1945); Ramon A. Klitzke, "Historical Background of the English Patent Law," 41 *J. Pat Off. Soc'y* 615, 616–21 (1959); Giulio Mandich, "Venetian Patents (1450–1550)," 30 *J. Pat Off. Soc'y* 166 (1948); Giulio Mandich, "Venetian Origins of Inventors' Rights," 42 *J. Pat Off. Soc'y* 378 (1960); Frank D. Prager, "A History of Intellectual Property from 1545 to 1787," 26 *J. Pat Off. Soc'y* 711 (1944); Frank D. Prager, "The Early Growth and Influence of Intellectual Property," 34 *J. Pat Off. Soc'y* 750 (1952); Edward C. Walterscheid, "The Early Evolution of the United States Patent Law: Antecedents," pt. 1, 76 *J. Pat Off. Soc'y* 697, 705–15 (1994); Pamela O. Long, *Openness, Secrecy and Authorship: Technical Arts and the Culture of Knowledge from Antiquity to the Renaissance* (Baltimore, Md.: Johns Hopkins University Press, 2001), 93–101.

[6] G. Doorman, *Patents for Inventions in the Netherlands during the 16th, 17th and 18th Centuries* (The Hague: M. Nijhoff, 1942); L. Hilarie-Perez, "Invention and the State in 18th Century France," 32 *Technology and Culture* 911 (1991); H. Pohlman, "The Inventor's Right in Early German Law," 43 *J. Pat Off. Soc'y* 121 (1961).

[7] There were a few incidents of grants of patents for invention prior to Elizabeth's reign. The earliest one known is probably the 1331 grant by Edward III to John Kempe for cloth making (Pat. 5 Edw. III p. I, m. 25). For a survey of early grants, see E. Wyndham Hulme, "The History of the Patent System under the Prerogative and at Common Law," 12 *L.Q.R.* 141–44 (1896); Harold G. Fox, *Monopolies and Patents: A Study of the History and Future of the Patent Monopoly* (Toronto: University of Toronto Press, 1947), 43–54. The early grants, however, were "letters of protection." This means that they lacked any element of exclusivity or a monopoly bestowed on the grantee. These letters of protection provided to foreigners the "King's protection" and a license to practice their trade in spite of guild and other restrictions. Klitzke compared these early grants to passports. Klitzke, "Historical Background," 624.

[8] Historians disagree which was the first "genuine" patent for invention in England. See Moureen Coulter, *Property in Ideas: The Patent Question in Mid-Victorian Britain* (Kirksville, Mo.: Thomas Jefferson Press, 1990), 9. Two patent grants that preceded Elizabeth but already took the standard form of the monopoly patent grant for invention were Smyth's 1552 patent for Normandy glass making under Edward VI and the Burchart Crancick 1554 mining patent under Queen Mary. See Fox, *Monopolies and Patents*, 60–61. Gomme points to a 1449 patent granted to John of Utynam that included twenty-year protection for the making of colored glass. Arthur A. Gomme, *Patents of Invention: Origin and Growth of the Patent System in Britain* (New York: Longmans Green, 1946), 6. Others point to Jacopo Aconio's 1565 patent for various machines as the first true patent. See Lyn White Jr., "Jacopo Aconcio as an Engineer," 72 *Am. Hist. Rev.* 2 (1967); Hulme, "History of the Patent System" (1896), 148, 151. See in general Klitzke, "Historical Background," 626–31.

under a focused policy introduced by her first Secretary of State, William Cecil (Lord Burghley).[9] Early English patents were very different from modern patents in respect to the two dimensions discussed above: the character of the entitlement and its object of reference.

The most important feature of English patents was being creatures of the royal prerogative. William Blackstone's relatively late and often-quoted description captured this character of patents. The king's grants, Blackstone wrote, "whether of lands, honours, liberties, franchises or ought besides are contained in charters, or letters patent that is, open letters, litterae patentae, so called because they are not sealed up, but exposed to open view."[10] Patents for invention were at first a completely undifferentiated category of dispensing royal policy through open letters granting various privileges. A unique, semi-independent category of invention patents was only gradually carved out with the emergence of the common law, the Statute of Monopolies framework, and much later a statutory patent regime. There were two significant, interlocking features to early patent grants. First, the grant was completely discretionary. No person, no matter how meritorious his case seemed, had a "right" to receive a patent, correlated by a duty to grant. It was, rather, within the discretionary power of the Crown and its organs to consider each case and make a specific policy decision of whether and under which conditions to grant a patent. Consequently, patents were granted on an ad hoc basis. There existed neither a general law of patents nor uniform practices or precedents followed by royal authorities. Each case was treated on its own terms, and similar cases could produce very different outcomes. Second, while sharing typical general forms, patents were highly tailored arrangements. Each grant was seen as a unique "deal" between the Crown and the grantee under which the parties exchanged case-specific "considerations." Individual patents were customized on both ends of this deal. Both the consideration given by the patentee

---

The debate over the first "genuine" patent for invention is somewhat anachronistic. The arguments revolve around the question of which patent was granted for a "genuine" invention in the modern sense. This focus tends to obscure the most significant fact, which is that the term "invention" did not yet acquire its modern meaning and was applied indiscriminately to different instances of introduction of new trades and industries.

[9] Fifty-five patents for inventions were issued during the reign of Elizabeth. Twenty-one of them were issued to foreigners. See E. Wyndham Hulme, "The History of the Patent System under the Prerogative and in Common Law: A Sequel," 16 *L.Q.R.* 44, 52 (1900).

[10] William Blackstone, *Commentaries on the Laws of England* (Oxford: Clarendon Press, 1766), vol. 2, 346.

and the privileges bestowed by the monarch varied from case to case and were subject to case-specific stipulations.[11]

These features of the patent privilege were embedded in a host of institutional characteristics of the grant practice. Patentees had to petition the Crown, plead for specific privileges and offer convincing reasons why the Crown should use its discretion to grant such privileges. Petitions contained recitals of utility. Though later degenerated into mere formalities, early recitals promised concrete and tangible benefits to the Crown and the public, ranging from the supply of a scarce commodity to the strengthening of the realm's defense.[12] When patents were granted, they often included special stipulations, including specifications of price, quality, or quantity of goods, and apprenticeship clauses that required the training of local apprentices.[13] Very common were "working clauses" that required, under a penalty of nullification, putting the invention into practice within a prescribed period.[14] The privileges granted by patents exhibited the same ad hoc discretionary quality. Individual privileges contained very different specific terms, such as varying duration, geographical limitations, definitions of the protected exclusive activity, and tailored exemptions from guild restrictions or other regulations.[15] Patent grant and revocation procedures completed this pattern. Patents were not granted on demand, but rather required a complex petition procedure that in the early period involved genuine substantive consideration by royal organs of

[11] Bracha, "Commodification of Patents," 183–91; Edward C. Walterscheid, "The Early Evolution of the United States Patent Law: Antecedents," pt. 2, 76 *J. Pat Off. Soc'y* 849, 859 (1994); Edward C. Walterscheid, "The Early Evolution of the United States Patent Law: Antecedents," pt. 4, 78 *J. Pat Off. Soc'y* 77, 91 (1996); Christine MacLeod, *Inventing the Industrial Revolution: The English Patent System 1660–1800* (New York: Cambridge University Press, 1988), 12.
[12] D. Seaborne Davies, "Early History of the Patent Specification," pt. 1, 50 *L.Q.R.* 88, 98 (1934); E. Wyndham Hulme, "On the Consideration of the Patent Grant Past and Present," 13 *L.Q.R.* 313, 315 (1897). For a survey of the changing character of the public benefits promised by patentees from the middle of the seventeenth century to the late eighteenth century, see McLeod, *Inventing the Industrial Revolution*, 158–81.
[13] For a general survey, see Bracha, "Owning Ideas," 17–20. See also Walterscheid, "Early Evolution," pt. 2, 857–58; Hulme, "History of the Patent System" (1896), 145–47; Klitzke, "Historical Background," 639–40; Davies, "Early History of the Patent," 104.
[14] See Hulme, "History of the Patent System" (1896), 143; Hulme, "On the Consideration of the Patent Grant," 313–14; Davies, "Early History of the Patent Specification," 97–98; Walterscheid, "Early Evolution," pt. 2, 856–57.
[15] Bracha, "Commodification of Patents," 187–88; Hulme, "History of the Patent System" (1900), 44–51; Hulme, "History of the Patent System" (1896), 145–50.

the effect and desirability of each grant.[16] Similarly, patents were subject to revocation procedures, usually conducted by the Privy Council. These revocation procedures often turned into policy debates about the public consequences and justifications of specific grants and allowed broad ex post discretion to the Crown.[17] All of these institutional features expressed and reproduced patents' nature as discretionary, ad hoc, and tailored privileges.

Just as important, early invention patents, despite the term, were based on a conception of invention thoroughly different from the modern one. Patents were seen neither as entitlements in informational entities nor as necessarily involving technological innovation. The consideration given by the patentee and the subject matter of his entitlements were seen in more dynamic terms. Patents for invention, inasmuch as they were distinguished from other patents, were thought and spoken of in terms of a policy strategy used to nourish and support the development of the English economy by encouraging the introduction of new industries or trades. The patentee offered to introduce an actual useful economic activity and received the exclusive right to exercise that activity. Thus, many invention patents established monopolies in activities such as the manufacture of a particular kind of glass, the production of salt or soap, or the weaving of a certain kind of cloth.[18] It was common that patents, such as the one granting the privilege "to take large fish ... called Bottled-nosed Whales ... in the North and South Seas,"[19] did not involve any new technological innovation or discovery.

Even when in the early seventeenth century new common law thinking about monopolies began to stress novelty as an essential element of lawful patents, the relevant frame of reference was the introduction of a new

[16] MacLeod, *Inventing the Industrial Revolution*, 12; Fox, *Monopolies and Patents*, 67–68; Walterscheid, "Early Evolution," pt. 2, 862; Davies, "Early History of the Patent Specification," 106.

[17] Bracha, "Commodification of Patents," 189–91; E. Wyndham Hulme, "Privy Council Law and Practice of Letters Patent for Invention from the Restoration to 1794," 33 L.Q.R. 63, 181 (1917); Davies, "Early History of the Patent Specification," 102–4; Hulme, "On the Consideration of the Patent Grant," 313–15.

[18] McLeod, *Inventing the Industrial Revolution*, 13; Davies, "Early History of the Patent Specification," 95–97.

[19] Davies, "Early History of the Patent Specification," 97. Davies referred to a 1707 patent mentioned in instructions to the Law Officers. MacLeod called such grants "heterodox uses" of patents, but the important point is exactly that at the time they were not conceived of as "heterodox." MacLeod, *Inventing the Industrial Revolution*, 81. See also Walterscheid, "Early Evolution," pt. 4, 79.

trade to the realm, rather than the disclosure of information, discoveries, or technological innovation.[20] To be sure, some patents did involve technological innovations and sometimes there were concerns about preserving technological knowledge. These were, however, unessential background elements. The focal concept was the introduction of a trade. Even when a technological development was present, patent grants were not usually designed to protect only the new technological innovation itself. The term "invention" encompassed indiscriminately development of new technology and introduction by way of importation of existing known technology, knowledge, or skilled workers.[21] Similarly, as expressed by patents' working clauses, revocation procedures, and other stipulations, the focus of the grant was not disclosure of information by patentees, but rather the performance in practice of some activity or service, deemed as publicly desirable: the manufacture of certain goods, the supply of some service, and so on. Both the patentee's entitlements and the basis of his grant were defined not in terms of technologically innovative information, but rather on the basis of practicing a useful trade or art.[22]

The early-seventeenth-century common law patent decisions and the 1624 Statute of Monopolies hold a special status in traditional patent history. These two developments are depicted as a moment of sharp break with the past when an abusive and corrupt royal grant practice gave way before a public interest–oriented regime, and the modern Anglo-American patent system was born.[23] More recent accounts acknowledge that the common law decisions and the statute created neither a sharp break with the past nor an early version of the modern institutional form of patents.[24] Far from being the dividing line between the early patent practices and the modern framework, both early common law and the Statute of Monopolies entrenched the conceptual scheme of patents as discretionary trade privileges. These two institutional developments were

---

[20] Hulme, "On the Consideration of the Patent," 313–14; Bracha, "Owning Ideas," 36–39.
[21] In Hulme's words, under such a concept "the rights of the inventor are derived from those of the importer and not vice-versa." Hulme, "History of the Patent System" (1896), 152. See also Hulme, "History of the Patent System" (1900), 53; Walterscheid, "Early Evolution," pt. 1, 870.
[22] See Edgar A.G. Johnson, "The Mercantilist Concept of 'Art' and 'Ingenious Labour,'" 2 *Econ. Hist.* 234 (1930–33).
[23] See e.g. Fox, *Monopolies and Patents*, 92–112; Klitzke, "Historical Background."
[24] See e.g. Chris R. Kyle, "'But a new button to an old coat': The Enactment of the Statute of Monopolies, 21 James I cap. 3," 19 *J. Legal. Hist.* 203, 210 (1988); McLeod, *Inventing the Industrial Revolution*, 17–18.

deeply rooted in the political battles and the ideological discourse of seventeenth-century England. They were part of the struggle between absolutist monarchists and their opponents, who strove to limit monarchical power and shift some of it to competing institutions such as parliament and the common law courts.[25] The attack on "odious" royal monopolies was a major part of the challenge to royal prerogative power.[26] During the early seventeenth century it gave rise to a fundamental distinction between bad or unlawful monopolies and good monopolies. The common law decisions and the Statute of Monopolies were part of this pattern. They outlawed most royal monopoly grants while recognizing exceptions: monopoly grants that served the public good and therefore were lawful. Patents for invention were one of these exceptions that with time developed to be the most important category.[27]

Although patents for invention were at first only a collateral issue, the common law developments and the Statute of Monopolies had two important implications within this field. First, invention patents were beginning to emerge as a differentiated category of grants. Second, royal discretionary power that was previously formally unchecked was subjected to some restrictions. The most important restrictions in the patents for invention context were: the principle that lawful patents could extend only to new inventions, and limiting the duration of patents to a maximum of fourteen years.[28] Beyond these two important implications the

---

[25] Bracha, "Commodification of Patents," 191–200; J.P. Sommerville, *Royalists and Patriots: Politics and Ideology in England, 1603–1640*, 2nd ed. (New York: Longman, 1999); J.P. Sommerville, "The Ancient Constitution Reassessed: The Common Law, the Court and the Languages of Politics in Early Modern England," in R. Malcolm Smuts, ed., *The Stuart Court and Europe: Essays in Politics and Political Culture* (New York: Cambridge University Press, 1996).

[26] Fox, *Monopolies and Patents*, 92–112; Mark Kishlansky, *A Monarchy Transformed: Britain, 1603–1714* (London: Penguin, 1996), 98–100; McLeod, *Inventing the Industrial Revolution*, 14–17.

[27] The main common law decisions that established this framework were *Devanant v. Hurdis* (the Merchant Tailor's Case), 72 Eng. Rep. 769 (K.B. 1599); *Darcy v. Allen*, 74 Eng. Rep. 1131 (K.B. 1602), 77 Eng. Rep 1260 (K.B. 1603); and *Cloth Workers of Ipswich*, 78 Eng. Rep. 147 (K.B. 1615). These decisions did not directly involve invention patents. Invention patents were referred to in the decisions as hypothetical examples of monopoly grants that under certain circumstances could be lawful. Section I of the Statute of Monopolies created a general ban on monopolies. Section VI of the statute, which was added late in the legislative process, exempted invention patents from the ban, subject to several conditions; 21 Jac. 1, c. 3. For an account of the legislative history, see Kyle, "'But a new button to an old coat,'" 208, 214.

[28] The novelty requirement was part of both the common law and the Statute of Monopolies. The maximal duration of fourteen years was imposed by the statute.

statute/common law structure incorporated and entrenched the existing framework of patents. No general patent regime or system was created. The statute's later role as the foundation of the English patent system was, in Christine MacLeod's words, "a curious side effect a quirk of history."[29] The focus of the new framework was not patent rights, but rather the liberties of Englishmen to be free from abusive monopolies. While subjected to external limitations that forbade unlawful monopolies, within the lawful zone the prerogative grant power remained as discretionary as ever. No universal patent rights were created, and grants were still issued on an ad hoc discretionary basis.[30] Similarly, despite the gradual creation of the category of patents for invention, the defining element of these grants remained not technologically innovative information but rather the exercise of a useful trade.[31] The authoritative commentary by Edward Coke in his *Institutes of the Laws of England* and the sparse common law decisions of the seventeenth century adhered to this basic framework of patents.[32]

The period stretching between the late seventeenth century and the end of the eighteenth century was characterized by a growing gap between formal legal concepts and actual practice. During this time the ways people and state authorities talked about patents and practiced related administrative procedures gradually and subtly changed. Until the late eighteenth century, however, formal legal concepts remained impervious to the change, still embodying the old conceptual orthodoxy. Only in the last decades of the century did the changes on the level of practice begin to percolate up and transform formal conceptions.

As for the character of patents as particularistic privileges, there occurred almost no formal change. Well into the nineteenth century patents were still issued as ad hoc royal discretionary privileges under

---

Edward Coke in his authoritative and influential commentary on the Statute of Monopolies identified seven requirements for a lawful invention patent. Edward Coke, *The Third Part of the Institutes of the Laws of England* (London: E. and R. Brooke, 1797), 184. For a detailed elaboration of Coke's commentary on the statute, see Walterscheid, "Early Evolution," pt. 2, 876–80; McLeod, *Inventing the Industrial Revolution*, 18–19.

[29] MacLeod, *Inventing the Industrial Revolution*, 15. See also Coulter, *Property in Ideas*, 13. The first legislative attempt to create a specific statutory framework for patents of invention was enacted only in 1835. It was the Patents Act, 1835, 5 & 6 Will. 4, c. 83, that dealt mainly with minor procedural reforms. Numerous successful and unsuccessful attempts of legislative reform occurred during the second half of the century.

[30] Bracha, "Commodification of Patents," 198. [31] Bracha, "Owning Ideas," 38–39.

[32] Coke, *Institutes*, 184. For elaboration, see Bracha, "Owning Ideas," 49–50.

the common law and Statute of Monopolies scheme.[33] The official legal position remained firmly entrenched: patents are granted as a matter of "grace and favour"[34] by the king and there exists "no right to demand a patent."[35] In practice, however, a gradual process eroded the character of patents as privileges. Since the late seventeenth century growing governmental disinterest caused increasing standardization.[36] Obtaining a patent involved a complicated and expensive bureaucratic procedure,[37] but, apart from exceptional cases, increasingly similar patent grants were issued as a matter of routine with little substantive discretion or investigation.[38] During the second half of the eighteenth century ex post discretionary procedures faded too. Privy Council patent revocation proceedings atrophied and eventually disappeared.[39] In addition there appeared new ideological strands of thought that began to conceptualize patents in terms of property rights and natural rights.[40] Often such views conflated indistinguishably new notions of rights and traditional concepts of privileges,[41] but late in the eighteenth century there appeared some

---

[33] Walterscheid, "Early Evolution," pt. 4, 92; Bracha, "Commodification of Patents," 201.

[34] W.A. Hindmarch, *Treatise Relating to the Law of Patent Privileges for the Sole Use of Inventions* (London: V. & R. Stevens and G.S. Norton and W. Benning, 1847), 3–4. See also *Ex parte O'Reily*, 30 Eng. Rep. 256 (Ch. 1790).

[35] The influential commentator Richard Godson included in his 1823 treatise on patent law a section entitled "No Right to Demand Patent." Richard Godson, *Law of Patents for Inventions and Copyright* (London: J. Butterworth and Son, 1823), 47.

[36] McLeod, *Inventing the Industrial Revolution*, 20–39; Fox, *Monopolies and Patents*, 154–56.

[37] See Coulter, *Property in Ideas*, 16–18; McLeod, *Inventing the Industrial Revolution*, 40.

[38] McLeod, *Inventing the Industrial Revolution*, 41, 42, 47; Bracha, "Commodification of Patents," 202–3.

[39] The exact time of the decline of Privy Council jurisdiction over patents is hard to locate. E.W. Hulme claimed that the Council divested itself of its power over patents in a dramatic 1753 case. Hulme, "Privy Council Law and Practice," 193–94. Yet Hulme's own account, as well as those of other scholars, describes later Privy Council patent proceedings. See id., 191–93; Davies, "Early History of the Patent Specification," 103. Legal commentators continued to refer to Privy Council power to revoke patents well into the nineteenth century, although in the later period it was acknowledged that such power was not recently used. Although the issue is somewhat obscured, it seems that Privy Council jurisdiction over patents, rather than being revoked in one dramatic moment, gradually declined and faded away toward the end of the eighteenth century. See Bracha, "Commodification of Patents," 204–6.

[40] See Adam Mossoff, "Rethinking the Development of Patents: An Intellectual History, 1550–1800," 52 *Hastings L. J.* 1255 (2001); McLeod, *Inventing the Industrial Revolution*, 199.

[41] Bracha, "Commodification of Patents," 206–7.

clearer voices that called for patents as standardized universal entitlements protected as a matter of right.[42]

The concept of invention underwent a similar process of gradual and incomplete transformation. Since the late seventeenth century the focus of invention patents on the introduction of new trades began to decline. Technological innovation gradually moved to the center and eventually became one of the main defining elements of patents.[43] By the mid-eighteenth century it became clear within the grant practices that the subject matter of invention patents was technological discoveries or developments. In 1776 this process received the belated imprimatur of formal law when Lord Mansfield overturned in *Morris v. Bramson*[44] the longstanding common law rule against patents in "mere improvements."[45] In the new intellectual climate in which technological innovation superseded the introduction of a trade as the constitutive element of invention, the notion that mere improvements could not be patented lost coherence.

Partly overlapping was the rise of the informational concept of invention that first emerged out of the administrative practices of patents and later found its way into formal legal thinking. Specifications – detailed written descriptions of the relevant technological innovation – appeared sporadically in seventeenth-century grants.[46] In the eighteenth

---

[42] Id., 207–8.
[43] Bracha, "Owning Ideas," 63–66. About the emerging nexus between technological innovation, entrepreneurship, and state patronage during the eighteenth century, see A.J.G. Cummings and Larry Stewart, "The Case of the Eighteenth Century Projector: Entrepreneurs, Engineers, and Legitimacy at the Hanoverian Court," in Bruce T. Moran, ed., *Patronage and Institutions: Science Technology and Medicine at the European Court, 1500–1750* (Rochester, N.Y.: Boydell Press, 1991).
[44] The case is unreported. It is known mainly from Justice Buller's reference to it in *Boulton & Watt v. Bull*, 126 Eng. Rep. 651, 664 (C.P. 1795).
[45] In the *Institutes* Coke famously explained that creating technological improvements was "but to put a new button on an old coat" and therefore did not merit a patent. Coke, *Institutes*, 183. The controlling precedents for this rule, that were regularly cited until the late eighteenth century, were the Mathey and the Bricot cases, probably decided late in the sixteenth century. None of these cases was reported. Bricot's case was decided in the Exchequer Chamber and is known mainly from Coke's reference. Mathey's case was decided in the Privy Council and involved a patent for manufacture of knives with a new kind of hafts. It is known from the reported argument in *Darcy v. Allen*. See 74 Eng. Rep. 1131.
[46] See MacLeod, *Inventing the Industrial Revolution*, 49; See also Edward C. Walterscheid, "The Early Evolution of the United States Patent Law: Antecedents," pt. 3, 77 *J. Pat. Off. Soc'y* 771, 783–85 (1991); Hulme, "On the Consideration of the Patent Grant," 315; Klitzke, "Early Background," 647.

century the specification became more common and eventually it was institutionalized as a mandatory, though somewhat ambiguous and flexible, requirement.[47] Gradually and ambiguously at first, disclosure of technological information was coming to be seen as the consideration given by the patentee in the patent deal in exchange for legal protection and also as an "object" that defined and demarcated legal protection.[48] Formal recognition and conceptualization arrived again in the last decades of the century. In a series of decisions in the 1760s and 1770s, most famously *Liardet v. Johnson*,[49] Mansfield introduced a new framework for understanding the patent deal under which the patentee exchanged the information disclosed in the specification in return for the patent's exclusive entitlements.[50] A decade later this became the new doctrinal orthodoxy of patent law.[51]

Around the same time, English jurists were beginning to describe patents as rights in intangible, informational objects. During the 1790s, in landmark cases such as *Boulton and Watt v. Bull*[52] these jurists were only beginning to grapple with the conceptual and practical difficulties of

---

[47] Hulme, "On the Consideration of the Patent Grant," 316; Walterscheid, "Early Evolution," pt. 3, 786–92; Coulter, *Property in Ideas*, 15; MacLeod, *Inventing the Industrial Revolution*, 49–51; John N. Adams and Gwen Averley, "The Patent Specification: The Role of *Liardet v. Johnson*," 7 *J. Legal Hist.* 156, 160 (1986); Erick Robinson, "James Watt and the Law of Patents," 13 *Technology and Culture* 115, 125 (1972).

[48] Bracha, "Owning Ideas," 168–69; Walterscheid, "Early Evolution," pt. 3, 792.

[49] There were two separate trials, neither of which was officially reported. Information on the cases is based mainly on newspaper reports. Reports of the first trial were published in the *Morning Post* and *Daily Advertiser* on February 23, 1778, and in the *London Chronicle* and *Daily Advertiser* on February 24, 1778. The *Morning Post* report is reproduced fully by Hulme. See E. Wyndham Hulme, "On the History of Patent Law in the Seventeenth and Eighteenth Centuries," 18 *L.Q.R.* 280, 283–84 (1902). Reports of the second trial were published in the *Morning Post*, *Gazeteer* and the *New Daily Advertiser* on July 20, 1778. A short summary that misstates the outcome exists in 1 Carp. P.C. 35. For surveys of the proceedings, see Adams and Averley, "Patent Specification," 162–65; Walterscheid, "Early Evolution," pt. 3, 793.

[50] It was recently discovered that Mansfield made some references to his new theory of the patent consideration prior to *Liardet v. Johnson*. These earlier, unreported cases were summarized in Mansfield's notebooks discovered in 1967. They are *Yerbury v. Wallace* (1768); *Taylor v. Suckett* (1770); and *Horton v. Harvey* (1781). See John Adams, "Intellectual Property Cases in Lord Mansfield's Court Notebooks," 8 *J. Legal Hist.* 18 (1987); James Oldham, *The Mansfield Manuscripts and the Growth of English Law in the Eighteenth Century* (Chapel Hill: University of North Carolina Press, 1992), vol. 1, 762.

[51] *Turner v. Winter*, 99 Eng. Rep. 1274, 1276 (K.B. 1787); *Boulton and Watt v. Bull*, 126 Eng. Rep. 651, 656 (C.P. 1795).

[52] 126 Eng. Rep. 656.

this new concept. Elaborating the implications of the new informational concept of patents for issues such as patentable subject matter or the scope of protection would last well into the nineteenth century.[53]

At the end of the eighteenth century the conceptual and institutional framework of English patents was in the midst of a paradigmatic shift. The traditional ad hoc privilege structure had eroded in practice for more than a century, but no firm and clear replacement took its place either in the bureaucratic practices or in formal legal thought. Despite new ideological and reform-minded voices, most jurists continued to express the privilege orthodoxy. New concepts of the invention that focused on technological innovation and depicted inventions as informational entities had appeared. Yet judges and practitioners were grappling to come to terms with these new concepts and were only beginning to pour concrete meaning into them.

COLONIAL AND STATE PATENTS

Beginning in the seventeenth century, the North American British colonies and later the American states developed a local version of the English patent grant.[54] Colonial patents were sporadic and were not granted in all the colonies.[55] The general framework of colonial patents was identical to that of English grants. As in England, colonial grants had two defining features: their character as discretionary ad hoc grants and an understanding of the object of rights as the exercise of an economic activity. At the same time the different material, ideological, and political conditions in the colonies resulted in specific administrative and institutional features that were unique to colonial grants. Moreover, the various

---

[53] See Bracha, "Owning Ideas," 72–88.

[54] About colonial patents, see Bruce W. Bugbee, *The Genesis of American Patent and Copyright Law* (Washington, D.C.: Public Affairs Press, 1967), 57–83; P.J. Federico, "Colonial Monopolies and Patents," 11 *J. Pat. Off. Soc'y* 358 (1929); E.B. Inlow, "The Patent Grant," 67(2) *John Hopkins University Studies in Political Science* 36–43 (1949). Edward C. Walterscheid, "To Promote the Progress of Science and Useful Arts: The Background and Origin of the Intellectual Property Clause of the United States Constitution," 2 *J. Intell. Prop. L.* 1, 14–17 (1994). The term "patent" is a misnomer when applied to grants made by colonial legislatures. As explained, Letters Patent was the technical term designating one of the forms of the royal prerogative exercised by the Crown and its agents. Nevertheless contemporaries sometimes used this misnomer.

[55] Walterscheid assesses that the total number of patents issued in the colonies that became the United States did not exceed fifty. The problems of exact quantification of colonial patents arise mainly from the absence of adequate records. See Walterscheid, "To Promote the Progress of Science," 15.

developments that gradually changed English patents in the seventeenth and eighteenth centuries were mostly absent or appeared only partially in the colonies and the states.

As in England, colonial patents were ad hoc, discretionary, and tailored privileges. Unlike England, however, the grants were issued as individual enactments by colonial legislatures. No coherent law or standard bureaucratic procedures governing patent grants developed during this period. Patent grants that bestowed on individuals exclusive privileges to engage in certain economic activities were one of many measures, such as subsidies, loans, or exemptions, employed by colonial legislatures[56] pursuing what they saw as the governmental duty of actively promoting the public good in the economic as well as all other social spheres. Each patent constituted a specific deal between the patentee and the colony. The patentee promised to supply a specific service or perform a useful activity such as the manufacture of a product of certain quality or the operation of a mill. In return the patentee received tailored, time-limited, exclusive privileges. Colonial patents often included working clauses that stipulated the privileges on practicing the invention. Sometimes there were stipulations of quality and price of the relevant product or service, as well as apprentice clauses that required training local apprentices. The exact terms of the privileges and their duration varied greatly from one grant to the other.[57]

Like their English cousins, colonial patents were based on a unique concept of invention. At the heart of this concept was not technologically innovative information but rather the exercise in practice of a publicly useful trade or art. The dominating figure in the grants was not the inventor in the modern sense but rather a combination of the economic entrepreneur and the artisan. Discoveries or technological innovation were neither an essential nor a defining element of colonial patents. An exclusive grant for operating a new machine was not categorically different from grants to the operators of mills, ferries, or docks. Similarly, as expressed by the ubiquity of working clauses, the emphasis of patents was not on disclosing information but rather on practicing the useful

---

[56] J. McCusker and Russel R. Menard, *The Economy of British America 1607–1789* (Chapel Hill: University of North Carolina Press, 2nd ed. 1991), 96, 343; Federico, "Colonial Monopolies," 360; Bugbee, *Genesis of American Patent and Copyright Law*, 57.

[57] Bracha, "Commodification of Patents," 213.

activity. Most colonial patents, whether or not new technology was involved, were "manufacturing" or "service" patents.[58]

Most of the processes that gradually transformed patent practices in England during the seventeenth and eighteenth centuries were almost completely absent in the colonies. The political struggle that engulfed England and produced the Statute of Monopolies and the common law framework was felt only as faint echoes in the colonies, at least in this context. Interestingly, some colonies such as Massachusetts and Connecticut legislated much diluted versions of the Statute of Monopolies.[59] These were, however, toothless declaratory measures. Unlike the English scheme, these colonial statutes did not attempt to check the granting authority or to transfer power to other institutional players. Neither statutory nor common law relating to patent grants developed in the colonies. In the absence of these normative sources the legislative grant power remained discretionary and unbound, free even from the external boundaries imposed in England on the royal prerogative power by the Statute of Monopolies and the common law. Similarly, the colonies did not experience a process of standardization of the grant procedures. Since colonial patents involved a legislative process rather than a bureaucratic apparatus, no dynamics of standardization developed. Periods of governmental disinterest in patents resulted in the absence of grants rather than, as happened in England, in their issuance on demand. Perhaps related to the absence of a standardized bureaucratic procedure, no specification or similar requirement of written disclosure appeared in colonial America. Apart from two failed, limited attempts in 1744 to legislate a rudimentary version of a general patent regime in South Carolina,[60] these trends persisted throughout the colonial period. By the Revolution, American patents were still completely discretionary and ad hoc legislative measures that dispensed

---

[58] Oren Bracha, "Geniuses and Owners: The Construction of Inventors and the Emergence of American Intellectual Property," in Daniel W. Hamilton and Alfred L. Brophy, eds., *Transformations in American Legal History: Essays in Honor of Professor Morton J. Horwitz* (Cambridge, Mass.: Harvard Law School, 2009), 372.

[59] "The Body of Liberties – 1641; A Copie of the Liberties of the Massachusetts Colonie in New England," in William Henry Whitmore, *The Colonial Laws of Massachusetts, Reprinted from the Edition of 1660, with the Supplement to 1672* (Boston: Rockwell and Churchill, 1889), clause 9, 34–35; Roger Ludlow, *The Laws of Connecticut: An Exact Reprint of the Original Edition of 1673*, ed. George Brinley (Hartford, 1865), 52.

[60] J.H. Easterby, ed., *Journal of the Commons House of Assembly, February 20 1744 – May 25, 1745* (Columbia: South Carolina Archives Dept., 1955), 245. See Bugbee, *Genesis of American Patent and Copyright Law*, 80–81.

state patronage in the form of exclusive entitlements to pursue certain useful economic activities.

Between independence and 1790, in the absence of a national patent system, grant activity occurred at the state level. While some of the young states experienced an upsurge of patent grants, no sharp break with colonial practices had occurred. Patents were still issued as ad hoc legislative enactments. Nevertheless, during this time a few embryonic developments, foreshadowing future changes, started to appear. One of those developments was the emergence of modern patent ideology. Starting in the late colonial era and intensifying after independence, there appeared a stream of utterances justifying the award of patents on general policy grounds of two kinds. The first ground was that of rewarding inventors for their useful services and mental labor with a just desert, or in the words of the Pennsylvania legislature: to "provide suitable recompense for those who, by their own expense, ingenuity or dint of application have made new and useful discoveries."[61] The other ground was a utilitarian-incentive argument premised on the need "to encourage useful inventions."[62] At this stage, however, both of these arguments remained justifications of ad hoc patent grants, rather than reasons for a general regime or for patent rights.

The states developed neither general patent regimes nor standardized legal or bureaucratic frameworks for issuing patents. South Carolina supplied, again, the partial exception to this rule. In 1784 the state created what is sometimes referred to as the first general patent act in America. It was, in fact, a provision in the newly enacted copyright law of the state providing that "the Inventors of useful machines shall have a like exclusive privilege of making or vending their machines for the like terms of fourteen years, under the same privileges and restrictions hereby granted to, and imposed on authors of books."[63] The South Carolina statute was an important landmark that signaled the changing understanding of patents, but the partial sources available show that it was not a decisive move to a general regime of universal patent rights. Despite its sweeping declaration about the entitlement of inventors, the statute did not create

---

[61] James T. Mitchell et al., eds., *Statutes at Large of Pennsylvania from 1682 to 1801* (Harrisburg: W.M. Stanely Ray, state printer of Pennsylvania, 1904), vol. 10, 131–32.

[62] This language appeared in the preamble of Maryland's 1787 grant to Robert Lemmon. See William Kilty, ed., *Laws of Maryland* (Annapolis, Md.: Frederick Green, 1799–1800), vol. 2, session of November 6, 1786–January 20, 1787.

[63] *Acts, Ordinances, and Resolves of the General Assembly of the State of South Carolina, Passed in the Year 1784* (Charleston, S.C.: Printed by J. Miller, 1784), 51.

any procedure or apparatus for issuing patents. It seems that after 1784 patents in South Carolina were still granted on a particularistic basis of specific petitions and legislation.[64] Thus the statute's significance was mainly declaratory, and possibly in introducing some standardization to subsequent South Carolina grants.[65]

More significant changes took place in regard to the concept of invention. Technological innovation gradually moved to the fore and became the defining element of patents for invention as a distinct category of grants. Around the time of the Revolution, technology increasingly captured the American mind and came to be seen as the key for prosperity and progress.[66] Growing public interest in the nation's struggle for technology diffusion from Britain and other European nations[67] and the proliferation of societies for the promotion of useful arts[68] contributed to the rise of technological awareness. Increasingly, invention patents were primarily identified with an effort to encourage technological innovation. Many of the state grants and the related discussions in state legislatures came to rest on the premise that technological innovation is the essence of invention and pointed to the "inventors of useful machines" as the proper recipients of patents.[69]

Somewhat more ambivalently, patentees came to be identified with inventors in the modern sense. To invent increasingly meant in this context the intellectual activity of creating or discovering new, useful ideas. The inventor was gradually distinguished from the artisan and the entrepreneur, and recast in the image of an intellectual genius who

---

[64] For examples of such grants, see Bugbee, *Genesis of American Patent and Copyright Law*, 93–95. One commentator observed that "in practice this section only operated as an invitation to inventors to request the legislature for patents." P.J. Federico, "State Patents," 13 *J. Pat. Off. Soc'y* 166, 167 (1931).

[65] Later patent grants in South Carolina generally adhered to a standard fourteen-year term.

[66] Hugo A. Meier, "American Technology and the Nineteenth Century World," 10 *Am. Quart.* 117 (1958); John F. Kassen, *Civilizing the Machine: Technology and Republican Values in America, 1776–1900* (New York: Grossman, 1976), 1–21; Jennifer Clark, "The American Image of Technology from the Revolution to 1840," 39 *Am. Quart.* 431 (1987).

[67] Doron S. Ben-Atar, *Trade Secrets: Intellectual Piracy and the Origins of American Industrial Power* (New Haven, Conn.: Yale University Press, 2004), 34–43; Kassen, *Civilizing the Machine*, 8–11.

[68] Ben-Atar, *Trade Secrets*, 93–103; Neil Longley York, *Mechanical Metamorphosis: Technological Change in Revolutionary America* (Westport, Conn.: Greenwood Press, 1985), 163–71.

[69] See e.g. the 1785 Pennsylvania patent grant to Arthur Donaldson for his "hippopotamus" dredging machine. See *Statutes at Large of Pennsylvania*, vol. 11, 412–15.

creates new ideas. A growing number of grants exhibited concern about this new meaning of invention by incorporating clauses that voided the patent if the patentee was not "the true and original" inventor.[70] The shift, however, was not complete. Traditional and new concepts of invention coexisted for a while. Thus, for example, in 1788 the Pennsylvania Society for the Encouragement of Manufacture and the Useful Arts praised the state legislature for issuing a monetary prize to Joseph Hague. Hague, breaking British technology-transfer restrictions, managed to smuggle a cotton-carding machine into the state. The society referred to Hague as "the ingenious Artizan, who counterfeited the Carding and Spinning Machine, though not the original inventor (being only the introducer)."[71] The "artizan" and the "introducer" were already relegated to a lower status compared with the "original inventor." Yet "counterfeiting" was still seen as both laudable and worthy of reward.

There were also signs of a new informational concept of invention both conceptually and within administrative practices. The patentee's invention – the consideration given by him in the patent deal and the referent of his exclusive entitlements – came to be identified with an abstract intellectual "object." The clearest indication of this change was the appearance in some grants of a rudimentary version of the specification, a requirement for deposit of a written description of the invention.[72] The common stated reason for written description requirements was to inform others of the exact coverage of the patent's exclusive privileges.[73] Yet latent in these practices was an emerging concept of the invention as an abstract, informational object. At least on one occasion, there appeared the notion that

---

[70] See e.g. the 1789 Pennsylvania grant to Robert Leslie and the 1787 Maryland patent to Robert Lemmon that were stipulated on the grantee being the true and original inventor. See *Statutes at Large of Pennsylvania*, vol. 12, 309–12; *Laws of Maryland*, vol. 2, session of November 6, 1786–January 20, 1787. See also the priority concerns around competing attempts to obtain state patents for steamboat innovations. Edward C. Walterscheid, "Priority of Invention: How the United States Came to Have a 'First-to-Invent' Patent System," 23 *AIPLA.Q.J.* 263, 269–80 (1995). The term "true and first Inventor" appeared in the 1624 Statute of Monopolies. However, it was only late in the eighteenth century that the term and its variations came to have the modern meaning of an independent developer or discoverer of new innovations.

[71] Cited in Ben-Atar, *Trade Secrets*, 79–80.

[72] See Bugbee, *Genesis of American Patent and Copyright Law*, 86–88; Bracha, "Owning Ideas," 114–15.

[73] For example, Peter Belin's 1784 South Carolina patent required him to deposit with the Secretary of the State plans or models of his devices in order to "prevent any person from pleading ignorance." Thomas Cooper and David J. McCord, eds., *The Statutes at Large of South Carolina* (Columbia, S.C.: A.S. Johnston, 1836–41), vol. 4, 755–56.

the consideration given by the patentee was "enabling" the public to use the invention by disclosing information about it.[74] Interestingly, some grants expressed the transitory character of patent thought during this period by including both working clauses and specification requirements.[75] In the absence of a body of patent law or standard bureaucratic procedures, the changing concept of invention remained obscure and unarticulated.

Ironically, at the eve of creating the national regime, the local American version of patent grants was closer to its English ancestors than were contemporary British patents. State patents, despite sporadic indications of change, were still issued on an ad hoc basis as discretionary grants of privileges by the sovereign. There appeared no standardized legal or administrative framework to govern patents. Patents came to be identified with technological innovation and patentees were increasingly seen as inventors in the modern sense. There were also the first signs of conceptualizing the invention as an abstract, informational object and patents as rights to control such information. But there appeared neither a clear and firm articulation of the new concept of invention nor attempts to elaborate the legal implications of such a concept. In short, by 1789 the intellectual framework of American patents, like that of their English cousins, was in a state of flux. It was as much rooted in the old paradigm as it was showing the first signs of change.

COPYRIGHT: ENGLISH ORIGINS

Like patents, copyright originated in practices that appeared first in the Italian republics and spread throughout Europe.[76] Although the

---

[74] Pennsylvania's grant to Henry Guest explained the requirement as follows: "in order that no person may unknowingly offend and that all after the expiration of the term of five years may be enabled to prosecute the said manufactures to their own advantage." *Statutes at Large of Pennsylvania*, vol. 10, 133.

[75] The Pennsylvania and New York grants to Henry Guest had such a dual requirement. See id.; *Laws of the State of New York* (Albany, N.Y.: Weed Parsons, 1886–87), vol. 1, 278.

[76] About the early origins of copyright in Venice and other Italian republics, see Bugbee, *Genesis of American Patent and Copyright Law*, 43–48; Brian Richardson, *Printing, Writers and Readers in Renaissance Italy* (New York: Cambridge University Press, 1999); Leonardas Vytautas Gerulaitis, *Printing and Publishing in Fifteenth-Century Venice* (Chicago, Ill.: American Library Association, 1976); Victor Scholderer, "Printing at Venice to the End of 1481," 25 *The Library* 4th ser., 130 (1924); Joseph Loewenstein, "Idem: Italics and the Genetics of Authorship," 20 *J. of Medieval and Renaissance Studies* 205 (1990). For an argument about a possible personal connection between one of the earliest English printing patents and Venice, see Joseph Loewenstein, *Author's Due:*

appearance of the printing press was the engine behind the spread of early copyright, the process was not technologically determined.[77] Copyright was shaped by the interaction of technology, economic elements, ideology, existing institutional practices, and other social factors. The general pattern was similar in most places: the emerging book trade's commercial interest intersected with state interest in censorship[78] and a well-ordered book trade,[79] and both were mediated through the guild and governmental structures of the time. The result was two institutional forms: ad hoc exclusive grants to print certain texts and more general arrangements of printing entitlements incorporated into the guild apparatus. England followed this pattern. Following the introduction of the printing press in 1477, there appeared in England two parallel tracks for copyright-like protection. The first – the printing patent– was directly based on the royal prerogative power. The second – the stationers' copyright – was rooted in guild powers and regulations.

Printing patents that first appeared at the beginning of the sixteenth century[80] were the equivalents of other patent grants. They were ad hoc, discretionary royal grants that bestowed on individuals – usually printers or booksellers – exclusive privileges to print and sell specific texts or

Printing and the Prehistory of Copyright (Chicago, Ill.: University of Chicago Press, 2002), 69, 75.

[77] The technological determinist account of the relationship between the printing press and social practices is a common, although not necessary, reading of Elizabeth L. Eisenstein, *The Printing Press as an Agent of Change: Communications and Cultural Transformations in Early Modern Europe* (New York: Cambridge University Press, 1979).

[78] Ronan Deazley, *On the Origin of the Right to Copy: Charting the Movement of Copyright Law in Eighteenth Century Britain (1695–1775)* (Portland, Ore.: Hart Publishing, 2004), 2; Lyman R. Patterson, *Copyright in Historical Perspective* (Nashville, Tenn.: Vanderbilt University Press, 1968), 43; John Feather, *Publishing, Piracy and Politics: An Historical Study of Copyright in Britain* (New York: Mansell, 1994), 15; Mark Rose, *Authors and Owners: The Invention of Copyright* (Cambridge, Mass.: Harvard University Press, 1993), 12.

[79] For a short survey of growing central royal involvement in economic regulation and the use of royal charters, monopolies and craft guilds in this respect since the fourteenth century, see Loewenstein, *Author's Due*, 60–62.

[80] About the printing patent in England, see Feather, *Publishing, Piracy and Politics*, 10–14; Loewestein, *Author's Due*, 66–82; Patterson, *Copyright in Historical Perspective*, 78–113. The first English printing patents are usually traced to the creation of the King's Printer office in 1485. The first King's Printer, Peter Actor, was given a right to import books and manuscripts but not an exclusive printing privilege. William Facques, who was appointed to this position in 1504, received a privilege to print royal proclamations, statutes, and other royal documents. See Feather, *Publishing, Piracy and Politics*, 11. Loewenstein argues that it is uncertain whether Facques received such formal privileges. Loewenstein, *Author's Due*, n. 64, 286.

classes of texts.[81] Printing patents had little to do with authorship[82] and were seen as exclusive privileges to pursue an economic activity rather than ownership of an intellectual work. Initially, printing patents covered the most valuable texts in the trade and were the dominant copyright-like device. In the late seventeenth and eighteenth centuries, however, printing patents gradually declined in importance[83] until they eventually decayed and disappeared.[84]

The stationers' copyright was an internal regulation system of the London book trade's Livery Company or guild: the Stationers' Company. It appeared around the mid-sixteenth century[85] and shared many of the characteristics of printing patents, but some of its institutional features were more complex. Much of this complexity derived from the duality at the core of the stationers' copyright: a universal guild practice founded on a particularistic royal grant.[86] In essence, it was a perpetual, exclusive license to publish a book or a "copy" issued by the Stationers' Company to a specific freeman. The company derived much of its status, powers and enforcement capability from a 1557 royal charter.[87]

---

[81] For a survey of the various categories of printing patents, see Bracha, "Owning Ideas," 122–24.

[82] A small number of printing patents were awarded to authors. This was the exception rather than the rule. Although grants to authors were the very early signs of some formal recognition of the role of authors, publishers remained the dominant figures in this system. Printing patents were granted to the person judged to be best suited for publishing the relevant text; in most cases this was a publisher or a printer, in others it was the author acting as, or cooperating with, a publisher. For examples of grants to authors, translators, editors, and relatives, see Feather, *Publishing, Piracy and Politics*, 12–13; Marjorie Plant, *The English Book Trade: An Economic History of the Making and Sale of Books*, 3rd ed. (London: Allen and Unwin, 1974), 109; Leo Kirschbaum, "Author's Copyright in England before 1640," 40 *Papers of the Bibliographical Society of America* 43, 47–51 (1946).

[83] Printing patents played an important role in consolidating the power of the Stationers' Company. The "English Stock" was the most important group of printing patents. The English Stock was a joint stock company that managed patents in some of the most valuable texts that were held directly by the Stationers' Company as a result of royal grants and purchase of conflicting rights. The English Stock was an important tool for implementing company policy, distributing benefits to members and striking internal compromises. See Cyprian Blagden, "The English Stock of the Stationers' Company," 10 *The Library* 5th ser., 163 (1955); Patterson, *Copyright in Historical Perspective*, 106–13.

[84] See Bracha, "Owning Ideas," 146–58.

[85] Since the earliest records of the company are lost it is impossible to date the exact appearance of the stationers' copyright, but it was probably a few years before the grant of the charter. See Patterson, *Copyright in Historical Perspective*, 42–43.

[86] Bracha, "Owning Ideas," 139–45.

[87] See Cyprian Blagden, *The Stationers' Company, A History, 1403–1959* (Cambridge, Mass.: Harvard University Press, 1977); Patterson, *Copyright in Historical Perspective*, 28–32; Rose, *Authors and Owners*, 12.

Was the stationers' copyright an ad hoc discretionary privilege like the printing patent or a universal right like modern copyright? The duality of the stationers' copyright complicates the answer. Externally, on the level of the relations between the Stationers' Company and the government, copyright was well grounded in the privilege form. The effective existence of the stationers' copyright depended on the monopolization of the trade by the company and on its enforcement powers, both of which derived chiefly from the company's royal charter and various licensing and censorship enactments that vested the company with unique powers.[88] Moreover, copyright was by no means a universal regime extended to all on equal terms. It was restricted to members of the book trade who were freemen of the Stationers' Company. Internally, on the level of the company's practices things were more ambiguous. Copyright was practiced as a general and standardized regime. There developed a standard registration process that combined the content-licensing and economic-regulation functions of the system.[89] As a rule, any stationer who completed the licensing and registration procedure could expect to receive, as a matter of routine, a conventional entitlement: the perpetual exclusive right to print the registered "copy."[90] A 1583 royal commission report on the printing patents conveyed this general sense of standardization. It explained that "the companie do order emongest them selves that he which bringeth a booke to be printed should use yt as a priviledge."[91] It went on to say that "everie of such Stationers hath divers copies severall to them selves ... evrie of them hath of order severall to him selfe any boke that he can procure any learned man to make or translate for him, or that can come to his hand to be the first printer of it."[92] This practice, however, never

---

[88] See Patterson, *Copyright in Historical Perspective,* 114–38.
[89] Id., 36–41; John Feather, "From Rights in Copies to Copyright: The Recognition of Authors' Rights in English Law and Practice in the Sixteenth and Seventeenth Centuries," in Martha Woodmansee and Peter Jaszi, eds., *The Construction of Authorship: Textual Appropriation in Law and Literature* (Durham, N.C.: Duke University Press, 1994), 195–200.
[90] It is not entirely clear whether registration was constitutive of the right or served only as an administrative and evidentiary tool, while copyright was recognized even in the absence of registration. See Patterson, *Copyright in Historical Perspective,* 55–64; Feather, "From Rights in Copies," 201–2.
[91] "The Final Report of the Augmented Commission from the Privy Council on the Controversy in the Stationers' Company [extracts]," in Edward Arber, ed., *A Transcript of the Register of the Company of Stationers, 1554–1640 A.D.* (London: Turnbull and Spears, 1876), vol. 2, 784.
[92] "Final Report of the Commissioners, with Autograph Signatures," in W.W. Greg, *A Companion to Arber* (Oxford: Clarendon, 1967), 127.

consolidated into a firm formal notion of a right. The governing bodies of the company retained a discretionary power to withhold or tailor its members' entitlements in specific cases. This usually happened during the adjudication of disputes and more rarely at the issuance stage. In such cases the company did not see itself as bound by a strict regime of rights, but rather intervened on an ad hoc discretionary basis.[93] While standard copyright entitlements were usually issued as a matter of routine, the company's occasional intervention preserved an important privilege aspect to the institution even on the internal level.

The conceptual framework of the stationers' copyright was much clearer in regard to the subject matter of the exclusive entitlements. The stationers' copyright, like the printing patent, was not seen as the ownership or control of an intellectual work. It was, rather, understood as an exclusive entitlement to engage in a specific economic activity, unique to the book trade: the printing and sale of a particular text.[94] During the sixteenth and seventeenth centuries there appeared several developments that indicate some subtle move toward a latent concept of owning intangibles. By the end of the sixteenth century the standard registration of copyright in the stationers' register changed from "license for printing" or similar forms to "entered for his copy." It is hard to assess whether this lingual shift from a license to print to ownership of a copy was more than merely formal.[95] Additionally, stationers came to treat copyrights as a commodified business asset. Copyrights were bought and sold, owned in shares, and used as security for debts.[96] Since the early seventeenth century stationers also occasionally referred to their copyrights as "property," especially in pamphlets and petitions.[97] A 1643 pamphlet that attempted to persuade parliament to create a new censorship system instead of the abolished Star Chamber[98] even included an early

---

[93] For a survey of the company's practices in this respect, see Bracha, "Owning Ideas," 140–44.

[94] Patterson, *Copyright in Historical Perspective*, 55.

[95] Patterson regarded the change as purely formal. Patterson, *Copyright in Historical Perspective*, 52–55. Rose agrees but adds that "the evolution in the form of entry indicates that a subtle conceptual change was occurring." Rose, *Authors and Owners*, 14.

[96] For examples, see Bracha, "Owning Ideas," 171–72; Feather, "From Rights in Copies to Copyright," 197–98. Wiliam Holdsworth inferred from these economic practices that copyright "was clearly regarded as a form of property." William Holdsworth, *A History of English Law* (London: Methuen, 1924), vol. 6, 365, 378.

[97] See Bracha, "Owning Ideas," 172–73.

[98] "The Humble Remonstrance of the Company of Stationers to the High Court of Parliament, April 1643 (attributed to Henry Parke Esq.)," in Arber, *Transcript of the Register*, 584.

rudimentary notion of intellectual property: "[T]here is no reason apparent why the production of the Brain should not be as assignable," the petition argued, "and their interest and possession (being of more rare sublime and publike use, demeriting the highest encouragement) held as tender in Law, as the right of any Goods or Chattels whatsoever."[99] Despite these developments, however, the dominant concept of copyright remained that of an exclusive privilege to exercise a trade. Occasional characterizations of copyright as "property" usually referred to the familiar guild regulations and trade privileges. More explicit conceptualization of ownership of intellectual works was rare, and there appeared no attempt to develop any legal or institutional framework based on it.

Another aspect of the stationers' copyright as a bookseller trade privilege was the marginality of authorship. Copyright was not founded on a general, abstract principle of rights in creative intellectual production. It was, rather, part of the unique regulation of the book trade. Copyright had little to do with authorship. It was a publisher's trade entitlement, rather than a right of authors. Stationers were the only ones who could register and hold copyright,[100] and authors enjoyed no formal entitlements under this system.[101] Neither was original authorship a requirement for protection. Many of the protected texts, such as bibles or classical works, had no known or relevant authors. In practice, authors were not always ignored. As book markets developed in the seventeenth century and a shift occurred from patronage to market-based production of texts, authors became an important source for publishable materials. This often entailed compensation for transferring the physical

[99] Id., 588.
[100] In 1598 the Court of Assistants of the Stationers' Company issued an order to be publicly read "Against printinge for forens to the Company" backed up by sanctions against such incidents. The Court reaffirmed it in a similar 1607 order. See W.W. Greg and E. Boswell, *Records of the Court of the Stationers' Company, 1576–1602* (London: The Bibliographical Society, 1930), 59; William Jackson, *Records of the Court of the Stationers' Company, 1602–1640* (London: The Bibliographical Society, 1957), 31. Authors, as such, could not enjoy copyright protection. There were attempts to bend the rules, as in cases where stationers registered copyright for others (occasionally authors) that in practice functioned as the publishers of the works. See e.g. G.E.B. Eyre, *A Transcript of the Register of the Worshipful Company of Stationers, 1640–1708 A.D.* (London, 1913), vol. 1, 392; id., vol. 2, 122, 166, 265, 304, 307; id., vol. 3, 27. For a comprehensive survey of such cases, see Kirschbaum, "Author's Copyright," 54–74. As a rule, however, the company jealously fought against ownership of copyright outside of its membership.
[101] Plant, *English Book Trade*, 68.

manuscript,[102] and sometimes more complex contractual arrangements.[103] As the system developed, authorial interests received some limited recognition beyond the dictates of mere economic necessity. Although there never appeared a general formal right of compensation, some company practices and adjudicated cases either implied or directly mandated the need to compensate authors.[104] In some instances there also occurred an ambivalent recognition of a norm under which authors had power to control first publication of their works.[105] That was the extent of the limited and haphazard formal recognition of authors' interests under the stationers' copyright system.

On occasion authors tried to manipulate the system to attain further control of their works, but such extensions of authorial power never received any formal sanction or institutional expression.[106] The stationer's copyright was and remained a publisher's trade privilege. To the extent authors' interests received any recognition, they derived from and were subservient to those of the stationers. In the words of Joseph Loewenstein, "contests within the book trade concerning the regulation of literary property had occasionally thrown off authorial protections, like regulatory sparks."[107] The publisher, rather than the author, was both formally and in practice the dominant figure under this system.

---

[102] Bracha, "Owning Ideas," 159–61. For a survey of typical sums paid and their gradual increase over time, see Plant, *English Book Trade*, 73–78.

[103] The most important early example of a complex author's contract is Milton's 1667 contract for the sale of *Paradise Lost* to Samuel Simmons. Reproduced in David Masson, *Life of John Milton* (New York: Peter Smith, 1880), vol. 6, 509–11. At the time the degree of sophistication of Milton's contract was the exception rather than the rule. See Peter Lindenbaum, "Milton's Contract," in Woodmansee and Jaszi, *The Construction of Authorship*, 175; Rose, *Authors and Owners*, 27–28; Patterson, *Copyright in Historical Perspective*, 74.

[104] Patterson, *Copyright in Historical Perspective*, 67–69.

[105] Id., 69; Bracha, "Owning Ideas," 162–64.

[106] Patterson maintains that under the stationers' copyright additional authorial "personal rights" to control the creative aspects and secondary uses of works were recognized – the equivalents of what in modern terms would be called rights of controlling derivative works. Patterson, *Copyright in Historical Perspective*, 70–77. The evidence does not support this claim. All indications are that the stationers' copyright left others, including the original authors, free to create and publish adaptations and secondary works based on registered texts. It does not follow and there is no evidence that the stationers' copyright vested an exclusive entitlement to make such secondary uses in authors. Sometimes authors tried to manipulate the system in order to attain such control, but there were no formal rights of this kind. See Bracha, "Owning Ideas," 165–69; Feather, *Publishing, Piracy and Politics*, 33.

[107] Loewenstein, *Author's Due*, 40.

The stationers' copyright system came to an end when the 1662 Licensing Act[108] lapsed in 1695. Despite numerous attempts[109] the Licensing Act was never renewed. A new ideological climate together with the changing structure of English politics brought about the decline of the censorship framework in which copyright was grounded for 150 years.[110] Only in the first decade of the eighteenth century did stationers grasp this change and revise their agitation strategy accordingly: they now advocated a statutory arrangement for copyright, based not on censorship but rather on the justice and public utility of protecting authors. A combination of stationers' agitation using the author as the new instrument for promoting their cause[111] and more sincere advocacy of authorial interests[112] resulted in 1710 in the creation of a new copyright system under the Statute of Anne. The statute vested in "the author of any book ... and his assign ... the sole liberty of printing and reprinting such book" for fourteen years.[113]

The Statute of Anne is often seen as the "first copyright act,"[114] a dramatic moment in which the old monopolistic guild-based system was replaced by modern authors' copyright. In reality, the statute did not form a complete break with the past. Alongside important innovation it contained much continuity with the longstanding institutional tradition of copyright. There were four main innovations introduced by the new regime. First, the Statute of Anne severed the formal link between governmental censorship and the economic regulation of printing rights. Second, it created, for the first time, a universal legal regime. The internal guild regulation whose benefit was limited to freemen of the company was replaced by general legal norms applicable to all. These general norms defined substantive and procedural requirements for the attainment of

---

[108] 13 and 14 Car. 2, c. 33.

[109] See Deazley, *On the Origin of the Right to Copy*, 1–29; Patterson, *Copyright in Historical Perspective*, 138–42; Feather, *Publishing, Piracy and Politics*, 50–58.

[110] Deazley, *On the Origin of the Right to Copy*, 29; Bracha, "Owning Ideas," 178–82.

[111] Feather, *Publishing, Piracy and Politics*, 61–63. Benjamin Kaplan made a similar argument. Benjamin Kaplan, *An Unhurried View of Copyright* (New York: Columbia University Press, 1967), 8–9. By contrast, according to Patterson it was the opponents of the company who used the author's figure in order to break its monopolistic power. Patterson, *Copyright in Historical Perspective*, 14, 143–44.

[112] Deazley, *On the Origin of the Right to Copy*, 45–46.

[113] 8 Ann., c. 19, sec. 1. The statute also provided for a twenty-one-year protection in works already published.

[114] Harry Ransom, *The First Copyright Statute: An Essay on an Act for the Encouragement of Learning, 1710* (Austin: University of Texas Press, 1956).

standardized rights. Third, with the vesting of the rights in authors and their assignees the formal focus of copyright shifted from publishers to authors. At least prospectively, authors became the original and main bearers of the rights, and publishers' entitlements were reduced to a derivative status.[115] Fourth, borrowing a page from patent's book, copyright was restricted to a term of fourteen years (once renewable).[116]

Alongside those significant innovations, important aspects of traditional copyright were retained. Under the Statute of Anne copyright remained the unique regulation of the book trade and was not founded on a new general principle of rights in creative intellectual works. Nor was copyright reconceptualized as ownership or general control of an intellectual object. The only entitlement bestowed by the statute was the publisher's privilege to print copies of a specific text. Authors were now the new formal center of copyright, but the full conceptual impact of this shift was only beginning to develop. The Statute of Anne did not define authors or try to limit protection to the kind of persons or works that conformed to its new authorial ideal. By the same token, it made no attempt to redefine the scope and character of copyright protection or the powers entrusted to copyright owners on the basis of the now dominant rationale of authors' rights. In essence the 1710 framework lifted the familiar trade privilege of the stationer, limited its duration, and conferred it on authors.

The final important piece of the English background of copyright that is essential for understanding the later American development is the literary property debate. The literary property debate was a series of legal disputes and public deliberations that stretched over four decades of the eighteenth century and revolved around the question of common law copyright.[117] The origin of this conflict was in the economic interest of the London booksellers. The claim that common law copyright existed independently of the statutory scheme was meant to restore perpetual

[115] In practice things were more complex. It was a gradual and slow process in which the formal legal changes transformed the actual realities and power divisions within the English book trade. See Bracha, "Owning Ideas," 189–96; Terry Belanger, "Publishers and Writers in Eighteenth Century England," in Isabel Rivers, ed., *Books and Their Readers in Eighteenth Century England* (New York: St. Martin's Press, 1982), 8.
[116] 8 Ann., c. 19, sec. 1, 11.
[117] Patterson, *Copyright in Historical Perspective*, 158–79; Rose, *Authors and Owners*, 67–112; Deazley, *On the Origins of the Right to Copy*, 115–210; Howard B. Abrams, "The Historic Foundation of American Copyright Law: Exploding the Myth of Common Law Copyright," 29 *Wayne L. Rev.* 1119, 1142–71 (1983); H. Tomás Gómez-Arostegui, "Copyright at Common Law in 1774," 47 *Conn. L. Rev.* 1 (2014).

protection, thereby counteracting the destabilizing effect of the limited statutory duration on the tight control of the trade by a small group of London publishers. The ensuing debate, however, had broader intellectual dimensions that left a lasting impression on copyright discourse. When proponents of common law copyright – lawyers, judges, and pamphleteers – were faced with the need to support their position with convincing and legitimate public arguments, they turned to the notion of literary property. As mentioned, casual reference to copyright practices as "property" and even rare claims about the equivalence between copyright and other forms of property occurred earlier. The literary property debate, however, produced for the first time elaborate philosophical justifications of literary property, and attempts to construct detailed legal models of property to match them. A series of pamphlets and court arguments created an intricate theory of copyright as property rights of authors in the product of their minds, justified by just desert for mental labor and public utility considerations.[118] Jurists labored to construct a general abstract model of property under which copyright would exhibit all the essential traits of a property right.[119]

Two elements of the new discourse of literary property had a particularly important lasting effect: the work and the author. The concept of the intellectual work was developed in order to answer the troubling question of the object of property. In a system that conceptualized property as control over things, an obvious objection to copyright as an author's property right was that "there is no subject nor *corpus* of which he can be said to be proprietor."[120] The intellectual work – a postulated intellectual entity created by the author – supplied the missing object of property. Copyright was now reinterpreted as ownership of "a set of intellectual ideas or modes of thinking ... equally detached from the manuscript, or any other physical existence whatsoever."[121] During the eighteenth century there emerged an increasingly crisp distinction between the physical

---

[118] Rose, *Authors and Owners*, 67–91; Deazley, *On the Origins of the Right to Copy*, 149–67; Sherman and Bently, *The Making of Modern Intellectual Property Law*, 11–42.

[119] Bracha, "Owning Ideas," 202–20.

[120] "Daniel Midwinter and Other Booksellers in London contra Gavin Hamilton &c.," in *Remarkable Decisions of the Court of Session from the Year 1730 to the Year 1752*, 2nd ed. (Edinburgh: Bell & Bradfute and William Creech, 1799), 157. This is a report of the *Midwinter v. Hamilton* (1743–48) case brought by English booksellers against Scottish publishers in the Scottish Court of Session, later appealed to the House of Lords as *Millar v. Kincaid* (1749–51).

[121] *Millar v. Taylor*, 98 Eng. Rep. 222, 251 (K.B. 1769).

object or the book and the intellectual work.[122] Ownership of the intel-lectual work gradually displaced the traditional privilege to engage in the art of printing as the dominant representation of copyright.

The notion of the author supplied the new focus of copyright thinking and the ultimate justification for the claim of literary property. The eighteenth-century debates completed the move started by the Statute of Anne. Authors were brought to the rhetorical and conceptual front of copyright, while publishers gradually faded into the background. There also appeared an elaborate concept of authors as owners. Authors came to be presented as individual geniuses who originate completely new intellectual creations through their mental labor. This, in turn, became the ultimate justification of copyright as a property right of authors in the product of their intellect.[123]

After a short-lived victory in the 1769 *Millar v. Taylor*,[124] the formal claim of common law copyright in published works was ultimately defeated. The House of Lords rejected the claim in the 1774 *Donaldson v. Becket*.[125] Despite the defeat, however, the literary property debate had a profound and lasting effect on Anglo-American copyright thinking. The scope and meaning of the House of Lords' decision remained con-tested.[126] More important, the notion of copyright as ownership by authors of their intellectual works based on the abstract principle of property in the creative product of the mind became the dominant view of copyright. During the eighteenth century this abstract notion was hardly instantiated in actual copyright doctrines and practices. Copyright doctrine was still heavily colored by the older publisher's trade-privilege framework. But the new conceptual elements and the new ideology of copyright they created were to be at the heart of the future developments of copyright in both Britain and the United States.

[122] Bracha, "Owning Ideas," 220–29. *Pope v. Curll*, 26 Eng. Rep. 608 (Ch. 1741), was an important landmark in this respect. In that case Chancellor Hardwick, who was faced with a dispute over the "property" in a letter, elaborated a clear distinction between the physical manuscript and the intellectual work embodied in it. See Mark Rose, "The Author in the Court: *Pope v. Curll* (1741)," in Woodmansee and Jaszi, *The Construction of Authorship*, 223–24; Rose, *Authors and Owners*, 64–66.
[123] Rose, *Authors and Owners*, 67–91; Mark Rose, "The Author as Proprietor: *Donaldson v. Becket* and the Genealogy of Modern Authorship," 23 *Representations* 51, 76 (1988).
[124] 98 Eng. Rep. 251.
[125] 98 Eng. Rep. 257; 1 Eng. Rep. 837; 17 Parl. Hist. Eng. 953 (H.L. 1774).
[126] See Gómez-Arostegui, "Copyright at Common Law."

By the end of the eighteenth century copyright was in a state of flux in Britain no less than patents. The ad hoc printing patents and the censorship-guild apparatus had evolved into a universal statutory regime of authors' rights. There developed an elaborate conceptual framework of copyright as ownership by authors of a postulated intangible entity – the intellectual work. The general ideological justifications of copyright, whether utilitarian or natural rights–based, came to revolve around the abstract principle of property rights in the product of the mind. However, on the more concrete level of the actual institutional details of copyright the change was less sweeping. For the most part,[127] by the end of the eighteenth century copyright was still the unique regulation of the book trade. Despite some embryonic developments,[128] copyright still had the basic institutional form of the stationers' trade privilege to print and sell a text, now bestowed on authors.

COLONIAL AND STATE COPYRIGHT

The American colonies never developed anything resembling a copyright system. During the colonial period there appeared no general statutory framework or common law rules regulating printing and publishing rights. Nor were there guild practices similar to the stationers' copyright. This is unsurprising given the dramatically different conditions in the colonies. During most of the period printing presses were extremely scarce. In some colonies presses did not appear or were banned altogether for protracted periods. Where printing presses were allowed they were treated as public resources. This entailed various mixes of public support and subsidy, on the one hand, and governmental regulation and suppression, on the other. Governmental interest in creating a local version of the stationers' copyright was absent. While censorship including prior

---

[127] For most of the eighteenth century the main extension of copyright beyond the realm of books was the 1735 Engravers Act, also known as the Hogarth Act. It extended copyright to makers of engravings; 8 Geo. 2, c. 13. A more decisive move in the direction of copyright based on the general principle of creative authorship occurred at the very end of the century with the 1798 Models and Busts Act, which extended protection to any new model, cast, bust and statutes of certain kinds; 38 Geo. 3, c. 7.

[128] These embryonic beginnings foreshadowing the future appeared in several cases and other legal texts. One example was in the form of 1735 and 1737 bills for amending the Statute of Anne that never passed. Deazley, *On the Origins of the Right to Copy*, 94–110. Probably the most important example was the 1735 Engravers Act, which contained, at least implicitly, a requirement of originality and explicitly extended protection beyond verbatim reproduction to cover evasive alterations. See id., 92–94.

restraint was common until the mid-eighteenth century, colonial authorities never developed a systematic licensing apparatus close in scale and
scope to the English one.[129] There was no central organization like the
Stationers' Company on which government could confer enforcement
powers. At the same time, printers and booksellers were relatively few,
even in later times and in places like Boston where a publishing trade
emerged. This situation made a censorship intermediary like the English
Stationers' Company unnecessary.

The printers' and booksellers' interest in copyright-like protection was
also relatively low for most of the period. Markets were often local and
insulated. The risk of local and out-of-colony competition was small.
Alternative mechanisms for securing investment were effective under such
conditions. These probably included occasional agreements or conduct
norms among publishers.[130] More conspicuous were various governmental "encouragements" such as the arrangement secured by William Bladen
in 1700 from the North Carolina legislature, under which various official
documents were required to be printed for set prices of "one penny or one
li Tobo per peece" (i.e., one pound of tobacco per piece) for some of
the documents and "Two pence or two pounds of tobbo" for others.[131]
In short, neither government nor publishers had a strong sustained interest in creating a local version of the English stationers' copyright.

There were scattered instances of ad hoc printing privileges granted by
colonial legislatures. These legislative grants resembled the English
printing patent, with the important difference that, like colonial patent
grants, they were issued by legislatures. The best known incident of this
sort is John Usher's 1672 grant from the Massachusetts General Court for
printing a revised edition of the colony's laws. The grant probably

---

[129] See John Tebbel, *A History of Book Publishing in the United States* (New York: R.R.
Bowker, 1972), vol. 1, 6–12; Helmut Lehmann-Haupt, *The Book in America: A History
of the Making, the Selling, and the Collecting of Books in the United States*, 2nd ed.
(New York: R.R. Bowker, 1951), 42–45; Lawrence C. Wroth, *The Colonial Printer*
(Portland, Me.: Southworth-Anthoensen Press, 1938), 42–46. In 1664 Massachusetts
came the closest of all the North American colonies to creating a local licensing system.
See Nathaniel B. Shurtleff, ed., *Records of the Governor and Company of the Massachusetts Bay in New England* (Boston: W. White, 1853–54), vol. 4, pt. 2, 141.

[130] See Tebbel, *History of Book Publishing*, vol. 1, 46. Social norms were described as "a
sense of mutual obligation" and as "common decency and enlightened self-interest."
Lehmann-Haupt, *Book in America*, 100. About contractual arrangements, see Tebbel,
History of Book Publishing, vol. 1, 42; Lehmann-Haupt, *Book in America*, 85.

[131] Quoted in Lawrence C. Wroth, *A History of Printing in Colonial Maryland, 1686–1776*
(Baltimore, Md.: Typothetae of Baltimore, 1922), 21.

originated in Usher's distrust of his printer, Samuel Green. Usher feared Green would make additional copies, thereby undermining his market.[132] The legislature ordered that "no printer shall print any more copies then are agreed & pajd for by the ouuner of the sajd coppie or coppies, nor shall he nor any other reprint or make sale of any of the same, wthout the sajd ouners consent."[133] One year later the grant was reaffirmed and explicitly limited to seven years.[134] While historians often claim that Usher's was the only colonial copyright-like grant,[135] there were other similar instances. North Carolina, for example, enacted in 1747 a statute for the publication of its laws. The statute conferred on "the Commissioners" entrusted with this project and their assignees "the Benefit and Advantage of the sole Printing and Vending the Books of the said Laws, for and during the Space or Term of Five Years."[136] Further research in colonial archives is likely to uncover similar examples. Colonial legislative printing privileges never consolidated into a copyright system or a general copyright law. These sporadic printing grants were a version of the colonial patent. They were ad hoc tailored measures meant to "encourage" specific entrepreneurs delivering a publicly beneficial service. The recipients of the grants were publishers, not authors. Indeed, the texts involved usually had no relevant authors. The encouragement took the form of exclusive privileges to engage in the economic activity of printing and selling a particular text and was not conceptualized as ownership of an intellectual work.

The next important development was the rise of authors' privileges. It occurred at the very end of the colonial period. In 1770 William Billings, a singing master from Boston who later would be considered the father of American choral music,[137] petitioned the Massachusetts legislature for protection for his newly written *The New England Psalm-Singer*. The authorship basis of the claim was reflected in the proceedings, which were fraught with concerns about authorship.

---

[132] Tebbel, *History of Book Publishing*, 25.

[133] *Records of the Governor and Company of the Massachusetts Bay*, 527.   [134] Id., 559.

[135] Bugbee, *Genesis of American Patent and Copyright Law*, 106; Lehmann-Haupt, *Book in America*, 99; Tebbel, *History of Book Publishing*, vol. 1, 46.

[136] "An Act for appointing Commissioners to Revise and Print the Laws of this Province, and for granting to his Majesty, for defraying the Charge thereof, a Duty of Wine, Rum and distilled Liquors, and Rice imported into this Province," sec. 4, in *A Collection of All the Public Acts of Assembly, of the Province of North-Carolina, Now in Force and Use* (Newbern: James Davis, 1751), 242–45.

[137] See Richard Crawford and David P. McKay, *William Billings of Boston: Eighteenth Century Composer* (Princeton, N.J.: Princeton University Press, 1975).

Billings' petition was delayed when suspicions arose that he was not the real author of the book, causing him to declare that "he is the sole Author, & should have been asham'd, to have expos'd himself by publishing any Tunes, Anthems or Canons; compos'd by Another."[138] When the legislature was finally convinced, it granted Billings a seven-year exclusive right to print and sell the book "in Order … to promote such a laudable performance,"[139] only for the bill to be terminated by Governor Hutchinson, who refused to sign it.[140] After independence, this trend intensified. State legislatures were faced with petitions by authors for legislative privileges in their works, and a few such privileges were granted.[141] Individual state grants continued even after most states enacted general copyright statutes in the 1780s.[142] The state grants, like the colonial ones, created ad hoc discretionary privileges that bestowed the traditional publisher's entitlement to print and sell copies. The novel element of these grants was the new, central status of authors, who were the direct recipients of the grants, rather than publishers. The changing ideological tide was also manifested in the justifications for such grants that increasingly relied on original authorship as the basis of either a moral-desert claim by authors or the public utility of encouraging writing.[143]

Unlike patents, copyright in the states developed beyond ad hoc grants. In 1783, following agitation from known literary figures such as Noah Webster and Joel Barlow, who relied among other things on the precedent of the Statute of Anne,[144] the Continental Congress issued a recommendation to the states to secure to authors or publishers of new books "the copyright of such books for a certain time, not less than fourteen years" (once renewable).[145] By that time three states – Connecticut,

[138] The petition is available in LVIII Massachusetts Archives 600. It was reprinted in Rollo G. Silver, "Prologue to Copyright in America: 1772," 11 *Papers of the Bibliographical Society of the University of Virginia* 259, 261–62 (1958).
[139] Id., 261.   [140] *Massachusetts House Journals* (1772), vol. 49, 134–35.
[141] Bracha, "Owning Ideas," 257–60; Bugbee, *Genesis of American Patent and Copyright Law,* 107, 124.
[142] See e.g. the 1784 Connecticut grant to Joel Barlow, Charles J. Hoadly, ed., *The Public Records of the State of Connecticut* (Hartford, Conn.: Case, Lockwood & Brainard, 1895), vol. 5, 458–59; or the 1792 South Carolina grant to Joseph Purcell for a map of the state; *Statutes at Large of South Carolina,* vol. 5, 219–20.
[143] Bracha, "Owning Ideas," 260–63.
[144] See Bugbee, *Genesis of American Patent and Copyright Law,* 104–24. See Barlow's letter to the Continental Congress in *Papers of the Continental Congress, 1774–1789,* vol. 4, 369–73 (no. 78).
[145] *Journals of the Continental Congress, 1774–1789* (Washington, D.C.: U.S. Government Printing Office, 1922), vol. 24, 326–27.

Massachusetts, and Maryland – already legislated general copyright laws, and in the following years all remaining states except Delaware followed suit.[146] The details of the state statutes differed but they all shared a family resemblance. All the state statutes followed the general model of the Statute of Anne, sometimes borrowing from it almost verbatim. All the statutes placed the author at the center of their ideological focus. The differences were in the exact doses of emphasis on natural-rights and utilitarian arguments. Some states, such as Massachusetts, emphasized the former, describing copyright as "one of the natural rights of all men there being no property more peculiarly a man's own than that which is produced by the labor of his mind."[147] Others, such as Connecticut, highlighted the need to "encourage men of learning and genius to publish their writings; which may do honor to their country, and service to mankind."[148] All statutes, however, had some reference to the two rationales and linked them to individual authorship. The state statutes created, for the first time in America, universal right-based regimes of copyright. As in Britain, however, there was no institutional expression to the new depiction of copyright as ownership by authors of their intellectual works. The statutes bestowed on authors the familiar printer's privilege of printing and selling copies.

Despite their different histories, at the eve of the federal regime the conceptual scheme of copyright in the United States was similar to the British one. Alongside persisting individual grants, universal copyright regimes emerged as a common institutional option, at this stage on the state level. Authors were now the direct recipients of rights and the unequivocal rhetorical center of copyright discourse. While America did not experience a literary property debate – a local version of which would take place only in the 1830s – some of the intellectual developments stimulated by the British debate clearly appeared in the United States. The most important of those developments was an elaborate

---

[146] The exact chronological order was: Connecticut, January 1783; Massachusetts, March 1783; Maryland, April 1783; New Jersey, May 1783; New Hampshire, November 1783; Rhode Island, December 1783; Pennsylvania, March 1784; South Carolina, March 1784; Virginia, October 1785; North Carolina, November 1785; Georgia, February 1786; New York, April 1786. See generally Francine Crawford, "Pre-Constitutional Copyright Statutes," 23 *Bull. Copyright Soc'y* 11 (1975).

[147] Thorvald Solberg, ed., *Copyright Enactments of the United States 1783–1906*, 2nd ed. (Washington, D.C.: G.P.O, 1906), 14.

[148] Id., 11.

ideology of copyright as ownership by authors of their intellectual product. These changes notwithstanding, in the United States as in Britain the
notions of authorship and of owning an intellectual work did not
yet receive an institutional instantiation or begin to reshape the actual
doctrines and practices of copyright.

THE INTELLECTUAL PROPERTY CONSTITUTIONAL CLAUSE

Until 1790 all patents and copyrights in the United States were limited to
the state level. The Continental Congress, despite several petitions,
legislated neither general enactments nor individual privileges. Members
of the Continental Congress probably saw themselves as lacking power
under the Articles of Confederation to pass national legislation in this
field.[149] The 1789 U.S. Constitution changed this situation and laid the
foundation for national patent and copyright regimes. The Constitution
contained a clause that would come to be known as the "intellectual
property clause." It granted Congress the power "[t]o promote
the progress of science and useful arts by securing for limited times to
Authors and Inventors the exclusive rights to their respective writings
and discoveries."[150] The intellectual property clause holds a paradoxical
position in American law, scholarship, and public debate. The clause
is usually treated as one of the most important developments in the
history of American intellectual property law, despite the fact that
contemporaries hardly perceived it as constituting a break with former
practices or concepts. It has received more scholarly attention than
any other historical episode in this field, despite the dearth of information about the purposes of its framers and the process leading to
its adoption.

As far as one can tell, the Founding Fathers did not see patent and
copyright as issues of great importance and did not devote much thought
or elaborate discussion to them or to the relevant clause of the Constitution. Copyrights and patents were not mentioned in the early proposals
for a national governance scheme presented by various states.[151] At the
eve of the constitutional convention in Philadelphia, James Madison
identified as one of the weaknesses of the Articles of Confederation's
scheme of government "the want of uniformity in the laws concerning

[149] See Walterscheid, "To Promote the Progress," 4–9.   [150] U.S. Const. art. I, §8, cl. 8.
[151] Edward C. Walterscheid, *The Nature of the Intellectual Property Clause: A Study in Historical Perspective* (Buffalo, N.Y.: W.S. Hein, 2002), 81–82.

naturalization & literary property."[152] He also designated the issue as one of "inferior moment."[153] Nor was the congressional power to legislate in the field mentioned in the first draft of the Constitution reported by the Committee of Detail to the convention on August 6, 1787, or in prior resolutions.[154] The issue made its first known appearance on August 18, almost three months after the convention began. The clause emerged out of various proposals for congressional powers relating to the encouragement of learning and technological innovation submitted by James Madison and Charles Pinckney on that day.[155] Almost nothing is known about the deliberative process that led from those various proposals to the final phrasing of the clause that was reported from the Committee on Detail on September 5, 1787, and approved with no debate.[156] The lack of known debate about this issue is sometimes construed as evidence of enthusiasm and consensus among the framers. It is just as plausible that it was the result of lack of interest, designation of the issue as one of "inferior moment," and perhaps general exhaustion at a late stage of the convention.[157]

The ratification process produced only scanty additional discussion of the clause or attempts to explain and justify it. The most famous reference was Madison's observation in the Federalist No. 43 that:

> The utility of this power will scarcely be questioned. The copyright of authors has solemnly adjudged in Great Britain to be a right at Common Law. The right to useful inventions seems with equal reason to belong to the inventors. The public good fully coincides in both cases with the claims of individuals. The States cannot separately make effectual provision for either of the cases, and most of them anticipated the decision of this point by laws passed at the instance of Congress.[158]

Apparently, Madison was scrambling for every available justification of Congress' new powers, caring little about inaccuracies or

---

[152] "Observations by J.M.," in *Documentary History of the Constitution of the United States of America, 1786–1870* (Washington, D.C.: Department of State, 1894–1905), vol. 4, 128.

[153] Id.   [154] Waltersheid, *Nature of the Intellectual Property Clause*, 100.

[155] *Documentary History of the Constitution*, vol. 4, 130–31. See Waltersheid, *Nature of the Intellectual Property Clause*, 101–5; Dotan Oliar, "Making Sense of the Intellectual Property Clause: Promotion of Progress as a Limitation on Congress's Intellectual Property Power," 94 *Geo. L.J.* 1771, 1789 (2006).

[156] Max Farrand, ed., *The Records of the Federal Convention of 1787* (New Haven, Conn.: Yale University Press, 1911), vol. 2, 505.

[157] Waltersheid, *Nature of the Intellectual Property Clause*, 80–81, 83.

[158] Benjamin F. Wright, ed., *The Federalist* (No. 43) (Cambridge, Mass.: Belknap Press, 1961), 309.

inconsistencies.[159] Thus for example, the reference to common law copyright in Britain suggests that Madison was familiar with the 1769 King's Bench *Millar v. Taylor*[160] decision that recognized copyright as a common law property right. However, Madison either did not know or chose to ignore the 1774 *Donaldson v. Beckett*[161] in which the House of Lords overturned *Millar* and rejected the notion of common law copyright after publication. Alternatively, Madison intended to offer a reading of *Donaldson v. Beckett* as recognizing a preexisting common law copyright that was limited to the statutory framework by the 1710 Statute of Anne.[162] Similarly, Madison's argument in the Federalist blended together indistinguishably individual natural-rights–based justifications of patent and copyright and social-utilitarian ones. All of this was probably of little concern, since Madison was not writing a philosophical argument, but rather was engaged in political rhetoric designed to attain approval for the Constitution. The other known attempts to justify the clause by James Iredell in North Carolina[163] and Thomas McKean in Pennsylvania[164] focused on points made by Madison: the need for national protection, the ineffectiveness of state regimes, and the British precedent.

The important innovation of the constitutional clause was the creation of a national power to legislate in the fields of patent and copyright. Against the background of an emerging national market and culture, state regulation of these fields was growing increasingly inadequate. Granting Congress the power of creating national arrangements was the framers' response to this inadequacy, which by 1787 was becoming apparent in both the patent and copyright context.[165] Yet, apart from

[159] About the difficulties with Madison's arguments in the Federalist No. 43, see Walterscheid, *Nature of the Intellectual Property Clause*, 220–26.
[160] 98 Eng. Rep. 222.   [161] 98 Eng. Rep. 257.
[162] See Edward C. Walterscheid, "Understanding the Copyright Act of 1790: The Issue of Common Law Copyright in America and the Modern Interpretation of the Copyright Power," 53 *J. of the Copyright Office Society of the USA* 313, 327 (2006).
[163] Merrill Jensen et al., eds., *The Documentary History of the Ratification of the Constitution, Commentaries on the Constitution, Public and Private, 1 February 1788, to 31 March 1788* (Madison: State Historical Society of Wisconsin, 1976), vol. 16, 382.
[164] Id., vol. 2, 415.
[165] In the copyright context it was the efforts of Noah Webster and others to secure state protection for their writings that vividly demonstrated these shortcomings. See Bugbee, *Genesis of American Patent and Copyright Law*, 128. The contest before various state legislatures between John Fitch and James Rumsey over protection for the steamboat invention and the troubles of other inventors did the same in the patent context. Frank David Prager, "The Steamboat Pioneers before the Founding Fathers," 37 *J. Pat. Off.*

the transition to the national level, the clause constituted no break with the past. Neither the text of the clause nor any known external contemporary reference to it betrays any hint that the framers saw the clause as diverging from existing concepts or practices. Some of the framers knew something about the British framework of copyright and patent. This fact is evidenced by the few public pronunciations on the subject by contemporaries and is made plausible by the legal education of many of the framers. Many of them must have had some familiarity with state and colonial practices in these fields. A substantial number of the framers were members of local legislatures, which handled copyrights and patents. Some of them, such as Pinckney and Madison, were involved in the proceedings surrounding some of the relevant enactments and petitions in their states. As far as one can say on the basis of the scanty record, it seems that the framers, to the extent they devoted any thought to the matter, simply saw themselves as granting the power to Congress to utilize the institutional forms they were familiar with from state and colonial governments and from the British context.

Congress was given the power to secure rights in writings and discoveries without elaborating what the particular form of these rights should be. Even the question of whether these rights should be secured by general enactments, as in the case of the state copyright statutes, or by ad hoc grants, as in the case of state printing and manufacture privileges, was left undecided. The rights were to be secured to authors and inventors only, but this was the general trend of patent and copyright grants since the Revolution. The clause supplied no guidance or elaboration on the defining traits of these figures or on the implications of placing them at the center of the definition of the federal power in this field. The securing of the rights was to be for limited times, but this had been a fixture of English patent and copyright thought since the seventeenth century and the uniform practice in colonial and state grants or enactments. Despite later attempts to read various innovations into the structure, text, or legislative process of the clause, it appears that there is little indication that the framers understood themselves as doing anything more than transplanting on the national level a familiar institutional practice.

To be sure, the constitutional clause became a unique feature of the American copyright and patent regimes. It created a peculiar set of debates and questions that did not appear in other nations. In addition

Soc'y 486 (1955); Andrea Sutcliffe, *Steam: The Untold Story of America's First Great Invention* (New York: Palgrave Macmillan, 2004), 26–85.

to normative questions about the wisdom or desirability of some arrangements and issues of interpretation and application of existing norms, American intellectual property discourse was to have a third layer, namely, debates and arguments about the very existence of legislative power to enact certain measures or use certain institutional forms. The existence of a constitutional source of power placed some alternatives, whether seen as desirable and just or not, beyond the power of legislatures. Arguments that relied on this understanding of the American patent and copyright regimes as limited by constitutional decree appeared at a very early stage. From the first federal Congress onward various arguments in public debate were based on this premise. In the first decades it was issues such as the power of Congress under the intellectual property clause to finance scientific expeditions[166] or to grant patents or monetary premiums to importers of foreign technology[167] that attracted arguments based on the assumption of limitations laid by the clause on congressional power. Despite these early beginnings, the rise in the importance of the constitutional element of American intellectual property law discourse was a gradual and long process. In the centuries following its passage, almost every word of the clause was utilized and debated as possibly significant in defining the scope of Congress' power in the field.[168] Much of this process, however, occurred in the late nineteenth and twentieth centuries.

How did the intellectual property clause that originally attracted little attention attain such a dominant status in American public discourse? The explanation resides not so much in the intrinsic importance of the clause at the moment of its creation as in various features of American culture and politics as they developed in later times. There are at least three overlapping such features. First, American culture and political discourse came to treat the Constitution as the embodiment of the nation's identity and fundamental values. The Constitution attained a

---

[166] This debate arose in the wake of John Churchman's petition to Congress that asked for both exclusive rights to sell maps and globes based on his method for calculating longitudes and funding for a Baffin's Bay expedition. "House of Representatives Journal," in Linda Grant De Pauw et al., eds., *Documentary History of the First Federal Congress of the United States* (Baltimore, Md.: Johns Hopkins University Press, 1977), vol. 3, 28–29. See Walterscheid, *Nature of the Intellectual Property Clause*, 166–68.

[167] See Walterscheid, *Nature of the Intellectual Property Clause*, 169–78, 313–27.

[168] Id.

status that has been described as the American "civil religion."[169] Against this backdrop the intellectual property clause offered lucrative rhetorical and justificatory opportunities to those engaged in public debate or persuasion in the field. Successfully tracing one's position in a particular debate to the constitutional clause was likely to attain substantial justificatory capital. Second, American legal and political thought, especially in the twentieth century, became fascinated with an interpretive approach known as "originalism," which seeks to interpret and apply legal texts in general and the Constitution in particular according to the framers' original intent, contemporaneous understandings and views or some other variation of the concept of original meaning.[170] In line with this popular approach, the intellectual property clause, dating to 1787, came to embody the supposed original and thus privileged meaning of copyright and patent in the United States. Third, and maybe most important, constitutional arguments based on the clause played a unique role within the dynamic of interest group politics that shaped intellectual property law. Such arguments, if successful, constituted "trump cards" that could circumvent the legislative process. The clause, by defining the contours of the legislative power, created an alternative power center in the courts and often attracted those who were likely to be the losers of the legislative process or simply preferred pursuing their objective through litigation.

Be that as it may, by 1789 the intellectual property clause laid the foundations for national copyright and patent regimes in the United States. The clause, however, did not constitute a sharp break with existing practices and did not introduce significant innovations. Both the framers who created the national power and the first federal Congress that acted on it worked against the background of conceptual traditions and institutional forms received from Britain, as well as from colonial and state practices. At the end of the eighteenth century this existing framework was itself in a state of flux. General rights regimes were supplanting ad hoc, discretionary privileges. Authors and inventors moved to the ideological foreground and became the common formal recipients of rights. There were early signs of conceptualizing patents and copyrights as rights in intangible objects. The first national copyright and patent regimes

---

[169] Sanford Levinson, *Constitutional Faith* (Princeton, N.J.: Princeton University Press, 1988), 10. For a discussion of American "civil religion," see Robert Bellah, "Civil Religion in America," 96 *Dedalus* 1 (1967).
[170] See Daniel A. Farber, "The Originalism Debate: A Guide for the Perplexed," 49 *Ohio St. L. J.* 1085 (1989).

created in 1790 reflected this transitory state of the field. They contained many traditional features alongside some newer ones rooted in the changing understandings. They also contained many ambiguities, unresolved tensions, and undeveloped new concepts. The bulk of the transformation that would bring about the modern framework of intellectual property would unfold in the following century.

2

The Rise and Fall of Authorship-Based Copyright

In May 1790 Congress passed the 1790 Copyright Act[1] and created the
first national American copyright regime. By that time, we are informed
by Mark Rose, "all the essential elements of modern Anglo-American
copyright law were in place" with the focal element being "the notion
of the author as the creator and ultimate source of property."[2] On one
level, the implication that the American copyright system was forged at a
time when copyright thought and practice already assumed new forms
infused with the notion of original authorship is accurate. By contrast to
the sporadic colonial printers' privileges, the Copyright Act, following
the state statutes and borrowing heavily from the British Statute of
Anne, created a universal regime of rights. The original holders of these
legal rights, at least as a formal legal matter, were authors, rather
than publishers or printers. More important, by 1790 American public
discourse about copyright came to be firmly fixed on authorship.
Whether they emphasized the notion of copyright as an inherent natural
right or as a positivist creature of the state, based on utilitarian considerations, Americans thinking, writing and disagreeing about copyright
shared a new conceptual framework. At the heart of this framework
were the concepts of authors as individuals who through their mental
labor create original intellectual works and of copyright as a standardized set of legal rights enjoyed by such authors owning the intellectual
works they created.

---

[1] Act of May 31, 1790, ch. 15, 1 Stat. 124.
[2] Mark Rose, *Authors and Owners: The Invention of Copyright* (Cambridge, Mass.:
Harvard University Press, 1993), 132.

On another level, however, the notion that by 1790 copyright law and discourse achieved its basic modern authorship-based framework is deeply misleading. Between 1790 and 1909 American copyright law underwent extensive and fundamental changes. If we could send forward in time an 1800 American copyright lawyer (nothing of the sort existed back then, of course) to 1890 and ask him to argue a copyright case, he would be bedazzled. Late nineteenth-century American copyright law would seem to him a strange and unfamiliar domain not merely because of the differences in legal technicalities. The more striking differences separating the copyright frameworks at either end of the nineteenth century are in the fundamental and constitutive elements of the legal regime and the assumptions embedded in them. In 1800 American copyright law was still the unique regulation of the book trade, which retained the traditional institutional features of the publisher's economic privilege, now bestowed on authors under a universal regime of rights. At the dawn of the twentieth century copyright had become a comprehensive field of law based on the abstract principle of authorial rights in original creative works of the intellect. The publisher's privilege in the shape of exclusive printing rights had been supplanted by a new institutional form pervaded by the concept of ownership of an intellectual "object" of property. These extensive conceptual changes roughly divide into two groups. One – to be discussed in this chapter – involves the complex and often paradoxical ways in which the notion of the original author was embedded in copyright doctrine. The other – discussed in the next chapter – revolves around the construction of the concept of owning an intellectual work. Although distinct, the two core concepts animating these changes were intertwined. Original works of the intellect were the hallmark of the author. Authorship was the justification of ownership of intellectual works and the basis for defining its boundaries.

The concepts of authorship and of the ownership of an intellectual work were not realized in one fell swoop. Nor was their instantiation in copyright law a straightforward manifestation of a predetermined logic. The process of converting abstract ideals into concrete legal concepts was fueled by the agency of interested actors. It was mediated through economic pressures as well as conflicting values, ideological commitments, and interests. The end result, far from a straightforward reflection of the ideals of authorship and intellectual ownership, was a curious and convoluted pattern. This pattern of the modern copyright framework was often ideological. It was ideological, not just in being an interlocking set of ideas, but also in the tendency of many of these ideas to present a distorted image of reality or at least to obscure the tensions between the realities of copyright law and its underlying ideals. Nowhere was the ideological nature of the nineteenth-century transformation of copyright more apparent than in the context of original authorship. By the dawn of the twentieth century original authorship was firmly established as a central principle of American copyright and was embedded in specific legal doctrines. These doctrines, however, were far removed from the abstract ideal of authorship, not just as an imperfect implementation but as the embodiment of a competing set of ideals. Thus American copyright law came to elevate original authorship to an unprecedented status, while at the same time extending copyright to works far removed from that ideal and frequently treating those who created works as wage laborers rather than authorial property owners. This chapter describes how this paradox came to be.

THE SHIFT TO AUTHORSHIP-BASED COPYRIGHT

The legislative dynamics that resulted in the 1790 Copyright Act highlights the extent to which Americans experienced the new federal power in the field as an extension of familiar patterns, rather than a break with them. Soon after the newly created federal Congress met for its first session, petitioners, aware of the intellectual property constitutional clause, started besieging it with pleas for protection of inventions and literary works. These early applications petitioned Congress for individual legislative privileges, rather than general enactments. Apparently, petitioners familiar with the practices of colonial and state grants assumed that the Constitution simply transferred this power to the national legislature and that Congress, like state legislatures, would grant individual privileges. The first two petitions of this kind arrived on April 15, 1789. Thomas Tudor Tucker from South Carolina presented to the House a petition from David Ramsay, a Charleston physician and a member of the state legislature as well as of the Continental Congress. Ramsay asked for protection for his recently written *The History of the American Revolution* and *The History of the Revolution of South Carolina from a British Province to an Independent State.*[3] The other petitioner was John Churchman from Nottingham Pennsylvania, a surveyor and a cartographer who claimed he "invented several different methods by which

---

[3] *House Journal*, 1st Cong., 1st Sess., April 15, 1789, 14. Ramsay's petition is available at *Primary Sources on Copyright (1450–1900)*, ed. L. Bently and M. Kretschmer, www.copyrighthistory.org (hereafter *Primary Sources on Copyright*).

the principles of magnetic variation are so explained, that a latitude of a place being given, its longitude may be easily determined."[4] Churchman asked that "a law may be passed for vesting in the petitioner, his heirs and assigns, an exclusive right of vending of spheres, hemispheres, maps, charts and tables, on his principles of magnetism."[5] These were followed by a steady trickle of pleas for individual grants by authors,[6] some of whom, such as Ramsay[7] or Jedidiah Morse,[8] expressly appealed to the new constitutional clause.

Congress' initial response to the petitions for individual privileges was favorable.[9] Events took a new turn, however, when the House responded to the report of a three-man committee charged with examining the Ramsay and Churchman petitions by ordering that "a bill or bills be brought in, making a general provision for securing to authors and inventors the exclusive right of their respective writings and discoveries."[10]

---

[4] *House Journal*, 1st Cong., 1st Sess., April 15, 1789, 14.   [5] Id.

[6] On May 12, 1789, Jedidiah Morse petitioned for protection of his *The American Geography or a View of the Present Situation of the United States of America. House Journal*, 1st Cong., 1st Sess., May 12, 1789, 40, 43. Nicholas Pike applied on June 8, 1789, for "an exclusive privilege" in his *A New and Complete System of Arthematic*; Charlene Bangs and Helen E. Veit, eds., *Documentary History of the First Federal Congress, Legislative Histories* (Baltimore, Md.: Johns Hopkins University Press, 1972), vol. 4, 508. Hannah Adams petitioned for protection on July 22, 1789. *House Journal*, 1st Cong., 1st Sess., July 22, 1789, 77, 80. The extent to which petitioners were immersed in the traditional framework of ad hoc petitions and private laws is exemplified by the petition of Enos Hitchcock dating May 26, 1790. At this time the general copyright bill was in the final stages of being passed into law. Hitchcock, who, as revealed by his petition, was aware of that, found it necessary nonetheless to ask that "the privilege of a late law, may be extended to him for securing the copy-right of a book which he has lately published." Id., 1st Cong., 2nd Sess., May 26, 1790, 115–16.

[7] Ramsay, after appealing to the justice of being compensated for his labor, mentioned that "the same principle [is] expressly recognized in the new constitution"; *Documentary History of the First Federal Congress*, 509.

[8] Morse slightly confused the articles when he mentioned that "provision is made in the 4th article ["eight" is struck out] Section of the first Article of the Constitution of the United Sates, for Securing to Authors the exclusive right to their respective Writings." Id., 511.

[9] The two first petitions were referred to a three-man committee whose members were Thomas Tudor Tucker, Alexander White, and Benjamin Huntington. On April 20 the House approved the committee's recommendation to grant individual privileges to Churchman and Ramsay; *House Journal*, 1st Cong., 1st Sess., April 20, 1789, 18. Churchman's additional plea for financing an expedition to Baffin's Bay, in order to investigate his theory, elicited a debate about the depleted state of national financial resources and even some doubts about congressional power under the intellectual property clause of the Constitution to support such an undertaking; Annals of Congress, 1st Cong., 1st Sess., 178–80.

[10] *House Journal*, 1st Cong., 1st Sess., April 20, 1789, 18.

There is no direct indication why the House responded to petitions for individual grants by ordering the creation of a general regime. The reason may have been concerns about adminstrability of a legislative grant system, given the volume of petitions that could be expected to flow from the entire nation to a busy national legislature. It is also likely that the institutional precedents of the British Statute of Anne and the states' copyright enactments that were known to members of Congress played a role in shaping this response. Whatever its reason, the House decision to order the preparation of a general legislation signified a crucial turn from ad hoc privileges to general, standardized copyright and patent regimes. Curiously, the committee appointed to prepare the legislation tried at first to treat copyright and patent under one legislative roof, which resulted in H.R. 10, "A bill to promote the progress of science and useful arts, by securing to authors and inventors the exclusive right to their respective writings and discoveries."[11] Later, however, at the suggestion of Aedanus Burke from South Carolina, the joint bill was split.[12] The result, following several more legislative rounds,[13] was the 1790 Copyright Act.

The 1790 act, which borrowed heavily from the Statute of Anne,[14] consolidated on the national level the two main developments of the preceding two decades in the colonies and the states. First, it completed the transition of copyright from ad hoc discretionary privileges to a universal private rights regime. Second, it firmly placed the author at the center of copyright doctrine and ideology, at the expense of publishers and printers, who, at least as a matter of formal doctrine and rhetoric, were relegated to a secondary status.

---

[11] No known copy of H.R. 10 has survived. The version referred to here is a typescript of a typescript of the original. In 1955 Wilma Davis, copyright office librarian, found a damaged typescript of the bill in the library of the office. She believed this typescript was made by Thorvald Solberg, U.S. register of copyright 1897–1930, who may have had a copy of the original in his private library before it was destroyed by fire in 1918. Ms. Davis had another typescript prepared. In 1968 the original typescript was not found in the Library of Congress where it was left. *Documentary History of the First Federal Congress*, 519. Frank Evina, Senior Copyright Specialist at the Copyright Office, located and provided a typescript of the bill, which is reproduced in *Primary Sources*.

[12] Annals of Congress, 1st Cong., 2nd Sess., 1080.

[13] See William F. Patry, *Patry on Copyright* (St. Paul, Minn.: Thomson Reuters, 2010), §1:19; Oren Bracha, "Commentary on the Copyright Act 1790," in *Primary Sources on Copyright*.

[14] For an analysis of the similarities between the two statutes, see Oren Bracha, "The Adventures of the Statute of Anne in the Land of Unlimited Possibilities: The Life of a Legal Transplant," 25 *Berk. Tech. L. J.* 1427, 1453–56 (2010).

The framework of the 1790 act was clearly that of a universal regime of private rights. The act specified in general terms the subject matter to which it applied, namely, any "map, chart, book or books."[15] It defined the potential recipients of protection in inclusive and universal terms as authors or (in regard to works already published) purchasers of copyright, who were citizens or residents of the United States, their administrators, executors, or assignees.[16] Standard requirements for protection were listed,[17] and a uniform set of entitlements[18] was extended, as a matter of right, to any eligible person who met those requirements.

Still, at the edges the act retained some of the traditional flavor of copyright as a governmental regulation of the book trade. This was most apparent in the fact that, following the Statute of Anne, the only remedies provided for the infringement of copyright were forfeiture and destruction of infringing copies and a fine of fifty cents per each sheet found in the possession of the infringer, to be equally divided between the United States and the copyright owner.[19] Indeed, the early bill H.R. 10 carried over from the original British statute what was probably a qui tam action by splitting the penalty sum between "the author . . . or the proprietor" and "any person or persons who shall sue for the same."[20] The lack of any other remedies was highlighted by the fact that in regard to the separate statutory protection extended to unpublished manuscripts the statute explicitly provided that an infringer "shall be liable to suffer and pay to the said Author and proprietor all damages occasioned by such injury to be recovered by a special Action on the Case."[21]

That this statutory restriction of the remedies conflicted with the new understanding of copyright as a private right is borne out by the extent to which later courts and commentators simply ignored it. Although the early practice of the lower courts in copyright cases is shrouded in

---

[15] 1 Stat. 124, §1.　　[16] Id.

[17] The act required registration of the work with the clerk's office of the local federal district court, publication of the registration record in public newspapers, and a deposit of a copy of the work with the Secretary of State. 1 Stat. 125, §§3–4.

[18] The act gave the copyright owner the exclusive right to print, reprint, publish, vend, and import the protected text for fourteen years, once renewable for another fourteen years by surviving authors. 1 Stat. 124, §§1–2.

[19] Id., §2.

[20] H.R. 10, 2. See Bracha, "The Adventures of the Statute of Anne," 1454–55.

[21] 1 Stat. 125, §6.

obscurity, it seems that American judges followed English courts[22] and read the full array of remedies into the copyright regime. In the first reported copyright case in the United States – the 1798 *Morse v. Reid*[23] involving an infringement of copyright in Jedidiah Morse's *American Geography* – the Circuit Court for the District of New York ordered an accounting of the defendant's profits arising from the infringement and a monetary relief based on it. The case record leaves it somewhat unclear whether the exact remedy was the equitable one of disgorgement of defendant's profits or common law damages for plaintiff's lost profit, but it is clear that the remedy was not the statutory penalty. The court simply awarded the remedy with no discussion or attempt to construe the Copyright Act. It is possible that the court assumed, as Lord Kenyon did in *Beckford v. Hood* decided that year in England, that "nothing could be more incomplete as a remedy than those penalties alone," and concurred in his observation that "I cannot think that the Legislature would act so inconsistently as to confer a right, and leave the party whose property was invaded, without redress."[24] Later nineteenth-century commentators flatly asserted the applicability of nonstatutory remedies with little discussion or support. Justice Joseph Story in his *Commentaries on Equity Jurisprudence* seems to have taken it for granted that both the common law remedy of damages and the equitable one of account were available in copyright infringement cases.[25] George Ticknor Curtis asserted in his 1847 treatise that "[n]o action on the case for damages is provided by statute; but there can be no doubt that here, as well as in England, such an action lies at common law."[26] He gave no reason whatsoever for this confident assertion. Only in 1908, when the

---

[22] *Beckford v. Hood*, 101 Eng. Rep. 1164 (K.B. 1798).

[23] A report of the case can be found in 5 *Collections of the Massachusetts Historical Society* 123 (1798). See John D. Gordan, "*Morse v. Reid*: The First Reported Federal Copyright Case," 11 *L. Hist. Rev.* 21 (1993).

[24] 104 Eng. Rep. 1164, 1167 (K.B. 1798). The English case had another significant aspect not present in *Morse v. Reid*. The court there awarded statutory damages for the infringement of a work that was not registered as required by the Statute of Anne and therefore was ineligible for the statutory remedies. In doing so the court partly revived the possibility of common law copyright, which was supposedly laid to rest in the 1774 *Donaldson v. Becket*. See Ronan Deazley, *Rethinking Copyright: History, Theory, Language* (Cheltenham: Edward Elgar, 2006), 30; Ronan Deazley, "Commentary on *Beckford v. Hood* (1798)," in *Primary Sources on Copyright*.

[25] Joseph Story, *Commentaries on Equity Jurisprudence as Administered in England and America*, 2nd ed. (Boston: Hilliard, Gray, 1839), vol. 2, 210.

[26] George Ticknor Curtis, *A Treatise on the Law of Copyright* (Boston: C.C. Little and J. Brown, 1847), 313.

question was of much less practical importance did the Supreme Court reject *Beckford v. Hood* and rule in regard to common law remedies that copyright protection was limited to the remedies provided in the statute.[27]

The new ideological focus on authors was as important as the shift to a universal rights regime. The act that placed initial ownership in the hands of the "author or authors of any map, chart, book or books"[28] made the author the primary owner of copyright and assigned all others, including publishers, to a derivative status. An implicit side effect of this arrangement was making authorship itself a precondition for protection, precluding the possibility of copyright in texts with no relevant authors such as classic ancient texts or the bible. As a formal doctrinal matter the author became the unquestionable center of American copyright, notwithstanding the fact that the little we know of early registration and ownership practices suggests that reality on the ground may have been more complex.[29]

On the ideological level too, the 1790 act expressed the shift of American copyright toward authorship. Unlike the Statute of Anne and some of the state statutes, it did not contain an elaborate preamble. The act was legislated, however, after a decade of public activity on the state and national level, which entrenched authors and authorship as the raison d'être of copyright. This shift started in individual petitions for state privileges. Some of those petitions, such as John Ledyard's 1783 appeal to the Connecticut legislature,[30] emphasized more traditional

---

[27] *Globe Newspaper Co. v. Walker*, 210 U.S. 356, 362–67 (1908). The practical importance of the question had declined by then because the statute had come to extend damages to many categories of works.

[28] 1 Stat. 124, §1.

[29] In the first decade of the regime many copyright registrations were for proprietors rather than authors. While authors could register copyright in their own works, proprietors were usually publishers or printers who registered works, presumably after the rights were assigned by the author. The relative share of registering proprietors was substantial from the start, but it steadily rose in the first decade. In Massachusetts between 1790 and 1794, forty-five books were registered by authors and twenty-five books registered by proprietors. Between 1795 and 1800, there were sixty-two registrations by authors and sixty-three by proprietors. The same trend occurred in other states, including some such as Pennsylvania and New York that were the home of important publishing centers. James Gilreath, "American Literature, Public Policy, and the Copyright Laws before 1800," in *Federal Copyright Records, 1790–1800* (Washington, D.C.: U.S. Government Printing Office, 1987), xxiii.

[30] Ledyard, a Connecticut adventurer who sailed with Captain James Cook's expedition, petitioned for protection in his *Journal of Captain Cook's Last Voyage*. In his petition Ledyard did not refer to authorship but rather emphasized the public utility of his essay

justifications and hardly mentioned authorship. Traditional justifications, however, were quickly supplanted by authorship-based arguments.[31] The lobbying for general state statutes, whether based on individual rights or utilitarian reasoning, already relied exclusively on authorship arguments. An early example of this was Samuel Stanhope Smith's allusion to "[m]en of industry or of talents ... [who] have a right to the property of their production" in the letter he provided Noah Webster for his copyright campaign in various states.[32] In his 1783 letter to the Continental Congress Joel Barlow observed that "[t]here is certainly no kind of property, in the nature of things, so much his own as the works which a person originates from his own creative imagination" and concluded that "it is more necessary, in this country than in any other, that the rights of authors should be secured by law."[33] Barlow's text was echoed in the resolution issued by the Continental Congress recommending that the states legislate copyright statutes.[34] The lobbying for these statutes as well as many of their preambles were rife with references to authors and their rights.[35] The 1789 constitutional clause spoke of securing the exclusive rights of "Authors,"[36] and the little public discussion it provoked focused on authors. In short, by 1790 copyright ideology, including both its natural rights and utilitarian strands, became the domain

---

consisting in "opening a most valuable trade across the north pacific Ocean to China & the east Indies." See Connecticut State Library: Manuscript (Colleges and Schools, 1661–1789), series I, vol. II, document 149, available in *Primary Sources on Copyright*. For an analysis of Ledyard's petition, see Oren Bracha, "Commentary on Andrew Law's Petition 1781," in *Primary Sources on Copyright*.

[31] See e.g. William Billings' Massachusetts petition, Massachusetts Archives, LVIII, 598–99, reprinted in Rollo G. Silver, "Prologue to Copyright in America: 1772," 11 *Papers of the Bibliographical Society of the University of Virginia* 259 (1958); Robert Ross' Connecticut petition, *The Public Records of the State of Connecticut*, ed. Charles J. Hoadly (1895), vol. 5, 245; Andrew Law's Connecticut petition, Connecticut State Library, Manuscript (Colleges and Schools, 1661–1789), series I, vol. II, document 147, available in *Primary Sources on Copyright*.

[32] Noah Webster, "Origin of the Copy-Right Laws of the United States," in *A Collection of Papers on Political, Literary and Moral Subjects* (New York: Webster & Clark, 1843), 174.

[33] *Papers of the Continental Congress, 1774–1789* (No. 78), vol. 4, 369, available in *Primary Sources on Copyright*.

[34] Journal of the Continental Congress, vol. 24, 326–27; *Papers of the Continental Congress* (No. 24), vol. 4, 91.

[35] See Francine Crawford, "Pre-constitutional Copyright Statutes," 23 *Bull. Copyright Soc'y U.S.A.* 14–16 (1975); Bracha, "The Adventures of the Statute of Anne," 1446–47; Oren Bracha, "Commentary on the Connecticut Copyright Statute 1783," in *Primary Sources on Copyright*.

[36] U.S. Const. art. I, §8, cl. 8.

of authors. This was borne out by the fact that, unlike earlier instances, all the petitions prior to legislating the federal act were by authors pleading for privileges in their own works. Members of the House were reminded of the authorial origin and focus of the act when it was pointed out during the legislative process that it "was solicited by some very ingenious men"[37] and that those "gentlemen had lately published the fruits of their industry and application, and were every hour in danger of having them surreptitiously printed."[38]

Whereas the 1790 act embodied a significant shift to a universal rights regime and expressed a new focus on authorship, in other respects it was firmly rooted in traditional patterns. The new regime lifted the old institutional form of the printer's privilege, generalized it, and bestowed it on authors. Authorship was now the underlying abstract justification of copyright and authors were the formal recipients of the right, but copyright law contained no mechanism whatsoever for defining or recognizing the all-important figure of the author. Copyright had come to be perceived in terms of rights of authors in their intellectual works, but the law provided no explanation of what a work of authorship was and made no attempt to target copyright protection to such subject matter. Indeed, the 1790 act that covered any "map, chart, book or books" simply extended copyright to its traditional centuries-old domain of the product of the printing press. Finally, copyright came to be described as the property rights of authors in the product of the intellect, but copyright law supplied no conceptual or doctrinal tools for coming to terms with this notion of ownership of an intangible "object" of property or for applying it. Under the 1790 act copyright still consisted of the familiar economic entitlement of the printer: "the sole right and liberty of printing, reprinting, publishing and vending,"[39] namely, the exclusive right of making and selling verbatim printed copies of a protected text.

The gradual process of converting the abstract principle of authorial ownership of the product of the intellect into concrete doctrinal and institutional forms unfolded during the nineteenth century. It was by no means a process in which a predetermined logic of authorship embedded in copyright at the end of the eighteenth century gradually manifested itself. Rather, the abstract concepts of authorial ownership operated as a repository of intellectual resources drawn on in order to construct arguments and legal doctrines. This shaping and bending of concrete

---

[37] Annals of Congress, 1st Cong., 2nd Sess., 1093.   [38] Id., 1117.   [39] 1 Stat. 124, §1.

authorship-based arguments was done in the service of a variety of interests and agendas, which were frequently in tension with each other. The outcome was a convoluted conceptual structure, the result of the interaction between copyright's new abstract principle of authorship, an array of powerful economic interests, and conflicting ideological commitments. The nineteenth century was thus the period of the rise and fall of authorship-based copyright. Paradoxically, the rise and fall happened simultaneously. As the ideology of authorial authorship was embedded in concrete legal doctrines, those doctrines took unexpected, tension-riddled, and often paradoxical forms.

THE MECHANIC AND THE AUTHOR: ORIGINALITY AS NOVELTY

In the first comprehensive treatise on American copyright published in 1847 George Ticknor Curtis observed that "[t]he statutes both in England and America, make use of the word *Author* which *ex vi termini* imports originality," but, he hastened to add, almost as an afterthought: "to some extent."[40] This sums up the curious career of the originality requirement in nineteenth-century American copyright law. Originality is often described as the heart of the new concept of individual or romantic authorship that took over copyright discourse in the eighteenth century.[41] The paradigmatic image of the author came to be that of an intellectual genius who introduces a radically new creation into the world. William Wordsworth famously described genius in 1815 as "the act of doing well what is worthy to be done, and what was never done before ... widening the sphere of human sensibility ... the introduction of a new element into the intellectual universe."[42] Prior to Wordsworth, others popularized similar concepts that identified originality as the defining feature of the author.[43]

---

[40] Curtis, *A Treatise on the Law of Copyright*, 169, n. 1.

[41] See Oren Brahca, "The Ideology of Authorship Revisited: Authors, Markets, and Liberal Values in Early American Copyright," 118 *Yale. L. Rev.* 186, 193 (2008); Martha Woodmansee, "The Genius and the Copyright: Economic and Legal Conditions of the Emergence of the 'Author,'" 17 *Eighteenth Century Stud.* 425, 427 (1984); James Boyle, *Shamans, Software and Spleens: Law and the Construction of the Information Society* (Cambridge, Mass.: Harvard University Press, 1996), 56; Peter Jaszi, "Toward a Theory of Copyright: The Metamorphoses of 'Authorship,'" 1991 *Duke L. J.* 455, 462–63.

[42] William Wordsworth, "Essay, Supplementary to the Preface," in Paul M. Zall, ed., *Literary Criticism of William Wordsworth* (Lincoln: University of Nebraska Press, 1966), 158, 184.

[43] See Woodmansee, "The Genius and the Copyright," 426–31; Rose, *Authors and Owners*, 114–24.

This vocabulary that fused together authorship and originality suffused Anglo-American philosophical copyright discourse beginning in the mid-eighteenth century. Authors and lawyers developed a conceptual system that closely bound together authorial originality and authorial ownership. The image of authors as the ultimate source of new ideas that were entirely their own was a powerful justification of their legal property rights in those intellectual products of their minds. As Blackstone put it in the *Commentaries*: "When a man by the exertion of his rational powers has produced an original work, he has clearly a power to dispose of that identical work as he pleases, and any attempt to take it from him, or vary the disposition he has made of it, is an invasion of his right of property."[44]

In light of this prominence of originality in general cultural notions of authorship and particularly in copyright's theoretical discourse, one may be surprised to learn that originality had no foothold whatsoever in late-eighteenth-century copyright doctrine in the United States. Virtually any map, chart, or text was eligible for protection as long as it had an author who was a citizen or resident of the United States. The term "author" was not understood to import any particular restriction in this regard. At its infancy American copyright law did not include a lax originality threshold. It included no doctrine or concept of this kind at all. This is borne out by the character of the works that were registered for protection in the first years of the regime. Practical, utilitarian, or informational texts of various kinds were the most common.[45] Of the first one hundred entries in Pennsylvania, almost half were textbooks, manuals, atlases, and commercial directories. The trend continued in later registrations.[46] American copyright may have been entangled with an ideology that celebrated the intellectual genius and the original author, but the most commonly copyrighted

---

[44] William Blackstone, *Commentaries on the Laws of England* (Oxford: Clarendon Press, 1766), vol. 2, 405–6.

[45] See Jane C. Ginsburg, "Creation and Commercial Value: Copyright Protection of Works of Information," 90 *Colum. L. Rev.* 1865, 1874 (1990); Meredith L. McGill, "Copyright in the Early Republic," in Robert A. Gross and Mary Kelly, eds., *A History of the Book in America: An Extensive Republic: Print, Culture, and Society in the New Nation, 1790–1840* (Chapel Hill: University of North Carolina Press, 2011) vol. 2, 199.

[46] Gilreath, "American Literature," xxii. See also Joseph F. Felcone, "New Jersey Copyright Registrations, 1791–1845," 104 *Proceedings of the American Antiquarian Society* 51, 54–5 (2004).

works had very little to do with the stereotypical image of original authorship in the romantic sense.

Originality as a doctrinal mode of argument began to appear only in the third decade of the nineteenth century. It developed in the course of court battles between interested parties. It is safe to assume that such parties had little concerns about the philosophical grounding of copyright. Copyright's new focus on authorship, however, supplied a store of ideological and rhetorical resources on which they could draw opportunistically. On one side of those disputes were parties trying to defend against charges of copyright infringement. As Curtis pointed out, the concept of authorship entailed the notion of originality, and that, in turn, held out the promise of a legal threshold for limiting the coverage of copyright protection and escaping liability. Litigants who exploited this opportunity developed two strands of argument in attempting to convince courts to convert the theoretical concept of originality into a doctrinal structure. The first relied directly on the romantic notion of the creation of radically new ideas as the essence of authorship. Arguments in this vein invited courts to regulate the entrance gate to the realm of copyright by imposing a robust or at least meaningful novelty requirement. The second emphasized the association of the author with creative genius, thereby claiming that only classes of works that involved a degree of scholarly or aesthetic merit, or in another variant creativity, by contrast to mere industriousness, were within copyright's purview. On the other side of those disputes were parties with a vested interest in keeping the gates of copyright protection wide open. Many of these were owners of copyright in useful works of the traditional variety, such as textbooks or maps. Others, especially in the second half of the century, operated in new emerging industries where the extension of copyright protection seemed a lucrative possibility. These parties fashioned arguments that shaped and bent the rhetorical resources available to prevent any strict threshold requirement for copyright protection. The legal doctrine of originality was forged between this hammer and anvil of competing claims.

Justice Joseph Story – probably the most influential figure in shaping early American copyright and patent law – established the basic framework for dealing with the issue of originality in a cluster of decisions and writings during the 1830s and 1840s. His decision in the 1839 *Gray v. Russell*[47] was an important landmark in this respect. The work

---

[47] 10 F. Cas. 1035 (C.C.D. Mass. 1839).

at issue was *Adam's Latin Grammar* by the Bostonian schoolmaster Benjamin Gould. This work was typical of the texts commonly protected by early American copyright. It was a popular textbook for the study of Latin written by the Scottish scholar Alexander Adam. Gould – the "author" and original copyright holder in the United States – created a revised and improved edition of the book suitable for the study of Latin in nineteenth-century America. He revised some parts of the text and added his own notes and supplementary materials. In producing this revised version Gould worked to correct the errors in earlier American editions of *Adam's Grammar* that were in circulation as early as 1799.[48] Although some of the revisions were substantial, Gould's purpose was to preserve "in all cases where it was practicable, the words of the original grammar."[49] The work, referred to by Gould as a "compendium," was, in short, the antithesis of the romantic notion of original authorship: a textbook that consisted of editor's revisions, consolidations, and commentary. This was hardly Woodsworth's "introduction of a new element into the intellectual universe."

The derivative nature of the copyrighted work was one of the main avenues of defense for the defendant, the publisher of C.D. Cleveland's edition of *Adam's Grammar*, a work described by a master appointed by the court as containing "the substance of all Mr. Gould's notes ... for the most part literally copied."[50] The defendant tried to convince the court to take seriously the notion of authorship as based on radical novelty. The argument was that copyright protection should be denied because "there is nothing substantially new in Mr. Gould's notes to his edition of Adam's Latin Grammar; and that all his notes in substance, and many of them in form, may be found in other works antecedently printed."[51]

Justice Story rejected offhand the strong version of originality offered by the defendant, observing "[t]hat is not the true question before the court." "The true question," he wrote, "is, whether these notes are to be found collected and embodied in any former single work."[52] In defining the pertinent legal question in this way Story constructed a version of

---

[48] Benjamin A. Gould, *Adam's Latin grammar, with some improvements and the following additions: rules for the right pronunciation of the Latin language; metrical key to the Odes of Horace; a list of Latin authors arranged according to the different ages of Roman literature; tables showing the value of the various coins, weights and measures used among the Romans* (Boston: Hilliard, Gray, Little, Wilkins, 1829), 3.
[49] Id.   [50] Master in Chancery Report in *Gray v. Russell* (case file).
[51] 10 F. Cas. 1037.   [52] Id.

originality and authorship strikingly different from the romantic one. Gould's original contribution, according to Story, was "[t]he plan, the arrangement, and the combination of these notes in the form, in which they are collectively exhibited," and these "belong[ed] exclusively to this gentleman."[53] This was also the correct understanding of the essence of authorship under which Gould was "justly to be deemed the author ... and entitled to a copyright accordingly."[54] By contrast to the defendant's proffered model of authorship, Story consciously emphasized the cumulative and cross-textual character of creation. "If no work could be considered by our law as entitled to the privilege of copyright, which is composed of materials drawn from many different sources," he explained, "then, indeed, it would be difficult to say, that there could be any copyright in most of the scientific and professional treatises of the present day."[55] Following prose that presented the entire intellectual corpus of Western civilization as an ongoing exercise of borrowing and standing on the shoulders of giants, Story gave an example that struck close to home. "Take the case of the work on insurance, written by one of the learned counsel in this cause, and to which the whole profession are so much indebted," he wrote, meaning Willard Phillips' *A Treatise on the Law of Insurance*.[56] Despite the fact that this treatise was "but a compilation with occasional comments upon all the leading doctrines of that branch of the law, drawn from reported cases, or from former authors ... none of us ever doubted, that he [i.e., Phillips] was fully entitled to a copyright in the work, as being truly, in a just sense, his own."[57]

Six years later, in *Emerson v. Davies*,[58] Story supplied an even stronger version of his minimalist conception of originality and authorship. The defendant whose book copied a few examples and exercises from the plaintiff's mathematics textbook tried his luck with an originality argument, claiming that Davies' book did not contain "any thing new and original, entitling him to a copy-right."[59] Had they looked at Story's opinion in *Gray v. Russell* or in the recent edition of Story's *Commentaries on Equity Jurisprudence*,[60] the defendant's lawyers might have had second thoughts about basing their defense on such a line of argument, natural though it may have seemed given copyright's grounding in authorship.

---

[53] Id.   [54] Id.   [55] Id., 1038.

[56] Id. See Willard Phillips, *A Treatise on the Law of Insurance* (Boston: Wells and Lilly, 1823).

[57] 10 F. Cas. 1038.   [58] 8 F. Cas. 615 (C.C.D. Mass. 1845).   [59] Id.

[60] Joseph Story, *Commentaries on Equity Jurisprudence*, vol. 2, 215–16.

Story had no sympathy for such arguments. He observed that "some of the learned witnesses, whose evidence is in the case, have entirely misunderstood the law upon this subject; and some portions of the argument at the bar seem to me to have proceeded upon an equally inadmissible ground."[61] "The question," he wrote, "is not, whether the materials which are used are entirely new, and have never been used before … The true question is, whether the same plan, arrangement and combination of materials have been used before."[62] Next came an antithesis of the romantic concept of authorship as radical originality even more striking than the one Story supplied in *Gray v. Russell*. It is worth quoting in length:

In truth, in literature, in science and in art, there are, and can be, few, if any, things, which, in an abstract sense, are strictly new and original throughout. Every book in literature, science and art, borrows, and must necessarily borrow, and use much which was well known and used before. No man creates a new language for himself, at least if he be a wise man, in writing a book. He contents himself with the use of language already known and used and understood by others. No man writes exclusively from his own thoughts, unaided and uninstructed by the thoughts of others. The thoughts of every man are, more or less, a combination of what other men have thought and expressed, although they may be modified, exalted, or improved by his own genius or reflection. If no book could be the subject of copy-right which was not new and original in the elements of which it is composed, there could be no ground for any copy-right in modern times, and we should be obliged to ascend very high, even in antiquity, to find a work entitled to such eminence.[63]

All the great authors of the past Story presented as bricoleurs, free borrowers of texts whose genius consisted in reworking and recombining existing knowledge and materials:

Virgil borrowed much from Homer; Bacon drew from earlier as well as contemporary minds; Coke exhausted all the known learning of his profession; and even Shakespeare and Milton, so justly and proudly our boast as the brightest originals would be found to have gathered much from the abundant stores of current knowledge and classical studies in their days. What is La Place's great work, but the combination of the processes and discoveries of the great mathematicians before his day, with his own extraordinary genius? What are all modern law books, but new combinations and arrangements of old materials, in which the skill and judgment of the author in the selection and exposition and accurate use of those materials, constitute the basis of his reputation, as well as of his copy-right? Blackstone's Commentaries and Kent's Commentaries are but splendid examples of the merit and value of such achievements.[64]

---

[61] 8 F. Cas. 620.   [62] Id., 618.   [63] Id., 619.   [64] Id.

This outlook resulted in a very low originality threshold, bestowing copyright on anyone "who by his own skill, judgment and labor, writes a new work, and does not merely copy that of another . . . if the variations are not merely formal and shadowy, from existing works."[65]

Thus, the moment that originality passed from the realm of abstract ideology into doctrinal discourse it was dramatically scaled down. The heroic notion of the author as a creator of radically new ideas ex nihilo had transformed into the thin requirement that he must not be a servile copier. This was no mere compromise or imperfect application of a theoretical principle due to practical difficulties. The diluted version of originality that Story planted at the heart of American copyright was backed by a conscious and explicit understanding of the creative process directly at odds with that of romantic authorship.

The minimalist interpretation of originality as a doctrinal requirement was grounded in traditional copyright practices and, as I will explain shortly, was in line with existing and emerging economic interests. It was not, however, the only possible future of copyright law. There were other available paths that were not taken. The most conspicuous example of this alternative path for copyright law – one that would have taken originality in the romantic sense more seriously – is the 1851 *Jolly v. Jacques*.[66] The case involved an American adaptation and rearrangement of a preexisting German musical composition. The German composition was adapted for use on stage as part of a comedy. The rights in the adapted version – explicitly recognized under the 1831 Copyright Act[67] – were assigned to the plaintiff, who published and sold it as sheet music. The defendant, who published a very similar musical composition under the same title, made a defense argument reminiscent of the defendants' in *Gray* and *Emerson*. The American author of the adaptation, he said, did not add "any new matter to the composition, or to the combination of the materials of the original air, but had simply adapted the old melody to the piano-forte."[68]

Justice Story (now deceased) would have instantly dismissed such an argument as a misunderstanding of copyright law. Justice Samuel Nelson, who heard the case, however, took the originality argument much more seriously. A year later in *Hotchkiss v. Greenwood*[69] Nelson would

[65] Id.

[66] 13 F. Cas. 910, 914–15 (S.D. N.Y. 1850). See also *Reed v. Carusi*, 20 F. Cas. 431 (C.C.D. Md. 1845).

[67] Act of Feb. 8, 1831, ch. 16, §1, 4 Stat. 436.   [68] 13 F. Cas. 913.

[69] 52 U.S. 248 (1851).

introduce into American patent law the nonobviousness requirement under which only inventions that demonstrated substantial innovation or, in Nelson's terms, inventions that are the work of a genius rather than that of a mere mechanic, could enjoy patent protection.[70] In *Jolly* Nelson attempted to create a similar threshold requirement in copyright law. He adopted an expert witness view that the adaptation "requires but an inferior degree of skill, and can be readily accomplished by any person practised in the transfer of music."[71] In light of this nature of the copyrighted work, Nelson explained, the question is whether it is a musical composition under the 1831 statute. In phrasing the question, Nelson already indicated that he was prepared to take the ideal of original authorship seriously. The question was pertinent, he wrote, because "[i]t is not claimed that [the adapter] is the author of the melody or air; but simply that, by skill and labor, he has adapted it to a new use, or to a new instrument."[72] The obvious subtext was a contrast between the author distinguished by the quality of radical novelty and a person who merely adapts an existing creation.

Nelson defined the litmus test for answering the question in terms of substantial novelty: "The musical composition contemplated by the statute must, doubtless, be substantially a new and original work; and not a copy of a piece already produced, with additions and variations, which a writer of music with experience and skill might readily make." He conjured up an opposition between the true work of authorship epitomized by "[t]he original air [that] requires genius for its construction" and "the adaptation or accompaniment" that could be made by "a mere mechanic in music."[73] Although falling short of enacting the strongest version of the romantic authorship ideal into law, *Jolly v. Jacques* with its requirement of innovation and distinction between the mechanic and the author embodied an alternative future for American copyright law. In this alternative future, copyright doctrine would be shaped to reflect the ideal that the essence of intellectual ownership and its ultimate justification is authorship defined by strong originality.

The actual trajectory of American copyright law in the second half of the nineteenth century involved the general acceptance of Story's view of originality and the decline of the alternative presented by Nelson. Whenever the issue arose, judges and commentators patiently explained

[70] 52 U.S. 267. See John F. Duffy, "Inventing Invention: A Case Study of Legal Innovation," 86 *Tex. L. Rev.* 1, 39–41 (2007).
[71] 13 F. Cas. 913.   [72] Id.   [73] Id.

that in copyright law originality is a technical and minimal threshold requirement that has nothing to do with heroic notions of radical novelty.[74] Some even followed in Story's footsteps and grounded their minimalist understanding of originality in elaborations of the creative process directly at odds with romantic authorship. Thus, in 1862 one court explained, when rejecting an originality challenge to the copyright in a dramatic adaptation of a novel, that "the plays of Shakespeare are framed of materials which existed long before his time, and were gathered by him from ancient chronicles, and other industry receptacles of anti-quated literature."[75] By the late nineteenth century originality as radical novelty, so it seemed, was a dead horse in American copyright discourse, perceived, at best, as a naïve concept of the creative process, having nothing to do with the doctrines of actual copyright law.

CREATIVE GENIUS AND MERE INDUSTRY: ORIGINALITY AS CREATIVITY

The second element of originality derived from the image of the author as a creative genius whose work introduces into the world not just novel ideas but works of beauty and merit. There were several strands of meaning to creativity in this sense that were frequently weaved together. Creativity often meant substantive merit, a form of creation that reached the level of high art or learning as opposed to merely vulgar amusement. Relatedly, creative originality was sometimes referred to as denoting elevating and civilizing qualities contrasted with lewd and debasing forms of expression. Finally, the concept of originality was invoked to conjure up the ideal of art or scholarly learning as higher forms of intellectual human activity by comparison to mere industriousness, which belonged to the world of utility and commerce. The three strands of meaning were grounded not just in copyright's association with authorship, but also in early American copyright discourse, which construed copyright as a vehicle for cultivating the high arts and spreading knowledge. This early outlook left its imprint on the Constitution's copyright clause and its

---

[74] Some of those judges and commentators did so by directly citing to Story's early opinions. See e.g. *Atwill v. Ferrett*, 2. F. Cas. 195, 198 (C.C.S.D. N.Y 1846); *Mead v. West Pub. Co.*, 80 F. 380, 383 (C.C.D. Minn. 1896); *Banker v. Caldwell*, 3 Minn. 94, 97 (Minn. 1859); Curtis, *A Treatise on the Law of Copyright*, 173. Others simply reiterated Story's views without referencing his writings. See e.g. *Ladd v. Oxnard*, 75 F. 703, 731 (C.C.D. Mass. 1896); *Brightley v. Littleton*, 37 F. 103, 104 (C.C.E.D. Pa. 1888).

[75] *Boucicault v. Fox*, 3 F. Cas. 977, 982 (C.C.S.D. N.Y. 1862).

stated purpose of promoting the progress of science. During the nine-teenth century the clause was often invoked as support and inspiration for arguments premised on originality in the sense of creative merit.

The legal treatment of originality as creativity followed a pattern similar to that of originality as novelty. Some early decisions demonstrated will-ingness by judges to take creativity seriously and derive from it meaningful threshold requirements. In 1829 in one of the first reported American copyright opinions – *Clayton v. Stone*[76] – Justice Smith Thompson, riding circuit, refused to extend copyright to a daily "price current." Technically, the decision was based on an interpretation of the scope of the statutory subject matter category of "books," but it was explicitly motivated by Thompson's view of publications of predominantly utilitarian/commercial nature as lacking the necessary connection to the realm of learning and arts. Finding that the question of the copyrightability of such publications should be decided by "inquir[ing] into the general scope and object of the legislature," he turned to the constitutional clause's reference to authors and its stated purpose of the copyright power as the promotion of progress of science. From this followed the conclusion:

> The act in question was passed in execution of the power here given, and the object, therefore, was the promotion of science; and it would certainly be a pretty extraordinary view of the sciences to consider a daily or weekly publication of the state of the market as falling within any class of them.[77]

In part, price currents (and interestingly, in Thompson's view, news-papers in general) were inadequate for copyright protection because of their "fluctuating and fugitive ... form ... the subject-matter of which is daily changing, and is of mere temporary use."[78] Among other things, the ephemeral nature of these publications meant that copyright's deposit and publication of notice requirements were practically impossible to fulfill. The opinion, however, also relied directly on a distinction between learn-ing and industry. "The title of the act of congress is for the encouragement of learning," Thompson wrote, and it "was not intended for the encour-agement of mere industry, unconnected with learning and the sciences."[79] Far from dismissing the utilitarian value of the work, Thompson con-ceded that "great praise may be due to the plaintiffs for their industry and enterprise."[80] But he concluded that since "the law does not contemplate

---

[76] *Clayton v. Stone*, 5 F. Cas. 999 (C.C.S.D. N.Y. 1829).   [77] Id., 1003.   [78] Id.
[79] Id.   [80] Id.

their being rewarded in this way," the work "must seek patronage and protection from its utility to the public and not as a work of science."[81]

The distinction of *Clayton v. Stone* between artistic or scholarly subject matter and utilitarian/commercial works excluded from the ambit of copyright reverberated in later nineteenth-century case law. Throughout the century, works predominantly associated with the world of commerce, such as product labels, advertisement posters, and catalogs, were treated with suspicion and doubt. Often such subject matter was denied entrance to the realm of copyright, seen as reserved for learning and art not tainted by the touch of commerce. In the 1848 *Scoville v. Toland*,[82] a case involving a claim for copyright protection for the label of a "patent" medicine, Justice John McLean rejected the idea that the copyright act encompassed purely commercial subject matter. He contrasted the label, which "[a]s a composition distinct from the medicine ... can be of no value" with "other compositions which are intended to instruct and amuse the reader, though limited to a single page," such as "lunar tables, sonata, music, and other mental labors."[83] His conclusion was that extending copyright to such a label and many like it was a construction that "the statute will not bear."[84]

In the following years various officials involved with copyright registration, including the Secretary of State, expressed similar views premised on the proposition that labels were unconnected to the constitutional mandate of promoting the progress or the statutory purpose of encouraging learning.[85] In 1859 the Patent Office that was charged with copyright responsibilities at the time instructed the District Courts not to register "stamps, labels, and other trademarks of any manufactured articles, goods, or merchandise." It reasoned that "the acts of Congress relating to copyright are designed to promote the acquisition and diffusion of knowledge, and to encourage the production and publication of works of art," a purpose that did not apply to such subject matter.[86] When in 1870 the floodgates were opened with the transfer of registration responsibility to the Library of Congress and a stream of registration for labels flowed in,[87] the result was the 1874 Prints and Labels Act. The act provided that no "prints or labels" designed for use with articles of

---

[81] Id.   [82] 21 F. Cas. 863 (C.C.D. Oh. 1848).   [83] Id., 864.   [84] Id.
[85] Zvi S. Rosen, "Reimagining Bleistein: Copyright for Advertisements in Historical Perspective," 59 J. *Copyright Soc'y U.S.A.* 347, 351–52 (2012).
[86] "The Law of Copyright," *New York Times*, July 25, 1859, 5.
[87] Annual Report of the Librarian of Congress 1872, Misc. Doc. 13, 42nd Cong., 3rd Sess. (1872).

manufacture "shall be entered under the copyright laws" but allowed them to be registered with the Patent Office.[88] It was ambiguous at its inception and resulted in later confusion and uncertainty. At the time, however, it was clear that the main purpose of the act was, as the Librarian of Congress put it, to remove from the realm of copyright subject matter that "clearly ha[d] no proper relation to it."[89]

As late as 1891 the Supreme Court in *Higgins v. Keuffel* strongly endorsed *Scoville v. Toland* and denied copyright protection to product labels.[90] Later, the opinion would be read narrowly, in a manner closer to the modern understanding of the originality requirement, as applying only to labels possessing "no artistic excellence"[91] such as the label at issue in Higgins, which consisted of a mere short textual description of the waterproof ink contained in the bottle to which it was attached. The language of Justice Stephen Field's opinion, however, was more capacious and could be read as almost a categorical condemnation of copyright in product labels. Field premised his opinion on the constitutional clause that "has reference only to such writings and discoveries as are the result of intellectual labor."[92] It followed that "[t]o be entitled to a copyright the article must have by itself some value as a composition, at least to the extent of serving some purpose other than as a mere advertisement or designation of the subject to which it is attached."[93] Mere product labels, however, have "no possible influence upon science or the useful arts," and therefore it cannot "be held by any reasonable argument that the protection of mere labels is within the purpose of the clause."[94] That this reasoning was understood for a time as a sweeping denial of copyright to product labels is borne out by the fact that in the years following the decision, registration of labels in the Patent Office fell sharply and was brought to a virtual halt.[95]

Six years after *Higgins* the Seventh Circuit drew on a similar theme when denying copyright protection to product catalogs and finding in the case law the broad principle that "mere advertisements, whether by letterpress or by picture, are not within the protection of the copyright law."[96]

[88] Act of June 18, 1874, ch. 301, §3, 18 Stat. 78.
[89] Annual Report of the Librarian of Congress 1872, Misc. Doc. 20, 43rd Cong., 1st Sess. (1872).
[90] 140 U.S. 428, 431 (1891).
[91] *Ex parte Palmer*, 58 O.G. 383 (Comm'r Patents, 1892). See also *Ex parte Mahn*, 82 O.G. 1210 (1898).
[92] 140 U.S. 431.   [93] Id.   [94] Id.   [95] Rosen, "Reimagining Bleistein," 364–65.
[96] *J.L. Mott Iron Works v. Clow*, the Seventh Circuit 82 F. 316, 321 (7th Cir. 1897).

The court described the illustrated catalogs as "mere advertisements of the appellant's wares, with nice cuts or illustrations of the goods accompanying and forming part of the advertisement, as an allurement to customers."[97] Drawing on the constitutional purpose of "dissemination of Learning, by inducing intellectual labor in works which would promote the general knowledge in science and useful arts," it conjured up a striking dichotomy. The constitutional clause, the court explained, "sought to stimulate original investigation, whether in literature, science, or art, for the betterment of the people, that they might be instructed and improved with respect to those subjects." It was "not designed as a protection to traders in the particular manner in which they might shout their wares."[98] Redundant though it may have seemed to point out on which side of this dichotomy the plaintiff's "pictures of slop sinks, washbowls, and bath tubs"[99] fell, the court supplied a lengthy description of the lack of artistic or scholarly merit. It could "discover nothing original in the treatment of the subject."[100] Such a detailed analysis of the aesthetic and scholarly deficiencies of the work made sense only within a conceptual universe where the notion of a merit-based threshold to copyright could still be taken seriously.

The rise of the advertisement industry in the late nineteenth century created another context where the traditional resistance to allowing predominantly commercial subject matter into the realm of copyright as well as emergent doubts about this approach were played out. Dicta in several Supreme Court and other courts' decisions expressly rejected the copyrightability of mere advertisements.[101] In 1880 a Circuit Court in New York denied protection to cards depicting paint samples because it was "an advertisement, and nothing more."[102] Two years later another New York federal court adopted a more moderate approach, distinguishing between the purpose and the substance of the work. Copyright, it explained, would not be denied categorically because of the mere purpose of the work as an advertisement, but any advertisement would still require "artistic merit" for receiving protection.[103] The court went

---

[97] Id., 318.   [98] Id., 319.   [99] Id., 321.   [100] Id., 318.
[101] *Baker v. Selden*, 101 U.S. 99, 106 (1880); *Higgins*, 140 U.S. 431; *J.L. Mott Iron*, 82 F. 321.
[102] *Ehret v. Pierce*, 10 F. 553, 554 (C.C.E.D. N.Y. 1880). See also *Collender v. Griffith*, 6 F. Cas. 104, 105 (C.C.S.D.N.Y. 1873).
[103] *Yuengling v. Schile*, 12 F. 97, 100 (C.C.S.D. N.Y. 1882). For a similar approach in regard to labels, see *Schumacher v. Schwencke*, 25 F. 466 (C.C.S.D. N.Y. 1885); *Schumacher v. Wogram*, 35 F. 210 (C.C.S.D. N.Y. 1888).

on to describe in much detail a beer advertisement chromolithograph as "a work of the imagination" with "obvious artistic qualities."[104] Even the 1903 Supreme Court decision in *Bleistein v. Donaldson Lithographing Co.*[105] – understood today as the iconic manifesto of a minimalist originality standard based on content neutrality – featured a diametrically opposed approach, albeit one that ultimately lost the day. Justice Harlan's dissenting opinion that was joined by Justice McKenna adopted the Sixth Circuit approach of refusing to extend copyright to a poster that "has no other use than that of a mere advertisement."[106] Harlan's only addition to the Court of Appeals opinion was observing dryly that "[t]he clause of the Constitution giving Congress power to promote the progress of science and useful arts" does not "embrace a mere advertisement of a circus."[107] Today this dissent is forgotten or, at best, appears in textbooks as a strange curiosity. At the time, however, it was a succinct expression of the traditional view of copyright, being delivered even at the moment of its downfall.

MERE SPECTACLES AND VULGAR SONGS

Another strand of cases stretching to the dawn of the twentieth century demonstrated willingness by some courts to employ a distinction between elevating art or scholarship and vulgar entertainment. To be sure, American copyright had never been limited to the belles-lettres. The predominant material copyrighted in the first decade of the copyright regime consisted of didactic and practical works such as textbooks, guides, or dictionaries. This trend continued and intensified throughout the nineteenth century. Nevertheless, under one influential approach access to copyright was denied to works that were seen as categorically falling short of the threshold of art or scholarship. Treatise writers analyzing this aspect of the law identified it with the English rule, a remnant of copyright's censorial ancestry, that copyright would not be enforced in regard to seditious, libelous, or blasphemous publications.[108] However,

---

[104] 12 F. 100.   [105] 188 U.S. 239 (1903).
[106] *Courier Lithographing Co. v. Donaldson Lithographing Co.*, 104 F. 993, 996 (6th Cir. 1900).
[107] 188 U.S. 253.
[108] Story, *Commentaries on Equity Jurisprudence*, vol. 2, 212; Curtis, *A Treatise on the Law of Copyright*, 147–66; Eaton S. Drone, *A Treatise on the Law of Property in Intellectual Productions in Great Britain and the United States* (Boston: Little, Brown, 1879), 181–96.

American judges refusing to extend copyright to what they described as lowbrow entertainment framed the principle differently. Infrequently and only briefly citing the English precedents, they anchored their approach instead in the constitutional purpose of promoting science and the useful arts – the noble realm of the human intellect to which the dismissed works clearly did not belong.

The 1867 *Martinetti v. Maguire*[109] is a striking example of this approach. The case involved a bitter dispute between two San Francisco theaters. According to Julien Martinetti's complaint the Metropolitan Theatre owned by him produced a vaudeville show entitled "The Black Rook." The court described the show as composed of "representations taken from . . . well known dramas and operas" and of "scenic effects."[110] During the production Martinetti learned that the competing establishment, Maguire's Opera House, managed to procure a manuscript copy of the show from one of his employees. Maguire introduced minor changes to the show, renamed it "The Black Crook," and exhibited it to the public. Maguire's counterclaim told a very different story. "The Black Crook," Maguire argued, was composed in New York by Charles M. Barras, from whom he purchased the right to exhibit the show in California. James Schonberg – the man described by Martinetti's complaint as the author of "The Black Rook" – was, in fact, employed by Martinetti to take a shorthand transcription of the show during one of its exhibitions in the Niblo's Theatre in New York. This transcription was the basis of Martinetti's "The Black Rook," whose exhibition in California was thus an infringement of Maguire's rights. Judge Mathew Paul Deady found Maguire's version of the events more credible, ruled that Martinetti had no legitimate rights in the show, and rejected his infringement claim.

Maguire, however, was robbed of a complete victory. His own claim for copyright infringement by Martinetti was rejected despite the fact that he established a good title to the work. The ground for this ruling was the frivolous and lewd character of the show. According to Judge Deady all the witnesses agreed that the show had "no originality."[111] The opinion describes in great detail what lack of originality meant in this case:

The Black Crook is a mere spectacle – in the language of the craft a spectacular piece. The dialogue is very scant and meaningless, and appears to be a mere accessory to the action of the piece – a sort of verbal machinery tacked on to a

[109] 16 F. Cas. 920 (C.C. Cal. 1867).   [110] Id., 922.   [111] Id.

succession of ballet and tableaux. The principal part and attraction of the spectacle seems to be the exhibition of women in novel dress or no dress, and in
attractive attitudes or action. The closing scene is called Paradise, and as witness
Hamilton expresses it, consists mainly "of women lying about loose" – a sort of
Mohammedan paradise, I suppose, with imitation grottos and unmaidenly
houris.[112]

In short, the "play," in the court's view, was vulgar and indecent entertainment appealing to the lower urges of the masses. One implication of
this was that being a mere "spectacle," the show was not encompassed
by the statutory subject matter category of a "dramatic composition."
Nor could it be said that the qualifier "suited for public representation"
attached in the statutory text to the term "dramatic compositions" applies
to such a show.[113] In Deady's words: "To call such a spectacle a
'dramatic composition' is an abuse of language, and an insult to the
genius of the English drama. A menagerie of wild beasts, or an exhibition
of model artistes might as justly be called a dramatic composition."[114]
While Congress could not interfere directly to prohibit such spectacles,
he explained, it could deny it "the benefit of copyright" and thereby
"to encourage virtue and discourage immorality."[115]

The opinion does not stop with the statutory interpretation but, rather,
goes on to argue that the Constitution itself bars the extension of copyright to works that are "grossly indecent, and calculated to corrupt the
morals."[116] The legislative power of Congress in the field, it explains,
is limited by the explicit purpose for which it was given. Since a work of
this kind "neither 'promotes the progress of science or useful arts,' but the
contrary," Congress has no power to protect it.[117] Thus *Martinetti v.
Maguire* stood for the proposition that the constitutional mandate of
promoting the progress limits copyright to the realm of art and learning.
It was also premised on the assumption that courts are entrusted with the
duty of scrutinizing the content of suspected works to make sure these
boundaries are not transgressed. Interestingly, the opinion drew a parallel
to patent law. It equated the denial of copyright to indecent works with
the denial of a patent to "an invention expressly designed to facilitate the
commission of crime, as murder, burglary, forgery or counterfeiting,
however novel or ingenious."[118] Judge Deady saw the common ideological infrastructure shared by courts willing to apply content-based
thresholds to copyright and decisions in patent law that scrutinized

---

[112] Id.   [113] Act of August 18, 1856, 11 Stat. 138, 139, §1.   [114] 16 F. Cas. 922.
[115] Id.   [116] Id.   [117] Id.   [118] Id.

inventions under the utility requirement by inquiring into their substantive merits.[119] Courts taking these positions in either copyright or patent assumed that both regimes were set up under the Constitution to encourage and reward higher and beneficial forms of creations of the human intellect. They understood their own role as actively making sure that the purpose of those regimes is not subverted by extending their reach to lower and less beneficial forms of creation.

Courts did not invoke explicit merit-based threshold requirements for copyright very often. Nor did they extend their reach very far. Thus when in 1860 a defendant in a common law copyright case ambitiously argued that in Massachusetts "all scenic exhibitions" were excluded from copyright because the Puritan founders of the commonwealth prohibited them as "immoral and pernicious," the Massachusetts Supreme Judicial Court was not impressed.[120] Accepting the basic principle of denial of copyright to "an immoral or licentious production" and referring to the argument as "ingenious and interesting," the court employed a dynamic interpretive approach attuned to changing social mores. Denying protection "in conformity with the peculiar opinions, sentiments or prejudices of one generation of men," it explained "will not control its application in a state of society where different views prevail."[121] Plays, contrary to the ingenious though perhaps overoptimistic argument of defendant's lawyer, were not categorically considered immoral in 1860 Massachusetts.

Still, the infrequent and moderate application notwithstanding, one established approach to originality called for courts' patrolling of copyright's borders to ensure that no content falling significantly short of the intended categories of art and learning slips in. Unsurprisingly, judicial interventions happened mainly in regard to traditionally suspicious expressive activities, such as vaudeville "spectacles"[122] and popular music, or to new forms of creation such as unconventional stage performances.[123] The 1898 case *Border v. Zeno Mauvais Music Co.*[124] demonstrates this tendency. Although the litigants were rival San Francisco music-publishing companies, the real battle took place between two artists who assigned their songs to the companies. The issue in

---

[119] On a content-based threshold in patent, see Chapter 4.
[120] *Keene v. Kimball*, 16 Gray 545, 548 (Mass. 1860).   [121] Id., 548.
[122] See Peter Decherney, "Gag Orders: Comedy, Chaplin, and Copyright," in Paul Saint-Amour, ed., *Modernism and Copyright* (Oxford: Oxford University Press, 2011), 136–37.
[123] See *Barnes v. Miner*, 122 F. 480, 492 (S.D. N.Y. 1903).
[124] 88 F. 74 (C.C.D. Cal. 1898).

the case was described by Judge Morrow as involving two "colored melodies" composed by "colored gentlemen," each alleging that the other had copied his song from him.[125] The court resolved this dispute in favor of plaintiff's assignor Bert A. Williams, alluded to as a "very clever vaudeville artist" and against Charles Sidney O'Brien, described as nothing "more than a street or saloon negro minstrel" who "played the banjo and sang negro songs in saloons and such like resorts, passing around the hat for his livelihood."[126]

An additional issue remained open, however. In earlier proceedings Judge McKenna refused to issue a preliminary injunction on the ground that Williams' song, "Dora Dean," contained an "indecent and obscene expression," namely the phrase "She's the hottest thing you ever seen."[127] By the time of the decision McKenna was already a Supreme Court Justice, and in five years he would join Justice Harlan's dissent in *Bleistein v. Donaldson Lithographing Company*, refusing to extend copyright to "a mere circus advertisement." Judge Morrow analyzed the question in depth, considered testimony on behalf of plaintiff that "the word 'hottest' . . . as understood by colored people, has no obscene or vulgar meaning," and found that the expression when applied to a female has "immoral signification."[128] He ruled that the relevant verse had an "indelicate and vulgar meaning and that for that reason the song cannot be protected by copyright," but suggested that copyright could be secured by republishing the song with the omission of the offensive word.[129]

"Dora Dean" was the perfect target for dismissal from the realm of art as vulgar and immoral expression by an 1898 federal judge. It was an entertaining piece of popular music, composed and sung by a black vaudeville artist, containing, at least in the eye of the beholder, sexual innuendo. But Judge Morrow's opinion was a product of its time also in the sense that it could be based comfortably and naturally on the assumption that copyright protection was denied to a creation seen as nothing more than vulgar, if somewhat popular, entertainment.

Denial of copyright protection on the ground that a work was immoral or constituted low entertainment rather than art or learning was infrequent. Unsurprisingly, such decisions were usually aimed at forms of expression that were frowned on by members of the judicial elite as vulgar and corrupting for the masses. Similarly predictable is the fact that, especially to observers looking backward, the criterion of immoral or

[125] Id.   [126] Id., 77.   [127] Id., 78.   [128] Id., 78–79.   [129] Id., 79.

vulgar works seemed a constantly moving target. A 1919 law review note pointed out that the show at issue in *Martinetti v. Maguire* "with its plentitude of pink fleshings, scandalous as it may have seemed in the days of crinolines, when legs – unless their very existence was gently denied – were vehicles, not spectacles, would probably bore a sophisticated modern audience, but would scarcely shock them."[130] Nevertheless, the rule was derived from and expressed the same fundamental assumption about copyright as the more common distinction between creativity and mere industry. The exclusion of both strictly commercial works and of vulgar or indecent entertainment assumed that copyright in the United States was reserved for the special realm of art and learning. Judges taking this approach saw the Constitution as mandating such distinctions. They regarded themselves as having both the power and the duty of substantively evaluating borderline works to determine to which category they belonged and to avoid contamination of the realm of copyright reserved for the higher forms of the product of human intellect.

VALERE QUANTUM VALERE POTEST

Throughout the nineteenth century parts of American copyright law and thought demonstrated willingness to take the different facets of the ideal of originality seriously. Such approaches, however, did not go unchallenged. As soon as originality began to take the form of legal arguments a competing line of cases appeared that construed the concept quite differently. We already saw Story's minimalist conception of originality as novelty developed in his early 1830s cases. The legal test that Story derived from his understanding of creation as reappropriation of existing materials was quite different from those of attempts such as Nelson's to introduce a more ambitious novelty standard into American copyright. The words "new and original," Story wrote in *Emerson v. Davies*, are to be understood in a particular sense in copyright cases. The question is not "whether the materials which are used are entirely new and have never been used before; or even that they have never been used before for that purpose." Rather, Story explained, "[t]he true question is, whether the same plan, arrangement, and combination of materials have been used before."[131] Later nineteenth-century courts almost uniformly

---

[130] Edward S. Rogers, "Copyright and Morals," 18 *Mich. L.Rev.* 390, 393 (1919–20).
[131] 8 F. Cas. 618–19.

followed this minimalist version of novelty, and attempts to introduce more demanding criteria, as in *Jolly v. Jacques*, remained marginalized.

The writers of American treatises that began to appear around the middle of the century went even further in their narrow constructions of the originality requirement. George Ticknor Curtis started his discussion of originality by explaining that copyright is based on authorship and that a person cannot be "the author of what he has borrowed from another."[132] He quickly went on to assert, however, that "[t]he law does not require that the subject of a book should be new, or that the materials of which it is composed should be original."[133] Here was an originality requirement that required no originality. What did originality mean then? Curtis explained that the claimant must show something "he produced by himself; whether it would be purely original thought or principle, unpublished before, or a new combination of old thoughts and ideas and sentiments, or a new application or use of known and common materials, or a collection, the result of his industry and skill." The test, in short, was the claimant's ability to show something, or rather anything "which the law can fix upon as the product of his and not another's labors."[134] This rendered the originality threshold almost nonexistent, except in cases of absolute plagiarism, as Curtis concluded that the rules of copyright "must include in their range everything that can be justly claimed as the peculiar product of individual efforts."[135] This included all derivative works, such as abridgments or translations, which in his chapter about infringement Curtis labored to reconstrue, contrary to older precedents, as mere copies in cases where the original was under copyright protection.[136]

In his authoritative treatise published thirty years later Eaton Drone took a similar approach, observing that "[a]lmost every product of independent literary labor is a proper subject of copyright."[137] Similar to Curtis, for Drone the originality test was only "whether the publication is a result of independent labor, other than that of mere copying."[138] Drone pushed the analysis one step further by stating clearly a general rule that no degree of similarity to a preexisting work would bar copyright to a later work as long as the identity is not the result of copying. "It is not probable that two authors, working independently of each

---

[132] Curtis, *A Treatise on the Law of Copyright*, 169.   [133] Id., 173.   [134] Id., 171.
[135] Id., 172.   [136] Id.., 186–92, 265–93.
[137] Drone, *A Treatise on the Law of Property in Intellectual Productions*, 199.
[138] Id., 202.

other," he wrote, "will produce two poems, novels, essays. &c., which will be precisely alike." Should this improbable occurrence come to pass, however, "each author will be entitled to copyright in his own production."[139] The independent creation rule, which became a staple of modern copyright, is the antithesis of novelty. It provides that even in the extreme case where the copyrighted work has not even token novelty the originality requirement is satisfied unless there was copying. Thus, the moment the ideal of originality, supposedly the bedrock of the copyright regime, passed into the hands of judges and legal commentators it was converted from the heroic romantic notion expressed by Wordsworth as "the introduction of a new element into the intellectual universe" into the barely related requirement of not being a slavish copier.

Similar to his early dismissal of the notion of originality as novelty, Justice Story laid the foundations for an approach to the issue of creativity that was at odds with the assumptions of those who sought to regulate the boundaries of copyright on the basis of the nature or substance of the work. In his *Commentaries on Equity Jurisprudence* Story expressed skepticism toward the English precedents that denied copyright to "clearly irreligious, immoral, libelous, or obscene" works.[140] The rule itself is stated ambiguously. Story first observes that "no copyright can exist" in such works, but then goes on to explain, in conformity with the procedural origin of the English rule, that in these cases "Courts of equity will not interfere by injunction ... but will leave the party to his remedy in law."[141] More important, while agreeing with "the soundness of this general principle," Story concluded that "[t]he chief embarrassment and difficulty lie in the application of it to particular cases."[142] Thus "[i]f a Court of Equity ... is to enter upon all the moral, theological, metaphysical, and political inquires which in the past times have given rise to so many controversies and in the future may well be supposed to provoke many heated discussions, and if it is to decide dogmatically upon the character and bearing of such discussions and the rights of authors growing out of them; it is obvious that an absolute power is conferred over the subject of literary property which may sap the very foundations on which it rests, and retard, if not entirely suppress, the means of arriving at physical as well as at metaphysical truths."[143]

---

[139] Id., 208. To support this proposition Drone cited a dicta in the English case *Jeffreys v. Boosey*, 10 Eng. Rep. 681 (H.L. 1854).

[140] Story, *Commentaries on Equity Jurisprudence*, vol. 2, 212.   [141] Id.   [142] Id., 213.

[143] Id., 213–14.

Story did not try to resolve the "embarrassment and difficulty," but rather left the reader to reflect on the absurdity, enabled by the legal rule, of a Trinitarian and a Unitarian judge "most conscientiously" reaching opposite results in regard to the same work.[144]

While he shifted the burden of dispelling "any real doubt" about the immoral nature of the work to the person who challenges its copyrightability,[145] Story was not prepared to simply reject the established English precedents. When it came to newer attempts to construct an originality requirement based on the substantive merits of the work, Story's aversion to content-based tests took a stronger form. When in *Emerson v. Davies* the defendant's witnesses challenged not just the novelty of plaintiff's arithmetic textbook but also whether it contributed anything to the field, Story responded that these arguments "entirely misunderstood the law upon this subject."[146] To dispel any notion that originality hinged on the substantive merits of the work, he added the following prose:

> I must confess, that it strikes me that the plaintiff's method is a real and substantial improvement upon all the works which had preceded his, and which have been relied on in the evidence; but whether to be better or worse is not a material inquiry in this case. If worse, his work will not be used by the community at large; if better, it is very likely to be so used. But either way, he is entitled to his copyright, "valere quantum valere potest."[147]

This was an early articulation of the notion that would follow minimalist versions of originality like a shadow: the idea that markets alone should determine the value of the work, or in a loose translation of Story's phrase, that the copyright owner should enjoy as much value as he can get. *Emerson*'s early rejection of any merit-based element of originality was emphatically echoed by later commentators. Curtis explained in 1849 that "[t]he mere utility of a book, or its adaptation to the end which it professes to answer – its value in a critical point of view – cannot determine its legal originality."[148] Drone similarly observed that a court "exercises no functions of criticism."[149]

Formally Story's early decisions did not conflict with later cases that refused copyright protection to subject matter excluded from the realm of

---

[144] Id., 214.
[145] Id., 212. Story acknowledged in a footnote that his assignment of the burden in cases of doubt was diametrically opposed to the English rule. Id., n. 5.
[146] 8 F. Cas. 620.   [147] Id., 620–21.
[148] Curtis, *A Treatise on the Law of Copyright*, 172.
[149] Drone, *A Treatise on the Law of Property in Intellectual Productions*, 210.

art and learning because it belonged either in the category of pure commerce or in that of vulgar entertainment. Story's logic, however, strongly hostile to any form of content-based threshold, gradually spread, and by the last quarter of the century its tension with relatively broad constructions of originality began to manifest itself in legal doctrine.[150] Thus in 1879, Drone, commenting on *Clayton v. Stone*, which denied copyright to a market prices publication, observed that "a more liberal doctrine now prevails."[151] Drone explained that "[t]he importance and value of the information often contained in prices currents, trade circulars, market reports &c., are well recognized in the commercial world."[152] The only case he cited in support, however, was a noncopyright New York decision that recognized a common law property right in unpublished financial news.[153] Drone did not mention that Justice Thompson in *Clayton* explicitly recognized the commercial value of financial information but saw it as irrelevant for copyright that was reserved for artistic or scholarly materials.

An 1894 opinion of a Massachusetts federal court in *Henderson v. Tompkins* demonstrates the increasingly hostile approach toward attempts to impose any content-based threshold requirement for copyright.[154] The defendant, who allegedly imitated a song out of the plaintiff's humorous play, claimed that the play was merely vulgar entertainment unworthy of protection under the mandate of promoting science and the useful arts or at least was too trivial "to demand the attention of the law."[155] This was exactly the reasoning of the court in *Martinetti* under similar circumstances twenty-seven years earlier. Judge Putnam, however, failed to be impressed. Dismissing the claim that plays of this class were outside copyright's scope as needing "but little consideration," Putnam refused to take a "narrow view" of the coverage of copyright. Copyright and patents, he explained, apply both to "what is essential to keep the physical, moral, and intellectual powers refreshed" and to subject matter "addressed to the taste, the imagination, or the capacity of being amused, and the enjoyment which immediately follows therefrom." Thus "the standard prescription from Euclid may

---

[150] See e.g. *Drury v. Ewing*, 7 F. Cas. 1113, 116 (C.C.S.D. Ohio 1862); *Mutual Advertising Co. v. Refo*, 76 F. 961, 963, (C.C.D. S.C. 1896); *Ladd v. Oxnard*, 75 F. 703, 731 (C.C.D. Mass. 1896).

[151] Drone, *A Treatise on the Law of Property in Intellectual Productions*, 210.   [152] Id.

[153] *Kiernan v. Manhattan Quotation Telegraph Co.*, 50 How. Pr. 194 (N.Y. 1876).

[154] *Henderson v. Tompkins*, 60 F. 758, 763–64 (C.C.D. Mass. 1894).   [155] Id., 763.

be useful, but an occasional one from the Book of Nonsense is not to be despised."[156] Patents are used in the opinion as both an analogy and an illustrative contrast to support this conclusion. The opinion draws a parallel between copyright's originality and a late-nineteenth-century strand of patent precedents interpreting patent law's threshold requirement that the invention be useful as setting an extremely minimal bar.[157] At the same time, it introduces a distinction between copyright's "author" and the "inventor" of the realm of "mechanical patents": "The latter carries an implication which excludes the results of only ordinary skill, while nothing of this is necessarily involved in the former."[158] In a striking contrast to the parallel drawn by Justice Nelson decades earlier between the legally recognized inventor and the legally recognized author, Putnam now maintained that the latter was not required to transcend the level of a mere mechanic.

Putnam's resounding rejection of a content-based originality criterion in *Henderson* is sealed by what was becoming a common trope in this context: reliance on the market value of the work as the conclusive proof of its originality. The opinion describes an unreported English case in which a song entitled "Slap, Bang, Here We Are Again?" received copyright protection despite "the impression which the title gives [that] would suggest little value, except what might be shown by sales." It goes on to report that "the copyright was worth from £1,000 to £2,000, and at the time of the trial as many as 90,000 copies had been sold."[159] As willingness to engage in any substantive evaluation of the work disappeared, market value stepped in to fill this vacuum. This shift, however was often more conceptual than practical. Market value was frequently used as a postulated abstract concept that established the work's assumed value, rather than as an actual doctrinal criterion requiring any empirical support. Thus, turning back to the work at hand, Putnam quoted an increasingly popular argument from Drone's treatise: "If it has merit and value enough to be the object of piracy, it should also be of sufficient importance to be entitled to protection."[160] From this perspective whatever was copied, by definition, had market value, which, in turn, was enough to satisfy any originality bar. In the newly emerging conceptual

---

[156] Id. [157] Id. [158] Id., 764.

[159] Id. The court probably derived its information about the unreported English case from Arthur Copinger's treatise on British copyright law. See Arthur Walter Copinger, *The Law of Copyright in Works of Literature and Art*, 3rd ed. (London: Stevens and Haynes, 1893), 327.

[160] 60 F. 765.

environment this tautological logic was powerful. To the extent it was taken seriously, it reduced originality to a triviality.

AFTER ALL IT WAS THE SUN WHICH DREW THE PICTURE

The treatment of photography technology demonstrates the gradual decline of the strand of nineteenth-century copyright thought that was ready to endow originality with meaningful content. Photographs were first recognized as copyrightable subject matter in 1865,[161] decades after photography first appeared. Even after the statutory recognition, however, serious doubts persisted about the copyrightability of photographs. A common early view of photography saw it as "the pencil of nature": a mechanical art involving the objective reproduction or recording of natural reality.[162] As such photography was seen as devoid of the essential, defining quality of subject matter suitable for copyright protection: creative human agency. Photographers, seen in this light, were operators of sophisticated recording machines rather than authors.[163] When copyright cases under the 1865 statute began to arrive at the courts, defendants' lawyers were quick to mount a challenge to photographic copyright based on this perception.[164]

Matters came to a head with the 1883 decision of the Supreme Court in *Burrow-Giles Lithographic Co. v. Sarony.*[165] The case involved mass reproduction of a photograph of Oscar Wilde by Napoleon Sarony (entitled "Oscar Wilde No. 18"). Sarony, who was known as the "Napoleon of photography," was one of the most famous and successful photographers of that time.[166] He specialized in portraits, and those of celebrities in particular. In the lower court the defendant's main defense was that the statutory grant "of copyright protection to photographs and negatives" was "unconstitutional and void" because a photographer

---

[161] Act of March 3, 1865, 13 Stat. 540, §1.

[162] See William H. Tablot, *The Pencil of Nature* (New York: Da Capo Press, 1969) (first published in 1846).

[163] See Christine Haight Farley, "The Lingering Effects of Copyright's Response to the Invention of Photography," 65 *U. Pitt. L. Rev.* 385, 395–402 (2003–4); Jane Gaines, *Contested Culture: The Image, the Voice, and the Law* (Chapel Hill: University of North Carolina Press, 1991), 52–65.

[164] See *Wood v. Abbot*, 30 F. Cas. 424 (C.C.S.D. N.Y. 1866); *Udderzook v. Pennsylvania*, 76 Pa. 340 (1874); *Schreiber v. Thornton*, 17 F. 603 (E.D. Pa. 1883).

[165] 111 U.S. 53 (1883).

[166] Farley "The Lingering Effects," 406–7; Helmut Gernsheim, *The Rise of Photography: 1850–1880, the Age of Collodion* (London: Thames and Hudson, 1988), 198.

is not an "author" under the Constitution.[167] Judge Coxe wrote a brief opinion, emphasizing the heavy burden borne by a challenger of the constitutional validity of congressional legislation, and found that the defendant did not manage to establish invalidity beyond reasonable doubt.[168]

In the briefs submitted to the Supreme Court the issues of originality and authorship as applied to photographs were argued in great length. While the parties obviously argued opposite sides of the copyrightability question, their arguments shared the assumption of a substantial and meaningful threshold requirement limiting the subject matter that could be considered a work of authorship under the constitutional clause. The defendant's brief continued its line of defense at the lower court and launched a wholesale attack on the constitutionality of copyright in photographs. The logic was straightforward: Congress has the constitutional power to extend copyright only to authors; the essential quality of authors is originality; and photographs necessarily lack originality. As the brief put it: if "the very idea of photography negatives the idea of originality, how can a photographer be called an author, the essential element of authorship being ... ORIGINALITY?"[169] This conclusion relied on an understanding of photography that effaced any trace of creative human agency from the process, captured by the observation, taken from a recent English photography decision: "AFTER ALL IT WAS THE SUN WHICH DREW THE PICTURE."[170] An artist such as a painter or a sculptor, the brief argued, shapes his work *"according to his own volition"* with "his *own mental originality* determining" the outcome. "The photographer," by contrast, "can do nothing of the kind; the camera acting by UNCHANGABLE LAWS OF NATURE, represents the scene AS IT IS; nothing is added nothing is omitted."[171]

The brief for Sarony denied neither the constitutional requirement of authorship nor originality as its defining quality. It relied on an understanding of photography in general and of Sarony's photograph in particular, which was very different from that of the defendant. The heart of the brief is a rejection of the image of the photographer as a mechanic

---

[167] *Burrow-Giles Lithographic Co. v. Sarony*, 111 U.S. 53 (1884). Transcript of Record, Defendant's Answer, 9–10.
[168] *Sarony v. Burrow-Giles Lithographic Co.*, 17 F. 591 (C.C.S.D. N.Y. 1883).
[169] *Burrow-Giles*, Transcript of Record, Statement and Brief for Plaintiff in Error, 17.
[170] Id., 8. The quotation was taken from the decision of the English Court of Appeals in *Nottage v. Jackson*, 11 Q.B. 627, 635 (C.A. 1883).
[171] Id., 16.

based on the proposition that "all a photographer does is to take his camera, get his focus, and produce his picture, just as the hunter aims his gun, pulls the trigger, and lodges a bullet in the mark."[172] The brief admitted that "there may be such cases, and such photographs,"[173] but claimed that Sarony's photograph was of a different sort. The true photographer, it explained, is identical to traditional artists such as the painter, the engraver, or the sculptor in that he creates and designs a "mental conception, invention or creation,"[174] the permanent, material form given to this conception being inconsequential. Thus after a lengthy description of Sarony's arrangement of the scene and subject, the brief concludes that "these various acts constitute an author … in the art of photography."[175] Sarony "had designed and set in order the whole scene or picture which he desired to discover or express or manifest."[176] The fact that he gave it a permanent form through a mechanical process was as irrelevant as an author's choice to put his literary work to paper by means of "the printing machine called the 'type writer.'"[177]

The Supreme Court sided with Sarony with an opinion by Justice Samuel Miller that echoed Sarony's brief. It found that "the Constitution is broad enough to cover an act authorizing copyright of photographs, so far as they are representatives of original intellectual conceptions of the author."[178] Far from a sweeping admittance of photographs to the realm of copyright, the court expressed sympathy to the claim that ordinarily photography is a mere mechanical process that "involves no originality of thought or any novelty in the intellectual operation." It observed in dictum that "[t]his may be true in regard to the ordinary production of a photograph," in which case copyright will be denied.[179] Miller's opinion conveys the impression that Sarony's photograph is the exception – the product of a member of a small elite who through extensive creative effort managed to cross the line separating a mechanical practice from art and create "an original work of art" of which he was "the author."[180] He quoted at length from the lower court's findings of fact that described the photograph as follows:

a useful, new, harmonious, characteristic, and graceful picture … that plaintiff made … entirely from his own original mental conception, to which he gave visible form by posing the said Oscar Wilde in front of the camera, selecting and arranging the costume, draperies, and other various accessories in said

---

[172] *Burrow-Giles*, Transcript of Record, Brief on the Part of the Defendant in Error, 12.
[173] Id.   [174] Id., 7.   [175] Id., 12.   [176] Id.   [177] Id., 13.   [178] 111 U.S. 57.
[179] Id., 58.   [180] Id., 60.

photograph, arranging the subject so as to present graceful outlines, arranging and disposing the light and shade, suggesting and evoking the desired expression.[181]

As observed by Peter Jaszi, this "evokes notions of individualistic artistic genius in a new technological context."[182] *Burrow Giles* was thus an affirmation of a relatively high standard of authorship and originality as applied to photographs.

Copyright cases involving photographs following *Burrow Giles* seemed at first to walk in its footsteps. In those cases, many of which owe their existence to the litigiousness of the photographer Benjamin J. Falk, courts generally looked in some depth into the creative process and sometimes scrutinized the final product to determine whether the photograph embodied an original intellectual conception that rose to the degree of authorship and separated it from ordinary photographs.[183] In most of the cases the conclusion was that the bar was met. Nonetheless, courts were unwilling to treat the requirement as a mere formality and appeared to undertake in each case a relatively substantial originality inquiry.[184] As time passed, however, the high standard gradually eroded.

Burrow Giles remained the controlling precedent and was duly cited, but courts used various techniques to stretch the meaning of what allowed a photograph to cross the originality threshold, resulting in the gradual dissolution of the distinction between the ordinary and the authorial photograph.[185] By 1921 Judge Learned Hand observed that "no photo-graph, however simple, can be unaffected by the personal influence of the author" and candidly concluded that "[t]he suggestion that the Constitution might not include all photographs seems to me overstrained."[186] In the course of fifty years, originality in photographs transformed from being seen as a rare quality found in a handful of elitist creations to a defining element of the medium whose absence became hard to imagine.

In the context of motion pictures this process was accelerated. During the early years of the technology motion pictures were treated under American copyright law as photographs.[187] This naturally led in the early

---

[181] Id.   [182] Peter Jaszi, "Toward a Theory of Copyright," 481.

[183] See Farley, "The Lingering Effects," 444–46.

[184] See *Falk v. City Printing Co.*, 79 F. 321 (C.C.E.D. La. 1897).

[185] Farley, "The Lingering Effects," 406–7; see e.g. *Altman v. New Haven Union Co.*, 254 F. 113, 115 (D.C. Conn. 1918) where the court made efforts to describe a standard high school class photo as an "*artistic* photograph."

[186] *Jewelers' Circular Pub. Co. v. Keystone Pub. Co.*, 274 F. 932, 934 (S.D. N.Y. 1921).

[187] *Edison v. Lubin*, 122 F. 240 (3rd. Cir. Pa. 1903).

litigated motion picture cases to originality-based challenges rooted in the *Burrow Giles* framework. The film at the heart of the first motion picture case – *Christening and Launching Kaiser's Wilhelm's Yacht "Meteor"* – shot in 1902 by the Edison Company, practically begged for such a challenge. The film, characteristic of the tendency of early motion pictures to "record" a mundane event or a spectacle with little narrative or editing, consisted of a single continuous shot of the yacht leaving the harbor. John F. Frawley, superintendent of film production for defendant, the Lubin Company, submitted an affidavit that described the film as follows:

> There is no peculiar skill or intellectual conception or original effect embodied in the photographs, representing the launching of the "Meteor." These photographs are purely the result of the functions of cameras, and a dozen different photographs with a dozen different cameras from the same general location necessarily would have obtained the same results. The cameras were placed in a convenient and obvious position and represents [*sic*] the objects as they subsequently arranged themselves.[188]

Edison's side countered within the *Burrow Giles* framework, taking pains to describe the film as the product of creative genius and artistic skill. The manager of Edison's film department, James H. White, explained in his own affidavit that:

> In taking moving pictures photographically, great artistic skill may be used ... artistic skill is required in placing the camera in such a position that the lights and shades of the picture, when taken, shall have proper values, and the grouping of the figures and the background shall constitute a harmonious whole and have a graceful composition.[189]

In rejecting the originality challenge the Third Circuit's opinion echoed White's affidavit by describing the film as embodying "artistic conception and expression" and as requiring "a study of light, shadows, general surroundings, and a vantage point adapted to securing the entire effect."[190] The analysis, however, hardly constituted a serious inquiry into the artistic quality of the film or the process of its creation. It briefly declared a few sweeping generalities and did not allude at all to the specific film at issue. When a similar originality challenge was mounted a few years later in a case involving the copying of the Biograph film *Personal*, Judge Lanning summarily rejected it simply by reciting the *Burrow Giles* formula and citing

---

[188] *Edison v. Lubin*, Affidavit of John J. Frawley, June 24, 1902.
[189] *Edison v. Lubin*, Affidavit of James H. White, June 9, 1902.   [190] 122 F. 242.

a string of decisions that found originality in various photographs.[191] As a rule, originality challenges to motion pictures within the *Burrow Giles* framework were rejected offhand, and they soon disappeared.[192] By the time motion pictures entered the realm of copyright, the moment for a radical originality challenge to photography as a subject matter suitable for copyright protection had already passed.

The decline of the originality standard applied to photographs was in part, as explained by Christine Farley, the result of a changing social concept of the medium and technology as well as a self-conscious struggle by professionals to attain social status, recognition, and commercial success.[193] It also reflected, however, the general trend in copyright thought – the demise of the approach that allocated courts an active role in scrutinizing the originality of works and the triumph of a minimalist view of originality that left the requirement devoid of most of its practical significance.

THE ROMANTIC AUTHOR IN THE LIBERAL MARKET

The basic social context for the changing landscape of originality and authorship was the transformation of the various economic spheres intersecting with copyright. Beginning in the late eighteenth century through the Civil War and beyond, the United States experienced a profound multifaceted transformation: the rise of the modern market society. The balance of economic activity shifted from mostly self-sustaining family households and traditionally organized artisans to increasingly large and concentrated workshops controlled and ran by entrepreneurs. This involved the rise of wage labor and a growing division between a small number of producers and masses of consumers. Limited and simple patterns of barter and commerce were supplanted by massive participation in and dependence on markets. These emerging markets were at first local, then regional, and finally national. Markets became

---

[191] *American Mutoscope & Biograph Co. v. Edison MFG. Co.*, 137 F. 262, 265–66 (C.C.D. N.J. 1905).

[192] The exception to this rule is *Barnes v. Miner*, 122 F. 480, 492 (S.D. N.Y. 1903). In this case the court denied protection to a film of the actress Hattie Delaro Barnes changing costumes in her dressing room projected as part of a stage show called "X-Rays of Society." The reasoning of the decision was based not on the *Burrow Giles* suspicious approach to photography as a noncreative process, but rather on the strand of cases denying copyright protection to material seen as vulgar or obscene.

[193] Farley, "The Lingering Effects," 412–25.

increasingly integrated as goods took the form of standardized commodities sold for a uniform price. More complex commercial mechanisms, instruments, and organizations developed and more sophisticated business strategies appeared.[194]

The immediate point of contact between these developments and copyright was the book trade. Since it first appeared, copyright had been the unique regulation of the book trade. In the nineteenth century this trade had undergone a radical transformation. Fundamental changes began in the second quarter of the century and accelerated dramatically in its second half. For the first time, conditions appeared for the emergence of a national market for books: broad demand, mass production capabilities, relatively cheap book commodities, the ability to create national distribution networks, and integrated national modes of production and marketing. In the decades leading up to the Civil War, the traditional organization of the industry was supplanted by new patterns. The artisan-based printing craft was gradually replaced by a capitalist commodity industry. The older pattern in which the roles of the printer, bookseller, and publisher were often blurred was replaced by a new system with a stricter differentiation of these roles in which the publisher was dominant.[195]

[194] See e.g. Michael Merrill, "Putting Capitalism in Its Place: A Review of Recent Literature," 52 *William & Marry Quart.* 315 (1995); Winfred Barr Rothenberg, *From Market Places to a Market Economy: The Transformation of Rural Massachusetts 1750–1850* (Chicago, Ill.: University of Chicago Press, 1992); Joyce Appleby, *Capitalism and a New Social Order: The Republican Vision of the 1790s* (New York: New York University Press, 1984); James A. Henretta, *The Origins of American Capitalism: Collected Essays* (Boston: Northeastern University Press, 1991); Christopher Clark, *The Roots of Rural Capitalism: Western Massachusetts 1780–1860* (Ithaca, N.Y.: Cornell University Press, 1990); Stuart Bruchey, *Enterprise: The Dynamic Economy of a Free People* (Cambridge, Mass.: Harvard University Press, 1990); Charles Sellers, *The Market Revolution: Jacksonian America 1815–1846* (New York: Oxford University Press, 1991).

[195] See Helmut Lehmann-Haupt, *The Book in America: A History of the Making, the Selling, and the Collecting of Books in the United States*, 2nd ed. (New York: R.R. Bowker, 1951), 122, and *A History of Book Publishing in the United States* (New York: R.R. Bowker, 1972), vol. 1, 206–7; James Gilreath, "American Book Distribution," 95 *Proc. Am. Antiquarian Soc'y* 501 (1986); Ronald J. Zboray, *A Fictive People: Antebellum Economic Development and the American Reading Public* (New York: Oxford University Press, 1993), 5–11; James N. Green, "The Rise of Book Publishing," in Robert A. Gross and Mary Kelly, eds., *A History of the Book in America: An Extensive Republic: Print, Culture, and Society in the New Nation, 1790–1840* (Chapel Hill: University of North Carolina Press, 2011), vol. 2, 75; Michael Winship, "Distribution and the Trade," in Scott E. Casper et al., eds., *A History of the Book in America: The Industrial Book, 1840–1880* (Chapel Hill: University of North Carolina Press, 2007), vol. 3, 117.

The outcome of these changes was a new, extremely competitive and commercialized publishing industry. The period of rapid expansion was described by one historian as "characterized by greed, ruthlessness, and small heed to the fundamental decencies of civilized business relations."[196] More generally, like other areas of market activity, the publishing industry came to be characterized by an increasingly self-conscious commercial drive, profit-maximizing focus, and ever more sophisticated strategies for capturing and cultivating market demand. Many of these market strategies had little to do with copyright. The bulk of printed publication occurred outside the copyright system, in part due to features of the copyright regime. As Meredith McGill has shown, a vibrant culture of print and reprint flourished in the United States with no reliance on copyright.[197] Indeed, this culture as well as some of the most financially lucrative publishing practices, such as the reprinting of popular British works, relied on the absence of copyright. Nevertheless, some of the new strategies for creating and exploiting market demand relied on the exclusivity promised by copyright protection.

A robust originality doctrine, in either its novelty or substantive merit guise, would have been an obstacle to obtaining copyright protection in regard to many of the publications for which it was sought. From the inception of the copyright regime in 1790 belles-lettres was not the prime subject matter for which it was used. Copyright was widely used to protect materials such as textbooks, dictionaries, encyclopedias, and a host of other "useful" works.[198] Throughout the nineteenth century, the largest relative share of the publishing market continued to be occupied by such works.[199] In addition to these traditional sources of income many of the new products and formats, designed to create and capture market demand that developed as the industry transformed, hardly resembled the ideal product of the creative genius. Magazines and journals of various kinds, the "dime novel," the "penny paper," and the

---

[196] Luke White Jr., *Henry William Herbert and the American Publishing Scene, 1831–1858* (Newark, N.J., Carteret Book Club, 1943), 7–8.

[197] Meredith McGill, *American Literature and the Culture of Reprinting 1834–1853* (Philadelphia: University of Pennsylvania Press, 2003).

[198] See Ginsburg, "Creation and Commercial Value," 1874.

[199] William Chavart, "The Condition of Authorship in 1820," in Matthew J. Bruccoli, ed., *The Profession of Authorship in America, 1800–1870: The Papers of William Chavart* (Columbus: Ohio State University Press, 1968), 34–35. It is estimated that, in 1860, textbooks constituted 30–40 percent of the books published in the United States. In later times, this relative share increased. Tebbel, *A History of Book Publishing*, vol. 1, 222.

highly popular illustration books were all aimed to appeal to a mass audience at attractive prices. As one of the first advertisements for commodity literature of this sort read: "BOOKS FOR THE MILLION! A DOLLAR BOOK FOR A DIME!! 128 pages complete, only Ten Cents!!!"[200] These new cheap formats often received scorn and criticism from contemporaries who lamented the deficiencies and even the supposed pernicious effect of "cheap" literature. But they tapped and created an unprecedented mass market, and they constituted a very lucrative opportunity for publishers. As for the novelty aspect of originality, numerous new products and formats, the result of new marketing techniques, embodied the opposite principle. Revised editions, serializations of existing works, and collected works volumes were variants of existing works with slight changes. To the extent that publishers wanted to rely on copyright, a substantial originality standard was out of the question.

In the later part of the nineteenth century and during the early twentieth century, as copyright expanded beyond its traditional province, the constituency with a firm interest against a substantial originality threshold grew. Various industries outside the book trade began to discover copyright and attempted to use it to achieve market advantages. Some of these fields would later be called the "content industries," whose products are considered to be part of the core of copyright, while others remained on its periphery. Photographers and later motion picture producers, makers of recorded music, the rising giant of advertisement, makers of sale catalogs, users of labels on commodities, and news agencies all discovered copyright and attempted to draft it into their service. Each new subject matter category for which copyright was procured challenged in different ways notions of strong originality and militated against their incorporation in legal doctrine. It is no accident that almost all the legal cases and policy debates involving originality in the second half of the nineteenth century involved such new copyright claimants rather than the traditional book trade actors. The new subject matter of copyright was the terrain where the border wars were fought and where the conceptual and legal frontier was steadily pushed outward. The demand for copyright beyond the domain of the book trade met varying degrees of success. However, whether the subject matter was admitted to the core of copyrightable materials or remained on the fringe, the demand created another powerful set of interests that generated constant pressure against a high originality bar.

---

[200] *New York Tribune*, June 7, 1860, 1.

The economic developments of the nineteenth century constitute a key element in understanding the evolution of originality doctrine. But on their own they provide an insufficient explanation. While in some cases, such as photography or labels, legal rules were changed by statutory decree, usually the relevant legal doctrines were shaped through adjudication. Even when statutory background existed, courts usually had the last word through statutory interpretation and application of general copyright principles. The adjudicative focus raises the question of how economic interests were translated into legal rules and concepts. A straightforward public choice model in which interests "purchase" the support of legislators hardly seems applicable to courts, even if one does not imagine adjudication as taking place in an isolated intellectual realm. Moreover, even a more nuanced conjecture that traces patterns in the results of adjudication to disparities in wealth and power of parties seems insufficient. He who can afford better legal representation, repeat litigation, and long-term legal strategies is likely to "come out ahead" in adjudication.[201] The constituencies of nineteenth-century copyright law did not always neatly divide, however, along lines of wealth and power. In many of the relevant battlegrounds of originality there existed countervailing interests with no obvious systematic disparities in resources or organizational ability. For most of the nineteenth century, there was a prospering and entrenched reprint industry in the United States whose members were as organized, sophisticated, and informed as other members of the book trade. In cases involving advertisements or labels there were no stable divisions between the profiles of plaintiffs claiming copyright and defendants objecting to it. Early motion picture fights over originality were held between commercial producers who switched roles as plaintiffs and defendants. The Edison Company lawyers, for example, argued for originality of a motion picture when they sued Lubin, but questioned it when defending a lawsuit by Biograph two years later.[202]

The explanatory gap left by economic interests is filled by ideological and conceptual factors. Changing values, practices, and fundamental assumptions gave meaning to the adjudicative process and shaped its outcomes. Such ideological factors constrained the arguments made by

---

[201] Marc Galanter, "Why the 'Haves' Come Out Ahead: Speculations on the Limits of Legal. Change," 9 *L. Soc'y Rev.* 95 (1974).

[202] See *Edison v. Lubin*, 122 F. 240 (3rd Cir. Pa. 1903); *American Mutoscope & Biograph Co. v. Edison MFG. Co.*, 137 F. 262, 265–66 (C.C.D. N.J. 1905).

lawyers and treatise writers or petitioners to Congress and informed the rulings of judges.

One important ideological influence on copyright law, operating in the interface between the economic and the intellectual realms, was the rise of a market concept of value. Prior to the nineteenth century it was common to see resources (the paradigmatic example was land) as having intrinsic value derived from their objective qualities and not dependent on subjective human desires. As market exchanges became a dominant feature of everyday life, defining the value of a growing number of things as measured by consumer demand became widespread. An earlier willingness to judge the fairness of transactions against a standard of inherent value was replaced by the assumption that value is synonymous with market price. The shift was reflected in many fields. In law the premarket concept of value was embedded in rules based on the idea of a fair transaction as the exchange of objectively equivalent values. As value became synonymous with market demand, the willingness to challenge the outcomes of market exchanges waned.[203]

The shift in the concept of value was most apparent in economic thought where an earlier distinction between market value and use value or true value lost coherence and gradually declined. As explained by Herbert Hovenkamp, a central attribute separating neoclassical from classical economics was a break with "the nearly sacred notion" of inherent value usually connected to the amount of labor invested in something.[204] Writing in the late eighteenth century, Benjamin Franklin could speak of "fair commerce" as the exchange of "equal values."[205] As late as 1853 Francis Wayland in his treatise on political economy distinguished between "intrinsic value" and "exchangeable value" and explained that "substances having an exchangeable value, do not possess that value, in proportion to their intrinsic value." For Wayland, even "exchangeable value" was defined by reference to some inherent objective

---

[203] See Morton J. Horwitz, *The Transformation of American Law 1780–1860* (Cambridge, Mass.: Harvard University Press, 1977), 160–88. Herbert Hovenkemp connects the shift in the concept of value in economic theory to other legal changes that occurred somewhat later during the progressive era, such as the decline of the wage-fund theory as a barrier to wage regulation or the demise of the rule against watered stock in corporate law. Herbert Hovenkemp, "The Marginalist Revolution in Legal Thought," 46 *Vand. L. Rev.* 305, 345–58 (1993).

[204] Hovenkemp, "The Marginalist Revolution," 310, 324.

[205] Benjamin Franklin, "Positions to Be Examined Concerning National Wealth," in J. Bigelow, ed., *The Works of Benjamin Franklin* (New York: Putnam's Sons, 1887), vol. 4, 236.

qualities rather than by the whims of market demand alone, since "the *degree* of the exchangeable value of any one substance depends chiefly upon the amount of labor and skill necessary to create that value."[206] As the assumption of extra-market objective value declined, the coherence of the distinction between intrinsic value and exchange value was undermined. "A thing may have an intrinsic utility," wrote Willard Phillips in his 1828 treatise, "but can hardly be said to have an intrinsic value, since its value depends upon the desire of others to obtain it from the possessor by giving something in exchange." Another writer explained that "practically, there is only this kind of value, and this kind of price known in the estimation of things. Commodities are exchanged for each other at their relative values and they are exchanged for money at their actual price."[207] Eventually the idea of inherent value was deserted altogether. William Stanley Jevons warned in 1871 of the tendency "to speak of such nonentity as *intrinsic value*" and explained that the term "value" in respect to a resource "merely expresses *the circumstance of its exchanging in a certain ratio for some other substance.*"[208] In 1872 Arthur Latham Perry similarly explained that value "is not an inherent and invariable attribute, but is the relative power which one thing has of purchasing other things." Thus, "[i]n one word, value is always relative, and never absolute. To say that anything has an absolute value is a simple contradiction in terms."[209]

In copyright thought a meaningful originality threshold was associated with assumptions about inherent value. Attempts to distinguish the work of the mere mechanic from that of the true genius author as well as willingness to draw a line between works of art or learning and vulgar entertainment all assumed that intellectual works have an inherent value that can be discerned apart from their market value. Given this assumption, the role of copyright law could be plausibly construed not just as encouraging valuable works but also as denying the reward to works lacking inherent value and protecting the public from them. Thus in one of the last opinions denying protection due to the questionable character

---

[206] Francis Wayland, *The Elements of Political Economy* (Boston: Gould and Lincoln, 1853), 15–24.
[207] Oliver Putnam, *Tracts on Sundry Topics of Political Economy* (Boston: Russell, Odiorne, 1834), 4.
[208] William Stanley Jevons, *The Theory of Political Economy* (London: Macmillan, 1871), 82.
[209] Arthur Latham Perry, *Elements of Political Economy*, 6th ed. (New York: C. Scribner, 1871), 51.

of a dramatic work, the court explained that "[s]ociety may tolerate, and even patronize, such exhibitions, but Congress has no constitutional authority to enact a law that will copyright them, and the courts will degrade themselves when they recognize them as entitled to the protection of the law."[210] The assumption underlying observations such as this was a distinction between market demand and inherent value. The decline of the concept of inherent value and its replacement by a market understanding pulled the rug from under this approach. Justice Story's early opinions that laid the foundations for the minimalist approach to originality were already colored by a market concept of value. When he dismissed the originality challenge in *Emerson v. Davies*, Story wrote that whether the author's work was "better or worse is not a material inquiry in this case," since "[i]f worse, his work will not be used by the community at large; if better, it is very likely to be so used." In the crucial conclusion, he found that a work "may be more useful or less useful," but the only significance of that is to "diminish or increase the relative values of ... works in the market."[211] A robust originality threshold was fundamentally at odds with the rising tendency to see the market as the only arbiter of value.

The change in economic theory and popular conception of value dovetailed with a shift in the understanding of the legitimate role of government in promoting social and economic welfare. Historians describe the dominant approach during the late colonial era and in the first quarter of the nineteenth century as the "commonwealth" style of government.[212] Under this framework, government enjoyed broad legitimacy for intervening in all aspects of economic and social life in order to promote the public good. Commonwealth-style American government was characterized by particular institutional forms. The ideal of active promotion of the public good was put into practice through a variety of methods. Many of those were general regulations of various sorts. More unique, however, was an eclectic group of techniques of ad hoc

---

[210] *Barnes v. Miner*, 122 F. 492.   [211] *Emerson v. Davies*, 8 F. Cas. 620.

[212] Some of the seminal works in this vein are Oscar Handlin and Mary Flug Handlin, *Commonwealth: A Study of the Role of Government in the American Economy: Massachusetts 1774–1861* (New York: New York University Press, 1947); Louis Hartz, *Economic Policy and Democratic Thought: Pennsylvania 1776–1860* (Cambridge, Mass.: Harvard Universty Press, 1948); Carter Goodrich, *Government Promotion of American Canals and Railroads 1800–1890* (New York: Columbia University Press, 1960); Harry N. Scheiber, "Government and the Economy, Studies of the Commonwealth Policy in Nineteenth Century America," 3 *J. Interdisciplinary Hist.* 135 (1972).

governmental involvement in economic life, such as bounties, monopoly privileges, land grants, franchise, and special incorporation grants. Underlying this extensive system of ad hoc privileges were several interlocking principles. First, these measures were particularistic rather than universal. Government's role was to choose a specific private party on which to confer special powers or benefits that were not granted to others, even if they were similarly situated. Second, these privileges and the process of their creation were overtly political. Each grant and its specific terms were directly authorized on a discretionary basis by the political representatives of the people, usually the legislature. Ideally, the role of the political representative was to assess the benefit offered to the public by a particular private party and to allocate an adequate reward or encouragement. Third, these practices were based on a paternalistic assumption that government officials know how to promote the public welfare and which private party could best serve that goal. Fourth, this entire framework was based on a conception of the public good as an identifiable cohesive set of interests common to all members of society.

Beginning in the 1830s, the commonwealth style of government and its underlying assumptions declined. It came under attack from competing Jacksonian ideals and was eventually replaced by an alternative framework that could be referred to as that of the liberal state. At least initially, extensive governmental regulation of the economy still enjoyed broad legitimacy. The commonwealth institutional forms, however, lost favor and were ultimately abandoned. Confidence in the existence of a cohesive set of interests common to all members of society and in the ability of government to reflect it waned. A distinction gradually appeared between a public sphere and a private sphere in which government could not legitimately intervene. Special privileges of various kinds became common targets of vehement attacks. These were increasingly considered the manifestation of corruption and of the hijacking of the republic by an aristocratic oligarchy. Government was now expected to regulate in the name of public welfare through universal regimes creating general rights rather than ad hoc privileges. These universal regimes were justified on the basis of their general utility rather than governmental evaluation of the merit of any specific case.[213]

---

[213] Handlin and Handlin, *Commonwealth*, 170–89; Scheiber, "Government and the Economy," 136; Lawrence Frederick Kohl, *The Politics of Individualism: Parties and the American Character in the Jacksonian Era* (New York: Oxford University Press,

In copyright the primary shift from ad hoc privileges to universal rights was completed early with the transition from colonial and state legislative printing privileges to the state copyright statutes of the 1780s and the 1790 federal regime. On a secondary level, however, the struggle between the two institutional forms continued within copyright law during the nineteenth century. The competing views were articulated in an 1807 public debate over the pages of the New York newspapers.[214] The exchange revolved around the propriety and the eligibility for copyright protection of a modified and "improved" American version of Murray's *English Grammar*. An anonymous correspondent who attacked the American practice of awarding copyright to revised British books relied, among other things, on an originality argument that questioned the substantive merit of such improved works:

> The public should lend their ear with great caution to all pretended "improvements" of European works; and when they see a bookseller, or any other mere money-making adventurer, hold up to view, a copy-right to secure him the profits arising from the exclusive sale of the article, they may safely regard it as the cloven foot, which leads to the detection of the unsoundness of the owner. What a contrast do these adventurers often form with the real authors of the works they profess to improve.[215]

This combined an elitist view of authorship, a confident assertion of the intrinsic value of works, and a paternalistic approach toward market demand. The answer, from the rival correspondent – "Vindex" – relied on different premises:

> How far he may have promoted the welfare of society, or advanced the interests of learning and literature, are other questions, to be determined upon by the public, to whom he appeals; but totally unconnected with his rights under the law – from that he claims the protection of his property, equally whether it proceeds from the exertions of his mind or the labour of his hands.[216]

While not denying altogether differences in the objective value of works, this argument maintained that these were matters to be decided not by copyright law, but rather by market demand.

This early, somewhat esoteric exchange nicely demonstrates the interlocking logic of competing views of value and of government's proper

---

1989), 133–44; Harry L. Watson, *Liberty and Power: The Politics of Jacksonian America* (New York: Hill and Wang, 1990), 34–35.

[214] Elise Tillinghast, "A Literary Controversy in 1807 New York: Early Americans' Competing Views of Copyright Law" (unpublished manuscript, 2002).

[215] *The Weekly Inspector*, February 28, 1807.   [216] *The People's Friend*, March 7, 1807.

role. When the legitimacy of government's ad hoc judgments about social utility declined, the market stepped into this vacuum as the alternative mechanism for determining and allocating value. In 1825, one writer, following this logic, supplied an eloquent attack on the traditional privilege system in the context of intellectual works:

In a free country where there exist no privileged orders, nor unequally protected institutions, it will generally happen that the value of every branch of human knowledge, as far as concerns such a community, will be very nearly indicated by the quantity of intellectual capital, to use the language of political economists, naturally determined to its cultivation.[217]

He concluded that "we consider the inference of all force whatever, in determining the channels through which physical or intellectual industry shall flow, as impertinent and oppressive."[218] The disdain for "privileged orders [and] institutions" professed by the writer was accompanied by the following vision: "The supply of literature and science will be in proportion to their demand and their demand in proportion to their usefulness. The elements of *really* valuable information, the principles of serviceable, practical and necessary knowledge, will receive the largest share of cultivation, because they will be most in request."[219] This vision of value determined and allocated by the market rather than by suspicious governmental preferences fueled the resistance to a strong originality requirement in copyright. It was expressed in Story's admonition that any person should be "entitled to his copy-right, 'valere quantum valere potest.'"[220]

Another force at work was the changing understanding of the judicial role. During the first half of the nineteenth century, the dominant perception of law and the common mode of legal reasoning was instrumentalist. Law was typically seen as a tool for advancing social goals and public welfare. Accordingly, legal questions were often argued openly in terms of their social consequences and by reference to underlying policies. The ideal judge was seen as interpreting and shaping the law to promote social welfare, common interest, and equity. In the last quarter of the century the understanding of legitimate legal reasoning and of the judicial role changed. Legal historians today disagree on whether late-nineteenth-century judicial formalism in the sense of a belief in law as a geometry-like gapless system based on logical deduction was a reality or a myth created in later

---

[217] *Atlantic Magazine*, February 1, 1825, 272, 273.   [218] Id., 280.   [219] Id., 273.
[220] F. Cas. 621.

generations.[221] It is somewhat less controversial that the judicial style and sources of legitimacy changed during that period. Judges became less prone to openly rest their decisions on social policies. Rather than prudent policy makers making choices in the name of the public good, they were more likely to present themselves as professional masters of a neutral set of techniques for deriving legal meanings and deciding specific cases.[222]

In copyright law, this meant that judges recoiled from a robust concept of originality that would require them to make regularly and overtly exactly the sort of substantive judgments they were claiming to abdicate. When in 1839 Story concocted his example of two judges of conflicting religious beliefs reaching opposite results on the copyrightability of a work, it was an extreme ad absurdum case. Later in the century, however, with the decline of a notion of a cohesive common interest that could guide the choices of judges as confident members of a socially responsible elite, the specter of subjectivism entailed by strict originality threatened judicial legitimacy. In 1894 one court rejected a defendant's claim that a work's value could not be simply equated with its box-office value. It tied together the new approach of judicial abdication with the notion of market value using the following prose:

> ... neither courts nor jurors have any certain rule for valuing it, except such as comes from evidence of effect which the composition in question has on masses of man. The claim made by the defendant that "the box-office value" fails to furnish any test under the copyright laws of the United States, with reference to dramatic compositions, is not sustainable ... with reference to matters like this at bar, touching which there are no rules except in the unmeasured characteristics of humanity, their reception by the public may be the only test on the question of insignificance or worthlessness under the copyright statutes.[223]

The ideas that the only kind of value is market value determined by subjective preferences and that judges should avoid basing legal conclusions on subjective value choices completed each other and doomed the possibility of a robust originality requirement.

---

[221] Cf. Morton J. Horwitz, *The Transformation of American Law 1870–1960: The Crisis of Legal Orthodoxy* (New York: Oxford University Press, 1992), 9–19, and Thomas C. Grey, "Langdell's Orthodoxy," 45 *U. Pitt. L. Rev.* 1 (1983), with Duncan Kennedy, *A Critique of Adjudication* (Cambridge, Mass.: Harvard University Press, 1997), 105, and David Rabban, *Law's History: Late Nineteenth-Century American Legal Scholarship and the Transatlantic Turn to History* (Cambridge: Cambridge University Press, 2013), 473–85, 512–19.

[222] Horwitz, *The Transformation of American Law 1870–1960*, 16–17.

[223] *Henderson v. Tompkins*, 60 F. 763–64.

The notion of originality as defining authorship could exist in its purity as long as it remained an abstract justification for copyright. As soon as it was translated into law, however, it met the economic and ideological realities of the day that reshaped and constrained it. The ideal of the romantic author was hamstrung by the liberal market.

THE SUPREME COURT SAYS THEY ARE ALL RIGHT

In the 1903 decision of the Supreme Court *Bleistein v. Donaldson Lithographing Co.*, which signifies the triumph of the modern, minimalist approach to originality, all of these threads came together.[224] The works at issue in the case were lithographic prints that served as advertisements for "The Great Wallace Shows" and depicted circus scenes alongside some simple text.[225] The commercial advertisement posters were a typical product of one of the rising industries external to the book trade that maintained constant pressure against strong notions of authorship and originality. Circus show advertisements accounted for a large share of the business of the commercial print industry in the nineteenth century.[226] The brief submitted to the Supreme Court on behalf of the *Courier Lithographing Company*, which owned the copyright in the posters, announced in a doomsday fashion that the fate of the industry hinged on the availability of copyright for its product:

It will be seen that the fundamental question of the right to copyright such show-bills or posters, is a question of great importance, involving the protection of an immense industry. If the proprietors of the lithographic establishments of the country cannot copyright and protect their designs for posters and show-bills, but these can be pirated and copied by cheaper competitors, then the entire lithographic business will have to be reconstructed, much capital which is now invested will be destroyed, the inducement to get up original and artistic designs will be at an end, and this great business, which has been steadily improving in the artistic quality of its productions; will surely deteriorate, and will have to be run on what may be described as a cheap and nasty basis.[227]

While the defense blurred statutory and constitutional arguments, by the time the case arrived at the Supreme Court it was clear that the central

---

[224] *Bleistein v. Donaldson Lithographing Co.*, 188 U.S. 239 (1903).
[225] Diane Leenheer Zimmerman, "The Story of *Bleistein v. Donaldson Lithographing Company*: Originality as a Vehicle for Copyright Inclusivity," in Jane C. Ginsburg and Rochelle Cooper Dreyfuss, eds., *Intellectual Property Stories* (New York: Foundation Press, 2006), 78.
[226] Id., 80.   [227] *Bleistein v. Donaldson*, Brief on Behalf of Plaintiffs in Error, 8.

question was whether the advertisement poster was eligible for copyright on grounds of originality. The defendant's brief recited a litany of precedents that denied copyright protection to works that fell outside the constitutional mandate of promoting the progress because they belonged to the realm of commerce or mere entertainment. The court of appeals decided the case on this ground after being unable to find in the poster anything "useful or meritorious" beyond being an advertisement.[228] This conclusion was echoed by the Supreme Court dissenters, who dismissed the poster as "mere advertisement of a circus" that fell outside the ambit of the constitutional clause.[229] Although mostly forgotten, the case also involved another aspect of originality doctrine that distinguished art from vulgar and immoral entertainment and denied copyright to the latter. The trial court made much in its statutory analysis of the "merely frivolous, and to some extent immoral in tendency" character of the posters. Judge Evans was particularly troubled by the poster "The Spectacular Ballet," which he described as representing "a dozen or more figures of women in tights, with bare arms, and with much of the shoulders displayed, and by means of which it is designed to lure men to a circus."[230] In the defendant's Supreme Court brief this became the basis for invoking the precedents that denied protection to vulgar and immoral subject matter accompanied by a moralistic warning of the influence of such images on the "young and immature and those who are sensually inclined."[231] A later personal note by Justice Oliver Wendell Holmes Jr. in which he described his decision as involving the copyrightability of "a poster for a circus representing décolletés and fat legged ballet girls" captured the various nuances of the originality objection in the case.[232]

Large parts of the plaintiff's Supreme Court brief were within the traditional contours of originality. It protested the trial's court characterization of the posters as "tawdry pictures" and argued at length within the framework of *Burrow Giles*, enumerating the aesthetic merits of the posters and explaining the creative choices and artistic skills required of their creators. The brief even made efforts to establish

---

[228] *Courier Lithographing Co. v. Donaldson Lithographing Co.*, 104 F. 993, 996 (6th Cir. 1900).

[229] *Bleistein v. Donaldson Lithographing Co.*, 188 U.S. 253.

[230] *Bleistein v. Donaldson Lithographing Co.*, 98 F. 608, 611 (C.C.D. Ky. 1899).

[231] *Bleistein v. Donaldson*, Brief for Defendant in Error, 23.

[232] Sheldon M. Novick, *Honorable Justice: The Life of Oliver Wendell Holmes* (Boston: Little, Brown, 1989), 254.

the place of commercial poster lithography as a respectable art, which it described as "a special and peculiar branch of pictorial art, and one into which many gifted artists, highly successful in other fields, have ventured."[233] As part of this effort the brief referred to poster exhibitions and literature and attached as an appendix parts of the book *Picture Posters* by Charles Hiatt.[234]

Another strand of the argument, however, offered a more open and radical challenge to traditional notions of originality. "[T]he value of such posters," the brief explained, "is in their attracting or drawing power." In fact, given their nature as advertisement, the market value of the posters was of a second order. It ultimately consisted not in the poster's own attraction but in the demand it created for whatever was advertised. Thus if the posters "advertise a show their value is proved practically by the number of people they bring to that show." This equated the value of the posters with their market value: "So in the case of such posters the 'box-office receipts,' spoken of in some of the copyright decisions, becomes an absolute test of the practical success and value of the picture."[235] Taking a market definition of value for granted, any additional doubts about the intrinsic value of the work seemed senseless. Thus the Circuit Court's observation that apart from serving as advertisement it was unclear the posters "have any intrinsic merit or value" provoked the comment that "[w]e are unable to imagine what standard the learned judges ... thought should be applied."[236] Any attempt to go beyond the "box office" test in ascertaining a work's value, the brief warned, would result in judges playing art critics and ruling on the basis of "a matter of taste," and thus: "If our courts in constructing the copyright law are to adopt the standards of New England Puritanism of two hundred years ago or of hypocritical art censors, there will be few works found of sufficient artistic merit to deserve the protection of copyright."[237] This second strand of argument no longer tried to push the boundaries of the traditional framework from within by demonstrating the work's artistic qualities and its creator's creativity. Instead it asserted that the market is the only mechanism for assessing value and that judges should avoid such judgments altogether.

Holmes upheld the copyrightability of the posters in a majority opinion that echoed the plaintiff's brief. It did not stop, as it might have, with finding that the posters embodied sufficient intellectual effort and

---

[233] *Bleistein v. Donaldson*, Brief on Behalf of Plaintiffs in Error, 10.   [234] Id., 10, 53.
[235] Id., 11.   [236] Id., 26.   [237] Id., 25–26.

creativity under *Burrow Giles*,[238] but continued with a radical challenge to the traditional originality framework. The passage that would become the foundation of modern originality doctrine was a manifesto of market value and judicial neutrality:

> It would be a dangerous undertaking for persons trained only to the law to constitute themselves final judges of the worth of pictorial illustrations, outside of the narrowest and most obvious limits ... if they command the interest of any public, they have a commercial value – it would be bold to say that they have not an aesthetic and educational value – and the taste of any public is not to be treated with contempt.[239]

This skillfully wove together the complete reduction of value to commercial value, the assumption that government should offer copyright to all on open and universal terms, leaving the market to determine its value, and the admonition that judges should refrain from any substantive evaluations of copyrighted works. The passage embodied, in short, the modern framework of originality. Following the decision, the *Chicago Record-Herald* published a cartoon that showed the judicial figure of Homes pointing at pictures of dancing women in ballet outfit. The text said, "THE SUPREME COURT SAYS THEY ARE ALRIGHT."[240]

PERSONALITY ALWAYS CONTAINS SOMETHING UNIQUE: THE IDEOLOGY OF ORIGINALITY

The economic and ideological forces that emerged during the nineteenth century prevented ideal notions of authorship and originality – the official justificatory foundation of copyright – from obtaining purchase in actual copyright law. But this is not the entire story. The constitutive image of the romantic author would not simply depart quietly. The dead corpse of originality was buried countless times, but its ghost kept coming back to haunt American copyright. This was true even of *Bleistein*. For a decision that banished the romantic author from copyright law, the majority opinion is overladen with images of genius artists. The names of Velasquez, Whistler, Degas, Goya, and Manet were all called on to justify the copyright in what the trial court called the "tawdry pictures." Holmes responded to the claim that the posters were merely banal representations of common circus scenes with his own theory of originality. "Personality always contains something unique," he explained, "and a very modest

---

[238] 188 U.S. 250.   [239] Id., 251.   [240] *Chicago Record-Herald*, February 3, 1903.

grade of art has in it something irreducible, which is one man's alone."
This expression of "singularity" a person "may copyright."[241]
Thus, Holmes did not dismiss originality. He banalized it. In a fit of fancy
rhetorical footwork, the quality that in romantic authorship discourse
was considered the hallmark of the genius few – the imprinting of one's
unique mark of personality on the world – became the standard quality of
any expression.

The same phenomenon appeared more generally and sometimes in
more curious ways in the copyright discourse of the era. Ironically,
as the prospects of a robust originality threshold dissolved and as the
standard applied by courts eroded, originality doctrine rose in status.
Drone included in his foundational treatise an elaborate section about
originality, which he started by declaring the "universally recognized"
rule that "originality is an essential attribute of copyright."[242] The section
was devoted, however, to cabining the concept and rejecting any
demanding notion of originality.

In the later part of the nineteenth century originality consolidated as a
fundamental principle of copyright law and formally acquired a constitutional status. The most important landmark in this process was the
1879 Supreme Court's decision in the *Trademark Cases*. In striking down
as unconstitutional the first federal trademark law enacted in 1870 the
Court found that Congress was powerless to legislate it under the intellectual property clause. Rejecting the possibility that trademarks could be
protected as "writings of authors" the opinion by Justice Miller reasoned
that the term extends only to intellectual creations that "are original,
and are founded in the creative powers of the mind." A trademark, whose
protection depends merely on registration or use in commerce, does not
necessarily possess the essential qualities of "novelty, invention, discovery, or any work of the brain." "It requires," Miller wrote, "no fancy or
imagination, no genius, no laborious thought."[243] Swirling together in
this reasoning were different conceptions of originality.[244] Whatever its
exact meaning, however, originality was positioned with unprecedented
clarity and force as a constitutive principle of copyright. It was also firmly
secured with constitutional moorings. Arguments about various aspects

[241] 188 U.S. 250.
[242] Drone, *A Treatise on the Law of Property in Intellectual Productions*, 198.
[243] *The Trademark Cases*, 100 U.S. 82, 94 (1879).
[244] See Robert Brauneis, "The Transformation of Originality in the Progressive-Era Debate
over Copyright in News," 27 *Cardozo Arts Ent. L. J.* 321, 326 (2009–10).

of originality as constitutional limits on congressional power had been floating around for decades, but this was the first time a court directly invalidated legislation on this ground, thereby formally sealing the requirement's constitutional credentials. Later courts continued this trend.[245] The lower the substantive threshold created by originality sunk, the higher rose its importance as a fundamental principle and as a constitutional defining feature of the field.

Given the economic and intellectual forces arrayed against it, one could expect originality to disappear or diminish into a triviality in copyright thought. It survived and flourished because of its ideological function. The ideological character of the concept accounts for the paradox of its declining practical significance accompanied by a rise in rhetorical and formal status. Since the late eighteenth century authorship – a construct wrapped inexorably with the notion of originality – had been the constitutive myth of copyright. The concepts of authorship and originality were embedded in the constitutive texts of copyright and permeated all common forms of copyright policy arguments, whether utilitarian or natural rights based. When the abstract ideals of authorship began to interact with concrete copyright law they met resistance not only from existing legal forms that were shaped when copyright was still the trade privilege of the publisher, but also from new economic and intellectual pressures. The result was a gap between copyright's constitutive ideals and its doctrinal realties. In the late nineteenth century, as the forces pulling away from a robust originality doctrine intensified and as legal doctrine came to reflect this, the rift expanded. Instead of a collapse of authorship and originality, the system developed mechanisms for containing the tension.

The elevation of originality to the level of a fundamental, constitutional principle reduced the dissonance between copyright's official ideals and its doctrinal realities. The greater the gap grew between the two, the stronger became the dissonance and the more necessary the means for its suppression. There was no false consciousness. Early-twentieth-century lawyers were not deceived to believe that copyright law reflected anything close to the ideals of romantic authorship. But the conceptual structure of copyright law mediated the tensions between the conflicting commitments

---

[245] See e.g. *Higgins v. Keuffel*, 140 U.S. 431; *Burrow-Giles Lithographic Co.*, 111 U.S. 57–60 (1884); *Am. Mutoscope & Biograph Co.*, 137 F. 265–67; *Courier Lithographing Co.*, 104 F. 994–95; *Falk v. City Item Printing Co.*, 79 F. 321; *Falk v. Donaldson*, 57 F. 32, 34 (C.C.S.D. N.Y. 1893).

and beliefs. It allowed the lawyerly knowledge that originality is a slim and technical requirement that rarely has practical significance to coexist with the premise that the ultimate animating principle of copyright is authorship. These mediated tensions underlie and explain the curiosities of the era's originality discourse: Holmes' simultaneous dismissal and embrace of the genius author by making the imprint of personality a standard trait of any expressive work, or the tendency of commentators to valorize originality while trivializing it, sometimes in the same sentence.

WHERE AUTHORSHIP PROPER ENDS AND MERE ANNALS BEGIN

The history of legal protection for news demonstrates the ideological intricacies of originality around the dawn of the twentieth century. As Robert Brauneis has shown, the era's battle for proprietary rights in news was a catalyst that helped shape modern originality doctrine.[246] For most of the nineteenth century it was a settled rule that copyright protection covers the factual content of works such as maps, directories, or chronologies.[247] This rule was adopted from English sources and became entrenched in an age when originality in its modern sense did not exist in American copyright law. The economic practices of the generation and exploitation of news, that by virtue of stringent registration and deposit requirements were left, as a practical matter, outside the domain of copyright, did not generate pressure for extending the same principle to news. The prevailing model of open exchange of news did not rely on commodification and was deeply rooted in the technological, economic, and social circumstances of the period.[248] This system was undermined in the last decades of the century when the spread of the telegraph and other developments changed the patterns of the industry and created fault lines within it over the question of exclusive rights in news. New, large, capital-intensive news organizations such as the Associated Press, Western Union, and the metropolitan newspapers developed a substantial interest in the legal appropriation of news. They were pitted against the "country

---

[246] See Brauneis, "The Transformation of Originality."

[247] *Blunt v. Patten*, 3 F. Cas. 763 (S.D. N.Y. 1828); *Lawrence v. Dana*, 15 F. Cas. 26, 60 (C.C.D. Mass. 1869); *Farmer v. Calvert Lithographic, Engraving & Map Publishing Co.*, 8 F. Cas. 1022, 1026 (C.C.E.D. Mich. 1872); *Banks v. McDivitt*, 2 F. Cas. 759 (C.C.S.D. N.Y. 1875); see generally Brauneis, "The Transformation of Originality," 328–32.

[248] Richard B. Kielbowicz, "News Gathering by Mail in the Age of the Telegraph: Adapting to a New Technology," 28 *Technology and Culture* 26, 28–38 (1987); Brauneis, "The Transformation of Originality," 339–45.

press" and others who had a stake in the traditional news exchange system.[249] A major move to propertize news first took place on the legislative front when in 1884 a "Bill Granting Copyright in Newspapers" was introduced in Congress.[250] The bill attempted to create an eight-hour-long exclusivity to newspapers in their content, attracting fierce opposition and stirring a lively debate.

The clash took place exactly at the moment when originality-based authorship was becoming the new ideological center of copyright doctrine. It is no surprise, then, that one of the main rhetorical weapons wrought by opponents of the bill, alongside allegations of monopolization, was characterizing news as lacking the essence of the proper subject matter of copyright, namely, authorial originality. Those who gathered news, the argument went, were not within the domain of authorship because, unlike authors, they did not create the news through their intellectual creative faculties. The *Nation* expressed this idea by observing that "it is absurd to talk of a man who picks up a piece of news or an 'item' as an author." It concluded that news is not the "fruits of original intellectual labor" whose protection is the purpose of copyright.[251] It is doubtful that originality arguments caused the ultimate defeat of the bill. The significance of the legislative debate was in creating a high-stakes context where interested parties were motivated to develop and articulate the new emerging rhetoric of originality as individual creativity.

This dynamics intensified when proponents of proprietary rights in news, defeated in the legislative arena, turned to the courts. Ironically, in this round it was these proponents who were strategically motivated to construct arguments about creativity-based originality as demarcating the outer boundaries of copyright. Given the nature of the news business, in the absence of statutory intervention relaxing the registration and deposit prerequisites, a judicial extension of statutory copyright to news would have been of little practical value. The argument was therefore that proprietary rights in news existed under the common law rather than statutory copyright. By this time, however, it was well settled that publication terminated common law copyright and triggered statutory protection requiring strict adherence to formalities. The solution was to extract news from the realm of copyright altogether.

---

[249] Brauneis, "The Transformation of Originality," 350–59.
[250] A Bill Granting Copyright to Newspapers, S. 1728, 48th Cong., 15 Cong. Rec. 1578; H.R. 5850, 48th Cong, 15 Cong. Rec. 1758.
[251] "Stealing News," *Nation*, February 21, 1884, 159.

This happened when in 1901 Western Union sued the National Telegraph News Company for interfering with its ticker machine operation.[252] Western Union deployed its tickers – machines that translated a telegraphic signal into text – in private companies and public establishments such as hotels and saloons interested in receiving news feeds including business or sport-related information. National Telegraph admitted to copying news items from Western Union tickers and using them in its own news ticker service. Following a district court injunction that prohibited the copying of the news for one hour, the case was appealed to the Seventh Circuit. Predictably, National Telegraph's main argument was that by publishing the news without registration or deposit Western Union had dedicated it to the public. Western Union responded in its brief that its news was "quasi – or pseudo – literary property; not within the purview of the copyright statutes ... but finding its protection ... in the principles of the common law."[253] Protection for news was thus shifted into the emerging field of unfair competition where the court could use its equitable powers to recognize a new quasi-property interest. But what was the basis for excluding news from the realm of copyright? The brief asserted "in the holy name of the art of letters" that such information "is not, properly speaking, literature."[254] The argument was explicitly rested on the image of the creative author:

Could you dignify by the name of "book," or "history," or "learning," or literature," or "writing" a telegraph message giving the result of a baseball match or a horse-race, or fluctuations of the stock market? Could you call the writer of the message an "author"? The very absurdity of the proposition is its own refutation.[255]

In his opinion upholding the injunction, Jude Grosscup adopted this reasoning and further developed the idea of the authorial use of the creative faculty as defining the purview of copyright. He wrote that the original meaning of the constitutional clause was that "literature, as Literature, had received an accession" and that "[u]nquestionably, the framers of the constitution ... had this kind of authorship in mind."[256] Grosscup explained the fact that copyright covered much more than literature as literature with a living constitution account. As conditions changed, the purview of copyright was gradually expanded to new

---

[252] *National Tel. News Co. v. Western U. Tel. Co.*, 119 F. 294 (7th Cir. 1902).
[253] *National Tel. News Co. v. Western U. Tel. Co.*, Brief for Appellee, 10.   [254] Id., 8.
[255] Id., 9.   [256] 119 F. 297.

subject matter under the principle of protecting "the labor of the brain." But he also observed that "obviously, there is a point at which this process of expansion must cease." What was that point? "[W]e may fix the confines," he wrote, "at the point where authorship proper ends, and mere annals begin." Authorship requires "that there has been put into the production something meritorious from the author's own mind; that the product embodies the thought of the author, as well as the thought of others; and would not have found existence in the form presented, but for the distinctive individuality of mind from which it sprang." The mere factual content of news clearly did not bear this distinctive mark of individuality and therefore rather than "the product of originality" it was "the product of opportunity."[257]

The conflict over propertizing news was an important moment in the development of originality. Together with a few other decisions *National Tel. News Co.* positioned originality as the defining feature of copyright and clearly articulated the criterion in terms of individual creativity. The specific new rule that the factual content of news could not properly be the subject of copyright protection was later followed as a matter of course.[258] But in what sense was it part of the ideology of originality? Placing some subject matter outside the purview of copyright was essential for maintaining authorship as the constitutive myth of copyright. As Grosscup observed, if original authorship was the basis of copyright, a line had to be drawn somewhere. The meaning of originality could be whittled down to encompass subject matter far afield from the creation of the romantic author. But the factual content of news (as opposed to the specific form of the report) seemed to be the antithesis of the product of the creative faculty of an author and offered little opportunity to square the circle with arguments about an ever-present mark of individuality. Extending copyright to encompass such subject matter threatened too much dissonance with its constitutive myth. Factual news had to be excluded or original authorship had to be explicitly repudiated.

Exclusion did not preclude, however, the possibility of proprietary rights. To the contrary, in *National Tel. News Co.* exclusion from the purview of copyright was a necessary prelude to providing common law protection free from cumbersome formalities. Deprived of the aura of original authorship these alternative rights could still be justified on the lesser ground of providing an incentive for a useful economic function.

[257] Id., 298.
[258] *International News Service v. Associated Press*, 248 U.S. 215, 234 (1918).

The *National Tel. News Co.* court phrased this as a rhetorical question: "Is the enterprise of the great news agencies, or the independent enterprise of the great newspapers or of the great telegraph and cable lines, to be denied appeal to the courts, against the inroads of the parasite, for no other reason than that the law, fashioned hitherto to fit the relations of authors and the public, cannot be made to fit the relations of the public and this dissimilar class of servants?" The answer was obvious: "We choose, rather, to make precedent – one from which is eliminated, as immaterial, the law grown up around authorship."[259]

Reclassifying the claim for ownership of news was not without implications. Proprietary rights under the newly minted common law misappropriation doctrine provided protection quite different from copyright (the injunction upheld in *National Tel. News Co.* precluded copying for one hour), and in the long run preclusion of the copyright option proved significant in regard to certain factual subject matter. Nevertheless, the ruling, upheld sixteen years later by the Supreme Court in *International News Service v. Associated Press*,[260] gave the industry interests seeking proprietary rights much of what they wanted: exclusivity in the factual content, creating a competitive advantage in regard to the "hot news" value. Authorship-based originality was thus not endlessly flexible. If the ideology was to survive, some subject matter had to be denied entry to the realm of copyright. But the principle was extremely malleable in two ways. First, through various doctrinal and rhetorical techniques much subject matter falling far short of the bar implied by the image of the original author was still covered by copyright. Second, even when the considerable internal elasticity was exhausted and some subject matter was excluded, the "outside" of copyright was no longer the "outside" of property. Non-authorship-based proprietary rights appeared at the external periphery of copyright and captured some of the subject matter that was excluded from it.

AS MUCH RIGHT AS AN AUTHOR: AUTHORSHIP UNIVERSALIZED

The rise of original authorship as the ideological heart of copyright exerted a measure of centrifugal force that placed some subject matter beyond copyright's confines. At the same time it generated centripetal

[259] 119 F. 301.   [260] 248 U.S. 234.

forces that helped pull much new subject matter into copyright's fold. When copyright was established in the United States it was still universally seen as the unique regulatory regime of the book trade. The 1790 Copyright Act covered maps, charts, and books,[261] and the 1802 extension to prints and engravings was well within the traditional domain of print.[262] Even the explicit addition of "musical works" in the 1831 statutory reform did not break this pattern.[263] This addition meant only that copyright protected sheet music against unauthorized reprints, which had already been the case from the earliest days of the regime.[264] It was only in the second half of the century that copyright was gradually extended through a series of incremental statutory amendments to new subject matter beyond the confines of the realm of print.

The gradual expansion of copyrightable subject matter is often conceived of in terms of technological and economic determinism. New information technologies, such as photography or audio recording, appeared and created new, valuable markets. This was followed by an economic need for, or at least a substantial private interest in, appropriation, resulting in the extension of copyright. No doubt, technological and economic developments played a crucial role in the spread of copyright to new domains. Ideology, however, had its own part to play. The ideology of original authorship had a universalizing effect. By making an abstract criterion – the use of one's creative power of the intellect – the raison d'être of copyright it opened the door for claims by new groups outside copyright's traditional domain of the book trade. The concept of original authorship facilitated the emergence of self-conscious groups of creators with a sense of a shared identity and interest. It supplied such groups with the vocabulary to articulate claims for social status as well as legal recognition. The claim for authorship status also aided, and gradually naturalized, the acceptance by others of these groups' demand for legal recognition. The history of the extension of copyright to dramatic compositions and to fine art demonstrates this process.

Dramatic compositions were not a distinct category of copyrightable subject matter in the United States until 1856. If published in print (and formal requirements were met) plays could be protected against

---

[261] 1 Stat. 124, §1.   [262] Act of Apr. 29, 1802, ch. 36, §2, 2 Stat. 171.
[263] 4 Stat. 436, §1.
[264] Oren Bracha, "Commentary on the U.S. Copyright Act 1831," in *Primary Sources on Copyright*.

unauthorized reprinting as a species of "book." In practice, playwrights, who for the most part adapted French and British plays, either offered their work in house to stock companies of which they were members or transferred their manuscripts for a lump sum.[265] Dramatic compositions as a separate subject matter category of copyright emerged out of the creation of a public performance entitlement for plays. Agitation for such an entitlement began to appear in the 1830s against the backdrop of economic and social changes in the profession. The number of theaters, the cost of production, and the demand for American drama all increased.[266] With the early emergence of the star system toward the middle of the century some playwrights started to write plays tailored for stars and achieved a measure of fame and better compensation.[267] This small new group of playwrights also began to see themselves as authors forming a special branch of the literary profession. Ironically, with the new claim for status came also a bitter sense of oppression and injustice. Playwrights were not getting the recognition and reward to which they started to see themselves as being entitled as authors. The *Albion Magazine* expressed this sentiment in the early 1840s when it observed in regard to drama that "[i]t is in vain to expect that the first talent in the country will exercise their faculties in this, the most difficult of all literary enterprises for so small a consideration," and demanded "European prices."[268] The new claim for authorship came with a new claim for compensation, which was soon translated into the language of copyright. In 1835 the playwright-actor John Howard Payne asked, "What are our laws on the subject?" and demanded a legal remedy.[269] A bill on the subject introduced in the Senate in 1841, most likely due to the efforts of the playwright Robert Montgomery Bird, framed the issue squarely within the

[265] See Alfred L. Bernheim, *The Business of the Theatre: An Economic History of the American Theatre, 1750–1932* (New York: B. Blom, 1964), 20; Thomas J. Walsh, "Playwrights and Power: A History of the Dramatists Guild," Ph.D. diss., University of Texas (1996), 10.
[266] Bernheim, *The Business of the Theatre*, 19.
[267] Felicia Hardison Londré and Daniel J. Watermeier, *The History of North American Theater: The United States, Canada, and Mexico: From Pre-Columbian Times to the Present* (New York: Continuum, 1998), 116–32; Bernheim, *The Business of the Theatre*, 27–28.
[268] Quoted in Montrose J. Moses, *The American Dramatist* (Boston: Little, Brown, 1925), 86–87.
[269] Id., 89.

vocabulary of authorial property.[270] The bill "To secure to the authors of dramatic works their property therein" proposed conferring a public performance entitlement on dramatic authors, but it was never passed.[271]

Following another failure to create a public performance right as part of Congressman Charles Jared Ingersoll's 1844 ambitious attempt of copyright reform, a new lobbying wave began in the 1850s.[272] The recognition of playwrights as authors and the need to place their just reward on par with those of literary authors pervaded the public campaign alongside the promise of encouraging American drama. The press highlighted the authorship argument and was almost uniformly supportive. "[T]here are no laborers in the literary field deserving more encouragement than those whose energies are devoted to the elevation and advancement of drama and the stage," observed "Acorn" in a published letter.[273] The *New York Daily Times* asked, "Why is that the author who writes successful novels should have it in his power to make a fortune, while the one whose bent leads him to produce successful plays should be unrewarded?"[274] Another newspaper conjured up a classic image from the pantheon of authorship when it referred to dramatists who "are treated in a manner more shameful than any authors have been treated since the days of Grab-street hacks."[275] The campaign led by playwrights George Henry Boker (encouraged by Bird, who did not live to see the victory) and Robert Taylor Conard[276] resulted in the 1856 act and its mandate that the copyright granted to "the author or

---

[270] Russell Sanjek, *American Popular Music and Its Business: The First Four Hundred Years* (New York: Oxford University Press, 1988), vol. 2, 33; Clement E. Foust, *The Life and Dramatic Works of Robert Montgomery Bird* (New York: Knickerbocker Press, 1919), 147–50.

[271] S. 227 A Bill to Secure to the Authors of Dramatic Works Their Property Therein, 26th Cong. (1841).

[272] H.R. 9, 28th Cong., 1st Sess. (January 3, 1844).

[273] "Letter from Acorn," *Spirit of the Times: A Chronicle of the Turf, Agriculture, Field Sports Life*, September 6, 1856.

[274] "Dramatic Copyright," *New York Daily Times*, June 24, 1856.

[275] "Copyright in a New Phase," *American Publishers' Circular and Literary Gazette*, June 28, 1856.

[276] See Oren Bracha, "Commentary on the U.S. Copyright Act Amendment 1856," in *Primary Sources on Copyright*. The actor and playwright Dion Boucicault claimed credit for playing the leading role in the lobbying that led to the 1856 Amendment. See Dion Boucicault, "Leaves from a Dramatist's Diary," 149 *N. Am. Rev.* 228, 230 (1889); Richard Fawkes, *Dion Boucicault: A Biography* (London and New York: Quartet Books, 1979), 91. There is little support in known contemporary sources for this claim.

proprietor of any dramatic composition, designed or suited for public representation" shall include an exclusive public performance entitlement.[277] On the Senate floor the chair of the Judiciary Committee, Senator James A. Bayard, observed that "the only value of a copyright to a dramatic author really is to protect the representation of his production in theaters."[278] The addition of a statutory public performance entitlement marked a new understanding of dramatic works as a separate category of copyrightable subject matter.[279]

Throughout the twenty-five-year-long process that led to the recognition of dramatic compositions and to the public performance entitlement, the vocabulary of authorship was both the stuff from which the emerging self-consciousness of playwrights was made and an effective legitimacy-conferring tool used in obtaining entrance to the domain of copyright. Even an account in the *New York Daily Times* following the enactment of the 1856 act lampooning the claimed beneficial results of the new act was riddled with the imagery of original authorship. It described sarcastically the stampede of "all the great American dramatists" to register their works under the new law:

For some days subsequent to the passage of the Act Murray-street was haunted by singular-looking men with long hair and inky finger-nails, each with a bundle of soiled paper under his arm or sticking out of his coat pocket, in case where the coat had a pocket that would hold anything. All these gentlemen wore an expression of mingled triumph and anxiety. They cast curious glances at each other, and eyed each other's bundles with ill-disguised curiosity. The fact was every one of the distinguished dramatists was alarmed, lest his companion should be about to copyright a version of his play; for these dramatic rivulets had one source-fountain-head – Paris.[280]

From this perspective, while original authorship did not appear out of thin air with the snap of the legislature's fingers, it was still the ultimate justification for the act and its desired outcome, hopefully to be achieved "in a year's time."

---

[277] 11 Stat. 139.   [278] 32 Cong. Globe 1647 (July 16, 1856).

[279] Drone had in his 1879 treatise a long section devoted to what he called "playright," by which he meant common law copyright in unpublished dramatic works that included a public performance entitlement. Drone, *A Treatise on the Law of Property in Intellectual Productions*, 533. Jessica Litman has shown that common law copyright in unpublished dramatic works did not predate the 1856 amendment but was "invented" by courts shortly after it. See Jessica Litman, "The Invention of the Common Law Play Right," 25 *Berkeley Tech. L.J.* 1381, 1404 (2010).

[280] "Plays and Playwrights," *New York Daily Times*, September 9, 1856.

The extension of copyright to works of fine art followed a similar pattern. For most of the nineteenth century American copyright did not apply to paintings, sculptures, or similar works. The precedent of the British 1798 Models and Busts Act notwithstanding, in the United States copyright seemed irrelevant to such nonprint creative forms.[281] A trickle of occasional lobbying by individual artists, usually casting their claim in the language of authorship and trying to persuade Congress to extend copyright to works of fine art, began in the 1820s. For decades such attempts were dismissed offhand, with legislators either rejecting the claim of authorship or turning it on its head to support the denial of copyright.

In 1820 Peter Cardelli petitioned Congress "to secure to him, and all other artists of his profession, the benefit of their labors ... for the same time allowed to authors for exclusive property in their writings."[282] Cardelli, a sculptor from Rome, was employed in the restoration of the Capitol in Washington and looked for his path to fame and fortune by making busts of great Americans – Jefferson, Madison, Monroe, and John Quincy Adams.[283] The Judiciary Committee reported negatively on his request.[284] The reasons it supplied are telling. The report explains that the petitioner "has not stated any new invention, or new combination of principles" and adds that the "art of sculpture" is not "within the meaning" of the intellectual property clause of the Constitution or alternatively that it is already covered by the Patent Act.[285] Ninety years later an observer commented on this reasoning: "Could stupidity go further?"[286] But in a climate in which copyright was still closely associated with the book trade such thinking was not remarkable. Cardelli and the committee were talking past each other. While he described himself as a creative author demanding rights in his original intellectual work, the committee, steeped in the print-bound notion of copyright, could classify his claim in his sculptural works only as belonging to the realm of the useful arts.

---

[281] An Act for Encouraging the Art of Making New Models and Casts of Busts, and other things therein mentioned, 1798, 38 Geo. III, c. 71.

[282] Senate Journal, 16th Cong., 1st Sess., March 1, 1820, 196.

[283] Charles E. Fairman, *Art and Artists of the Capitol of the United States of America* (Washington, D.C.: G.P.O., 1927), 46.

[284] Senate Journal, 16th Cong., 1st Sess., May 8, 1820, 384.

[285] Serial Set Vol. No. 27, Session Vol. No. 2, 16th Congress, 1st Sess., May 8, 1820, S. Doc. 129.

[286] Gustavus Myers, *History of the Great American Fortunes* (Chicago: C.H. Kerr, 1910), vol. 1, 137.

When four years later the painter Rembrandt Peale tried to convince Congress to extend "the benefit of copy-rights to the authors of paintings and drawings," he had only little more success.[287] The occasion for this attempt was the completion of Peale's celebrated portrait of Washington. Although the bill was favorably reported by the Judiciary Committee,[288] it was subsequently defeated on the Senate's floor. In debate Senator Lowrie explained that Peale was willing to sell his Washington portrait only if he could "have the same privilege of profiting by his work as writers of books have in theirs." The reply from Senator Mills relied in part on denying Peale's originality by claiming that his portrait was "but a copy, with some little embellishment" of the one by Gilbert Charles Stuart. Mills also provided, however, a more general account of the relationship between authorship and copyright, observing that the proposed act "would have a great tendency to retard the progress of the art of painting, as it would do away the right to imitating and attempting to excel paintings already in existence."[289] Ironically, Mills' argument echoed Peale's own description of how when working on the portrait he assembled in his room "every Portrait, Bust, Medallion, and Print of Washington."[290]

In another failed attempt in 1838 John A. Brevoort and O.S. Fowler relied even more explicitly on the generalized claim of authorship. "By what principle of right or justice," their petition asked, "should the artist who takes a lithograph or engraving of an individual's features be protected by copyright, while the artist who takes a likeness of the same individual in plaster ... is excluded from legal protection"?[291]

Only in 1870 did Congress finally extend copyright to paintings and sculptures after a concentrated lobbying effort by artists, such as the prominent Bostonian painter William Morris Hunt, who wielded the authorship argument with more confidence and success.[292] By this

---

[287] 41 Annals of Congress Senate, 18th Congress, 1st Sess., April 12, 1824.
[288] S. 77 A Bill Extending the Benefit of Copyrights to the Authors of Paintings or Drawings, 18th Cong., 1st Sess., March 23, 1824, in Senate Journal, 18th Cong., 1st Sess., March 30, 1824.
[289] 41 Annals of Congress Senate, 18th Congress, 1st Sess., April 12, 1824.
[290] Edward C. Lester, *The Artists of America: A Series of Biographical Sketches of American Artists* (New York: Baker & Scribner, 1846), 210.
[291] Memorial of John A. Brevoort and O.S. Fowler, Serial Set Vol. No. 319 Session Vol. No. 6, 25th Congress, 2nd Session, S. Doc. 475, June 8, 1838, 25th Congress, 2nd Session.
[292] Journal of the Senate, 41st Cong., 1st Sess. 17, March 8, 1869.

time the American market for art had grown considerably.[293] Art became a more prosperous economic area and artists gained in social recognition and status.[294] A self-conscious artistic community with an articulate leadership had developed. Art academies and professional associations proliferated and trade journals appeared.[295] Tellingly, in the early stages of this process it was common for artists to associate with literary authors – a group that enjoyed a higher social status.[296] By comparison with previous rounds, in 1870 it was a much more confident artistic community, in terms of both its self-image and social status, that demanded legal recognition. This time no one mistook artists for artisans or assigned their claim to the area of the useful arts.

The argument in the lobbying efforts was based again on the parallel between artists – described as authors – and other authors already recognized by copyright. Thus the petition of the Officers of the Cincinnati Academy of Fine Arts complained that "existing laws do not afford to the authors of paintings, drawings, statuary and models, being works of the fine arts, protection in the nature of copy-right" and asked for the extension to artists of the same rights that are "conferred on authors of books, charts, engravings, prints and photographs."[297] This time, this logic was taken for granted. Authorship, understood in a broad sense by contrast to its old association with the book trade, justified treating all creators of original creative works equally. As Representative Jenckes remarked in the House: "an artist has as much right to the exclusive reproduction of his works as an author or engraver."[298] No one objected.

The process of universalizing authorship fed on its own momentum. Each incremental extension of copyright to new subject matter eroded its traditional strong association with the book trade and helped establish the new universal understanding of copyright's scope as defined by the criterion of authorship. The universal authorship arguments employed in each succeeding wave of subject matter expansion seemed increasingly

[293] Neil Harris, *The Artist in American Society: The Formative Years: 1790–1860* (New York: G. Braziller, 1966) 254–55; Lillian B. Miller, *Patrons and Patriotism: The Encouragement of the Fine Arts in the United States, 1790–1860* (Chicago, Ill.: University of Chicago Press, 1966), 213.
[294] Harris, *The Artist in American Society*, 258–61.
[295] Ibid., 255; Miller, *Patrons and Patriotism*, 85–138.
[296] Harris, *The Artist in American Society*, 113–15.
[297] The Petition of the undersigned officers of the Cincinnati academy of fine arts and others, N.A. 41A-H.8-1 Committee on Patents.
[298] Congressional Globe, 41st Cong., 2nd Sess., April 20, 1870.

self-evident. The natural culmination of universalization was abstraction. Thus, by contrast to the lengthening lists in preceding copyright statutes, the 1909 Copyright Act defined the scope of copyright with one inclusive term: "all the writings of an author."[299] This was followed by a long list of specific categories of subject matter, reflecting the many incremental extensions of the previous half-century. But the drafters of the act made sure to clarify that the purpose of the specific categories was classificatory and administrative and that it did not limit the abstract and inclusive definition of subject matter coverage.[300] The modern understanding of copyright as a universal field defined by the abstract principle of creative authorship, by that time already the new orthodoxy, received a formal expression in law. Universalizing the principle of authorship and diluting its practical meaning to the vanishing point went hand in hand.

[299] Act of March 4, 1909, ch. 320, §4, 35 Stat. 1075, 1076.   [300] Id., §4, 1077.

3

Objects of Property

Owning Intellectual Works

The flip side of authorship was ownership. As we have seen, nineteenth-century jurists had to translate the abstract ideal of authorship, placed at the center of copyright, into specific institutional arrangements. They faced much the same challenge with the related concept of owning intellectual objects. Who is the owner of the product of the mind? If property is a relationship between an owner and an object, what exactly is the object in which property subsists? And if property defines the rights and powers of the owner regarding other people in relation to the owned object, what does it mean to own an intangible object that has no readily apparent material boundaries that could be fenced in or trespassed?

Answering the first question was supposed to be easy. If the ideal of authorial property demanded anything, it was that authors would be the owners of the intellectual product of their minds. It is no surprise, then, that the 1790 copyright regime was based on the formal principle that initial ownership is vested in authors. In the late nineteenth century, however, strong forces pushed against a universal application of this principle. Many valuable works were now produced in hierarchical and collaborative settings. Works such as maps, advertisement lithographs, catalogues, and later motion pictures were produced through an employment, often corporate employment, relationship, rather than by independent artists or artisans. This relationship increasingly involved close supervision by an entrepreneur or a managerial hierarchy that often exercised tight control over both the production and the economic exploitation of the works. Many of these works required the collaboration of multiple creators whose labor was coordinated by the entity controlling the process. All of this produced a demand, usually sounded in the name of economic "need," for vesting initial ownership in the coordinating entity rather than the creator. By the dawn of the twentieth century, a judicially crafted work for hire doctrine, backed by a 1909 statutory imprimatur, mandated that in many cases authors were no longer owners. But the ideal of authorial ownership was never completely abandoned even in those areas where all that was left of it was an empty shell. As a result, copyright ownership became a conceptual terrain where the ideology of authorship took particularly twisted forms, forms that often ignored the principle of authorial property and at the same time refused to let go of it.

The questions of the intangible object of property and the nature of owning it were handled, at first, through concepts taken from the traditional framework of the printer's privilege. Latent in the doctrines that governed scope of protection and infringement was a narrow, semi-materialist understanding of copyright's object of property as the "copy." It dovetailed with a thin notion of ownership as the exclusive right to multiply copies of the protected text in print. Thus when in 1834 Americans experienced their own version of a literary property debate, defenders of copyright as a common law property right could claim that "the question is not as to property in ideas but in books."[1] By the end of the century, however, the printer's privilege to print a copy was supplanted by the radically different idea of ownership. The new model treated copyright as a polymorphic right, an entitlement to the full economic value of an intellectual commodity through the control of the markets for all its possible specific forms. As copyright was plainly becoming property in ideas rather than in books, there arose an anxiety that had to be repressed: the specter of private ownership as a means for controlling the dissemination of ideas and knowledge. New doctrinal boundary-setting mechanisms, such as the fair use doctrine and the idea/expression dichotomy, were developed instead of the old ones that were swept away. Along with their practical use of regulating copyright's burgeoning scope, these mechanisms had another function, every bit as ideological as copyright's concept of authorship: mediating the tension between a deep commitment to free access to knowledge and legal forms allowing unprecedented private control of it.

---

[1] Richard Peters, *Report of the Copy-right Case of Wheaton v. Peters Decided in the Supreme Court of the United States* (New York: James Van Norden, 1834) (an independent report hereinafter referred to as *Wheaton v. Peters*), 19.

THE SCULPTOR SELDOM TOUCHES THE MARBLE:
AUTHORS AS OWNERS?

Sometimes copyright's authorship framework prevented the law from taking forms manifestly inconsistent with it. At other times, however, the tension between official ideology and doctrinal reality was glaring. The development of the rules governing the ownership of copyright is a striking example of the latter. In 1846 Justice Levi Woodbury rejected offhand an employer's claim for the fourteen-year renewal period of the copyright in his employee's book. "It is the genius which conceived and the toil which compiled the book that is to be reward," he wrote, and added that the employer's claim was based on a principle that "aids those kinds of patrons, who fatten on the labors of genius."[2] Fifty-three years later another federal court found it exceedingly obvious that "the literary product" of a salaried employee was the property of the employer in which the employee "would have no more right than any stranger to copy or reproduce."[3] How were employee authors turned in the course of half a century from proprietors of their creations to nonowner, wage laborers?

The tension between the interests of creators and of those who exploit their product commercially is as old as copyright. In the days of the stationers' copyright or colonial privileges the law's priorities were clear. The publisher or the entrepreneur was officially the primary bearer of legal rights. The interest of authors was either ignored or weakly recognized at the margin. The new focus of copyright on authorship in the eighteenth century changed this. A fundamental implication of authorship as the justificatory basis of copyright was that those whose intellectual labor produced the owned work must be the primary bearers of legal rights. The state statutes and the 1790 act firmly placed authors in this position. The interests of entrepreneurs did not disappear, of course, but rather were shifted to a derivative status. The legal mechanism that enabled this was assignability. There is nothing inevitable in making copyright assignable.[4] Yet the institutional precedent of the statute of Anne and hundreds of

---

[2] *Pierpont v. Fowle*, 19 F. Cas. 652, 660 (C.C.D. Mass. 1846).

[3] *Colliery Engineer Co. v. United Correspondence Schools Co.*, 94 F. 152, 153 (C.C.S.D. N.Y 1899).

[4] Many continental countries ended up distinguishing rights of economic exploitation from rights designed to protect a personal interest of the author and significantly limited the alienability of rights in the latter group. On the history of the development of these personal rights in France and Germany, see David Saunders, *Authorship and Copyright* (London: Routledge, 1992), 75–121.

years of British practice going back to the early days of the stationers' copyright made assignability a foregone conclusion. Americans simply took assignability for granted when they created their copyright regime.[5] Making copyright assignable played, however, an important mediating role. Assignability left untouched the status of authors as the formal primary bearers of copyright and at the same time allowed for actual ownership and management of the rights by entrepreneurs. The large numbers of registrations by "proprietors" in the first decade of the federal copyright regime attests to the fact that this division often occurred.[6]

For the first half of the nineteenth century courts vigilantly guarded the status of authors as the primary owners of their creation. Direct challenges to authorial ownership from those who would lay a claim for their product were rare. The question typically arose in two other kinds of cases: lawsuits against infringers by authors who created the work as employees or from whom the work was commissioned[7] and, more commonly, lawsuits against infringers by employers or commissioning entities.[8] In these cases courts simply assumed authorial ownership or analyzed ownership by nonauthors on the basis of a clear per se rule: the creator of a work was its copyright owner, unless there was express assignment of the rights.[9] As one court put it: "The title to literary property is in the author whose intellect has given birth the thoughts and wrought them into the composition, unless he has transferred the title, by contract, to another."[10] In the rare case of a direct conflict between an author and another claiming the copyright, such as *Pierpont v. Fowle* – the 1846 case producing Woodbury's decisive support of authorial ownership – the same rule was applied.[11] The rule was grounded in the assumption that authorship entailed both intellectual labor and a personal connection between the author and his creation,

[5] See Oren Bracha, "The Ideology of Authorship Revisited: Authors, Markets, and Liberal Values in Early American Copyright," 118 *Yale L. J.* 186, 256 (2008).

[6] During the first decade of the federal copyright regime, proprietors registered 46.6 percent of copyrights. B. Zorina Khan, *The Democratization of Invention: Patents and Copyrights in American Economic Development, 1790–1920* (Cambridge: Cambridge University Press, 2005) 236.

[7] See e.g. *Heine v. Appleton*, 11 F. Cas. 1031 (C.C.S.D. N.Y. 1857).

[8] See e.g. *Binns v. Woodruff*, 3 F. Cas. 421 (C.C.D. Pa. 1821); *Atwill v. Ferrett*, 2 F. Cas. 195 (C.C.S.D. N.Y. 1846); *Little v. Gould*, 15 F. Cas. 612 (C.C.N.D. N.Y. 1852).

[9] See e.g. *Binns v. Woodruff*, 3 F. Cas. 423; *Atwill v. Ferrett*, 2 F. Cas. 197–98; *Heine v. Appleton*, 11 F. Cas. 1033; *Little v. Gould*, 15 F. Cas. 613; *De Witt v. Brooks*, 7 F. Cas. 575 (C.C.S.D. N.Y. 1861).

[10] *Boucicault v. Fox*, 3 F. Cas. 977, 980 (C.C.S.D. N.Y. 1862).   [11] 19 F. Cas. 659.

resulting in a strong proprietary interest. Another court explained this rationale in the same year: "A man's intellectual productions are peculiarly his own and, although they may have been brought forth by the author while in the general employment of another, yet he will not be deemed to have parted with his right."[12]

The situation on the ground may have been more complex than suggested by the formal rule. At least in some enclaves where creation was traditionally collaborative and supervised by a coordinating entity, creators were not treated as owners. Cartography was the main example. Evidence suggests that in this area the publisher who coordinated the production of a map was treated as the original owner whether or not the surveyors, engravers, and printers explicitly assigned their rights.[13] The large number of early copyright registrations by proprietors raises the question of whether assignment by authors in these cases represented real, remunerative exchanges or mere nominal acts.[14] Nevertheless, the fundamental, substantive rule during the first half-century of the copyright regime was one of firm authorial ownership.

This rule began to destabilize in the second half of the nineteenth century. Challenges to authorial rights from those who employed or commissioned works from them became more frequent and on occasion were met by courts with more receptiveness. The main legal mechanism that emerged for negotiating the conflicting ownership demands of authors and entrepreneurs was implied intent. The harbinger of this trend was the 1861 case *Keene v. Wheatley*, which recognized the rights of a theater owner in an adapted play produced by one of her actors.[15] The decision was based not on copyright law but on "equitable

---

[12] *Atwill*, 2 F. Cas. 198.
[13] Catherine L. Fisk, "Authors at Work: The Origins of the Work-for-Hire Doctrine," 15 *Yale J.L. & Human.* 1, 26–27 (2003).
[14] Khan, *The Democratization of Invention*, 236; James Gilreath, "American Literature, Public Policy, and the Copyright Laws before 1800," in *Federal Copyright Records, 1790–1800* (Washington, D.C: G.P.O., 1987), xxiii. Evidence on the question of whether and how many registrations by proprietors involved real transactions with authors is lacking. The main indication of a common practice of preregistration assignment is that in most, although not all, of the cases in which copyright was registered for a proprietor, there was also an explicit reference in the record to the name of the author. There is a gap between mentioning the name of the author and a real remunerative transaction, but the former provides some indication that the interest of authors was not completely ignored. See generally Joseph F. Felcone, "New Jersey Copyright Registrations, 1791–1845," 51 *Proceedings of the American Antiquarian Society* 104 (2004).
[15] See e.g. *Keene v. Wheatley*, 14 F. Cas. 180 (C.C.E.D. Pa. 1861).

principles,"[16] but wrapped in this formalistic distinction was a radically new proposition. Since the employee created the adaptations "in the course of his willing performance of this duty," the court reasoned, the employer "became the proprietor of them as products of his intellectual exertion in a particular service in her employment."[17] The court did not base this conclusion on an actual contractual assignment by the employee. It relied instead on a series of new contract and trade secret cases to deduce the general "duties of theatrical performers to their employers."[18] In later years, gradually abandoning a clear default rule, courts came to see the allocation of ownership as determined by the parties' implied intent, embedded in the nature of the relationship between them. The highly influential dictum of the 1869 case *Lawrence v. Dana*, which vested initial ownership in the person who commissioned a work, relied on the proposition that "the title to the same vested in the proprietor ... as necessarily implied by the terms of the arrangement." The court explained that "an equitable title may vest in one person to the labors of another, where the relations of the parties are such that the former is entitled to an assignment of the production."[19] Other cases of the era, whether they adhered to the traditional rule of author's ownership or allocated the rights to the employer, cast their analysis in similar terms.[20]

The crucial element in the new approach was that the relevant intent was implied. In short, this meant that rather than requiring actual assignment for any deviation from the default rule, courts now inferred the intent of the parties from the circumstances of their relationship. This construct of implied intent helped cushion the retreat from a firm commitment to authorial ownership. The concept obscured the difference between an externally imposed rule that deprived the creator of ownership and the traditional, voluntary assignment based on private agreement.[21]

---

[16] Id., 186–87. The court found that the additions to an existing play were not copyrightable. Nevertheless, it decided that the plaintiff had equitable rights against third parties who procured the additions from her employee–actor who was the person who created them.

[17] Id. 187.   [18] Id., 186.

[19] *Lawrence v. Dana*, 15 F. Cas. 26, 51 (C.C.D. Mass. 1869). The allocation of ownership away from the author was dictum in this case because there was an express contract in which the commissioning party agreed not to make further use of the work with no authorization from the author.

[20] *Callaghan v. Myers*, 128 U.S. 617, 647 (1888); *Root v. Borst*, 36 N.E. 814, 814 (N.Y. 1894); *Donaldson v. Wright*, 7 App. D.C. 45, 58 (D.C. Cir. 1895).

[21] This function of implied intent in the copyright context had a very similar structure to what Duncan Kennedy described as the central role of implied intent in "pre-classical"

In the last quarter of the nineteenth century the pressures to allocate ownership away from creators intensified. The economic background for these pressures was the rising importance of collaborative and hierarchically coordinated forms of creation. These patterns of creation, traditionally common in industries such as cartography or lithography, spread to other areas. In the late nineteenth century a dictionary or a catalogue that earlier was likely to be a solo project was much more likely to involve multiple contributors whose work was coordinated and supervised by an entrepreneur. Production in new copyright-related industries, such as advertising, magazine publishing, and later motion pictures, was firmly organized in such collaborative and hierarchical patterns. In many cases creators were formally employees of the coordinating entrepreneur, often in a corporate context. In these settings entrepreneurs who controlled the work of creators began to assert that economic efficiency required that they or the corporation of whose management they were part would be the initial owner of the copyright in the expressive product of employee–creators. Assignment, they argued, was too burdensome or even infeasible, especially when renewal rights that returned to the author or his successors in title at the end of the first fourteen-year term sent publishers "searching all over the world for widows and legitimate children."[22] Such claims were met with gradually growing sympathy by courts, thereby undermining the mediating mechanism of implied intent and leading to its eventual collapse. The disarray of the law of employee copyright ownership around the 1880s attests to the inability of implied intent to contain the mounting conflict between the principle of authorial property and the intensifying claim by entrepreneurs for original ownership in the creative product of their subordinates.[23]

American private law. According to Kennedy, implied intent was frequently used in antebellum private law in a way that blurred the distinction between public government-imposed decisions and private, individual choices. See Duncan Kennedy, *The Rise and Fall of Classical Legal Thought* (Washington, D.C.: Beard Books, 2006), 157.

[22] "Stenographic Report of the Proceedings of the Librarian's Conference on Copyright, Held at the New York City Club, New York, N.Y., May 31–June 2, 1905 Inclusive," in E. Fulton Brylawski and Abe Goldman, eds., *Legislative History of the 1909 Copyright Act* (South Hackensack, N. J.: Rothman, 1976), vol. 1, 56.

[23] The disarray in this area of copyright law is apparent in the section devoted to it in Eaton Drone's 1879 treatise. While the treatise is otherwise a model of coherence, this particular section is confused. In the space of five pages it states at least three conflicting versions of the rule: the employment relationship does not change the default rule of author's ownership; employers generally own the copyright in their employees' works; and in each case ownership is determined by the implied intent of the parties deduced from all the specific circumstances. See Eaton S. Drone, *A Treatise on the Law of Property in*

Around the turn of the century the default rule in the case law had flipped. A new rule under which, in the absence of express assignment, an employer owned the copyright in the creative product of his employee was put in place.[24] Employers now became the primary legal owners of intellectual works produced within the employment relationship. The legislature followed suit in 1909, after lobbying from publishers. Initial ownership by an employer of both copyright and the right of renewal, they argued, is an economic necessity in cases such as encyclopedias or directories, and prior assignment is impractical when works are produced through the collaboration of numerous contributors.[25] The lobbying efforts resulted in a short but significant sentence in section 62 of the 1909 Copyright Act declaring that "the word 'author' shall include an employer in the case of works made for hire."[26] The plain meaning of this opaque legal phrasing was that for purposes of works produced within an employment relationship, employers were to be treated by the law as the authors and therefore the original copyright owners.

Bernard Edelman described the parallel legal development in France and Germany with respect to film copyright as a process in which *"the determinant influence of capital* becomes, for the law, the *creative influence; financial direction* becomes *creative direction;* the *authors* become *proletarians* who are payed [sic] for the job which accomplishes 'a task' work and not a creative activity, halfway between the man and the machine."[27] The immediate cause for the decline of employee–creators' ownership was the growing commodification of copyrighted works.

Intellectual Productions in Great Britain and the United States (Boston: Little, Brown, 1879), 255–60. See also Fisk, "Authors at Work," 48–50.

[24] See *Schumacher v. Schwencke*, 25 F. 466, 468 (C.C.S.D. N.Y. 1885); *Mut. Adver. Co. v. Refo*, 76 F. 961, 963 (C.C.D. S.C. 1896); *Colliery Eng'r Co. v. United Correspondence Sch.*, 94 F. 152, 153 (C.C.S.D. N.Y. 1899); *Dielman v. White*, 102 F. 892, 894 (C.C.D. Mass. 1900); *Edward Thompson Co. v. Am. Law Book Co.*, 119 F. 217, 219–20 (C.C.S.D. N.Y. 1902); *Nat'l Cloak & Suit Co. v. Kaufman*, 189 F. 215, 217 (C.C.M.D. Pa. 1911). Later courts came to distinguish between an employee and an independent contractor and applied a default rule that deprived authors of ownership only to the former category. See *W.H. Anderson Co. v. Baldwin Law Publishing Co.*, 27 F. 2d 82, 88 (6th Cir. 1928).

[25] "Stenographic Report of the Proceedings of the Librarian's Conference on Copyright," 41. For a discussion of the legislative history of the work for hire doctrine, see Fisk, "Authors at Work," 62–67.

[26] Act of March 4, 1909, ch. 320, §62, 35 Stat. 1075, 1088.

[27] Bernard Edelman, *Ownership of the Image: Elements for a Marxist Theory of Law* (London: Routledge & Kegan Paul, 1979), 58 (emphasis in original).

The production of many of these works came to resemble that of other commodities: a process that involved the coordination of the labor of many contributors under the hierarchical supervision of an entrepreneur or his or her agents, often in the form of a corporate management. Such production patterns gave rise to employers' demand for ownership of their employee–creators' product in the name of economic efficiency. They also made the demand seem natural. After all, what was the difference between a physical industrial product where it was clear to all that the entrepreneur owned the product of his employees' labor with no need for an express contractual assignment and an expressive work produced in much the same way? When creative production became industrial production, applying the ownership patterns of the latter became obvious. Employer ownership seemed to be inherent in the nature of the employment relationship. The fact that creators in these contexts increasingly appeared as subordinate wage laborers doing the bidding of others, rather than as individual creating spirits, made it even easier to discard the ideal of authorship and its demand for authorial ownership. Thus at one point in the legislative discussions preceding the enactment of the 1909 Copyright Act the secretary of the American Authors' Copyright League, Robert Underwood Johnson, expressed an objection to the proposed work for hire doctrine. He did not dispute the vesting of original ownership in employers but rather argued that an employer "ought to be considered the proprietor and not the author."[28] It was important for Johnson to differentiate the proprietor and the author; that employee–creators were deprived of both the status of authorship and ownership of copyright was never an issue.

By the beginning of the twentieth century the most fundamental element of authorship-based copyright was gone in regard to a wide swath of works. Creators were no longer even nominal owners of the product of their intellectual labor. A considerable tension was building up between ownership rules and the premise underlying the originality doctrine that copyright was founded on the principle of authorship. Even in the areas of copyright where authorship was subdued, however, it was not discarded. Instead, the concept of authorship kept cropping up in twisted and perverse forms. As Catherine Fisk notes, there was something strange in the combination of copyright's intensifying emphasis on the nature of authorship as an irreducibly individual, intellectual creation and its embrace of

---

[28] "Stenographic Report of the Proceedings of the Librarian's Conference on Copyright," 56–57.

hired creativity owned by another.[29] In *Bleistein v. Donaldson Litho-graphing Co.*, for example, as Holmes was celebrating the author's irreducible mark of personality that made every work unique, he was also taking for granted that the creators of the lithographs at issue were simply a hired workforce whose intellectual production was owned by the firm that employed them.[30] Strange though it may seem, this conceptual hybrid was not accidental. Authorship in its ideological form was mobilized to justify the very rules that turned creators into nonowner, wage laborers.

One common form of this logic was projecting the authorship of the creators on the employer, who now owned their intellectual product. A defendant accused of infringing the copyright in the *American and English Encyclopaedia of Law*, for example, tried to challenge the idea that the plaintiff – a corporation – could be an author and therefore an original owner, rather than an assignee of copyright. A corporation, it claimed, was a "mere legal fiction, and not an author entitled to copyright within the meaning of the laws of the United States, in that it is incapable of intellectual labor, incapable of begetting children."[31] Unimpressed, the court responded that plaintiff's publication "is the result of the intellectual labor of the editors and compilers" employed by it. It then added that "[i]t is unnecessary, as it might be impracticable, to set forth the names of the persons engaged in the preparation of the work."[32] Authorship's hallmark – the unique mark of personality – was now attributed to an abstract, nameless mass of "editors and compilers" that could not even be specified. The original authorship of these nameless laborers could not make them owners, but it was attributed to their corporate employer and justified its property rights.

The decision in *Schumacher v. Schwencke*,[33] involving a painting probably produced as a design for a cigar box label, took this logic one step further. The reasoning of the decision conjures up an image of agency in which the plaintiff corporation, described as the "originating, inventive and master mind," is endowed with all the creative subjectivity. The employee–artist, on the other hand, is imagined as a mechanical extension that simply carries out instructions.[34] The decision conveys

---

[29] Catherine Fisk, *Working Knowledge: Employee Innovation and the Rise of Corporate Intellectual Property 1800–1930* (Chapel Hill: University of North Carolina Press, 2009), 219.

[30] 188 U.S. 239 (1903). See Fisk, *Working Knowledge*, 237.

[31] *Edward Thompson Co.*, 119 F. 219.   [32] Id.   [33] 25 F. 466.

[34] On the metaphor of agency, see Gerald E. Frug, "The Ideology of Bureaucracy in American Law," 97 *Harv. L. Rev.* 1276, 1297–98 (1984).

the uncreative nature of the painter's role by describing the painting as
having been "actually painted by one Charles Stecher, a resident of this
country and an artist in the complainant's employ." How could a corporation, however, be made a creative master mind? The decision achieves
this rhetorical feat by identifying the corporation with the subjectivity of
its managerial stuff. Thus, Theodore Schumacher – the corporation's
president – is described as "himself an artist of respectable attainments"
who "suggested and designed" the concept of the painting.[35] By combining the subordinate role of the painter and the control and creativity of the
corporation's management the agency construct is made complete:

> The fact that the artist Stecher executed Schumacher's design cannot defeat the
> copyright. The sculptor seldom touches the marble from which his statues are
> carved. The fact that the brush which embodied Schumacher's idea was held by
> another artist rather than by himself cannot be important in considering a ques-
> tion of this character.[36]

It is hard to say to what extent Schumacher actually acted as a
Michelangelo-like master whose creative vision and direction controlled
the actions of an apprentice mechanically carrying out allotted tasks. It is
clear, however, that the court's reasoning combined elements of authorship and agency to rhetorically justify corporate ownership of intellectual
creation, in two moves: locating all creative subjectivity with management
rather than the employee and then attributing this subjectivity to the
corporation itself. In this regard *Schumacher* is an application of the logic
of corporate liberalism to the area of copyright. The decision's reasoning
fits the trend of the period's jurisprudence toward shifting rights and
duties from individuals associated with the corporation to the corporation itself, identified with its managerial hierarchy.[37]

There was no false consciousness. Copyright lawyers understood very
well that copyright never fully embodied the principles of ownership
based on original authorship and that parts of it were moving even further
away from that ideal. But there was an uneasy coexistence between this
sober understanding and an ongoing use of the authorship framework –
an odd mixture of simultaneous dismissal and reverence. The discussions
of the work for hire provision in the preparatory conference preceding the
legislation of the 1909 act exemplify this dynamics. The final statutory

---

[35] 25 F. 466.   [36] Id., 468.
[37] See W.M. Geldart, "Legal Personality," 27 L. Q. Rev. 90, 97 (1911); Morton J. Horwitz,
The Transformation of American Law 1870–1960: The Crisis of Legal Orthodoxy
(New York: Oxford University Press, 1992), 94–100.

provision assigned ownership to the employer by defining it as the author. It was clear to everybody involved, however, that the principle of authorial ownership was being deserted rather than upheld. Representatives of the publishing industry were clear throughout the conference that what they wanted was vesting of rights in the employer that would fully deprive actual creators of both original and renewal rights.[38] The early suggested text did not refer to employers as authors.[39] Defining an employer as an author was introduced largely as a result of a desire to simplify the structure of the act by using a uniform comprehensive term to refer to all original copyright owners.[40] And yet throughout the conference the substantive question of authorship kept emerging. The main concern was that the constitutional clause limited the grant of original rights to authors only. As Samuel James Elder explained to participants in the conference: "When you come down to the question of who can take out copyright you are confined by the language of the Constitution to authors and by the broadening of the idea that the courts have given it to the assignees of author[s]."[41] The whole point of the claimed economic need for employers' ownership, however, was to make the employer an original owner rather than to rely on the derivative status of an assignee. Throughout the conference the participants continued to express concerns that the constitutional mandate's exclusive reference to authors could restrict original employer ownership.[42] At the end, the agreed-on solution was simply defining employers as authors. The Librarian of Congress, George Herbert Putnam, explained that when Richard Bowker of the American Authors' Copyright League suggested this strategy, his "impulse originated in the authority under which Congress provides copyright laws, and that is the Constitution ... and then he had to define what 'author' might include."[43] Bowker himself explained

---

[38] "Stenographic Report of the Proceedings of the Librarian's Conference on Copyright," 41, 56.
[39] Section 26 of the early draft bill provided: "The publisher of a composite or collective work (a 'series,' a 'library,' or an encyclopaedia) which has been produced at his instance and expense, may claim copyright in the same." Memorandum Draft of a Bill to Amend and Consolidate the Acts Respecting Copyright," in *Legislative History of the 1909 Copyright Act*, vol. 2, xxxvi.
[40] "Stenographic Report of the Proceedings of the Librarian's Conference on Copyright," 40–41.
[41] Id., 54.   [42] Id. 34, 41, 45, 56, 85.
[43] "Stenographic Report of the Proceedings of the Second Session of the Conference on Copyright, Held at the New York City Club, New York, N.Y., Nov. 1–4, 1905 Inclusive," in *Legislative History of the 1909 Copyright Act*, vol. 2, 146.

the strategy succinctly: "In other words, everybody is an author."[44] Authorship was thus simultaneously revered and dismissed. It was treated as an enshrined constitutional principle that could lay real restriction on the allocation of copyright ownership and then was conveniently bypassed through a statutory definition that made everybody an author. Nowhere was the paradoxical state of authorship ideology more apparent than in the area of ownership.

A LITERARY PROPERTY BATTLE REDUX: *WHEATON V. PETERS*

Treating copyright as literary property, which since the late eighteenth century had become the conventional wisdom, entailed considerable conceptual challenges. William Blackstone famously described property in his influential *Commentaries* as the "sole and despotic dominion which one man claims and exercises over the external things of the world, in total exclusion of the right of any other individual in the universe."[45] Fitting copyright into this schema required, at a minimum, an owner and an owned external thing. Defining copyright's object of property proved even more challenging than identifying its owner. What exactly is the external thing over which a copyright owner exercises "sole and despotic dominion"? The answer usually was not offered in philosophical or theoretical discussions of the nature of copyright, which were rare in the early nineteenth century. It was, rather, implicit in the legal rules that Americans adopted and developed to deal with the practicalities of copyright, mainly determining the scope of the right and deciding infringement questions.

The 1834 case of *Wheaton v. Peters* stands out against this backdrop.[46] This first copyright decision by the Supreme Court offers a unique glimpse at how Americans conceptualized ownership of intangibles in one of the rare occasions when they faced the question head-on in theoretical terms. *Wheaton v. Peters* was a "great case" first and foremost because it hit close to home. Henry Wheaton was the third reporter of the Supreme Court. Richard Peters Jr. was the fourth reporter. By all accounts the quality of Peters' reports did not match that of his

---

[44] Id., 143. Bowker tried to suggest an explicit comprehensive definition of an "author," but the participants could not agree on such a definition. Eventually no statutory definition was included, and the work for hire provision simply defined the employer as an author without delineating who else might be included in that term.

[45] William Blackstone, *Commentaries on the Laws of England* (Oxford: Clarendon Press, 1766), vol. 2, 2.

[46] 33 U.S. 591 (1834).

predecessor. He made up for what he lacked in scholarly inclination and analytic precision, however, with a developed business sense. Identifying the business opportunity, Peters embarked on republication in a condensed and cheaper series the decisions of the Supreme Court reported by the three previous reporters – Dallas, Cranch, and Wheaton. After attempts to settle the affair amicably had failed, Wheaton and his publisher Robert Donaldson sued Peters and his publisher John Grigg.[47] The litigants, advocates, and judges involved all came from the same circles of the nation's legal elite. Wheaton and Peters had a professional relationship and in some cases personal ties with the Justices. The issue in controversy implicated the Supreme Court's work and was of direct interest to the legal community.[48] And sharp substantive disagreements between the Justices resulted in tensed interpersonal dynamics among them that became apparent when the opinion was delivered.[49] There could scarcely be a more dramatic first appearance to copyright law in the Supreme Court.

There were three main legal questions in the case. The first was whether the legal formalities in force at the time – registration, deposit of copies with the Secretary of State, and a copyright notice published both in a newspaper and on the title page – were complied with by Wheaton and whether noncompliance was fatal to the validity of copyright. The majority opinion written by Justice McLean and joined by three others ruled that complying with the formalities was necessary for a valid copyright, although it left the exact ruling somewhat ambiguous.[50]

The second question was about the subject matter eligible for copyright protection. Could the opinions of the Supreme Court be protected by copyright? This issue attracted much argument from the parties, who offered competing accounts of the division between the public

[47] See Craig Joyce, "The Story of *Wheaton v. Peters*: A Curious Chapter in the History of Judicature," in Jane C. Ginsburg and Rochelle Cooper Dreyfuss, eds., *Intellectual Property Stories* (New York: Foundation Press, 2006), 42–49.

[48] For a comprehensive description of the complex personal and institutional story behind the case, see Edward G. White, *The Marshall Court and Cultural Change, 1815–1835* (New York: Macmillan 1988), 408–24; Craig Joyce, "The Rise of the Supreme Court Reporter: An Institutional Perspective on Marshall Court Ascendancy," 83 *Mich. L. Rev.* 1291, 1364–86 (1985).

[49] See White, *The Marshall Court*, 421–22; Joyce, "The Story of *Wheaton v. Peters*," 64–65.

[50] 33 U.S. 663–64. For a discussion of the ambiguity surrounding the ruling on the issue of formalities, see Joyce, "The Story of *Wheaton v. Peters*," 68–69.

and the private in copyright law. Wheaton's attorneys presented the opinions as the ultimate case of private property. The opinions produced by judges, they argued, were "their own to give away," which they did, thereby transferring their property right to the reporter.[51] J.R. Ingersoll, arguing for Peters, conjured up a very different picture. Describing the opinions as *"the law of the land,"* he appealed to civic-republican values. "[T]he law cannot and ought not to be made the prisoner or the slave of any individual," he argued, and "the entrance to the great temple itself, and the highway that leads to it, cannot be shut without tyranny and oppression."[52] This being the only issue on which all the Justices were able to agree, the majority opinion disposed of it in one sentence, ruling that "no reporter has, or can have any copyright, in the written opinions delivered by this court."[53] Two years later in his *Commentaries on Equity Jurisprudence* Justice Story explained that what the Court had actually meant was that while there could be no copyright in the opinions themselves, the reporter could copyright supplementary materials such as notes or summaries of the counsels' arguments prepared by him.[54]

It was the third question – that of common law copyright – that presented the challenge of conceptualizing copyright as a property right in intangibles. The basic legal logic was simple. Seeing that the validity of Wheaton's copyright was threatened by the claim that he did not comply with the formalities required by the statute, his attorneys resorted to the same maneuver used by English publishers in the previous century. They argued that copyright was protected under the common law, independently of the statute. Common law copyright not only would be unrestricted by the statutory limited duration, it would also make available common law and equitable remedies (by contrast to the statutory remedial penalties), irrespective of compliance with any formal requirement imposed by statute.

Much of the argument on this third issue revolved around technical questions: Was common law copyright recognized in England at the relevant time?[55] Was the English rule adopted into the local common

[51] *Wheaton v. Peters*, 71.   [52] Id., 74, 77.   [53] 33 U.S. 668.

[54] Joseph Story, *Commentaries on Equity Jurisprudence as Administered in England and America*, 2nd ed. (Boston: Hilliard, Gray, 1839), vol. 2, 247–48.

[55] Justice McLean's majority opinion found that the question of common law copyright in England involved "great doubt and perplexity" and that the final ruling by the House of Lords in *Donaldson v. Becket* was against the existence of such a right; 33 U.S. 660.

law, be it the common law of Pennsylvania or the federal one?[56] The moment the argument of common law property rights was raised, however, there was no escaping the more theoretical question of property in intangibles. Here, the arguments of parties and judges were firmly rooted in the framework of the British literary property debate. A century after English stationers first turned to the common law to bypass the limited duration of copyright imposed by the Statute of Anne and half a century after the question was decided in the great case of *Donaldson v. Becket*, Americans experienced their own version of a literary property debate.[57] The British precursor supplied more than precedents. The decades-long conflict left a trail of philosophical and theoretical arguments about property in intangibles that framed the American debate.[58]

The basic question was this: How could copyright fit the mold of common law property rights, traditionally conceived of as absolute control of tangible objects? To contemporaries the concept of common law rights meant much more than simply judge-made law. It was defined by a series of interlocking features that distinguished it from statutory law. While statutes were seen as political, the common law was prepolitical. This meant that common law rights were derived from objective, "natural" principles, while statutes were "arbitrary" in the sense of reflecting subjective human policy judgments. Finally, while statutory law was "made" by legislatures, the common law was "discovered" by judges who through the common law process of elaboration uncovered the rules derived from its prepolitical, natural principles.[59] The property

---

[56] Justice McLean's majority opinion denied the existence of federal common law – a proposition to which it is doubtful that Story and Marshall agreed. It found that even if common law copyright was recognized in England, it was never adopted in Pennsylvania; 33 U.S. 658–60.

[57] *Donaldson v. Becket*, 98 Eng. Rep. 257; 1 Eng. Rep. 837; 17 Parl. Hist. Eng. 953 (1774 H.L).

[58] On the British literary property debate, see Mark Rose, *Authors and Owners: The Invention of Copyright* (Cambridge, Mass.: Harvard University Press, 1993), 67–112; Brad Sherman and Lionel Bently, *The Making of Modern Intellectual Property Law: The British Experience, 1760–1911* (New York: Cambridge University Press, 1999), 11–42.

[59] Morton J. Horwitz, *The Transformation of American Law 1780–1860* (Cambridge, Mass.: Harvard University Press, 1977), 4–9. Horwitz describes the understanding of the common law as reflection of natural rights as an eighteenth-century conception that was replaced in the nineteenth century by an instrumentalist conception of the common law. See also Willard J. Hurst, *The Law and Conditions of Freedom in the Nineteenth-Century United States* (Madison: University of Wisconsin Press, 1956);

inflection of this concept of the common law was that of natural property rights, based on one or another variant of labor theory.

Both proponents and opponents of common law copyright started with the proposition that the question of whether such a right existed could be answered only by reference to a general theory of property. As George Ticknor Curtis put it in his discussion of *Wheaton v. Peters*, thirteen years after it was decided, "there are certain great characteristics which mankind have universally attributed to the right" of property. Only after answering the question of "[w]hat constitutes property," he wrote, shall we "be able to say whether any supposed subject of the right possesses the general attributes of property, and whether it is agreeable to justice and fitness that it should be so recognized."[60] Also common to both parties was the acceptance of labor-based natural rights theory as the basis of property. Elijah Paine, one of Wheaton's attorneys and his former law partner, cited from the annotations of Edward Christian to Blackstone's *Commentaries*: "But the true mode of ascertaining a moral right, is to inquire whether it is such as the reason, the cultivated reason, of man kind must necessarily assent to. No proposition seems more comfortable to that criterion, than that every one should enjoy the reward of his labour; the harvest where he has sown; or the fruit of the tree which he has planted."[61] The argument for common law copyright progressed from this starting point by following the strategy introduced in England by William Warburton almost a century earlier in his foundational pamphlet on literary property: equating intellectual labor and its product with physical labor and its product.[62] The dissenting Justice Thompson explained this argument as follows: "The great principle on which the author's right rests, is, that it is the fruit or production of his own labour,

William E. Nelson, "The Impact of the Antislavery Movement upon Styles of Judicial Reasoning in Nineteenth Century America," 87 *Harv. L. Rev.* 513 (1974). In the mid-nineteenth-century debate over literary property, however, traditional natural law understating of property rights played a major role.

[60] George Ticknor Curtis, *A Treatise on the Law of Copyright* (Boston: C.C. Little and J. Brown, 1847), 4.

[61] *Wheaton v. Peters*, 20. The quotation was taken from William Blackstone, *Commentaries on the Laws of England by the Late Sir W. Blackstone: to which is added an analysis by Barron Field Esq.: A New Edition with Practical Notes by Christian, Archbold, and Chitty* (New York: E. Duyckinck, 1827), vol. 1, 306, n. 14.

[62] See William Warburton, *A Letter from an Author to a Member of Parliament Concerning Literary Property* (1747), reprinted in Stephen Parks, ed., *Horace Walpole's Political Tracts 1747–1748* (New York: Garland, 1974).

and that labour, by the faculties of the mind may establish a right
of property as well as by the faculties of the body."[63]

One challenge to this argument was the novelty of the claim for
literary property. The argument was that property in intangibles
"possesses every feature, which Puffendorf considers necessary, to give
any subject the character of property."[64] But the seventeenth-century
natural rights theorists never contemplated literary property, and their
theories were oriented toward physical labor and physical objects.
Paine brushed this aside by citing Christian again for the proposition
that "[n]othing is more erroneous than the practice of referring the
origin of moral rights, and the system of natural equity, to that savage
state which is supposed to have preceded civilized establishment, in
which literary composition, and of consequence the right to it, could
have no existence."[65] In other words, reason, rather than pseudo-
history, was the basis of natural rights. In his treatise Curtis supplied a
more elaborate account:

It is, of course, impossible to look to the mere light of nature for a solution of this
question, or to find it in any speculation upon the condition of man in that
imaginary state, which has been called the state of nature ... it is to be observed,
that the act of committing ideas to any corporeal substance, by means of signs,
and the multiplication and delivery of copies, thus produced, for a valuable
consideration are things that can only take place after society is formed and an
advanced stage of civilization has been reached ... we have reached an artificial
and refined condition of mankind, in which the mere light of nature will no longer
guide us. We must have recourse to those general principles of justice and right,
which mankind are supposed to have brought originally from the state of nature,
but by which they have agreed to be bound in a state of civilization, where they
have become modified, enlarged and strengthened.[66]

This line of argument shifted the emphasis of natural rights from static,
immemorial principles traceable to the state of nature to a dynamic
process of progress in which reason was gradually unveiled as humanity
ascended from savagery into civilization.

On the other side, opponents of common law copyright shifted the
ground of the debate. Accepting labor as the basis of property, they
nevertheless asserted that there were other conditions necessary for
natural property rights to exist. Justice McLean, writing for the
majority, borrowed from the dissent of Justice Yates in the 1769 case of

---

[63] *Wheaton v. Peters*, 110.   [64] Id., 24.   [65] Id., 20.
[66] Curtis, *A Treatise on the Law of Copyright*, 2–3.

Millar v. Taylor, the major English case to recognize common law copyright. "That every man is entitled to the fruits of his own labour must be admitted," he wrote, "but he can only enjoy them, except by statutory provision, under the rules of property which regulate society, and which define the right of things, in general."[67] Ingersoll, arguing for Peters, also relied on the dissent by Yates, but supplied more details:

> The notions of personal property of the common law, which is founded on natural law, depend materially on possession, and that of an adverse character, exclusive in its nature and pretensions. Throw it out for public use, and how can you limit or define the use? How can you attach possession to it at all, except of a subtle and imaginative character?[68]

This statement bundled together indistinguishably two different strands of argument. Partly the argument was about the so-called nonexcludable nature of ideas. Unlike physical objects, it was nearly impossible to prevent others from using and enjoying ideas, at least once published. This deprived the supposed object of property of a central hallmark of property. Published ideas were permanently in a state of an object thrown out on the highway, unpossessed by anyone, denied to none, and, in a common variant of the argument, intended by the person who published them to be open to all. Thompson in his dissent rejected this argument as a non sequitur. He explained that ideas were no different in this regard from any other object of property. A public use necessary for economic exploitation did not imply intent to abandon control by the owner, and the ability of others to intrude was a reason for the law to intervene and restore excludability rather than for its inapplicability.[69]

The second strand of the argument posed, however, a different challenge to property in ideas. Physical possession seemed to supply a self-defining character to the object of property. A physical object had the markers of property built in, so to speak. By virtue of its physical existence, it had a ready-made demarcation of what was owned and what constituted trespass, and when physically possessed there was an ostensibly natural connection between the owner and the owned. When it came to elusive intangible ideas this self-defining character, grounded in physicality, seemed to disappear in what Ingersoll described as a "subtle and imaginative" haze. This challenge went to the heart of the concept of common law property as a natural, prepolitical right. Property rights were supposed to be a reflection of an objective, natural reason of the

---

[67] *Wheaton v. Peters*, 100.   [68] Id., 79.   [69] 33 U.S. 673–77.

world, not an artificial creation. Judges were supposed to discover this reason and enforce objectively predefined rights, not make law based on arbitrary policy calls as legislators did. Ingersoll pushed this logic to its conclusion:

If you may read, you may print. The possession is not more absolute and entire in one case than the other. It is an artificial and therefore arbitrary rule which draws the distinction; and in order to render it available, the lesson must be read in the statute.[70]

From this perspective the problem with property in ideas was not non-excludability but a lack of objective, self-defining borders. To be sure, where no natural physical borders existed, the law could create legal ones. The law might mandate, for example, that certain books could be read freely but not reprinted. This sort of line-drawing was, however, arbitrary in the sense of exercising political will, rather than reflecting the natural state of things in the world. Rights in intangible ideas were, in short, within the traditional province of the legislature and not part of the prepolitical property rights discovered and enforced by judges.

When American proponents of common law copyright searched for a response to this second challenge to property in intangible ideas they discovered that their English predecessors had devised one. More precisely they found the concept of the "copy." Paine argued that the objections to the fluid and undefined nature of ideas as objects of property had one fatal flaw: ideas were not the object of literary property rights. Copyright was ownership of the particular language and expression used by the author, rather than of his ideas. And that is what critics of literary property going all the way back to Yates missed. Their mistake was "forgetting that books are not made up of ideas alone, but are and necessarily must be, clothed in language, and embodied in a form which gives them individuality and identity that make them more distinguishable than any other personal property can be." Thus: "A watch, a table, a guinea, it might be difficult to identify; but books never."[71] Arguing that "the question is not as to property in ideas but in books"[72] allowed Paine to construct an owned object more amenable to natural property rights theory. He borrowed this maneuver from Blackstone, who first deployed it in one of the early English literary property cases – *Tonson v. Collins*[73] – and then at more length in the

---

[70] *Wheaton v. Peters*, 79.   [71] Id., 18.   [72] Id., 19.
[73] 96 Eng. Rep. 169, 189 (K.B. 1761).

Commentaries.[74] Paine cited Blackstone's argument that "the identity of literary composition consists intirely in the *sentiment* and *language*; the same conceptions cloathed in the same words."[75]

Shifting the ground from ownership of ideas to ownership of specific language seemed to restore to the object of property the materiality whose absence haunted arguments for common law property rights. The book, the copy, or the "*sentiment* and *language*" constituted a semi-material entity, a seemingly fixed and stable object in which to ground the property right. In fact, as Meredith McGill argued, Paine's description of the text elevated it to a new level of materiality, one marked by an even higher degree of individuality than ordinary material objects.[76] "A watch, a table, a guinea, it might be difficult to identify; but books never." This constructed uber-object of property had two merits for justifying literary property. The stability of the specific language played a role equivalent to that of a physical object. It endowed ownership with fixed, predetermined boundaries and made arbitrary line-drawing unnecessary. As important, this notion of the object of property offered a view of a world in which texts carried with them inerasable marks of their origin and inseparable bonds to their authors. Books, Paine explained, "may be copied or pirated, but no one ever supposed that others would or could accidentally produce the same work as a previous author. It is impossible even to produce the same paragraph."[77] In a happy happenstance the hallmark of originality – the author's personal mark embedded in the text – became also an instrument of property rights: a permanent stamp communicating to the world the identity of both the owned and the owner.

In his dissent Thompson explicitly turned to the renewed sense of materiality supplied by fixing the object of property in specific expression. The fallacy of the defendant's argument, he wrote, was assuming that "the claim was to a mere idea not embodied or exhibited in any tangible form or shape." Literary property subsisted, however, in "the very language and sentiment of the author, which constitute the identity of his work."[78] Several years later Curtis provided his own version of this semi-material object of property. What an author seeks property right in, he explained, is "the exclusive multiplication of copies of the particular

---

[74] Blackstone, *Commentaries*, vol. 2, 405–6.   [75] Id.
[76] Meredith L. McGill, "The Matter of the Text: Commerce, Print Culture, and the Authority of the State in American Copyright Law," 9 *Am. Lit. Hist.* 1, 7–11 (1997).
[77] *Wheaton v. Peters*, 27.   [78] Id., 114.

combination of characters, which exhibit to the eye of another the ideas that he intends shall be received."[79]

Wheaton v. Peters was one of the last great moments of the old conceptual framework of copyright as ownership of intangibles. The debate over literary property in the case was dominated by the concept of the property object as specific language – what Lord Mansfield called "somewhat intellectual communicated by letters."[80] This was in line with the traditional understanding of copyright as the publisher's right to print a specific text or a copy. Ironically, at this stage it was copyright maximalists, arguing for common law copyright, who were most invested in this narrow concept of ownership. While the copy was a constructed object of property that could fit smoothly with traditional natural rights theory, it also prescribed a restrictive scope to ownership.

All of that would soon change. The ruling of *Wheaton v. Peters* limited common law copyright to unpublished works and refused to extend it to published works. Hope for recognition of postpublication copyright as a common law property right persisted for a while.[81] But such arguments gradually disappeared from disputes about actual law and survived only as an ideological story about the origin and nature of copyright told mainly in debates over international copyright and in the opening chapters of legal treatises.[82] More generally, the relationship between property in intangibles and general property theory would flip. In *Wheaton* the intangible object of property was constructed so it would fit a traditional theory of natural property rights. In later decades, the growing recognition of property in intangibles – what Morton Horwitz called "the de-physicalization of property" – challenged the general theory.[83] By the early twentieth century, natural rights theory of common law property rights collapsed under this pressure and was replaced by a positivist conception. At the end, rather than intangibles being fit into the mold of natural rights, property in intangibles helped bring about the decline of that theory. Within copyright law, the concept of the copy on which the property argument in *Wheaton* relied would soon come under fire and gradually be abandoned. Expansion of copyright would not come about through the recognition of common law property rights

---

[79] Curtis, *A Treatise on the Law of Copyright*, 12–13.
[80] *Wheaton v. Peters*, 18, citing *Millar v. Taylor*, 98 Eng. Rep. 201, 251 (K.B. 1769).
[81] See Oren Bracha, "The Statute of Anne: An American Mythology," 47 *Houston L. Rev.* 877, 900 (2010).
[82] Id., 902–5, 914.
[83] Horwitz, *The Transformation of American Law 1870–1960*, 139.

based on a narrow concept of the object of property. Instead, it took the route of expanding the notion of copyright's object of property.

THIS IS WHAT THE LAW TERMS "COPY"

On March 11, 1853, Harriet Beecher Stowe and her husband Calvin Ellis Stowe filed suit in equity in the federal Circuit Court of the Eastern District of Pennsylvania against F.W. Thomas, the publisher of the Pennsylvania German newspaper *Die Freie Presse*. With *Uncle Tom's Cabin*, published in book form a year earlier, already a bestseller and Stowe a celebrity, this was a high-profile case. Thomas published a German translation of the novel as a serialization in his newspaper and in pamphlet form beginning on January 1, 1853, just a few weeks prior to the date when Stowe and her publisher John P. Jewett planned to launch their own authorized German translation. Thomas also had plans to publish a full book version of his translation. Stowe argued that she, as the copyright owner of the book, "ever had, and still hath the sole and exclusive right, to translate, print, publish and sell the same, for her own private benefit and advantage."[84] Thomas replied that "Harriet Beecher Stowe hath not the sole and exclusive right to translate the said work" and that he did only what "he had and still has a right to do under the laws of the United States."[85] Presiding over the case was Justice Robert Grier of the U.S. Supreme Court in his capacity as a Circuit Court judge. Grier was an active and outspoken enforcer of the Fugitive Slave Act. The irony of the courtroom encounter between him, Stowe, and her *Uncle Tom's Cabin* was not lost on contemporaries.[86] Grier ruled against Stowe. The "only property" which the author has, he wrote in his opinion, "is the exclusive right to multiply the copies of that particular combination of characters ... This is what the law terms copy, or copyright."[87] Since a translation was clearly not a copy in this sense, the unauthorized translation could not infringe the copyright in the book.

To modern eyes, Grier's reasoning is likely to appear outlandish. At the time, however, it was an accurate statement of the traditional framework of copyright, albeit a framework that was already under attack and that

---

[84] *Stowe v. Thomas*, Complainant's Bill.   [85] *Stowe v. Thomas*, Defendant's Answer.

[86] See Melissa J. Homestead, *American Women Authors and Literary Property, 1822–1869* (New York: Cambridge University Press, 2005), 129–44; Melissa J. Homestead, "'When I can Read my Title Clear': Harriet Beecher Stowe and the *Stowe v. Thomas* Copyright Infringement Case," 27 *Prospects* 201 (2002).

[87] *Stowe v. Thomas*, 23 F. Cas. 201, 206–7 (C.C.E.D. Pa. 1853).

would soon decline. How could the view that a full commercial translation of a literary work in direct competition with the author's own translation did not infringe copyright make sense? Within copyright's traditional understanding as the publisher's privilege of printing a text, it made perfect sense. This understanding emerged in the days of the stationers' right and reflected its nature as a trade privilege: the right gave exclusivity to publishers in their core economic activity, namely, printing and selling printed texts. This meant that copyright's core scope encompassed only verbatim reprinting. Pressures to expand the scope of this right and to prevent evasion by reproduction with minor changes had always existed. In the early days of copyright they were handled through ad hoc compromises and rulings of the Stationers' Company's organs and through occasional accommodations in royal printing patents.[88] The core of copyright protection and the focal concept underlying it remained, however, verbatim reproduction in print.

The 1710 Statute of Anne adhered to this framework, by conferring on the copyright owner only the very limited entitlement of the "sole liberty of printing and reprinting" of "books."[89] This diverted the pressures to expand and redefine the scope of copyright to the courts that during the eighteenth century were presented with cases of alleged infringement by various secondary uses such as translations or abridgments. Eighteenth-century English courts, however, did not only adhere to copyright's narrow concept but developed and explicated what earlier had been a latent understanding. The basic rule that dominated the case law was that the core of copyright protection was limited to verbatim reproduction or reprint of the same text. To prevent emptying the right of any significance through evasion, the rule added a narrow penumbra of protection: any nonverbatim reproduction of the work was deemed infringing if and only if the changes made were only "colourable" ones constituting a "mere evasion" of copyright protection against reprinting.[90]

---

[88] On the compromises and rulings of the Stationers' Company, see Oren Bracha, "Owning Ideas: A History of Anglo American Intellectual Property," S.J.D. diss., Harvard Law School (2005), 140–43; Lyman Ray Patterson, *Copyright in Historical Perspective* (Nashville, Tenn.: Vanderbilt University Press, 1968), 33. On the scope of the right in printing patents, see Ronan Deazley, "The Statute of Anne and the Great Abridgment Swindle," 47 *Hous. L. Rev.* 793, 810–15 (2010).

[89] 8 Ann., c. 19, sec. 1.

[90] *Gyles v. Wilcox*, 26 Eng. Rep. 489, 490 (Ch. 1740). See also *Tonson v. Walker*, Eng. Rep. 1017, 1019–20 (Ch. 1752); *Sayre v. Moore*, 102 Eng. Rep 139, 140 (K.B. 1785); *Cary v. Kearsley*, 170 Eng Rep. 679, 680 (K.B. 1802).

There were three interlocking features to this doctrine. First, the core of copyright's scope was narrowly defined as requiring exact identity between the protected text and the infringing reproduction. In the 1740 *Gyles v. Wilcox*, for example, Lord Chancellor Hardwicke framed the critical question as "[w]hether this book ... which the defendant has published, is the same with Sir Mathew Hale's Histor. Placit. Coronce, the copy of which is now the property of plaintiff."[91] Second, the additional penumbra of protection was defined in narrow terms interwoven with a strong connotation of fault or bad intentions. There was no unequivocal formal rule that required proving a separate element of intention, but the framing of the critical question in terms of "evading" copyright contrasted with "bona fide" secondary uses colored the infringement analysis with strong shades of a fault inquiry. A work was deemed infringing only inasmuch as its differences from the original were such that it was reasonable to assume that they were introduced simply for the purpose of evading the prohibition on reprinting. Lord Ellenborough expressed this attitude in dictum in the 1802 *Cary v. Kearsley* where he explained that the fundamental inquiry in cases of alleged infringement is whether the purpose of the publication "was to convey to the public the notes and observation fairly, or only to colour the publication of the original essay, and make that a pretext for pirating it." This criterion rested on a broader principle:

[A] man may fairly adopt part of the work of another: he may so make use of another's labours for the promotion of science, and the benefit of the public: but having done so, the question will be, Was the matter so taken used fairly with that view, and without what I may term the *animus furandi*?[92]

As late as 1844, Richard Godson still cited this rule in his treatise and talked about "*animus furandi*" – intention to steal – as the critical element of the analysis.[93] Third, the doctrine rejected a rigid hierarchy between original and derivative creation. Secondary uses of protected texts, even if they drew heavily on the original, were not seen simply as excused transgressions. As long as these secondary works did not cross the line to the territory of mere evasive reprinting, they were seen as "new and meritorious work[s],"[94] in their own right, and their creators were seen as authors as much as those who created the works on which they drew.

---

[91] *Gyles v. Wilcox*, 26 Eng. Rep. 490.   [92] *Cary v. Kearsley*, 170 Eng Rep. 680.
[93] Richard Godson, *A Practical Treatise on the Law of Patents for Inventions and of Copyright*, 2nd ed. (London: W. Benning, 1844), 477.
[94] *Newbery's Case*, 98 Eng. Rep. 913 (Ch. 1773).

As Justice Willes put it in *Millar v. Taylor*: "Certainly bona fide imitations, translations and abridgments are different, and in respect of the property may be considered new works: but colourable and fraudulent variations will not do."[95] What catches the eye most in this formula is the "bona fide imitation" – a term that a century later would become an unfathomable contradiction.

The upshot of these rules was a strong immunity given to secondary uses of copyrighted works such as translations, abridgments, or works improved by corrections and commentaries. Whoever obtained a book, wrote Justice Aston in *Millar v. Taylor*, "may improve upon it, imitate it, translate it; oppose its sentiments: but he buys no right to publish the identical work."[96] Latent in the doctrine was a concept of the protected object of property as a semi-material object. The "copy" was an imagined immaterial object different from the physical book, but it was still bounded by the rigid bonds of what Blackstone described as "the same conceptions cloathed in the same words."[97] This narrowly defined object of property dovetailed with the strict definition of copyright as "the sole and exclusive right of multiplying printed copies for sale."[98] Underlying copyright's restrictive infringement rules was the same concept of the object of property on which British proponents of common law copyright and their American counterparts in *Wheaton v. Peters* relied in their search for fixity and objective boundaries to literary property.

The United States inherited this framework. The 1790 act followed the Statute of Anne's basic structure. It covered "maps, charts and books" and defined the exclusive entitlement conferred by copyright as "the sole right and liberty of printing, reprinting, publishing and vending" such maps, charts, and books.[99] Occasional pressures to expand copyright's narrow scope existed from the outset. Jedidiah Morse in one of the earliest copyright petitions to Congress asked for (but never received) specific legislative protection of his work that "might be so expressed as effectually to secure the Petitioner, against all mutilations, alterations and abridgments ... as may operate to his injury."[100] The drafters of

---

[95] 98 Eng. Rep. 205.   [96] Id., 226.   [97] Blackstone, *Commentaries*, vol. 2, 406.

[98] Francis Hargrave, *An Argument in Defence of Literary Property* (1774), reprinted in Stephen Parks, ed., *Four Tracts on Freedom of the Press, 1790–1821* (New York: Garland, 1974).

[99] Act of May 31, 1790, ch. 15, §1, 1 Stat. 124.

[100] Charlene Bangs and Helen E. Veit, eds., *Documentary History of the First Federal Congress, Legislative Histories* (Baltimore, Md.: Johns Hopkins University Press, 1972), vol. 4, 511.

the 1802 amendment to the Copyright Act, which added protection of prints, were apparently cognizant of the problem of evasion. The amendment explicitly prohibited copying prints "in the whole or in part, by varying, adding to, or diminishing from the main design."[101] But there was no break with the English rule. In fact, for the first several decades of the regime there were no known American cases on the issue. This was probably a result of a combination of the low economic stakes of the question in the undeveloped American market and of taking the traditional English framework for granted.

Toward the middle of the century the established rules began to destabilize. The main trigger was the deep changes in the publishing industry: an emergence of a national market for books and the rise of a centralized publishing industry with patterns of mass production, distribution, and marketing. For one thing, this meant higher stakes. By the 1850s the numbers of books sold had risen dramatically, which meant that primary markets for books became more valuable and that secondary markets such as the domestic translation ones became worth investing in.[102] At the same time, competition became fiercer, causing many publishers to identify the main challenge in their trade as that of "overproduction."[103] The industry grew increasingly geared toward identifying and cultivating market demand. Publishers came to see books as commodities out of which they had to squeeze any available market value. This meant investment in efficient distribution networks, product differentiation strategies, and advertisement.[104] In 1854 George Putnam offered the same publication – Irving's works in fifteen volumes – in the following variety of covers: cloth cover ($19); sheep ($20); half calf ($30); half morocco, gilt tops ($33); calf, extra ($37.50); calf, antique ($40); and morocco, super extra ($48).[105] Cover varieties had little to do with copyright, but some of the strategies for maximizing the market value of the book commodity

[101] Act of April 29, 1802, ch. 36, §3, 2 Stat. 171, 172.
[102] In the 1830s, one hundred books were published on average each year in the United States. In 1859, the figure rose to 1350. In 1820, the value of books manufactured and sold in the United States was $2.5 million. In 1856, this value was $16 million. John Tebbel, *A History of Book Publishing in the United States* (New York: R.R. Bowker, 1972), vol. 1, 221.
[103] A.D. Van Nostrand, *The Denatured Novel* (Indianapolis, Ind.: Bobbs-Merrill, 1960), 14.
[104] Susan Geary, "The Domestic Novel as a Commercial Commodity: Making a Best Seller," 70 *Bibliographical Society of America Papers* 365, 371 (1976).
[105] Ronald J. Zboray, *A Fictive People: Antebellum Economic Development and the American Reading Public* (New York: Oxford University Press, 1993), 11.

relied on exploiting secondary markets: translations, dramatizations, serializations, abridgments, and annotated and revised editions. All secondary markets became potential revenue streams; copyright offered the means for securing these sources of profit; and the old rule immunizing secondary markets became a stumbling block.

The economic pressures and the changing concept of books as commodities produced by them had counterparts in public conceptions of authorial entitlement. Gradually it became common to assert that an author's right to enjoy the fruits of his intellectual labor meant a right to all the revenue streams from all secondary markets. In one of the earlier examples of this trend, Curtis explained in his 1847 treatise that "while the public enjoys the right of reading the intellectual contents of the book, to the author belongs the exclusive right to take all the profits of publication which the book can, in any form, produce."[106] Occasional descriptions of the author's entitlement in terms of appropriating the market value of his work circulated since the eighteenth century.[107] The telling change was the new emphasis on "any form." In 1847 Curtis conceded that the legal question of a translation entitlement was an open one. His new understanding of copyright's object of ownership dictated the answer. "Upon principle," he said, it was inconceivable that the translator by "merely incorporating with the matter of the book the fruit of his own industry ... can entirely absorb the rights of the original author."[108]

Stowe v. Thomas was a microcosm of these economic and ideological changes. *Uncle Tom's Cabin* was the first true American bestseller. A market success of unprecedented scale, it sold more than 300,000 copies in the first year following its publication and probably more than a million copies before the Civil War.[109] Stowe wrote that "the idea of making money by a book which I wrote just because I could not help it never occurred to me."[110] Yet she was revealed as a savvy player

---

[106] Curtis, *A Treatise on the Law of Copyright*, 237–38.
[107] See e.g. *Tonson v. Collins*, 96 Eng. Rep. 169 (K.B. 1761).
[108] Curtis, *A Treatise on the Law of Copyright*, 291.
[109] Homestead, *American Women Authors*, 108. Claims that the novel sold millions of copies before the Civil War were recently challenged. See Michael Winship, "'The Greatest Book of Its Kind': A Publishing History of *Uncle Tom's Cabin*," 109 *Proceedings of the American Antiquarian Society* 309 (1999). There is no doubt, however, that the book was sold in substantial and unprecedented numbers in the American market.
[110] Harriet Beecher Stowe to Eliza Follen, February 16, 1853, in Annie Fields, ed., *Life and Letters of Harriet Beecher Stowe* (Boston: Houghton Mifflin, 1897), 176.

in the literary marketplace. Unlike many others, she had the foresight to register the copyright in *Uncle Tom's Cabin* prior to its early publication by serialization, thus avoiding a forfeiture of the copyright.[111] Although she would later accuse her publisher John P. Jewett of exploiting her naïveté, Stowe learned quickly. In the 1850s she became a sophisticated business player, conscious, among other things, of the commercial possibilities offered by a calculated use of copyright law.[112] Jewett was one of the publishers who perfected the new techniques for maximizing profits from book commodities.[113] In the wake of the book's success, Jewett and Stowe identified the potential of the American translation markets and less than a year from publication moved to capture them by arranging a German translation and, according to the bill of complaint, also authorizing a Welsh one.[114] The sense of entitlement to the profit arising from such secondary markets was clear. In the affidavit she submitted to the court Stowe declared that she "has been greatly injured in respect of her sole and exclusive right ... and will be, as she fears, greatly injured and damnified in respect of and deprived of the receipt of large profits which she reasonably expects to receive from the sale" of her own translation.[115]

The quality of Stowe's sponsored translation was ridiculed by the local German press, and even more sympathetic observers felt compelled to agree that the translation published by Mr. Thomas was "superior to that made for Mrs. Stowe" since "the latter has some very gross faults, which prove that the translator neither understands English thoroughly, nor knows how to write German with respectable correctness."[116] Stowe's moral claim garnered more support among most observers. A commentary in the *New York Weekly Tribune*, for example, professed: "As for the absolute moral right, we see nothing in the nature of things to limit the ownership of the author. It is his work, and it ought to be for him to say on what terms others shall enjoy it, in whatsoever time, place, or tongue."[117] Even this supportive account, however, estimated that Stowe's chances of success were rather grim. It referred to American

---

[111] E. Bruce Kirkham, *The Building of Uncle Tom's Cabin* (Knoxville: University of Tennessee Press, 1977), 70.

[112] See Susan Coultrap-McQuin, *Doing Literary Business: American Women Writers in the Nineteenth Century* (Chapel Hill: University of North Carolina Press, 1990), 89.

[113] See Geary, "The Domestic Novel as a Commercial Commodity," 375–76.

[114] *Stowe v. Thomas,* Complainant's Bill.

[115] *Stowe v. Thomas,* Affidavit of Harriet Beecher Stowe.

[116] "'Uncle Tom' at Law," *New York Weekly Tribune,* April 16, 1853, 10.   [117] Id.

case law that immunized abridgments of copyrighted works and concluded that the legal rule laid "a very considerable limitation upon the
absolute right of property" that "may very easily be construed to extend
to translations."[118]

The argument for Thomas was deeply rooted in this traditional
rule of copyright. Its logic was straightforward: the Copyright Act "uses
the term 'copy' in the sense of reprint"; "[i]n no parlance – either
ordinary or legal – does 'copy' mean 'translation'"; and "the prohibition
is only against printing, publishing or importing 'any copy of such
book.'"[119] A translation, the defendant argued, is neither a "verbatim
copy" nor within the penumbra of "colourable variations" or
"servile and mechanical imitation."[120] Underlying the argument was
the traditional rejection of a sharp authorial hierarchy between an
original and a translation. The translation was presented as "original
with the translator," and therefore as being not a "work such that any
body, if ordered like a tradesman or mechanic, to make it, would have
produced substantially in the same shape," but rather the "the creation
of genius."[121]

Samuel H. Perkins and Samuel C. Perkins, a father and son team of
Philadelphia lawyers representing Stowe, conceded at the outset the
novelty of their claim and the absence of any statutory or case law
guidance on it. Consequently, much of their argument departed only
slightly from the traditional understanding of copyright as a narrow
right of reprinting. Their strategy was to present the translation as a
form of verbatim reproduction: "The translator aims to convey to the
mind of his reader the ideas and thoughts of the author; nay, the very
shades of his ideas and thoughts; his exact manner and form of expression, and even his words, so far as represented by similarly constructed
expressions in the new language. All changes, all variations in any of
these particulars, are failures, and are studiously guarded against."[122]
Aided by a theory of language in which words were inconsequential,
transparent signs for conveying signified ideas, the argument conjured
up an image of the "mere translation," unlike a "paraphrase or
rendering from prose to poetry," as being "the same book."[123] Only
toward its end did the plaintiff's argument start to grope more ambitiously toward a new concept of copyright. Quoting from the treatise
by Curtis, published six years earlier, the argument presented the

[118] Id.   [119] 23 F. Cas. 205.   [120] Id.   [121] Id.   [122] Id., 202.   [123] Id.

touchstone for infringement as follows: "Has the original author suffered, or will suffer injury from the act complained of?" It goes on to ask rhetorically, "Has any one doubted that congress meant to secure to authors the profits from their work throughout the length and breadth of this country?" and to assert that an unauthorized translation "would deprive them of any profits as respects a vast class of our people."[124] Invoking the theme of injury to a potential stream of market profit was the hallmark of a new understanding of copyright, which was no longer limited to the sphere of reprints.

Grier would have none of it. He described the legal question as "what constitutes literary property" and responded with a resounding answer. The author's "exclusive property in the creation of his mind," he wrote, "cannot be vested in the author as abstractions, but only in the concrete form which he has given them, and the language in which he has clothed them ... the only property which he reserves to himself, or which the law gives to him, is the exclusive right to multiply the copies of that particular combination of characters which exhibits to the eyes of another." The protected "copy" he defined as "a transcript of the language in which the conceptions of the author are clothed."[125] The contrast of a transcript with a new secondary work also led to the rejection of an authorial hierarchy between an original and a derivative. "[I]n questions of infringement of copyright," Grier explained, the inquiry is whether the defendant's "composition may be considered a new work, requiring invention, learning and judgment, or only a mere transcript of the whole or parts of the original, with merely colourable variations."[126] Under this scheme it was self-evident that translations in general and the one by Thomas in particular were new and noninfringing works. Grier put it this way: "I have seen a literal translation of Burns' poems into French prose; but to call it a copy of the original, would be as ridiculous as the translation itself."[127] The opinion in *Stowe v. Thomas* was an eloquent manifesto of the old view of copyright as a limited right to produce reprints. It was also the swan song of that view. Grier's views were already under fire when he uttered them. They would soon become obsolete, and in seventeen years the rule pronounced by the decision would be overturned by Congress.[128]

---

[124] Id., 204.   [125] Id., 207.   [126] Id.   [127] Id.
[128] Act of July 8, 1870, ch. 230, §86, 16 Stat. 198, 212.

THE ABRIDGMENT SWINDLE, AMERICAN EDITION

In 1860 British author and playwright Charles Reade railed against what he called "the abridgment swindle."[129] He described the rules that allowed the "swindle" of unauthorized abridgments as well as other secondary uses as "[m]onstrous, idiotic, heartless, illegal, and iniquitous."[130] In America too the abridgment rule was one of the main fronts of the assault on copyright rules friendly to secondary uses. In his 1847 treatise Curtis declared that "the general doctrine of the English law on the subject of Abridgments needs revision."[131] Curtis accepted the traditional image of the good faith abridgment as a work of "invention, learning and judgment." Nevertheless, he concluded that the abridgment was still taking "the property of the original owner," which could not be justified by "any amount of learning, judgment or invention, shown in the act by him who thus appropriates the property of another."[132]

Why did the unauthorized abridgment that was obviously justified and commendable for eighteenth-century English judges become so reprehensible? The main reason was that the abridgment exposed most clearly the rift between the old and new concepts of copyright ownership. The abridgment, by definition, was a market substitute for the original. Its very purpose for most consumers was to forgo the need to read the original, and this presumably reduced the copyright owner's profit not just in the secondary market but in the primary one for the original work.[133] In a conceptual climate in which copyright ownership became synonymous with control of market profits, the abridgment rule that allowed this became an anathema.

The Curtis treatise signified this shift toward market value analysis. For Curtis it was obvious that the principle that allows "some use of all antecedent literature ... will not sanction direct and palpable injuries to the author in whom the law invested the sole right to take the profits of his own book and every part of it." Thus the "most material inquiry" in each

---

[129] Charles Reade, *The Eighth Commandment* (Boston: Ticknor and Fields, 1860); see generally Deazley, "The Great Abridgment Swindle."

[130] Reade, *The Eight Commandment*, 152.

[131] Curtis, *A Treatise on the Law of Copyright*, 265.   [132] Id., 271.

[133] Curtis thought that any argument that an unauthorized abridgment did not reduce or even increased profits in the primary market should not be allowed to be heard, just like the defendant who produced verbatim copies was not allowed to argue that as a matter of fact his actions did not decrease the sales of authorized copies. Id., 276–77.

case came to be "whether the author has sustained or is likely to sustain an injury by the publication of which he complains."[134] This framing of the question doomed the abridgment. Curtis made explicit the connection between a concept of ownership of intangibles as control of market value and his attack on secondary uses:

When we consider the incorporeal nature of literary property, it will be apparent that no writer can make and publish an abridgment, without taking to himself profits of literary matter which belong to another.[135]

The abridgment according to Curtis "of necessity tends to the injury of the true proprietor" because "[t]he real object of most abridgments is to undersell the original work."[136] At some point Curits shifted the focus of his attack from adverse effects in the primary market of the book to effects in secondary markets. The author's copyright, he explained, "must be held to have secured to him the right to avail himself of the profits to be reaped from all classes of readers, both those who would purchase his production in a cheap and condensed form, and those who would purchase it in its more extended and costly shape."[137]The "right to publish an abridgment" is "a valuable part of the copyright," and therefore "[i]f, during the existence of the copyright, the work is abridged by a stranger, the copyright is shorn of an incident, the loss of which may greatly affect its value as property."[138] The moment copyright became the right to control every "incident" of market profits, the rule shielding unauthorized abridgments – a danger to both the primary and secondary markets – had to go.

Story v. Holocombe,[139] decided six years prior to *Stowe* in the year of the first publication of Curtis' treatise, exposed the transitory nature of American copyright ownership jurisprudence at the time. By the time of the decision Joseph Story had been dead for two years, but his hand was still reshaping American copyright law. The lawsuit was brought by Story's estate against James Philemon Holcombe, a professor of law at the University of Virginia, a future confederate politician, and an apologist of slavery. At issue was Holcombe's 1846 book *An Introduction to Equity Jurisprudence: On the Basis of Story's Commentaries*. Holcombe described the book as "substantially, an abridgment" of Story's celebrated *Commentaries on Equity Jurisprudence*, meant to be "an introduction, a companion, and a supplement" for "the young man, who has

[134] Id., 240.   [135] Id., 275–76.   [136] Id., 276.   [137] Id., 278.   [138] Id., 279.
[139] 23 F. Cas. 171 (C.C.D. Oh. 1847).

no previous knowledge of the principles of the science, confused amid a labyrinth of particulars."[140]

A special master appointed by the court reported after "a very able and laborious examination of the two works" that "the work of Holcombe is a fair abridgment of the Commentaries of Judge Story."[141] Under the settled English precedents this should have easily decided the controversy. Justice McLean, however, found the case anything but easy. He opened his opinion with the agonized confession that "[t]his controversy has caused me great anxiety and embarrassment."[142] The cause of this great anxiety was a dissonance between the established rules and what McLean saw as the logic of copyright ownership. Observing that the decision must turn on "the question of abridgments," he declared: "If this were an open question, I should feel little difficulty in determining it."[143] McLean meant he would have ruled that an abridgment was an infringement. Unfortunately, he also had to concede that "a contrary doctrine has been long established in England ... and in this country the same doctrine has prevailed." As a result he saw himself as "bound by precedent" to which he had to yield "more as a principle of law, than a rule of reason or justice."[144]

The reason for this dissonance between law and reason was that McLean had already taken for granted the new understanding of copyright as control of market value of the work. An abridgment was, by definition, a market substitute for the original: "An abridgment should contain an epitome of the work abridged – the principles, in a condensed form of the original book." As a result "it would be difficult to maintain that such a work did not affect the sale of the book abridged."[145] Because the abridgment "does, to some extent in all cases, and not unfrequently to a great extent, impair the rights of the author," McLean explained, "[t]he reasoning on which the right to abridge is founded, therefore, seems to me to be false in fact."[146] The same quality that constituted the worth of the abridgment for eighteenth-century jurists – its usefulness to the reading audience – was for McLean its chief evil. This happened once public value came to be seen as market value defining the scope of the author's entitlement: "Now an abridgment, if fairly made contains the principle of the original work, and this constitutes its value."[147]

---

[140] Joseph Holcombe, *An Introduction to Equity Jurisprudence: On the Basis of Story's Commentaries* (Cincinnati, Ohio: Derby, Bradley, 1846), iii–iv.
[141] 23 F. Cas. 172.   [142] Id.   [143] Id.   [144] Id., 173.   [145] Id., 172.
[146] Id., 173.   [147] Id.

McLean devised a tortuous route to escape his predicament. "To abridge," he said, "is to preserve the substance, the essence of the work, in language suited to such a purpose."[148] Holcombe's work, how- ever, not only failed to be entitled "an abridgment," it also did not achieve the task of preserving the entire substance of the original work in a condensed form. McLean seized Holcombe's declaration in the preface that the book was not meant to be a substitute for Story's work and turned it against him. He found that at least the first third of the book was a mere "compilation" of extracts that did not enjoy an abridgment's safe haven.[149] Thus, the abridgment rule survived *Story v. Holcombe*, but the growing emphasis in copyright jurisprudence on market value was clearly robbing it of its justification, breeding hostility toward it and bringing about an erosion of its practical effect. *Story v. Holcombe* was never officially overturned either by a subsequent court or by Congress. There was no need to. As the conceptual scheme that grounded the rules to which the decision adhered (albeit in a wooden way) lost power, these rules and their protection of good faith abridgements stopped making sense and eventually dissolved.

THAT WHICH CONSTITUTES THE ESSENCE AND VALUE OF LITERARY COMPOSITION: INTELLECTUAL COMMODITIES

In a process that began in the 1830 and intensified after the Civil War, treatise writers, judges, and lawyers created a new conceptual framework of copyright ownership. This framework fused together an understanding of copyright ownership as an entitlement for all streams of market profit, a metaphysics of the expressive work as an intellectual essence that could be manifested in numerous concrete forms, and legal rules that expanded and abstracted the reach of copyright protection.

The first move in the assault on the traditional framework was purging copyright of any fault element. Curtis put it this way:

[T]he question of intention does not enter directly into the determination of the question of piracy. The exclusive privilege that the law secures to authors, may be equally violated, whether the work complained of was written with or without the *animus furandi* – the intention to take what belongs to another, and thereby to do an injury.[150]

---

[148] Id., 174.   [149] Id., 174–75.   [150] Curtis, *A Treatise on the Law of Copyright*, 238.

As long as copyright's scope was understood as covering reprints and a thin penumbra of evasive copies it made perfect sense to inquire about fault. But under the new focus of preventing market injury, inquiring after fault seemed out of place. For Curtis, "[t]o decide the question of piracy upon the motives of the party charged with the infringement, would reduce the exclusive right secured to authors by the law to a much lower scale of value and efficiency than the law intends to give it."[151] Thus, he rebuked the English treatise writer Godson for still adhering to the *animus furandi* rule in the context of quotations: "If an injury is caused there is no occasion to prove the intention ... If part of one author's book is found in that of another, the question will be, what effect is it to have? Not whether it was taken with bad intent."[152] In *Story v. Holcombe* Justice McLean similarly declared he could not perceive how the intention "can bear upon the question." The inquiry, he said, must be about effect. If secondary uses render the protected work "less valuable by superseding its use, in any degree, the right of the author is infringed; and it can be of no importance to know with what intent this was done."[153] Eaton Drone included a section in his 1879 treatise called "Intention to Pirate Not Essential," the gist of which was that in copyright infringement the "thing done and its effect, and not the intention with which it is done, are the controlling considerations."[154] Traces of fault elements survived in copyright doctrine until the end of the nineteenth century.[155] As the focus became protecting the value of the work, however, injurious market effect displaced fault as the constitutive element defining copyright infringement.

The demise of fault, however, was a sideshow. The heart of the transformation of copyright was the decline of the idea of the "copy" and its replacement by a much more capacious notion. Drone put it this way:

The definition that a copy is a literal transcript of the language of the original finds no place in the jurisprudence with which we are concerned. Literary property, as has been shown, is not in the language alone; but in the matter of which language is merely a means of communication. It is in the substance and not in the form alone. That which constitutes the essence and value of literary composition ... may be capable of expression in more than one form of language different than the original.[156]

---

[151] Id., 238–39.   [152] Id., 252, n. 3.   [153] 23 F. Cas. 173.

[154] Drone, *A Treatise on the Law of Property in Intellectual Productions*, 401. See also *Lawrence v. Dana*, 15 F. Cas. 60.

[155] See Anthony Reese, "Innocent Infringement in U.S. Copyright Law: A History," 20 *Colum J. L. Arts* 132, 154–75 (2007).

[156] Drone, *A Treatise on the Law of Property in Intellectual Productions*, 451.

Here were all the components of the new framework of copyright: a rejection of the notion of reprinting copies, a focus on protecting market value, and a concept of the protected work as a polymorphic intellectual essence. The two last elements dovetailed with each other. Various specific "forms" were manifestations of the same intellectual "substance" because they created secondary markets offering potential profits. The author was entitled to these profits because the secondary markets were for his own intellectual work in a different form. The logic was circular but powerful.

The doctrinal upshot of this framework was a firm rejection of the precedents that shielded secondary uses. The criticism of these rules started around the middle of the century in the two editions of the Curtis treatise and culminated in Drone's 1879 uncompromising attack. "It is no defence of piracy," Drone wrote, "that the work entitled to protection has not been copied literally; that it has been translated into another language; that it has been dramatized; that the whole has not been taken; that it has been abridged; that it is reproduced in a new and more useful form." Rather, "[t]he controlling question always is, whether the substance of the work is taken without authority."[157] At the time Drone was writing, Congress already created by statute a right of translation and dramatization, albeit with the possible limitation of the author having to "reserve the right."[158] For Drone it was imperative, however, to show that the entitlement of translation derived from "established principles" of copyright law, rather than being an arbitrary statutory intervention.[159] Starting with the premises that "literary property is not limited to a precise form of words, the identical language in which the composition is expressed," and that "the author of a literary composition may claim it as his own, in whatever language or forms of words it can be identified as his production,"[160] it was little wonder that Drone's conclusion was that "[t]he doctrine that an unlicensed translation of a protected work is no invasion of the copyright in the original, as was held in Stowe *v.* Thomas, is contrary to justice, recognized principles, and the copyright statutes of the United States as judicially construed."[161]

Another implication of the idea that the intellectual essence of the work covers a multitude of concrete forms was the emergence of an increasingly hierarchical distinction between the original and a derivative. Thus,

---

[157] Id., 385.   [158] 16 Stat. 198, 212, §86.
[159] Drone, *A Treatise on the Law of Property in Intellectual Productions*, 446.
[160] Id., 384–85.   [161] Id., 454.

according to Drone, "the translator creates nothing," but merely "takes the entire creation of another, and simply clothes it in new dress."[162] And similarly:

The dramatist invents nothing, creates nothing. He simply arranges the parts, or changes the from, of that which already exists ... in making this use of a work of which he is not the author, he avails himself of the fruits of genius and industry which are not his own, and takes to himself profits which belong to another.[163]

Gone was the old premise that the creator of the secondary work is an original author in his own right to which even Curtis felt compelled to pay some lip service thirty years earlier.

The shift in the case law toward this new model of copyright ownership started in the 1840s. By the late 1860s, an expansion and abstraction of the scope of copyright protection that stood in sharp contrast to the right to reprint a copy described by Grier in *Stowe v. Thomas* became unmistakable. Judges usually avoided the theoretical version of the question in terms of defining the owned object of property. Instead, they focused on more practical aspects such as the legal formula for determining infringement. Implicit in the legal rules, however, there emerged a notion of the protected work as an abstract intellectual commodity similar to the one developed explicitly in the treatises.

The 1845 decision of Justice Story in *Emerson v. Davies* signified the beginning of this process. The lawsuit was brought by Fredrick Emerson, the writer of a popular arithmetic textbook, against Charles Davies and his publisher. Emerson did not argue that Davies reprinted his book but alleged that "the defendants have adopted the same plan, arrangement, tables, gradation of examples and illustrations by unit marks, in the same page, in imitation of the plaintiff's book."[164] Finding for the plaintiff, Story wrote a subtle opinion. It did not directly attack the old English precedents. But Story wove in a new strand of reasoning that began to undermine the familiar distinction between evasive reprinting with colorable changes and a new, good faith secondary work. He described "the true test of piracy" as follows:

[W]hether the defendant has, in fact, used the plan, arrangements, and illustrations of the plaintiff, as the model of his own book, with colorable alterations and variations only to disguise the use thereof; or whether his work is the result of his own labor, skill, and use of common materials and common sources of

---

[162] Id., 451.   [163] Id., 464.
[164] *Emerson v. Davies*, 8 F. Cas. 615, 620 (C.C.D. Mass. 1845).

knowledge, open to all men, and the resemblances are either accidental or arising from the nature of the subject. In other words, whether the defendant's book is, quoad hoc, a servile or evasive imitation of the plaintiff's work, or a bona fide original compilation from other common or independent sources.[165]

All the traditional catchphrases were here, but Story began to change their ultimate meaning. The precedents that limited the scope of copyright allowed secondary uses of the protected work as long as they did not amount to being disguised reprints. But in Story's formula a subsequent bona fide original work could draw only on "other common or independent sources." In other words a resemblance, even on a nonliteral level, either was not attributable to borrowing at all or was by definition a "servile imitation." The shift from reprints to protecting market value became apparent with the observation that "to amount to an infringement, it is not necessary that there should be a complete copy or imitation in use throughout; but only that there should be an important and valuable portion, which operates injuriously to the copy-right of the plaintiff."[166] And the result was deserting the "copy" for a broader definition of the intellectual object of copyright's protection: "In truth, every author of a book has a copy-right in the plan, arrangement and combination of his materials, and in his mode of illustrating his subject, if it be new and original in its substance."[167] This was very different from the earlier identification of the protected copy with a particular combination of signs. Stealthily, almost unnoticeably, Story started the process of abstracting and expanding the scope of copyright's intellectual work.

Two years later in his agonizing attempt to deal with the established abridgment rule, Justice McLean identified this process of moving away from the "copy" and analogized it to the parallel trend in patent law. In patent law, McLean wrote, "[t]he construction of any other machine which acts upon the same principle, however its structure may be varied, is an infringement on the patent ... if it act up on the same principle of the one first patented, the patent is violated." He asked rhetorically: "Why, then in reason and justice, should not the same principle be applied in a case of copyright as in that of a patented machine?"[168] The "principle" that McLean identified as the object of protection in patents supplied an abstract essence to the invention, an identity that was preserved in every subsequent use, irrespective of changes to the specific design. Drawing the parallel to copyright anticipated Drone's

---

[165] Id., 624.   [166] Id., 625.   [167] Id., 619.   [168] *Story v. Holocombe*, 23 F. Cas 173.

later focus on the "thing itself" that remained the same, no matter the exact "means of communication."

After the Civil War this trend intensified. Judges still used the language of evasive and colorable reproductions, but they were constantly moving away from the notion of the reprint and expanding the scope of copyright. Some of these cases were within the familiar terrain of printed texts.[169] But other cases involved nontextual media such as dramatic performances, photographs, or lithographs.[170] The significance of this broadening sweep of copyright was twofold. Most important, it meant that the economic base generating the demand for broader copyright was expanding. No longer was it only book publishers who saw the potential of copyright for extracting profit out of their intellectual commodities. In other industries (many of which were new), such as theater, advertisement, photography, music, and later motion pictures, many began to rely on copyright as a tool for maximizing profit in both primary and secondary markets. On the conceptual side, moving beyond texts facilitated the process of expansion and abstraction. The old notion of the copy dovetailed with copyright's traditional focus on printed texts and the publisher's right of reprinting. To be sure, even in the context of books the concept of copyright as covering only a specific series of characters had declined. Broadening copyright's focus beyond printed texts, however, accelerated this process. As the idea that copyright could subsist in something other than texts – images, dramatic effects, performed music – took root, it became more natural to see the object of property as a polymorphic entity – an intellectual essence that could appear in a manifold of concrete forms or media.

The 1868 case of *Daly v. Palmer* was an important landmark in this respect. The plaintiff Augustin Daly, a towering figure in the American theatrical scene, wrote, produced, and copyrighted the play *Under the Gaslight*. The play featured what came to be known as "the railroad scene," involving a rescue of a character tied to the tracks from an onrushing train. Dion Boucicault, another important figure in the annals of both American theater and copyright, wrote the play *After Dark*, which contained a similar scene. Various details of the scene and

---

[169] See *Lawrence v. Dana*, 15 F. Cas. 58; *Simms v. Stanton*, 75 F. 6, 10 (C.C.N.D. Cal. 1896); *Gilmore v. Anderson*, 38 F. 846, 849 (S.D. N.Y. 1889).

[170] See e.g. *Daly v. Plamer*, 6 Fed. Cas. 1132 (S.D. N.Y. 1868); *Falk v. Brett Lithographing Co.*, 48 F. 678 (S.D. N.Y. 1891); *Falk v. Donaldson*, 57 F. 32 (S.D. N.Y. 1893); *Maxwell v. Goodwin*, 93 F. 665 (C.C.N.D. Ill. 1899).

especially the dialogue were different. Thus when Henry Palmer, who produced *After Dark*, was sued by Daly, it seemed he had a strong defense. As the case was based on the newly created public performance entitlement, the defendant's argument necessarily conceded that copyright extended its reach here beyond strict reprinting. Nonetheless, some early understandings of dramatic copyright still limited it to a narrow verbal realm, as in the case of one treatise that identified the protected essence of drama as the "delivery of a dialogue."[171]

Despite the difference in dialogue and other details, however, Judge Blatchford found the scene to be infringing. He relied on a new-vintage English case in which an adaptation of an opera into dance music was ruled to be an infringement. The English court found that "the piracy is where the appropriated music, though adapted to a different purpose from that of the original, may still be recognized by the ear. The adding variations makes no difference in the principle."[172] Finding that this line of reasoning is "eminently sound and just, and ... applicable to the case of a dramatic composition," Blatchford concluded that "[a]ll that is substantial and material in the plaintiff's 'railroad scene' has been used ... in a manner to convey the same sensations and impressions to those who see it represented, as in the plaintiff's play." He explicitly described copyright's object of ownership as follows:

The original subject of invention, that which required genius to construct it and set it in order, remains the same, in the adaptation. A mere mechanic in dramatic composition can make such adaptation, and it is a piracy, if the appropriated series of events, when represented on the stage, although performed by new and different characters, using different language, is recognized by the spectator, through any of the senses to which the representation is addressed, as conveying substantially the same impressions to, and exciting the same emotions in the mind, in the same sequence or order.[173]

The abstraction was twofold. First, this formula detached copyright not just from printed text, but from verbal language altogether. In the case of drama the commodified object was "a series of events" or represented human behavior.[174] Second, this intellectual entity was defined on an abstract and elusive level. It survived any "adaptation" and consisted in

---

[171] T.H. Lacy, *A Handy Book on the Law of the Drama and Music* (London: T.H. Lacy, 1864), 20.

[172] *D'Almaine v. Boosey*, 160 Eng. Rep. 117, 123 (Ex. 1835).

[173] *Palmer v. Daily*, 6 Fed. Cas. 1138.

[174] See Derek Miller, "Judicial Criticism: Performance and Aesthetics in Anglo-American Copyright Law 1770–1911," Ph.D. diss., Stanford University, (2013), 108–25.

the "impressions" and the "emotions" conveyed to the mind of the spectator rather than in any concrete set of expressive forms.

In 1869 T.W. Clarke, who represented Palmer, published a short comment in which he highlighted the decision's novelty. He argued that it was the first time that "a property in incident" was recognized and sharply diagnosed the parallelism with the developments in patent law. The decision, Clarke thought, followed in the footsteps of *Emerson v. Davies* and "may be said to advance in literary law the doctrine of romantic equivalents, analogous to the doctrine of mechanical equivalents of the patent or mechanical law."[175]

THE METAPHYSICS OF THE LAW: BALANCING MECHANISMS

Two modern copyright rules are broadly seen today as the most important built-in safety valves against overbroad copyright: the fair use doctrine that renders certain, otherwise infringing uses of copyrighted works permissible and the principle that copyright extends only to concrete expression rather than abstract ideas. Historically, however, the emergence of both rules was a central part of the process of expansion and abstraction of copyright. While this historical role of the two doctrines may seem surprising to modern eyes, it makes perfect sense when understood against the backdrop of the conceptual changes of copyright during the nineteenth century. As the narrow concept of reprints was supplanted by the new idea of protecting the market value of an elusive intellectual work, its integral boundary-setting mechanism was swept away. If copyright extended to protecting the value of an intellectual work in any form and any market, what would stop private ownership from binding in "cobweb chains" the spread of knowledge and science as Lord Camden feared in 1774?[176] The new doctrines that emerged gradually played a dual role in responding to this challenge. One role was functional. When the old limiting mechanisms decayed, the new rules supplied alternative analytical and conceptual tools for managing copyright's external boundaries, for stopping short of the unacceptable point of total control. These rules ensured that the cobweb chains were not as tight as they otherwise might have been. The other role was ideological. As they became foundational parts of this area of the law, fair use and the idea/expression dichotomy worked to suppress the anxiety accompanying

---

[175] "Copyright," 3 *Am. L. Rev.* 453 (1869).
[176] *Donaldson v. Becket*, 17 Parl. Hist. Eng. 1002.

modern copyright like a shadow. In an environment in which private control of ideas was gaining unprecedented strength, these doctrines allowed to assert that the cobweb chains did not exist at all, that all knowledge remained as free as the air.

Contrary to a common view that the fair use doctrine originated in the 1841 *Folsom v. Marsh* decision,[177] Mathew Sag has recently argued that there is a "surprising continuity" between eighteenth-century English case law and modern fair use doctrine and identified several "constants" that connect the two.[178] There is much truth in this view. As Sag shows, much of the legal formulas that became part of the American fair use doctrine originated in English case law going back to eighteenth century.[179] What this view plays down, however, is the subtle craft of the common law. It was this craft that allowed judges to cite the old English precedents and pledge allegiance to them while gradually changing their meaning. This process obscured the break with the past, but its ultimate result was a radical change of the old framework of copyright. Justice Joseph Story was a master of this common law craft, if there ever was one. In 1847 McLean railed and protested against the senseless fair abridgment precedents by which he saw himself as bound. Story, by contrast, did what a master craftsman of the common law does. He cited all the old eighteenth-century formulas and wove them together with newer-vintage English precedents into a seemingly coherent whole, as if there was no tension. At the same time he was filling the old bottles with new wine and laying the ground for a radical departure from the overall scheme of copyright. Only by understanding this subtle, common law process one can explain how while the questions that courts ask in fair use cases "have remained largely constant," the answers "have changed markedly."[180] Only by perceiving the logic of this process can one see the radically new meaning of fair use in modern copyright, relative to eighteenth-century copyright jurisprudence.

In his *Commentaries on Equity Jurisprudence* Story expressed ambivalence toward the existing rules. While citing the traditional English precedents that shielded secondary uses, he also observed that what

---

[177] 9 F. Cas. 342 (C.C.D. Mass. 1841).

[178] Mathew Sag, "The Prehistory of Fair Use," 76 *Brook. L. Rev.* 1371, 1393 (2011).

[179] Id., 1393–409. Sag identifies the following constants of fair use: the case-by-case nature of the analysis, the role of the amount taken from the original, the weight given to the market effect of the use, and the importance of the transformative nature of the secondary use.

[180] Id., 1411.

constituted a bona fide use of this kind was "often a matter of most embarrassing inquiry."[181] The distinction between a "fair exercise of a mental operation deserving the character of a new work" and a "mere colorable curtailment of the original work, and a fraudulent evasion" he found to be "another mode of stating the difficulty, rather than a test affording a clear criterion."[182]

The 1839 *Gray v. Russell*[183] afforded the first opportunity to start reshaping these categories. The case involved two American revised editions of *Adam's Latin Grammar*. As Story acknowledges at the end of the opinion, the case could be easily decided under the traditional rules because the master's report found that all of Benjamin Gould's additions and revisions in the first American edition were copied and "for the most part literally copied" by the defendant's edition.[184] Story, however, devoted long paragraphs to unpacking the observation that "[a]lthough the doctrine is often laid down in the books, that an abridgment is not a piracy of the original copyright; yet this proposition must be received with many qualifications."[185] He explained that "[t]he question, in such a case, must be compounded of various considerations," including "whether it be a bona fide abridgment, or only an evasion by the omission of some unimportant parts; whether it will, in its present form, prejudice or supersede the original work; whether it will be adapted to the same class of readers; and many other considerations of the same sort, which may enter as elements, in ascertaining, whether there has been a piracy, or not."[186] Story cited the old formulas while subtly, almost unnoticeably moving the analysis beyond a clear focus on whether subsequent changes were merely a disguised attempt of reprinting. In doing this Story cited newer English cases that had moved in the same direction and particularly *Bramwell v. Halcomb*,[187] which stood for the proposition that "[i]n many cases, the question may naturally turn upon the point, not so much of the quantity, as of the value of the selected materials."[188]

In the 1841 *Folsom v. Marsh* Justice Story built on the foundations he laid in *Gray* and introduced to American copyright law what came to be known as the fair use doctrine. At issue was a publication by Charles W. Upham "in which Washington is made mainly to tell the story of his own life, by inserting therein his letters and his messages, and other written documents."[189] The publication made extensive use of the letters

---

[181] Story, *Commentaries on Equity Jurisprudence*, vol. 2, 242.   [182] Id.
[183] 10 F. Cas. 1035 (C.C.D. Mass. 1839).   [184] Id., 1039.   [185] Id., 1038.   [186] Id.
[187] 40 Eng. Rep. 1110 (Ch. 1836).   [188] 10 F. Cas. 1038.   [189] 9 F. Cas. 345.

of Washington previously published in eleven volumes together with his biography. Like *Wheaton v. Peters*, the case struck close to home. The heir of George Washington's letters was his nephew, Supreme Court Justice Bushrod Washington. Jared Sparks, the compiler of Washington's papers and the writer of the published biography, acquired the letters together with Chief Justice John Marshall, who was deceased by the time of the decision.[190]

According to Story, "the real hinge of the whole controversy" was whether the subsequent use of the letters was a new work in its own right that only abridged and selected materials from the original work, as it was allowed to do according to the English precedents.[191] Story started with his famous observation that "[p]atents and copyrights approach, nearer than any other class of cases belonging to forensic discussions, to what may be called the metaphysics of the law, where the distinctions are, or at least may be, very subtle and refined, and, sometimes, almost evanescent."[192] The exact scope of copyright had always been an elusive matter, and it had long been acknowledged that questions of bona fide secondary uses required a case-by-case analysis. But the "metaphysical" nature of the inquiry forcefully came to the surface only once judges moved beyond the organizing concept of evasive reprints. Despite its hazy borderlines, the traditional notion of the right to reprint a "copy" supplied a relatively fixed definition of the scope of copyright. Story made it clear that he was expanding protection beyond those boundaries and that it was in that expanded zone that the metaphysical questions arose:

So, in cases of copyright, it is often exceedingly obvious, that the whole substance of one work has been copied from another, with slight omissions and formal differences only, which can be treated in no other way than as studied evasions; whereas, in other cases, the identity of the two works in substance, and the question of piracy, often depend upon a nice balance of the comparative use made in one of the materials of the other; the nature, extent, and value of the materials thus used; the objects of each work; and the degree to which each writer may be fairly presumed to have resorted to the same common sources of information, or to have exercised the same common diligence in the selection and arrangement of the materials.[193]

---

[190] For the background of the case, see R. Anthony Reese, "The Story of *Folsom v. Marsh*: Distinguishing between Infringing and Legitimate Uses," in Ginsburg and Dreyfuss, eds., *Intellectual Property Stories*, 261–71.

[191] 9 F. Cas. 347.   [192] Id., 344.   [193] Id.

Story was obviously concerned with the new terrain in which "the question of piracy" depended on "a nice balance" rather than with the traditional rule that was focused on disguised reprints. Opening up this new terrain destabilized the relatively clear traditional rules.

In order to define the new fair use rule, Story appealed to a list of specific considerations that were later canonized as the fair use factors: the nature, extent, and value of the materials used; the object and character of the original and the secondary work; and the effect on the market of the original work. All of these factors had antecedents in English case law, especially in newer, nineteenth-century cases. The linchpin holding them together in Story's opinion was the last consideration of effect on the market value of the copyrighted work. Rejecting the reprint concept, Story wrote that "[i]t is certainly not necessary, to constitute an invasion of copyright, that the whole of a work should be copied, or even a large portion of it, in form or in substance." What mattered was whether "the value of the original is sensibly diminished, or the labors of the original author are substantially to an injurious extent appropriated."[194] The formal questions then were very similar to the ones that could be found even in the eighteenth-century cases. Their analysis, however, was reconfigured by the conceptual shift of copyright. Deciding whether the taking was excessive, whether the secondary work was a substitute for the original, and whether it embodied independent authorship was heavily colored by a new focus on protecting the market value of an intellectual essence that could take many forms rather than on evasive reprinting.

Folsom v. Marsh did not instantly achieve its modern canonical status.[195] Nineteenth-century courts cited it only infrequently. Unlike the modern doctrine, fair use was not treated as a defense that exempted uses otherwise found to be infringing. Rather, the question of fair use blended into the infringement analysis.[196] The significance of fair use as developed by Story in *Folsom v. Marsh* and *Gray v. Russell* was in subtly but fundamentally changing the structure of copyright. In the eighteenth century the core of copyright extended to reprints and the rule was that

---

[194] Id., 348.

[195] Reese discusses the various contexts in which *Folsom v. Marsh* was cited by later courts and traces its rising significance in the area of fair use to a 1954 *Chicago Law Review* comment by Chief Judge Leon Yankwich. See Reese, "The Story of *Folsom v. Marsh*," 292; Leon R. Yankowich, "What Is Fair Use?," 22 *U. Chi. L. Rev.* 203 (1954).

[196] See L. Ray Patterson, "*Folsom v. Marsh* and Its Legacy," 5 *J. Intell. Prop. L.* 431 (1997–98); Reese, "The Story of *Folsom v. Marsh*," 288–90.

secondary uses were permissible, unless they were not fair, meaning bad faith attempts to evade the reprint prohibition. Beginning with Story's early decisions, and more clearly later in the century, this structure was flipped. Now the baseline became that all secondary uses were infringing. As Drone put it in 1879: "[I]t is no defence of piracy that the work entitled to protection has not been copied literally; that it has been translated into another language; that it has been dramatized; that the whole has not been taken; that it has been abridged; that it is reproduced in a new and more useful form."[197] Excluded from this sweeping scope were only exceptional cases where the metaphysical and "most difficult" inquiry showed that a particular use was fair.[198] In 1869 one court described this new narrow idea of fair use as the "privilege of a subsequent writer to make what is called a fair use of a prior publication," a privilege that must be limited "so that it shall not be exercised to an extent to work substantial injury to the property which is under the legal protection of copyright."[199] This new doctrine was now hailed as "essential to the growth of knowledge" because "it would obviously be a hindrance to learning if every work were a sealed book to all subsequent authors."[200] But in the context of the general changing structure of copyright, its effect was to substantially limit the freedom previously afforded to secondary uses.[201]

Much like fair use, the modern idea/expression dichotomy seems to have deep roots tracing back at least to the mid-eighteenth century. There are multiple statements in early English judicial opinions of the proposition that "all the *knowledge*, which can be acquired from the *contents* of a Book, is *free for every man's use*".[202] These observations were typically made as a response to complaints that copyright, and particularly common law copyright, creates a monopoly of a particularly odious kind: a monopoly in knowledge. The response to this accusation was that because copyright only prevents reprints and leaves all ideas unshackled, it forms neither a monopoly nor a constraint on knowledge. As described earlier, the later American literary property debate in *Wheaton v. Peters* followed exactly the same pattern. Responding to

---

[197] Drone, *A Treatise on the Law of Property in Intellectual Productions*, 385.

[198] Id., 387.   [199] *Lawrence v. Dana*, 15 F. Cas. 60.

[200] Drone, *A Treatise on the Law of Property in Intellectual Productions*, 386.

[201] For this argument, see Patterson, "*Folsom v. Marsh* and Its Legacy," 431; Bracha, "The Ideology of Authorship Revisited," 229; John Tehranian, "Et Tu, Fair Use? The Triumph of Natural Law Copyright," 38 *U.C. Davis L. Rev.* 465, 481 (2005).

[202] *Millar v. Taylor*, 98 Eng. Rep. 216.

warnings of monopolization of knowledge, early American proponents of common law copyright pointed out that at issue was a narrow right to reprint a text, not property in ideas. This early version is fundamentally different from the modern idea/expression dichotomy that began to appear in the late nineteenth century. The early statement of the principle was based on the assumption that copyright was limited to the multiplication of printed copies. It was a theoretical observation that received its meaning from the doctrines that instantiated the narrow copy-based notion of copyright. By contrast, the modern idea/expression dichotomy appeared exactly at the time that this framework of copyright as the right to reprint a text was collapsing. Thus, the meanings and functions of the traditional and modern idea/expression distinction were radically different.

In the last quarter of the nineteenth century it became common for treatises to include bold statements declaring that "ideas, thoughts, sentiments, &c., wherever found, may be appropriated by anyone."[203] Typically, these statements were accompanied by no citations and nestled among long discussions that elaborated the new, expansive approach to copyright's scope. Soon enough courts analyzing the scope of copyright began to make similar statements.[204] Just as actual copyright scope was being extended to increasing levels of abstraction, the assertions that copyright was limited to concrete expression and left all ideas completely untouched grew gradually stronger. This tension is particularly apparent in the few turn-of-the-century cases where some litigants seized on the idea/expression distinction and implored courts to make good on the promise that copyright was limited to concrete expression. In these cases defendants invoked the old meaning of the distinction. They argued that "there is no inherent property right in ideas, sentiments, or creations of the imagination expressed by an author, apart either from the manuscript in which they are contained, or the concrete form which he has given them, and the language in which he has clothed them."[205] Courts repeatedly rejected such attempts to transform the old theoretical principle into an operative legal rule.[206] Whether they ultimately found infringement or not, they stressed that "the author of a literary

---

[203] Drone, *A Treatise on the Law of Property in Intellectual Productions*, 385. See also James Appleton Morgan, *The Law of Literature* (New York: J. Cockcroft, 1875), vol. 2, 669.

[204] *Holmes v. Hurst*, 174 U.S. 82, 86 (1899).   [205] *Maxwell v. Goodwin*, 93 F. 666.

[206] See e.g. *Falk v. Donaldson*, 57 F. 35; *Maxwell v. Goodwin*, 93 F. 665–66; *Kalem Co. v. Harper Bros.*, 222 U.S. 55, 63 (1911).

composition may claim it as his own in whatever language or form of words it can be identified as his production."[207] Looking backward, a writer of a 1917 treatise saw clearly that what he called "the classical definition" of the idea/expression dichotomy could not be squared with modern copyright jurisprudence. Using a real property metaphor he likened the specific expression of a work to "the title deeds" that "are not comparable to the property to which they refer."[208] Surveying the broad scope of copyright, he observed that the "right of variation, of re-birth ... is only consistent with the conception that copyright is in ideas rather than in their expression."[209] This was the exception. The typical approach was to declare that copyright is limited to concrete expressions while giving full effect to the "right of variation."

At the heart of this paradox was a deep-seated anxiety about private control over the flow of knowledge. "Encouragement of learning" had been one of the primary stated goals of copyright since the 1710 Statute of Anne and before.[210] In the late-eighteenth-century United States this ideal received new meaning colored by republican values. The emphasis now was on the political and moral dimensions of the spread of knowledge as a precondition for civic virtue and political participation.[211] By contrast to the elitist notion of encouragement of learning, there was also a new egalitarian streak to the ideal that stressed the broad dissemination of knowledge and the enlightenment of all members of the citizenry.[212] A new confidence in the dissemination of knowledge as the road to both material and intellectual progress accompanied these convictions.[213]

---

[207] *Maxwell v. Goodwin*, 93 F. 666.

[208] Arthur W. Weil, *American Copyright Law with Especial Reference to the Present United States Copyright Act* (Chicago, Ill.: Callighan, 1917), 379.

[209] Id., 380. Weil proposed an unpersuasive formula for resolving the tension between his candid admission that copyright was not limited to expressions and the proposition that copyright did not create a monopoly in ideas. The property, he wrote, "*such as it is*, is in ideas," but the monopoly is not in ideas but in certain uses "of the author's expression of ideas." Id., 384.

[210] The full title of the Statute of Anne is "An act for the encouragement of learning, by vesting the copies of printed books in the authors or purchasers of such copies, during the times therein mentioned." The preamble of the act made a long reference to the goal of the "encouragement of learned men to compose and write useful books." 8 Ann., c. 19. For a discussion of antecedents of this justification of copyright, see Bracha, "Owning Ideas," 178–83.

[211] Michael Warner, *The Letters of the Republic: Publication and the Public Sphere in Eighteenth-Century America* (Cambridge, Mass.: Harvard University Press, 1990), 63–67.

[212] Id.; Carl F. Kaestle, *Pillars of the Republic: Common Schools and American Society 1780–1860* (New York: Hill and Wang, 1983), 91–92.

[213] Michael D. Birnhack, "The Idea of Progress in Copyright Law," 1 *Buff. Intell. Prop. L.J.* 3, 17–21 (2001).

The ideal of the free flow of knowledge in various incarnations continued to be a major ideological force throughout the nineteenth century. Toward the middle of the century, it animated the movement for common schools and general education in the United States.[214] It also inspired the mid-century proliferation of societies for the diffusion of knowledge and various initiatives such as the short-lived American Library of Useful Knowledge.[215] Importantly, the ideal was closely associated with the book industry. The revolutionary era identification of printing with a vital sphere of broad and unimpeded flow of information was cast into new updated versions in the nineteenth century.[216] The popular self-image in the industry was a blend of technological advancement and democratic progress.[217] In 1855 one writer argued that "[t]he Cheap Press – its importance cannot be estimated! It puts every mind in direct communication with the greatest minds ... It is the great leveler, elevator and democratizer. It makes this huge Commonwealth, else so heterogonous and disunited, think with one mind, feel with one heart, and talk with one tongue."[218]

The transformation of copyright threatened to cast a shadow on this self-image. By the late nineteenth century copyright's built-in tension – being a private exclusion power over information for the purpose of maximizing access to information – was becoming increasingly apparent. As copyright protection steadily expanded beyond its formerly narrow sphere, the constraints it laid on the free flow of information were no longer limited to the verbatim copier or the reprinting publisher. They extended to a steadily expanding sphere of information exchanges that were now seen as derivative markets. The United States became a society strongly committed to the ideal of the uninhibited flow of information that developed massive mechanisms for regulating that flow. The danger that the legal structure erected in order to promote knowledge might be impeding its dissemination had become more palpable than ever.

---

[214] Kaestle, *Pillars of the Republic*, 4–8, 78–81.

[215] Tebbel, *A History of Book Publishing in the United States*, vol. 1, 241–42.

[216] On the association of printing with the public sphere in republican ideology, see Warner, *The Letters of the Republic*, 4; Richard D. Brown, "The Revolution's Legacy for the History of the Book," in Robert A. Gross and Mary Kelly, eds., *A History of the Book in America: An Extensive Republic: Print, Culture, and Society in the New Nation, 1790–1840* (Chapel Hill: University of North Carolina Press, 2011), vol. 2, 59.

[217] Zboray, *A Fictive People*, 4–5.

[218] J. Parton, *The Life of Horace Greeley, Editor of the New York Tribune* (New York: Mason Brothers, 1855), 138–39.

The new idea/expression dichotomy was a mechanism for reducing the tension between these conflicting commitments. By asserting that copyright protection did not extend to ideas, it enabled courts to simultaneously claim that copyright protected the full market value of all forms of the work and that the free flow of knowledge remained completely uninhibited. The dichotomy mediated and repressed the inherent conflict between the two propositions. One early twentieth-century court clearly articulated the anxiety underlying the idea/expression dichotomy. "If an author, by originating a new arrangement and form of expression of certain ideas or conceptions," it said, "could withdraw these ideas or conceptions from the stock of materials to be used by other authors, each copyright would narrow the field of thought open for development and exploitation, and science, poetry, narrative, and dramatic fiction and other branches of literature would be hindered by copyright, instead of being promoted."[219] Fortunately copyright did not extend to "ideas, conception, or facts," and "[o]ther authors have a right to exploit the facts, experiences, field of thought, and general ideas, provided they do not substantially copy a concrete form."[220]

The new idea/expression dichotomy was neither false nor devoid of any practical significance. In the several decades bracketing the turn of the century, courts had developed a group of new rules that helped to demarcate copyright's boundaries after the old rules faded away. The 1879 *Baker v. Selden* was an important landmark. Ruling for a defendant accused of reproducing from the plaintiff's book charts necessary for the use of a new bookkeeping system, Justice Joseph Bradley declared that "the truths of a science or the methods of an art are the common property of the whole world, an author has the right to express the one, or explain and use the other, in his own way."[221] Bradley's distinction between "the book" and "the art which it is intended to illustrate" became the basis for the modern principle that copyright does not extend to methods, systems and other functional subject matter.[222] As in this, somewhat distinct, branch of doctrine courts began to use the distinction between abstract ideas or themes and concrete expressions more generally

---

[219] *Eichel v. Marcin*, 241 F. 404, 408 (S.D. N.Y. 1913).   [220] Id., 408–9.

[221] *Baker v. Selden*, 101 U.S. 99, 100–101 (1879).

[222] See Pamela Samuelson, "The Story of *Baker v. Selden*: Sharpening the Distinction between Authorship and Invention," in Ginsburg and Dreyfuss, eds., *Intellectual Property Stories*, 180–92; Pamela Samuelson, "Why Copyright Law Excludes Systems and Processes from the Scope of Its Protection," 85 *Tex. L. Rev.* 1921, 1924–36 (2007).

as an actual doctrinal means for regulating the scope of copyright.[223] Unlike the failed attempts to interpret the old idea/expression dichotomy as limiting copyright to exact reproduction, these decisions actually worked in tandem with the expanded scope of copyright. They relied on the principle that while copyright extended well beyond reprints, some general informational elements were still left unprotected. Rather than being empty rhetoric, the new conceptual vocabulary was thus translated into legal doctrines with real effects.

Still, the idea/expression dichotomy had an important ideological aspect. It played a crucial role in alleviating the anxiety over the monopolization of knowledge in a world of expanded legal control of information. The strategy relied on drawing a sharp, supposedly bright line between expression and knowledge. Depicting the two as two completely separate spheres allowed locking property and free access to knowledge in two provinces that never touched each other. Private control could be exercised within the proper sphere of "expression" while leaving completely unaffected the sphere of free "knowledge."[224] This picture made sense because it left in the shadow the considerable flexibility built into the concepts of expressions and ideas, flexibility that allowed the idea/expression dichotomy to coexist with the ever-growing abstraction and expansion of copyright's scope. It would be only in 1930, on the cusp of legal realism, that Judge Learned Hand would recast the doctrine in a new form, one that traded the bright-line dichotomy of absolute spheres for a continuum of levels of abstractions, accompanied by the judicial craft of drawing copyright's boundary at the right level.[225]

TO PROTECT THE AUTHOR AGAINST EVERY FORM OF PIRACY

In 1897 the *Bouvier Law Dictionary* described the term "copyright" as "confined to the exclusive right secured to the author or proprietor of a writing or drawing, which may be multiplied by the arts of printing in any

---

[223] See e.g. *Holmes v. Hurst*, 174 U.S. 82; *Eichel v. Marcin*, 241 F. 404; *London v. Biograph Co.*, 231 F. 696 (2d Cir. 1916); *Stodart v. Mut. Film Corp.*, 249 F. 507 (S.D. N.Y. 1917).

[224] This absolute and distinct sphere structure of the idea/expression dichotomy bears close resemblance to the public/private distinction that Duncan Kennedy described as the fundamental organizing concept in late-nineteenth-century classical legal thought. See Kennedy, *The Rise and Fall of Classical Legal Thought*, xi. See also Morton J. Horwitz, "The History of the Public/Private Distinction," 130 *U. Pa. L. Rev.* 1423 (1982).

[225] *Nichols v. Universal Pictures Corp.*, 45 F.2d 119 (2nd Cir. 1930).

of its branches."[226] At that time this definition was becoming obsolete. It emphasized not only the narrow scope of the copy, but also the traditional association of copyright with the book trade. Historically, being the unique regulation of the book trade, copyright protected texts as texts. The core model of copyright was protection against reproduction in print. For more than half a century the American copyright regime adhered to this model. Despite the inclusion of maps and charts in the 1790 act and the 1802 extension to prints and engravings, early American copyright protected printed material against reproduction in print.[227] In the second half of the nineteenth century, however, this model came under steadily increasing pressure. Two intertwined factors generated the pressure: economic interests and ideological changes.

Various demands for legal exclusivity in increasingly valuable nonprint uses of expressive works intensified. Texts could be adapted into other textual uses such as dramatizations or translations or converted into profit-generating, nontextual forms such as dramatic performances, musical performances and later recordings, or motion picture versions. As the markets for such uses became more lucrative, the clamor for bringing them into the fold of copyright grew in strength. Economic rent seeking dovetailed with the conceptual transformation of copyright. The book-trade–centric concept of copyright that emphasized "the art of printing" element was gradually supplanted by the notion of a general entitlement for market profits that could be extracted from an abstract intellectual work in any form or media. The two factors fed on each other. As economic demands achieved a measure of success and copyright was extended to nontextual uses, the traditional print-bound concept of copy-right lost its coherence and the broader new model became instantiated in the institutional details of the law. At the same time, the new concept of copyright that unmoored it from printed texts colored the economic demands with legitimacy. In a world where copyright was no longer defined by its association with the art of printing, extending its reach to a growing domain of nontextual uses seemed increasingly natural.

Much of this process unfolded through statutory developments. The 1870 statutory recognition of distinct entitlements of dramatization and translation was an important landmark.[228] The new entitlements

---

[226] John Bouvier, *Bouvier's Law Dictionary: A New Edition Thoroughly Revised and Brought Up to Date* (Boston: Bostob Book Co., 1897), vol. 1, 436.

[227] 1 Stat. 124, §1; Act of April 29, 1802, ch. 36, §2, 2 Stat. 171.

[228] 16 Stat. 198, 212, §86.

recognized the principle of protecting intellectual works in multiple forms, but remained bounded to the textual domain. In this respect the emergence of a public performance right was a more decisive move in breaking away from the print-bound model of copyright. Unsuccessful attempts to obtain a public performance right for dramatic works first appeared in the early 1840s and produced a failed bill in 1841.[229] The issue soon reemerged in the ambitious 1844 copyright bill by Congressman Charles Jared Ingersoll.[230] Interestingly, the later version of this bill included a performance entitlement applicable to both dramatic and musical works, but only if the works were not published in print.[231] The bill that was ahead of its time in many respects was aborted after a short time. Finally, in 1856, after extensive lobbying by several playwrights, Congress added a public performance right for any "dramatic composition, designed or suited for public representation."[232]

The emergence of a public performance right in music was later in coming. It took fifty-three more years after the short appearance in the Ingersoll bill before such a right was created in the 1897 Cummings bill.[233] The bill's focus was beefing up remedies for infringement of the dramatic public performance right, including the creation of criminal sanctions. Adding a music performance right was introduced by a later amendment almost as an afterthought. It was possibly induced by involvement of the newly minted Music Publishers Association, whose establishment in 1895 was a testament to the growth of the industry and its intensifying interest in soliciting legal protection.[234] The committee's report on the bill demonstrated how the logic of expanding copyright beyond the realm of print tended to feed on its own momentum. In support of a music performance right, the report simply noted that

---

[229] S. 227, 26th Cong. (1841).

[230] H.R. 9, 28th Cong. (1844) *as amended* January 18, 1844 (hereinafter H.R. 9). See Zvi S. Rosen, "The Twilight of the Opera Pirates: A Prehistory of the Exclusive Right of Public Performance for Musical Compositions," 24 *Cardozo Art Ent. L. J.* 1157, 1159–67 (2007).

[231] H.R. 9, §19.

[232] Act of August 18, 1856, 11 Stat. 138, 139, §1. See Oren Bracha, "Commentary on the U.S. Copyright Act Amendment 1856," in *Primary Sources on Copyright (1450–1900)*, ed. L. Bently and M. Kretschmer, www.copyrighthistory.org (hereafter *Primary Sources on Copyright*).

[233] Act of March 3, 1897, ch. 392, 29 Stat. 694. See Rosen, "The Twilight of the Opera Pirates," 1200–216.

[234] Rosen discusses the possibility that the bill was attributable to the influence of the Music Publishers Association and concludes that the issue remains unclear. See Rosen, "The Twilight of the Opera Pirates," 1210.

"[t]here can be no reason why the same protection should not be extended to one species of literary property ... as to the other." It concluded that the "omission" of a public performance right in music "was doubtless the result of oversight."[235]

The development of the public performance right stopped short of enacting into law a general principle that extended the coverage of copyright to all profit-generating forms of an intellectual work. At first, the public performance right itself was understood as a limited legislative extension to specified subject areas. Drone, for example, described copyright and the dramatic public performance right that he called "playright" as "two independent and distinct rights." The former applied to all printed publications, the latter only to dramatic compositions. "Copyright may be infringed by publication in print," he wrote, "but not by public performance; playright by representing but not by printing the play."[236] Even Drone, who never tired of arguing that copyright must protect against any use of the intellectual work irrespective of change of form, had to admit that the law did not fully reflect this ideal. After some impressive interpretive maneuvers designed to bring the music of dramatic-musical works into the fold of the performance right, he conceded that "the statute does not give to the composer the exclusive right of playing a piece of music."[237] The 1897 extension of the performance right to music still followed this pattern by simply adding yet another specific area where copyright was extended beyond reproduction in print. By the time of the 1909 Copyright Act the cumulative effect of such extensions was substantial, but the general pattern was unbroken. Rather than a small group of comprehensive entitlements generally applicable, the act contained a long list of specific subject matter, such as musical works, lectures, or photographs, and the various entitlements that attached to each.[238]

The picture was somewhat different in respect to unpublished works. The rule following *Wheaton v. Peters* was that common law copyright protected unpublished works and that only statutory protection applied after publication. In the 1870s commentators led by Drone started to assert that "an author, whether in literature, sculpture, painting, or in any department requiring creative power, has unlimited control over the

---

[235] Report to accompany H.R. 1978, 54 Cong., 1st Sess., Rep. No. 741 (1896). Available in *Primary Sources on Copyright*.

[236] Drone, *A Treatise on the Law of Property in Intellectual Productions*, 601.

[237] Id., 640.   [238] 35 Stat. 1075–77, §2.

products of his brain until they have been abandoned to the public."
This meant that the author "has the exclusive right of using it in any
manner which does not interfere with the rights of others, and he may
prevent others from making any use of it which invades his own
rights."[239] This was a self-fulfilling prophecy, not a restatement of a
timeless principle. There are no pre–Civil War American cases that extend
common law copyright to anything other than reproduction in print.
When recognition of a public performance right in unpublished dramatic
works began to appear in the 1860s, it was nothing like the "unlimited
control" imagined by commentators. At first courts following some
English case law imposed various limitations on the existence and scope
of the public performance common law right.[240] The same happened with
music where public performance litigation started a few decades later.[241]
It was a gradual process that led around the turn of the century to broad
control of the author of an unpublished work of all uses and formats of
his work. Only in the 1880s courts began to gravitate toward the position
that "[e]very new and innocent product of mental labor is the exclusive
property of its author" and that all such products are "equally inviolable
while they remain unpublished, and their owner may exercise the same
supreme dominion over them that the owner of any other species of
property may exercise over it."[242] At this point common law copyright
came closer than statutory protection for published works to embodying
a principle of general control of all valuable uses of an intellectual work,
irrespective of form.

What explains the gap between the treatment of published and unpublished works? Most important, common law copyright posed fewer obstacles for implementing the newfound principle. To be sure, there were a
few inconsistent precedents. But unlike statutory copyright, there was

---

[239] "Authors' Rights before Publication: The Representation of Manuscript Plays," 9 *Am. L. Rev.* 236 (1874–75). See also Drone, *A Treatise on the Law of Property in Intellectual Productions*, 102.

[240] See e.g. *Keene v. Wheatley*, 14 F. Cas. 180; *Crowe v. Aiken*, 6 F. Cas. 904 (C.C.N.D. Ill. 1870). See generally Jessica Litman, "The Invention of Common Law Copyright," 25 *Berkeley Tech. L. J.* 1381, 1403–10 (2010).

[241] See e.g. *Thomas v. Lennon*, 14 F. 849 (C.C.D. Mass. 1883); *Carte v. Ford*, 15 F. 439, 442 (C.C.D. Md. 1883); *Carte v. Duff*, 25 F. 183, 186 (S.D. N.Y. 1885). See generally Rosen, "The Twilight of the Opera Pirates," 1169–78.

[242] *Aronson v. Baker*, 43 N. J. Eq. 365, 367, 12 Atl. 177, 180 (Ch. 1887). See also *Tomkins v. Halleck*, 133 Mass. 32, (1882); *Frohman v. Ferris*, 87 N.E. 327, 328 (Ill. 1909), affirmed by 223 U.S. 424 (1912). See generally Litman, "The Invention of Common Law Copyright," 1412–15.

much less constraining legal text, the product of centuries when copyright was defined by its association with the printing arts. Commentators and courts could simply explain why the inconsistent precedents were wrong and state the new rule as a timeless principle of the common law. Common law copyright also offered an ideological environment that was more naturally hospitable to the total control principle. Rights in unpublished works were seen as literary property – a branch of common law property rights. These were still strongly associated with natural rights theories that emphasized the absolutist nature of the right or, in the Blackstonian version, the "absolute dominion" of the owner over the object of property. In the days of *Wheaton v. Peters* an absolute right simply meant that it was perpetual and not subject to statutory preconditions or formalities. In the new conceptual climate half a century later, however, an absolute right came to denote the idea of control of all uses of an intellectual work in its manifold of concrete forms. Common law copyright invoked natural property rights, and the theory of natural property rights easily lent itself to justifying the new meaning of absolute dominion.[243]

At the dawn of the twentieth century, embedding in doctrine the principle that copyright encompasses all profit-generating uses of a polymorphic intellectual work was incomplete. Copyright would never become absolute control in this sense. But the overall trend both conceptually and doctrinally headed in the direction of generalized control. Two early-twentieth-century cases, decided by the Supreme Court three years apart from each other, demonstrate this dynamics: *White-Smith Music Pub. Company v. Apollo Company*[244] and *Kalem Company v. Harper Brothers*.[245]

White-Smith revolved around the question of nonprint reproduction of music. White-Smith Music sued Apollo for reproducing copyrighted music in the form of perforated rolls used to operate the popular player piano. The larger looming question was whether copyright would play a major role in structuring the emerging lucrative market for recorded music. Two similar copyright lawsuits had failed in the previous decades, but now the stakes were much higher.[246] During the litigation it became

---

[243] For a similar explanation in the context of common law copyright in dramatic works, see Litman, "The Invention of Common Law Copyright," 1415–16.

[244] 209 U.S. 1 (1908).   [245] 222 U.S. 55.

[246] See *Kennedy v. McTammany*, 33 F. 584 (C.C.D. Mass 1888); *Stern v. Rosey*, 17 App. D. C. 562 (C.A.D. D.C. 1901). For a general description of the background for *White-Smith* and previous cases, see Stuart Banner, *American Property: A History of*

apparent that White-Smith was just a pawn. The real mastermind and deep pocket behind the lawsuit was the New York–based Aeolian Company, the biggest manufacturer of player pianos and rolls. Aeolian supported the litigation because it had entered exclusive licensing deals with most of the major music publishers, the contracts for some of which were submitted as exhibits during the trial. The licensing deals were to take effect only once it was established that copyright covers music reproduction in piano rolls. In other words, Aeolian was after the goal that Apollo's lawyers described as "prostituting a lawful copyright monopoly to producing an unlawful monopoly" over the recorded music business.[247]

Modern scholars usually understand the White-Smith case as being about the question of technological neutrality. The Supreme Court's decision that refused to recognize the rolls as an infringing copy of the sheet music is seen as based on the premise that copyright's scope depends on arbitrary distinctions between reproduction technologies. Thus described the decision seems a bizarre, perhaps incomprehensible, relic of the past. The question of technological neutrality was certainly an important aspect of *White-Smith*, but the case is better understood against the broader backdrop of the changing models of copyright. The decision was one of the last rearguard battles of the old print-bound model that was about to be swept away.

Apollo's lengthy Supreme Court brief included a variety of arguments, many of which will be familiar to modern copyright lawyers: anything from the interpretive significance of the fact that Congress could not had been aware of the technology not yet in existence when it enacted the statute to the claim that the player piano market actually increased the sales of copyright holders in the protected sheet music market. The heart of the brief, however, was an elaboration of the traditional view of copyright's core as defined by association with printing. Copyright, the brief argued, is limited to "*multiplication of copies.*" Its reach never extends to "*collateral, secondary* or derived *presentations*" such as translations, dramatizations, or public performances, except by circumscribed statutory extensions.[248] Directly rejecting the idea of a polymorphic intellectual work, it asserted that what copyright protected were certain

---

How, Why and What We Own (Cambridge, Mass.: Harvard University Press, 2011), 111–13.

[247] *White-Smith Music Pub. Company v. Apollo Company*, Appellee's Brief, 4–5.

[248] Id., 61.

"tangible and legible embodiments," not the "intangible intellectual product" as such.[249] The brief therefore concluded that, in the absence of
special legislative extension, copyright did not extend to a "record,"
meaning any tangible embodiment of the intellectual work. Copyright
covered only the "copy," meaning the traditional object in the book trade
in the form of printed text.[250] White-Smith's brief, by contrast, was
founded on the new model of copyright as a protection of all profit-
generating forms of a polymorphic intellectual work. Boiled down, it
argued that "the policy of the law is to protect the author against every
form of piracy" and that reproducing and selling a musical composition
"is just as culpable" as any other form.[251]

The Supreme Court's opinion, written by Justice William Day, was a
sweeping endorsement of the first view and the traditional print model of
copyright in which it was grounded. Echoing Apollo's brief, Day wrote
that "Congress has dealt with the concrete and not with an abstract right
of property in ideas or mental conceptions."[252] While admitting that the
perforated rolls embodied the musical composition, he ruled that copyright was limited to the "exclusive right of printing or otherwise multiplying copies of those sheets of music, – i. e., of the bars, notes, and other
printed words and signs on those sheets."[253] Day's adherence to the print
model of copyright was no blind formalism. He understood full well that
embedding the musical composition in the perforated rolls allowed
"the manufacturers thereof to enjoy the use of musical compositions for
which they pay no value."[254] But he had an institutional competence
theory to support his position: the role of courts was to enforce what he
still saw as the conceptual core of copyright, namely, reproduction in
print; Congress, where it deemed appropriate, could intervene by statute
and add additional circumscribed protection in specific contexts, as it had
done with the public performance entitlement.

Justice Holmes' concurrence was cut of a very different cloth. Holmes
felt compelled to concur due to the weight of authority, but he made it
clear that "the result is to give to copyright less scope than its rational
significance and the ground on which it is granted" demand.[255] While
embracing the new model of copyright, he was beginning to articulate a
new theory of property to support it. From the 1870s onward, treatise
writers and commentators tended to ground broad, polymorphic

---

[249] Id., 75.   [250] Id., 82.
[251] *White-Smith Music Pub. Company v. Apollo Company*, Appellant's Brief, 32.
[252] 209 U.S. 16.   [253] Id., 13.   [254] Id., 18.   [255] Id., 19.

copyright in natural property rights assumptions. Holmes, by contrast, highlighted the positivist character of copyright. While the notion of property, he wrote, starts with "confirmed possession of a tangible object, and consists in the right to exclude others from interference with the more or less free doing with it as one wills," in copyright "property has reached a more abstract expression." It was copyright's lack of a tangible object that made it a right "in vacuo" that restrains "the spontaneity of men where, but for it, there would be nothing of any kind to hinder their doing as they saw fit" and that "may be infringed a thousand miles from the owner and without his ever becoming aware of the wrong." This clearly made copyright a positivist rather than a natural right, which at this point still meant for Holmes "a product of statute."[256] In ten years Holmes would take this insight one step further in *International News Service v. Associated Press*, not incidentally yet another intellectual property case.[257] In his dissent there Holmes came to the realization that all property is a creation of law.[258]

The evolving property thought of Holmes exemplified the changing course of the effect of intellectual property on property theory. Mid-nineteenth-century Americans, like their eighteenth-century English predecessors, struggled to develop a natural property rights theory that could accommodate the new concept of property in intangibles. Late-nineteenth-century commentators used the idea that a natural property right meant absolute dominion as an anchor for the polymorphic model of copyright. In *White-Smith*, however, grappling with the implications of owning intangibles, Holmes was on his way to concluding that all property is a positivist creation of man. On this emerging property positivism Holmes grafted the new model of copyright. The collocation of expressive elements that is copyright's object of property, he argued, had to be protected "according to what was its essence." Thus copyright protection must be "coextensive not only with the invention ... but with the possibility of reproducing the result which gives to the invention its meaning and worth," except "so far as some extraneous consideration of policy may oppose."[259] The dominant underlying property theory of copyright was on its way to shifting from natural rights to positivism. The positivist model required a policy justification for creating the right and setting its boundaries, but it remained heavily colored by the assumption that had developed in the natural rights environment under which the

[256] Id.   [257] 248 U.S. 215 (1918).   [258] Id., at 246.
[259] White Smith, 209 U.S. 19–20.

rule was protection of all valuable forms of the intellectual work. The fundamental concept of the polymorphic intellectual work proved to be remarkably resilient by working itself into both natural rights and positivist theoretical accounts of copyright.

One year after it was decided, the outcome of *White-Smith* was overturned by the 1909 Copyright Act, which gave the owner of a musical composition copyright the exclusive right of making sound recordings subject to a compulsory license arrangement.[260] After two more years Holmes got the opportunity to implement his views of copyright as protecting the work's essence in all its possible forms. *Kalem* involved a different doctrinal question than *White-Smith*'s, but the fundamental conceptual issue was identical. Harper and Bros., the publisher of Lew Wallace's *Ben Hur*, and Klaw and Erlanger, the exclusive licensee of the dramatization right, sued the Kalem Company for copyright infringement. Kalem followed the practice of many early motion picture producers hungry for new materials who in their films often drew on preexisting works, especially plays, novels, or short stories. Kalem produced a fifteen-minute motion picture representing several scenes from *Ben Hur* and advertised it as "A ROMAN SPECTACLE PICTURES ADAPTED FROM GEN. LEW WALLACE'S FAMOUS BOOK BEN HUR."[261] Not only did Kalem follow a very common practice, it also had good reasons to assume that it had not transgressed the law. In fact, an earlier attempt by Harper and Bros. to control visual adaptations of *Ben Hur* was a complete failure. In 1896 it brought together with Wallace a lawsuit in New York against Riley Brothers, which made and sold a set of magic lantern slides illustrating the Ben Hur story used for purposes of narrated slide presentations.[262] The court rejected the lawsuit and summarily dismissed the argument that copyright in the novel gave the owner the right to exclude photographic images based on it.[263] *The Photographic News* report of the case observed: "[T]he decision of the Court is in harmony, not only with United States law, but with the dictates of common sense."[264] More generally, early copyright case law relating to

---

[260] 35 Stat. 1076, §2(e). For a description of the lobbying process that led to the provision, see Banner, *American Property*, 113–19.

[261] *The Billboard*, December 7, 1907, 100.

[262] The case was not reported. See "To Restrain a Magic-Lantern Lecture of 'Ben-Hur,'" 49 *The Publisher's Weekly* 768 (May 2, 1896).

[263] "Infringement of Copyright. Wallace and others v. Riley Bros.," *The Photographic News*, September 25, 1896, 618.

[264] Id.

motion pictures, perhaps still somewhat suspicious of the new media, tended to limit copyright's scope in this area. In 1905 a New Jersey federal district court ruled that an Edison Company exact remake of Biograph's popular film *Personal* was not an infringement.[265] If exact remakes of motion pictures and slide-show versions derived from a text were not infringing, why would a motion picture adaptation be?

By 1911, however, the winds of copyright thought were changing. Kalem had reason to be worried. The stakes were high. In 1908 after Kalem had lost in both the trial and appeal courts, the *New York Times* explained that "[t]he decision will have a most important effect on the motion picture business all over the country."[266] The Motion Pictures Patent Company – the Edison-Company–dominated trust of the major motion picture companies – covered Kalem's appeal cost.[267] In its Supreme Court brief Kalem relied heavily on the print-bound model of copyright. The brief included a section entitled "Book and Picture Are Essentially Different," which unpacked this proposition over many pages.[268] Once again the argument resorted to the distinction between a "copy" denoting a print-based physical embodiment of the work and a "record" referring to any embodiment of the intellectual work. In the motion picture adaptation, the brief argued, "the author's thoughts are transformed, by the alchemy of the artist's mind, into ideals that may be realized by the eye, and copied not as specimens of General Wallace's composition, but as a record of the artistic ideals produced in the mind of another."[269]

The Supreme Court opinion by Holmes upheld the lower court's decision and ruled that Kalem was a copyright infringer. But it did not rule that the motion picture version was a direct infringement of the copyright in the book. The reasoning, rather, followed a more circuitous route plotted by the Court of Appeals opinion and the briefs by appellees.[270] The opinion reasoned that the exhibition of the motion picture constituted an infringement of the dramatization right in the book and that Kalem, as the maker of the film, was liable as a contributor to the primary infringement by the exhibitors because it sold and advertised the

---

[265] *American Mutoscope & Biograph Co. v. Edison MFG. Co.*, 137 F. 262 (C.C.D. N.J. 1905).
[266] "Must Pay Royalties on Moving Pictures," *New York Times*, May 6, 1908, 5.
[267] Kerry Segrave, *Piracy in the Motion Picture Industry* (Jefferson, N.C.: McFarland, 2003), 47.
[268] *Kalem Co. v. Harper Bros*, Brief for Appellant, 12.   [269] Id., 17.
[270] See *Harper & Bros. v. Kalem Co.*, 169 F. 61 (2d Cir. N.Y. 1909).

film fully aware of the infringing use by the exhibitors. Modern readers are often perplexed by this complex legal reasoning. Why didn't the court simply rule that creating the motion picture was a direct infringement? Indeed, the reasoning was not only circuitous, but also dubious. A critical law review note was quick to observe that when the dramatization right was created, dramatization "had the meaning strictly of using, or preparing for use, a story or a novel in a drama to be lived by living persons on a scenic stage."[271] Applying the term to the projection of a motion picture was a stretch.

The reason for the intricate legal acrobatics in *Kalem* was that the courts involved faced the same dilemma that Holmes encountered three years earlier in *White-Smith*. Many, including Holmes, had already internalized the new model of copyright in which the intellectual work must be protected according to its valuable "essence" across the full range of different expressive forms.[272] A motion picture was yet another profit-generating form of the same intellectual essence. But at this point Holmes also had to admit that legal doctrine was not quite there yet. Holmes kept quiet on this point, but the Court of Appeals' opinion that he affirmed explicitly said that motion pictures "do not infringe a copyrighted book or drama" and cited *White-Smith*.[273] The law did not seem to recognize a general right of control of a textual work, irrespective of media or form, hence the need to resort to the complicated reasoning: first locate the projection within one of the limited statutory extensions, namely, dramatization, and then attribute liability to the maker of the film through a contributory infringement construct.

The *Kalem* decision was thus a crucial transitory moment. The decision's rationale was already based on the new model of copyright, but its legal reasoning still relied on manipulating the doctrines that were rooted in the traditional print-bound model. By instantiating the new polymorphic concept of copyright in doctrine and practice the Supreme Court's decision entrenched and fortified it.[274] Soon nobody would

---

[271] "Copyright: Moving Pictures as Dramatization," 73 *Central L.J.* 442, (1911). See also later correspondence in regard to the note in 74 *Central L. J.* 36 (1912).

[272] For a similar argument describing the opinions by Holmes in *White-Smith* and *Kalem* as based on the same logic, see Peter Decherney, *Hollywood's Copyright Wars: From Edison to the Internet* (New York: Columbia University Press, 2012), 53.

[273] *Harper & Bros. v. Kalem Co.*, 169 F. 63.

[274] *Kalem* changed legal practice by pushing the film industry to strict adherence to a licensing model for the textual materials it used for its motion pictures. See Decherney, *Hollywood's Copyright Wars*, 55–56.

bother with *Kalem*-like complex reasoning to justify the possibility of cross-media infringement. It would become obvious that infringing copying applied across media and expressive forms and was not limited to the realm of texts.[275] Early in the twentieth century copyright law did not become absolute control of all forms of the protected intellectual work. There was no unlimited right of making derivative works based on the original. But copyright did become generalized control. Despite the incomplete implementation in doctrine, the logic of derivative works – an underlying principle that copyright ownership should cover all forms and media of a polymorphic intellectual essence – became a bedrock premise in the field.

---

[275] For cases making this assumption in regard to film adaptations of literary works, see e.g. *Photo Drama Motion Picture Co. v. Social Uplift Film Co.*, 213 F. 374 (S.D. N.Y. 1914); *London v. Biograph Co.*, 231 F. 696 (2nd Cir. 1916); *Brady v. Reliance Motion Picture Corp.*, 229 F. 137 (2nd Cir. 1916); *Bobbs-Merrill Co. v. Equitable Motion Pictures Corp.*, 232 F. 791 (S.D. N.Y. 1916); *International Film Serv. Co. v. Affiliated Distribs.*, 283 F. 229, 234–35 (S.D. N.Y. 1922).

4

Inventors' Rights

The effort of the first Congress to translate its new constitutional power to promote the progress of science and the useful arts into concrete legislation started early in its first session with a joint copyright–patent bill. In April 1790, after the joint bill was bifurcated, Congress passed into law the first U.S. Patent Act.[1] The system it created is often described as the "first modern patent regime."[2] In fact, as in the case of copyright, the 1790 patent regime combined the old and the new. The most important innovation was the creation of a general legislative and administrative patent framework. Instead of the states' ad hoc legislative grants, the 1790 act created uniform substantive standards and a general bureaucratic procedure for the grant of patents. Following the late colonial and state practice, the new regime was firmly focused on technological innovation as a distinct and unique category of governmental encouragement of beneficial economic activity. But many of the elements of the modern patent framework had not yet fully developed. In 1790 patents were not so much inventors' rights as the artisan's traditional economic privilege, generalized and bestowed on inventors.

The unifying theme of the new conceptual framework of patents was the patent as an inventor's property right in his mental creation. It was not immediately clear, however, how this new concept of patent rights changed the nature of the inventor's claim on the state, compared with the privilege system. Nor were there clear criteria for identifying the

[1] Act of April 10, 1790, ch. 7, 1 Stat. 109.
[2] B. Zorina Khan and Kenneth L. Sokoloff, "History Lessons: The Early Development of Intellectual Property Institutions in the United States," 15 *J. Econ. Persp.* 233, 235 (2001).

privileged category of invention within the broader field of technological tinkering and use. Inventors were now singled out as a unique subset of agents in the technological field and as the only legitimate owners of patent rights. But who was an inventor and what was an invention? There was little guidance on those critical questions. Similarly, patents were reconstrued as ownership of an informational object known as the invention, but there was little to explain and operationalize this idea. What exactly could be owned under a patent and what could not? How could one identify the boundaries of patents' elusive, immaterial object of property? What exactly did it mean to own such an intangible object?

The answers to these fundamental questions would emerge gradually during the nineteenth century. As in the area of copyright, the answers did not emerge through a linear unfolding of a predetermined logic. Nineteenth-century patent law and the concepts underlying it did not simply come to embody the abstract ideology of inventors' property that had taken over patent thinking at the end of the eighteenth century. The new framework of ownership of inventions supplied a repository of arguments and concepts that was used by agents pursuing specific agendas for giving concrete meaning to this abstract idea. This concrete meaning was shaped by the interests of the agents, their economic constraints, and their ideological commitments. Because the material and ideological forces at work were often similar, many of the specific features of the framework of owning inventions as it emerged in the late nineteenth century resembled those of copyright's authorial property. This included the built-in tensions and paradoxes produced by conflicting ideological and material commitments. At other critical junctures copyright and patents' respective schemes of property in intangibles diverged. The following two chapters explain how this process of creating the modern framework of ownership of inventions unfolded. This chapter examines the specific ways in which patent thought came to understand the figure of the inventor and the nature of his claim on the state. The next chapter focuses on conceptualizing the invention as patents' intangible object of property and the meaning of ownership of such objects.

AS A MATTER OF PROPERTY AND AS A MATTER OF RIGHT

Soon after the enactment of the 1790 Patent Act, some Americans began to argue that the Act and the constitutional power on which it was based had fundamentally changed the nature of patents. John Fitch, an inventor and entrepreneur who engaged in a fierce patent battle over the steamboat, succinctly expressed this claim. "[P]atents," he said, "are now obtained as a matter of property and as a matter of right."[3] In 1792 Joseph Barnes – the attorney and brother-in-law of James Rumsey, who was one of Fitch's rivals in a patent skirmish over the steamboat – pushed the point further. He argued that "each American citizen has a constitutional right to claim that his property in the product of his genius, should be secured by the National Legislature."[4] The shift from privileges to rights was indeed a fundamental one. Colonial and state patents were discretionary political grants made on an ad hoc basis and endowing no individual with a right to claim a patent. This practice was firmly grounded in the English patent tradition, in which patents were granted under the discretionary royal prerogative. The milestones of English patent law – the 1624 Statute of Monopolies and the common law rules – merely defined the outer limits of the royal grant power. They neither changed the discretionary nature of the grant within the permissible sphere nor created an individual right to claim a patent. At the end of the eighteenth century this basic structure was unchanged in Britain despite the fact that at the time patents were granted as a matter of routine and with little selectivity to those who managed to go through the complex and expensive bureaucratic process involved. In fact, the discretionary nature of patents – the antithesis of the patent right idea – was a common feature of all early European patent grants. With the possible exception of one episode more than three hundred years earlier in Venice, the full recognition of patents as rights was a great novelty at the end of the eighteenth century.[5]

---

[3] Cited in F.D. Prager, "The Steamboat Interference 1787–1793," 40 *J. Pat. Off. Soc'y.* 611, 633 (1958).

[4] Joseph Barnes, *Treatise on the Justice, Policy, and Utility of Establishing an Effectual System for Promoting the Progress of Useful Arts, by Assuring Property in the Products of Genius* (Philadelphia: Francis Bailey, 1792), 16.

[5] The 1474 Venetian patent statute is often celebrated not only as anticipating all the principles of modern patent law, but also as recognizing that every inventor has a "substantive right, arising from the very fact of his invention and not merely a privilege." Giulio Mandich, "Venetian Patents (1450–1550)," 30 *J. Pat. Off. Soc'y* 166, 180 (1948). See also B. W. Bugbee, *Genesis of American Patent and Copyright Law* (Washington, D.C.: Public Affairs Press, 1967), 23; Christopher May, "The Venetian Moment: New Technologies, Legal Innovation and the Institutional Origins of Intellectual Property," 20 *Prometheus* 159, 162 (2002). Other scholars, however, argue that the main significance of the Venetian statute was declaratory and that it did not change the practice of individual, legislative privileges. See Joanna Kostylo, "Commentary on the Venetian Statute on Industrial Brevets (1474)," in *Primary Sources on Copyright (1450–1900)*, ed. L. Bently and M. Kretschmer, www.copyrighthistory.org.

It was this basic reconfiguration of the relationship between the individual and the state – treating a patent as a claim that could be asserted against the state and enforced on it by an entitled individual – that stands at the heart of the view that the 1790 act created the first modern patent regime. In 1793 Congressman William Vans Murray presented to the House this very contrast between a privilege and a right as the fundamental feature separating the new American patent from its old English ancestor. Speaking of the "doctrine of patents in England," he observed:

> There is a strong feature which distinguishes that doctrine in that country from the principles which we must settle in this. These patents are derived from the grace of the Monarch, and the exclusive enjoyment of the profits of a discovery is not so much a right as it is a privilege bestowed and an emanation of the prerogative. Here, on the contrary, a citizen has a right in the inventions he may make, and he considers the law but as the mode by which he is to enjoy the fruits.[6]

Murray's statement was perceptive, but premature. A closer look at the first American patent system shows that the strong assertions by some contemporaries of a clear shift to a right-based system were founded on inaccurate assumptions and wishful thinking.[7] These assertions attest that at this time a strong ideological support for patent rights had consolidated, not that the corresponding institutional forms had been implemented in practice.

Barnes was clearly overenthusiastic in declaring a constitutional patent right. The constitutional clause merely bestowed legislative power on Congress and created no individual right. Moreover, despite its reference to the "rights" of inventors, the clause contained no indication of a shift from privileges to rights. The constitutional text did not speak to the question of patents' nature as a right or privilege. At first, contemporaries simply assumed that the clause bestowed on Congress the power to issue nationally the same patent grants practiced by state legislatures and that Congress would use this power in the familiar ad hoc manner. As with copyright, prior to legislating the Patent Act, Congress was presented with numerous petitions for individual grants.[8] The same John Fitch

---

[6] 3 Annals of Cong. 855 (1793). For an example of taking this declaration at face value, see George Ramsey, "The Historical Background of Patents," 18 *J. Pat. Off. Soc'y.* 7, 16 (1936).

[7] For a similar view, see Edward C. Walterscheid, *To Promote the Progress of Science and Useful Arts: American Patent Law and Administration, 1798–1836* (Littleton, Colo.: F.B. Rothman 1998), 170.

[8] For a survey of early patent petitions to Congress, see Walterscheid, *To Promote the Progress*, 82–87, 115–16; Bugbee, *Genesis of American Patent and Copyright Law*, 131–41.

who preached that patents were now obtained "as a matter of right" was among the first petitioners to plead for a special legislative privilege.[9] Like Fitch, who tried to obtain national protection for his steamboat, other early petitioners were veterans of the state patent practice and they followed the patterns they knew. Early patent petitions to Congress detailed specific public benefits offered to the nation by the relevant inventions such as increased productivity, reduced labor needs, or prevention of counterfeiting. They pleaded for private laws granting case-specific exclusive privileges as "encouragements" or rewards for the offered benefits. Sometimes the petitions bundled the request for exclusive privileges with pleas for other "encouragements," such as the commission of an official printer or the financing of a scientific expedition.[10] As far as petitioners were concerned, nothing had changed except for the transfer of the ad hoc patent grant from the state to the national level.

Members of Congress did not seem to think otherwise. While at least in one case doubts were expressed on whether the constitutional clause had given Congress the power to award peripheral encouragements such as financing an expedition, no one doubted its power to issue ad hoc legislative grants.[11] The individual privilege petitions were referred for consideration on the merits by a special committee. In regard to the first petition submitted by John Churchman, a committee appointed by the House recommended a law securing to him for an unspecified term of years "the exclusive pecuniary emolument" derived from the inventions related to navigational methods.[12] At least in one case – Francis Bailey's petition for protection in his printing-related invention – a private enactment was imminent, being passed in the House but not in the Senate.[13]

[9] L.G. De Pauw et al., eds., *Documentary History of the First Federal Congress of the United States* (Baltimore, Md.: Johns Hopkins University Press, 1992), vol. 3, 59–60; vol. 4, 512–13.
[10] In his April 15, 1789, patent petition for items utilizing his method of determining longitude based on magnetic variation John Churchman also asked for funding of an expedition to Baffin's Bay. *Documentary History*, vol. 3, 22. Francis Bailey included a request for the position of official printer in his petition for a patent in his printing-related invention. See House Journal, 1st Cong., 2nd Sess., January 29, 1790. The petition is reproduced in "Proceedings in Congress during the Years 1789 and 1790, Relating to the First Patent and Copyright Laws," 22 *J. Pat Off. Soc'y.* 352, 353 (1940).
[11] See *Documentary History*, vol. 10, 213–14, 220; Walterscheid, *To Promote the Progress*, 77–79.
[12] *Documentary History*, vol. 3, 28–29.
[13] Walterscheid, *To Promote the Progress*, 77–79. The text of H.R. 44 – the bill for Bailey's patent that was passed in the House – is available in *Documentary History*, vol. 3, 353–55.

What cut short the processing of individual petitions was Congress' decision to pursue general copyright and patent legislation.[14] Petitions for individual patents would now wait for the impending general regime.[15]

Wasn't then the 1790 act the definitive shift to patent rights? A close look at the first Patent Act and its operation in practice reveals that this was not the case. In some respects the 1790 regime did break with previous traditions. For the first time, the act created a general framework for a patent system. It defined general substantive criteria of patentability, the most important of which were novelty of the invention and a requirement for depositing a description of it.[16] These criteria were rooted in the English patent law tradition, but they also differed in some details.[17] The act also defined general uniform entitlements to be bestowed by all patents: "the sole and exclusive right and liberty of making, constructing, using and vending" the invention.[18] On the administrative side, standard, uniform procedures for granting patents were established. These were important moves toward generalization and standardization. Patents were no longer tailored legislative grants. For the first time in the United States, the act laid down the foundation of what could be fairly described as a patent system.

But the 1790 act stopped short of creating patent rights. The heart of the new patent system was an institution that came to be known as the "Patent Board."[19] Its members were the Secretary of State, the Secretary of War, and the Attorney General. The act mandated that for any two members of the board "it shall and may be lawful ... if they deem the invention or discovery sufficiently useful and important, to cause Letters Patent to be made out in the name of the United States" for a term "not exceeding Fourteen years."[20] This framework is often described as an

---

[14] *Documentary History*, vol. 3, 29.

[15] Apparently, petitions submitted to Congress were not automatically transferred for consideration under the 1790 act. Interested petitioners had to reapply, which they did in only some of the cases. Walterscheid, *To Promote the Progress*, 173.

[16] The major substantive patentability criteria defined by the statute were patentable subject matter, priority of invention, novelty of the invention, and enabling disclosure. See 1 Stat. 109, §§1–2.

[17] For a detailed discussion, see Walterscheid, *To Promote the Progress*, 109–43.

[18] 1 Stat. 109, §1.

[19] It was also referred to as the "Commissioners for the Promotion of the Useful Arts" or the "Patent Commission." See P.J. Federico, "Operation of the Patent Act of 1790," 18 *J. Pat. Off. Soc'y*. 237, 238 (1936).

[20] 1 Stat. 109, §1.

"examination system."[21] But it was no examination system in the modern sense. To be sure, some role was contemplated for the board in certifying that the standard patentability requirements were satisfied. This is borne out by the statutory requirement that the Attorney General would certify that each patent is "comfortable to this Act" and in making issued patents prima facie evidence that the patentability requirements were satisfied.[22] Unlike the modern meaning of examination, however, the board's role was not limited to ascertaining that the patentability requirements were met. The legislative history does not supply any explicit indication on this point, but the clear logic underlying the statute is that of giving the board full discretionary power to weigh public policies and decide whether the benefits offered by a petitioner justified the grant of a patent. As Thomas Jefferson, who as Secretary of State was deeply involved in the board's work, observed decades later, the board's task was to identify in each case whether the social benefits offered by the invention "are worth to the public the embarrassment of an exclusive patent."[23]

The best indication that the board was endowed with discretionary power to make policy decisions is its composition. It seems highly unlikely that the top-ranking officials, specifically designated by the statute as members, were expected to limit themselves to the strictly bureaucratic task of certifying standard patentability requirements and were subject to a duty to issue a patent whenever these requirements were met. A much more plausible reading is that the board was endowed with a broad discretion. Far from stating a duty to issue, the statutory language merely provided that it "shall and may be lawful" to issue a patent if the board finds that the invention is "sufficiently important and useful."[24] The statute did not even specify a standard term for patents, but only capped the maximal patent duration at fourteen years, much as the Statute of Monopolies did.[25] Yet another indication that no patent rights were contemplated is the fact that there was no enforcement mechanism against governmental decisions not to grant. The validity of issued patents could be challenged in a court endowed with a power to review the board's certification that the patentability requirements were satisfied.[26]

---

[21] Khan and Sokoloff, "History Lessons," 236 n. 3; Bugbee, *Genesis of American Patent and Copyright Law*, 144.

[22] 1 Stat. 109, §§1, 6.

[23] Thomas Jefferson to Isaac McPherson, August 13, 1813, in J. Jefferson Looney, ed., *The Papers of Thomas Jefferson, Retirement Series* (Princeton, N.J.: Princeton University Press, 2009), vol. 6, 379.

[24] 1 Stat. 109, §1.   [25] Id.   [26] 1 Stat. 109, §6.

In contrast, there was no available review procedure for rejections. In the absence of a remedy or an enforcement procedure in cases of refusal to grant, there was no meaningful right to receive a patent.

The logic of the 1790 statutory scheme was that of a republican version of the traditional English patent framework. In this version the Patent Board replaced the Crown. In the absence of a royal prerogative, it was the high-ranking officials of the executive who were vested with the discretionary power of making ad hoc decisions. As in England, these were public policy decisions based on weighing the social costs and benefits underlying each grant. There was neither a governmental duty to grant a patent nor an individual right to receive one. Following the centuries-old pattern of the Statute of Monopolies and the common law, the logic of the American act was not that of protecting a right to receive a patent but of shielding the rights of the public to be free from abusive patents by defining the outer limits of the grant power. The act, in other words, defined the permissible sphere within which patents could be granted and left untouched the nature of the grant as a discretionary political decision.

So much for law in the books, but what about law in action? How did board members and patent petitioners act in practice? Did their behavior imply an assumption of a right to receive a patent on satisfying standard patentability requirements or did they operate under the very different assumption that the board possessed plenary discretion to make ad hoc policy judgments? Unfortunately, the sources from which the board's practice during its operation between 1790 and 1793 can be reconstructed are extremely limited.[27] Still the picture that arises from the fragmentary extant evidence is that both the board and petitioners assumed a plenary, discretionary power. The board did not grant patents on demand. In fact, it rejected more than half the petitions during the period of its operation.[28] It is unknown whether any of the rejections were made on the basis of considering whether the invention was "sufficiently useful and important." Yet this is unknown because the board probably

---

[27] An 1836 fire in the Patent Office destroyed all original records. A few records relating to early patents were later reconstructed from various sources. See B.M. Federico, "The Patent Office Fire of 1836," 19 *J. Pat. Off. Soc'y.* 804 (1937).

[28] Fifty-seven patents were issued under the 1790 act. It is unknown how many petitions were rejected. A 1792 internal State Department report indicates, however, a high rejection rate. The report listed 114 patent applications under active consideration at the time, and it is likely that the total number was higher. See Federico, "Operation of the Patent Act," 244.

did not provide reasons for rejections – a practice that is indicative of the members' perception of their role.[29]

The board often asked petitioners for additional information and sometimes would summon them to appear in person. The few surviving patent petitions and communications between the board and petitioners convey a strong impression that both parties assumed a discretionary power rather than a right to receive a patent. Nathan Read, for instance, took in his long correspondence with the board regarding his steam engine the position that "[h]ow far my improvements merit an exclusive privilege, the Honorable Board will judge."[30] Reade's petition was potentially in conflict with three other petitions for steam engine–related patents submitted by John Fitch, John Rumsey, and John Stevens.[31] Six months later Reade was informed by State Department clerk Hennery Remsen that "[t]he Commissioners at their meeting in April, agreed to grant patents to all the claimants of steam-patents."[32]

The indications of the board's discretionary power are not limited to the humble attitudes of petitioners. The bulk of the more detailed petitions is devoted not to establishing the novelty of the inventions or even discussing their technical details, but rather to expounding on the substantial social benefits they were expected to produce. The impression is that petitioners, much as in the era of state and colonial privileges, devoted most of their energy to convincing the granting power that the promised social benefits justified the grant. William Pollard, for example, petitioned in July 1790 for a patent in what he argued was an improvement on Arkwright's spinning machine, but was probably just an imported version.[33] His petition is overwhelmingly devoted to describing in detail and exalting the substantial social benefits offered by his invention to the nation. Pollard cited from a short compilation of data

[29] Walterscheid, *To Promote the Progress*, 174.

[30] Nathan Read to Thomas Jefferson, January 8, 1791, in David Read, *Nathan Read: His Inventions of the Multi-Tubular Boiler and Portable High-Pressure Engine, and Discovery of the True Mode of Applying Steam-Power to Navigation and Railways* (New York: Hurd and Houghton, 1870), 53.

[31] See Prager, "The Steamboat Interference"; Walterscheid, *To Promote the Progress*, 184–94.

[32] Hennery Remsen to Nathan Read, July 1, 1791, in Read, *Nathan Read*, 115.

[33] See National Archives, Records of the Patent Office, Record Group 241, Copies of Specifications for "Name and Date" Patents, Volume 1, 1790–1803 (hereinafter *Patent Records*). For a discussion of whether Pollard made any improvement to Arkwright's design, see A.F.C. Wallace and D.J. Jeremy, "William Pollard and the Arkwright Patents," 35 *Wm. & Mary Q.* 404 (1977); Walterscheid, *To Promote the Progress*, 164, n. 61.

called "An account of the Cotton Mills in Great Britain and an Estimate
of the Cotton Manufacture of that Country."[34] It contained statistics
indicating dramatic increase in productivity in the years 1781–1787,
presumably attributable to Arkwright's machine. The following prose
followed:

[I]n the Southern states where young negroes & weakly disabled Men & Women
are at present a [Burden?] to their owners they may in these cotton mills be
employed to advantage, and the same observations may be extended to the poor
white inhabitants in all our large towns ... One girl or boy from eight to fourteen
years of age will tend from 30 to 50 spindles, & it is necessary to have man or
woman to every ten children, to keep order no exertion of strength is required in
the spinning apartment ... Your Petitioner therefore prays that in consideration of
the expense & trouble he hath been at ... so as to perfect a machine which
promises such extensive advantages to these United States ... that your honorable
board will be pleased to grant him ... the sole and exclusive rights and liberty of
making constructing & using of & of vending to others ... for fourteen years.

To this Pollard added a promise to charge a reasonable price for the
machine and submit his prices to inspection by the board. In 1792, after
he had received his patent, Pollard wrote Jefferson and suggested that the
board (and possibly also "our worthy President") would visit to inspect
his invention and see "to what extent it may be carried, and its usefulness
in such a Country as ours."[35]

John Fitch followed a similar strategy in a June 1790 patent petition
for his steamboat engine. Most of the petition is devoted to demonstrating the "great immediate utility and the important advantages which
would in future result therefrom not only to America but to the world
at large." Fitch supplied long descriptions of these public benefits,
including "increased value [that] will be given to the western territory"
due to the fact that "[t]he western waters of the United States, which
hitherto been navigated with great difficulty and expense may now
be ascended with safety, conveniency, and great velocity." To that he
added "the great saving in labour of men and horses, as well as expense
to the traveler." In return he asked for "public countenance and
encouragement."[36]

[34] 4 The American Museum or Repository of Ancient and Modern Fugitive Pieces &c. Prose
and Political 346 (1788).

[35] William Pollard to Thomas Jefferson June 26, 1792, in John Catanzariti, ed., *The Papers
of Thomas Jefferson* (Princeton, N.J.: Princeton University Press, 1990), vol. 24, 126.

[36] The petition is reprinted in William Thornton, *Short Account of the Origin of Steam
Boats* (Washington, D.C.: Rapine and Elliot, 1814), 13–14.

The 1792 petition by Oliver Evans for a patent in his invention for "propelling land Cariages without Cattle" was more succinct. Nevertheless, Evans too made a point of arguing that "[t]hese engines are of such simple Construction that they may with Convenience be applied to move any kind of machinery that requires either Circular or Vibrating motion And to the propelling of land Cariages with heavy burdens in an easie cheap and powerful manner." Evans prayed that the board "will be pleased ... to Cause letters patent to be made out granting to your petitioner his heirs Executors Administrators and assigns for the Term of fourteen years the sole and exclusive right and liberty of propelling land Carriages by the power of steam."[37] He never received this extremely broad patent.

A handful of surviving petitions from the period immediately following the transition to the new 1793 patent regime demonstrate similar tendencies of describing in detail the social benefits offered by the invention.[38] Although under the 1793 new framework patents were registered on demand, and the board ceased to exist, it seems that institutional inertia continued to influence petition phrasing for a while.

Probably the most striking episode related to the nature of the 1790 regime is that of the enticed immigration of William Pearce. In April 1791, Thomas Digges, a descendant of a prominent Maryland Catholic family and an acquaintance of George Washington, wrote Jefferson on a subject of "importance to the Manufactures of our country."[39] He reported that the Yorkshire mechanic William Pearce,

---

[37] "Copy of Oliver Evans's Petition presented Dec 1st 1792," *The Papers of Thomas Jefferson*, vol. 24, 683.

[38] Eli Whitney's cotton gin patent petition from June 1793 mentions that the machine "may be turned by horses or water with the greatest ease" and that it "requires no other attendance than putting the Cotton into the hopper." "One of its peculiar excellencies," it goes on to elaborate, "is that it cleanses the kind called green seed cotton almost as fast as the black seed." And it ends with the familiar promise of progress: "If the machinery is moved by water, it is thought it will diminish the usual labour of cleaning the green seed cotton at least forty nine fiftieths." Unnumbered Cotton Gin Eli Whitney, June 20, 1793, in *Patent Records*. Jacob Perkins's 1795 petition for a nail-making machine promises that "much manual labor may be saved," and goes on to explain, echoing Pollard's petition, that "one boy of ten or twelve years of age can with ease supply six Engines so that the labor of one Boy can cut three thousand Nails pr minute." Unnumbered, Machine for Making Nails, Jacob Perkins. Id.

[39] Thomas Digges to Thomas Jefferson, April 28, 1791, *The Papers of Thomas Jefferson*, vol. 20, 313. For a discussion of this episode, see Doron Ben-Atar, *Trade Secrets: Intellectual Piracy and the Origins of American Industrial Power* (New Haven, Conn.: Yale University Press, 2004), 143–47.

whom elsewhere he described as a "second Archimedes,"[40] was disappointed with his failure to obtain patronage from the Irish Parliament and "has finally determined to go for America with his Invention." Digges promised that Pearce would be bringing with him a box previously shipped to New York "containing the materials and specifications for a new Invented double Loom." The purpose, he wrote, was "Inspection of the President and yourself as to obtain for the Inventors Pearce and McCabe a Patent, or such exclusive Benefit as the Laws of America provide for Artists who furnish new and usefull Inventions." This scheme was a flagrant violation of British prohibition on the emigration of skilled artisans. Digges mentioned that the plan was "highly dangerous to those concerned" and later reported to Washington that he had to engage in some maneuvers to evade pursuit.[41]

The most remarkable aspect of this episode is its striking resemblance to early English patents that were often used to entice foreign craftsmen to immigrate and bring their skill and knowledge with them. Three hundred years later, here were the President of the Untied-States, his Secretary of State, and soon also his Secretary of the Treasury cooperating in a scheme to entice a foreign artisan, partly through the promise of a patent. It appears that everybody involved took for granted the basic notion that patents were discretionary tools used for dispensing government patronage in pursuit of specific industrial policies.

On July 12 Pearce arrived and called on Washington and Jefferson, armed with the recommendation letters written by Digges. Washington wrote Jefferson a short note observing that if Pearce lived up to Digges' description he "will unquestionably merit encouragement" and instructing Jefferson that "you can put him in the way to obtain it."[42] Jefferson was uneasy about the impropriety of high American officials taking part in a scheme of industrial espionage of criminal nature under British law, something of which he had warned Washington a few months earlier.[43]

---

[40] Thomas Digges to Alexander Hamilton, April 6, 1792, in Harold C. Syrett, ed., *The Papers of Alexander Hamilton* (New York: Columbia University Press, 1966), vol. 11, 241.

[41] Thomas Attwood Digges to George Washington, November 12, 1791, in Mark A. Mastromarino, ed., *The Papers of George Washington, Presidential Series* (Charlottesville: University Press of Virginia, 2000), vol. 9, 182.

[42] George Washington to Thomas Jefferson, July 12, 1791, in *The Papers of George Washington*, vol. 8, 335.

[43] The earlier warning was made in the context of a Virginia plan for encouraging local textile manufacture through premiums and enticement of foreign craftsmen. Jefferson had originally written a favorable opinion, but later he joined Attorney General Edmund

He maneuvered out of the broad duty to "encourage" Pearce by landing him in the care of Alexander Hamilton and Tench Coxe, who recently with the publication of the *Report on Manufactures* had become the public champions of encouragement of manufacture.[44] But there is no indication that Jefferson objected to the patent aspect of the scheme. The day following Washington's instruction, Coxe wrote Jefferson informing him that he had received his note relating to Pearce and "prevailed on him to deposit his articles at once in the patent office." The articles referred to were Pearce's specifications and models kept in New York, and Coxe promised to call on Jefferson the following day to "submit the proceeding, which appears proper in the Case."[45] Coxe proceeded to draft a patent petition on Pearce's behalf.[46] It is unknown whether the patent petition was ever submitted or granted. It is known, however, that in June 1792 Washington, Jefferson, and Hamilton inspected Pearce's "Cotton Manufactory" in Philadelphia.[47] Six months later Jefferson wrote Pearce and expressed interest in his most recent invention – a cotton gin. Jefferson did not mention a patent, but he did express the hope that "the benefit of it will reach us in such time and way as you shall find convenient" and invited Pearce to call on him in Philadelphia.[48] On the last day of 1792 Pearce and Thomas Marshall, another English immigrant and Pearce's codeveloper, replied with some technical details. They expressed a wish to avoid discussing "Particulars" and told Jefferson that they wanted to "ernestly and Respectfully Solicit a line of Advice" from him.[49] If Pearce and Marshall ever applied for a patent it probably was under the later 1793 act.

In sum, the surviving documents convey a clear picture: everybody involved in the process of issuing patents under the 1790 regime assumed that the board's role was to make judgments about the social benefits of inventions and exercise its discretion in deciding whether these benefits

Randolph in expressing doubts about the propriety of Washington's involvement with the scheme. See Jefferson's "Opinion on Proposal for Manufacture of Woolen Textiles in Virginia," December 3, 1790, in Julian P. Boyd, ed., *The Papers of Thomas Jefferson*, (Princeton, N.J.: Princeton University Press, 1971), vol. 18, 120–24, editor's note.

[44] Jefferson's note to Coxe was not found, but it is mentioned in Coxe's reply. See Tench Coxe to Thomas Jefferson, July 13, 1791, id., vol. 20, 623.

[45] Id.   [46] See Thomas Digges to Thomas Jefferson, April 28, 1791, editor's note.

[47] Gazette of the United States, June 9, 1792.

[48] Thomas Jefferson to William Pearce, December 15, 1792, *The Papers of Thomas Jefferson*, vol. 24, 745.

[49] A letter to Thomas Jefferson from William Pearce and Thomas Marshall, December 31, 1792, id., 805.

merited governmental patronage. In some other respects, the board's administrative practice did break with previous patterns of patents as case-specific privileges. Gradually, there appeared signs of standardization. Despite some variations, patent grants were phrased rather uniformly. This was true of form as well as content. Unlike the colonial and state grants, federal patents contained no ad hoc limitations or conditions and no working clauses that required putting the invention into practice. Even the term of the patent, in regard to which the statute explicitly defined only an upper limit, was uniform at the maximum length of fourteen years. Under Jefferson's guidance the board began developing uniform rules of patentability that guided its decisions even within the discretionary zone defined by the statute. The degree to which these self-imposed uniform rules existed and were applied up to 1793 is unclear. In his 1813 letter to Isaac McPherson, Jefferson described three such rules, but went on to observe that "there were still abundance of cases which could not be brought under rule."[50] Thus it seems that during the three years of the board's operation its practice developed some momentum toward the standardization of patents, including some procedural and substantive norms that increased the probability of a similar treatment of individual cases. Despite these developments, no formal patent right had appeared. Under the 1790 regime patents remained a form of discretionary government patronage as a matter of both formal law and administrative practice.

THE ADVANTAGES WHICH THE PUBLIC ARE TO DERIVE FROM IT

The 1790 regime was short lived. There were some complaints from patentees, but, as Jefferson observed years later, the main reason for its demise was that the board members were overwhelmed by the work load.[51] A scheme in which busy, high-ranking officials were expected to evaluate in an ad hoc manner the stream of patent petitions from the entire nation proved impractical. In 1793 a new Patent Act was legislated. It swung the pendulum to the opposite extreme. Whereas the 1790 regime was based on discretionary issuance, the 1793 act created a registration system. This meant that patents were issued on demand whenever an applicant followed a few procedural requirements and "alleged" that he

[50] Thomas Jefferson to Isaac McPherson, August 13, 1813.   [51] Id.

met the substantive patentability criteria. Although the text of the 1793 act still mandated simply that "it shall and may be lawful for the . . . Secretary of State to cause Letters Patent to be made out," it was clear to everyone involved that patents would be issued on demand.[52] Gone was the Patent Board with its high-ranking officials. Under the new framework patents were handled by clerks of the State Department and, from 1802, by the Patent Office that was established by Madison as a subdivision of the department. Even the first dominant head of the Patent Office, William Thornton, who tended to assert broad powers on behalf of his organization, had to concede this point. In an 1811 guide to patent applicants he observed that "there is at present no discretionary power to refuse a patent."[53] Decades later, in 1836 a congressional select committee observed that "[t]he granting of patents . . . is but a ministerial duty. Everyone who makes application is entitled to receive a patent."[54] Not only did the new regime do away with government discretion, it also eliminated any examination of the statutory patentability requirements.

In the absence of meaningful prior review, the task of deciding the validity of patents now fell to the courts and was postponed entirely to the stage after the patent was issued. Courts were given the power to examine the validity of a patent and declare it void in repeal procedures up to three years from issuance[55] or on a challenge by a defendant in an infringement lawsuit.[56] Jefferson later claimed that he favored prior examination by "a board of academical professors" and was skeptical of the chosen arrangement because "we might in vain turn over all the lubberly volumes of the law to find a single ray which would lighten the path of the mechanic or the mathematician." The reason for the court-centric system, he wrote, was that "England had given it to her judges, and the usual predominancy of her examples carried it to ours."[57] The irony was that as a matter of formal law the 1790 regime with

---

[52] Act of February 21, 1793, Ch. 11, 1 Stat. 318, §1.

[53] William Thornton, *Patents* (1811), reprinted in 6 *J. Pat. Off. Soc'y.* 98 (1923).

[54] John Ruggles, *Select Committee Report on the State and Condition of the Patent Office*, S. Doc. No. 228 (1836), reprinted in "1836 Senate Committee Report," 18 *J. Pat. Off. Soc'y.* 853 (1936).

[55] 1 Stat. 323, §10. The section gave courts power to void a patent in repeal proceedings if the patent "was obtained surreptitiously, or upon false suggestion."

[56] 1 Stat. 322, §6. The section specifies specific grounds on which a defendant could challenge the validity of a patent. Later courts, however, treated it as giving them power to invalidate a patent on the basis of any recognized ground, including ones not specified in the section.

[57] Thomas Jefferson to Isaac McPherson, August 13, 1813.

its discretionary review by the sovereign was much closer to the English framework. The 1793 act, however, tracked more closely the way the English patent system functioned de facto in the late eighteenth century. By this time preissuance procedures had become mainly a complex set of formalities, and ex post review of patents by the Privy Council – formerly an important forum for policy review of patents – had degenerated.[58] Jefferson was not the only one who noticed that the 1793 regime was modeled after the de facto system in England. In the discussion preceding the legislation Congressman Williamson explained that the proposed act was "an imitation of the Patent System of Great Britain" and was meant to "circumscribe the duties of the deciding officer within very narrow limits."[59]

To an extent, the new registration system resolved the question of patents as rights. Under this new system, the validity of only a fraction of all patents – those challenged in litigation – was scrutinized at all. In those cases the institutional character and the ethos of courts dictated a strong focus on applying uniform patentability criteria, rather than ad hoc evaluation of the social benefits offered by a specific invention. But this was true only to an extent. Even when courts assumed the key position in the patent system, the shift to patent rights was not complete. For more than half a century some courts would continue to treat patents as privileges by asserting a broad discretionary power to void them on the basis of particularistic evaluations of the social costs and benefits involved.

In the decades following the passing of the 1793 act, many saw courts as entrusted with a function similar to that formerly carried out by the Patent Board. In his 1821 opinion in *McGaw v. Bryan*, Judge William Van Ness described the transition in exactly these terms.[60] Contrasting the American patent system with the English one, he explained that in England the proceedings for obtaining a patent are "tedious" and involve ample opportunity for challenging the patent and considering its merits (by this time the latter part was true only in theory).[61] Similarly the 1790 American regime created the Patent Board and "made the duty of these officers to inquire into the utility and importance of the proposed

---

[58] Christine MacLeod, *Inventing the Industrial Revolution: The English Patent System, 1660–1800* (New York: Cambridge University Press, 1988), 40–55; Oren Bracha, "The Commodification of Patents 1600–1836: How Patents Became Rights and Why We Should Care," 38 *Loy. L.A. L. Rev.* 177, 200–206 (2004).

[59] 3 Annals of Cong. 855 (1793).   [60] 16 F. Cas. 96 (S.D. N.Y. 1821).   [61] Id., 98.

patent before it issued."[62] But under the new system, Van Ness wrote, "it seems to me equally required by considerations of expediency and public safety that when all preliminary inquiries are abolished, and monopolies and patents freely and gratuitously given to all who present themselves in the character of inventors or discoverers there should be some easy and summary mode of investigating their merit and deciding on their validity."[63] Three years earlier Charles Jared Ingersoll, who represented Oliver Evans in one of his attempts to enforce his milling technology patent, made an almost identical argument with one crucial difference. He argued that under the 1793 act "[t]he jury are substituted for the *board*, which, under the first law, was to decide whether the supposed invention was 'sufficiently useful and important' for a patent."[64] Van Ness and Ingersoll were thus arguing that courts – either judges or juries – filled the gap left by the abolition of the board. In postgrant proceedings courts both examined whether the standard patentability requirements were met and decided whether the social benefits of a particular invention justified a patent.

The statutory grounding for this view was the act's reference to a patentable invention as "useful."[65] In the early nineteenth century a strong line of decisions construed this as an important requirement of patentability that empowered courts to evaluate the social utility of patented inventions. Thus when Eli Whitney's cotton gin patent was challenged in the 1810 case of *Whitney v. Carter*, testimonies were produced "to prove the origin and progress of his invention."[66] When arguing the utility question, Whitney's counsel rhetorically stated that "the court would deem it a waste of time to dwell long on this topic" and went on to an extensive dwelling of his own. He provided the following dramatic description of the public benefits of the cotton gin:

The whole interior of the Southern states was languishing, and its inhabitants emigrating, for want of some objects to engage their attention, and employ their industry, when the invention of this machine at once opened views to them which set the whole country in active motion. From childhood to age, it has presented us a lucrative employment. Individuals who were depressed with poverty, and sunk in idleness, have suddenly risen to wealth and respectability. Our debts have been paid off, our capitals increased, and our lands have trebled in value. We cannot express the weight of obligation which the country owes to this invention; the extent of it cannot now be seen. Some faint presentiment may be formed from the

[62] Id., 102. [63] Id., 99. [64] *Evans v. Eaton*, 16 U.S. 454, 488 (1818).
[65] 1 Stat. 319, §1. [66] 29 F. Cas. 1070, 1071 (C.C.D. Ga. 1810).

reflection that cotton is rapidly supplanting wool, flax, silk, and even furs, in manufactures, and may one day profitably supply the want of specie in our East-India trade. Our sister states also participate in the benefits of this invention; for, besides affording the raw materials for their manufactories, the bulkiness and quality of the article afford a valuable employment for their shipping.[67]

The reported cases of the time indicate that this was not an exception. When the utility question arose courts were often provided with substantive evidence and arguments regarding the social effects of the relevant inventions.[68]

The 1822 decision of *Langdon v. De Groot* allows a glimpse at the assumptions undergirding the approach that made utility an instrument for court evaluation of the social value of inventions. The case involved a challenge to jury directions, according to which the patented invention was not useful and therefore could not be patented. The patented invention was a mode of packaging cotton for retail that made the product more attractive and increased its sale. Supreme Court Justice Henry Brockholst Livingston, riding circuit, supported the conclusion of lack of utility in strong terms.[69] "[I]f the utility of an invention is also to be tested by the advantages which the public are to derive from it," he said, "it is not perceived how this part of his title is in any way whatever established."[70] Livingston's basic assumption was that courts now played the role of assessing whether the invention's social value justified governmental patronage. Thus he described the utility inquiry as whether the invention's "benefits are of sufficient consequence to be protected by the arm of government."[71]

Embedded in this reasoning were the further assumptions that inventions have an intrinsic value distinct from subjective market demand and that judges or juries can discern and assess that value. Responding to the objection that the public was willing to pay "an enormous additional price" for cotton sold in the new packaging, Livingston wrote that this "extravagant premium" was exactly what the consumer who

---

[67] Id., 1072.

[68] See e.g. *Langdon v. De Groot*, 14 F. Cas. 1099 (S.D. N.Y. 1822); *Stanley v. Whipple*, 22 F. Cas. 1046, 1048 (C.C.D. Ohio 1839). In his 1830 treatise Willard Phillips referred with disdain to "some of the earlier cases in Pennsylvania and Massachusetts" in which substantive inquires into the merits of inventions were undertaken. Willard Phillips, *The Law of Patents for Inventions* (Boston: American Stationers' Co., 1837), 137.

[69] Livingston believed, however, that the decision on utility should have been left to the jury and therefore rejected the challenge to the trial court decision.

[70] *Langdon v. De Groot*, 14 F. Cas. 1100.   [71] Id.

"literally receives no consideration" had to be protected from.[72] Utility, in other words, was to be evaluated by a court entrusted with protecting the public interest and not by the market. This was exactly the point of fusion between assumptions about the social value of inventions and about the court's institutional role. Within a worldview that refused to hand over completely the measure of public utility to the market, the court remained the only institution with both the power and the duty to act as a discretionary arbiter of objective social value. In the words of Livingston: "When congress shall pass a law, if they have the right so to do, to encourage discoveries by which an article, without any amelioration of it, may be put off for a great deal more than it is worth, and is actually selling for, it will be time enough for courts to extend their protection to such inventions"[73]

THE SUPPLY OF LITERATURE AND SCIENCE WILL BE IN PROPORTION TO THEIR DEMAND

The line of utility cases that made patents contingent on courts' evaluation of the objective social value of the invention they protected was not unchallenged. From the very beginning there emerged an opposing line of cases based on very different assumptions. The early landmark case was *Lowell v. Lewis*, decided in 1817 by none other than Justice Joseph Story.[74] Winslow Lewis, the defendant accused of infringing a patent for a new water pump design, argued that the patent failed to meet the utility requirement. The patented design, his lawyer contended, was not superior in any way to water pumps already in common use. Under the traditional view of substantive utility the argument made perfect sense. If the invention supplied no actual public benefit, it was within the court's power to find that it was not worth the "embarrassment" of an exclusive privilege and to declare the patent void. Justice Story had, however, a very different conception of the law. The patentee is required to show, he wrote, only "that the invention should not be frivolous or injurious to the well-being, good policy, or sound morals of society."[75] This moralistic framing often misleads modern observers to conclude that *Lowell* was in line with other early utility cases that gave judges broad discretionary

---

[72] Id., 1100–101.   [73] Id., 1101.
[74] 15 F. Cas. 1018 (C.C.D. Mass. 1817). See also *Earle v. Sawyer*, 8 F. Cas. 254, 256 (C.C.D. Mass. 1825).
[75] Id., 1019.

power to evaluate the social value of inventions.[76] Far from writing within this orthodox view, Story was creating a very different understanding of utility. "Useful," he explained, "is incorporated into the act in contradistinction to mischievous or immoral."[77] This meant that judges were not given an open ticket to evaluate the social value of inventions, but could void patents only in a narrow set of extreme cases. Story's examples of cases falling within the mischievous or immoral zone were inventions "to poison people, or to promote debauchery, or to facilitate private assassination," which he obviously regarded as equally depraved.[78] This position was analogous to Story's views on copyright law where he rejected any evaluation of a work's substantive merit under the originality doctrine and begrudgingly accepted content-based judicial denial of protection only with respect to a narrow category of seditious and blasphemous materials.[79]

Story's version of the utility requirement challenged the two dovetailing assumptions of the orthodox view. Under it, judges were no longer the successors of the members of the Patent Board wielding broad discretionary power of deciding whether to extend government patronage on the basis of the public value of inventions. Their role now became identifying the rare case of an invention that crossed the extreme line of being "mischievous" or "noxious." Whether the invention was "more or less useful," Story said, was irrelevant.[80] Who then shall judge the value of inventions and protect the public from useless inventions? Story entrusted this role to the market. If the invention's "practical utility be very limited," he wrote in another utility opinion, "it will follow, that it will be of little or no profit to the inventor; and if it be trifling, it will sink into utter neglect."[81] This reduced value to subjective market demand and restricted government's role to defining and enforcing universal standard patentability criteria, leaving all evaluative judgments to the market. It was the antithesis of Justice Livingston's vigilant scrutiny of the invention's objective value to the point of willingness to protect the public from its own unfounded subjective preferences.

Throughout most of the nineteenth century these two conflicting views of utility competed in American patent law. In 1837 Willard Phillips

---

[76] Even George Armstrong, who keenly identified the transformation of the utility requirement, mistook the *Lowell* decision as being representative of the traditional conservative line of cases. See George M. Armstrong Jr., "From the Fetishism of Commodities to the Regulated Market: The Rise and Decline of Property," 82 *Nw. U. L. Rev.* 79, 91 (1987).
[77] 15 F. Cas. 1019.   [78] Id.   [79] See Chapter 2.   [80] 15 F. Cas. 1019.
[81] *Bedford v. Hunt*, 3 F. Cas. 37 (C.C.D. Mass. 1817).

identified in his patent treatise the opposing understandings of utility and declared that "the construction of Mr. Justice Story is now universally adopted in the United States."[82] But the acceptance of Story's line was far from universal at this time. In an unreported 1823 decision Judge Van Ness explicitly rejected Story's thin version of utility in favor of a "more enlarged and comprehensive signification" that "may safely, and properly, be ascribed to the term." Useful, he wrote, meant "not mischievous to the State, or generally inconvenient."[83] These were code words from the Statute of Monopolies used in seventeenth-century England as a hook for scrutinizing the validity of patents by the courts and the Privy Council on the basis of a policy-oriented evaluation of the social utility of inventions.[84] For the first half of the century variants of this orthodox view of utility were widespread. Courts often heard detailed arguments about the social benefits offered by patented inventions or the lack thereof and engaged in substantive evaluations of these benefits.[85] As long as this approach survived so did a somewhat diluted form of the concept of patents as governmental patronage rather than universal rights. Postgrant discretionary review by courts preserved the fundamental premises of this concept even when the short-lived privilege-oriented grant process disappeared. In the second half of the century, however, the orthodox approach to utility gradually declined, and within a few decades Story's alternative version was completely victorious. By the end of the century all that was left of the privilege concept of patents was a faint echo.

---

[82] Phillips, *The Law of Patents for Inventions*, 142. See also George Ticknor Curtis, *A Treatise on the Law of Patents for Useful Inventions in the United States of America*, 2nd ed. (Boston: Little, Brown, 1854), 37. For early cases that followed Story's approach, see *Kneass v. Schuylkill Bank*, 14 F. Cas. 746 (C.C. Pa. 1820); *Whitney v. Emmett*, 29 F. Cas. 1074, 1077 (C.C.E.D. Pa. 1831).

[83] *Thompson v. Haight*, unofficially reported in "Law of Patents: Decision of Judge Van Ness," *United States Law Journal and Civilian's Magazine*, April 1823, 563.

[84] See Bracha, "The Commodification of Patents," 203–6.

[85] See e.g. *Stanley v. Whipple*, 22 F. Cas. 1046, 1048 (C.C.D. Ohio 1839); *Parker v. Stiles*, 18 F. Cas. 1163, 1175 (C.C.D. Ohio 1849); *Many v. Sizer*, 16 F. Cas. 684, 685–86 (C.C.D. Mass. 1849); *Wilbur v. Beecher*, 29 F. Cas. 1181, 1185 (N.D. N.Y. 1850); *Judson v. Moore*, 14 F. Cas. 17, 20–21 (C.C.S.D. Ohio 1859); *In re Corbin*, 6 F. Cas. 538 (C.C. D.C. 1857); *Colt v. Massachusetts Arms Co.*, 6 F. Cas. 161, 165 (C.C.D. Mass. 1851); *Carr v. Rice*, 5 F. Cas. 140, 145 (S.D. N.Y. 1856); *Wayne v. Holmes*, 29 F. Cas. 473, 476 (C.C.S.D. Ohio 1856). In *Page v. Ferry*, 18 F. Cas. 979, 982–83 (C.C.E.D. Mich. 1857), the court applied Story's formula but proceeded to bend its spirit by declaring that "new inventions in regard to some trifling article or dress, such as hoops, or crinolines" are "frivolous" and hence unpatentable.

The statutory reform of 1836 was an important landmark in this process.[86] The 1836 Patent Act was legislated after a long period of dissatisfaction with the existing framework. Complaints about the registration system varied, but most of them revolved around the insecurity of registered patents and the vagueness surrounding them. Issuing patents on demand with no prior examination resulted in their validity being highly questionable. Patentees often discovered their patents were invalid or that other patents overlapping with theirs had been issued. Purchasers of patented goods were harassed with dubious patents or paid licensing fees only to discover later that the goods they bought were covered by other conflicting patents.[87] According to a report by Henry L. Ellsworth, the Superintendent of Patents, the "villainy" included cases of people proceeding from copying models in the Patent Office display room to applying for patents on similar inventions in the adjoining room.[88] The only way to reduce the fog of uncertainty was litigation that usually occurred after reliance by patentees or the public had taken place.

The remedy of the 1836 act for these problems was a shift to an examination system. Unlike the 1790 regime, this was an examination system in the modern sense. The act specifically established the Patent Office as a subdivision of the State Department, defined its structure, and established a corps of examiners. It also provided for "an examination of the alleged new invention"[89] and mandated that "if the Commissioner shall deem it to be sufficiently useful and important, it shall be his duty to issue a patent."[90] Despite the "sufficiently useful and important" language it was clear that the newly organized Patent Office was meant to be nothing like the old Patent Board. It was set up not as a semi-political forum with discretionary powers to grant privileges, but rather as a bureaucracy whose role was to certify the satisfaction of standard patentability criteria. The underlying concepts were universality and uniformity. Decisions to reject applications could be appealed, underscoring the fact that applicants now had a right to receive a patent on meeting the patentability criteria. At first the appeal was to the board of examiners, an ad hoc tribunal composed of "three disinterested persons," one of whom possesses "knowledge and skill in the particular art."[91] But an

---

[86] Act of July 4, 1836, ch. 357, 5 Stat. 117.

[87] See Walterscheid, *To Promote the Progress*, 424–25.

[88] "Report from the Hon. Henry L. Ellsworth to the Secretary of State, and Transmitted to the Select Committee on the Patent Laws," reprinted in 8 *Mechanic's Magazine* 175, 177–78 (1836).

[89] 5 Stat. 119, §7.   [90] Id., 119–20.   [91] Id., 120.

1839 amendment replaced the board of examiners with the Chief Justice of the United States District Court for the District of Columbia.[92] The same amendment subjected to review in the federal courts "all cases where patents are refused for any reason whatever," including by decisions of the Chief Justice.[93]

The new examination system was not just a functional response to the ailments of the registration system. It was also an institutional expression of the period's Jacksonian ideology with its emphasis on formal equality and antipathy for privileged classes. Patents as government patronage were an embodiment of Whig ideals. They were based on the assumption that government could identify an objective interest common to all members of society and promote it by conferring particularistic privileges on individuals well positioned to serve that interest.[94] Colonial and state patents were deeply rooted in this "commonwealth tradition."[95] Much like corporate charters, they were particularistic governmental privileges given to specific individuals as encouragements for activities identified as promoting the public welfare.[96] This understanding of patents was transferred to the federal regime and survived even in the registration days within the judicial orthodox approach to utility.

The fundamental assumptions of the privilege concept of patents were an anathema to Jacksonian ideals that gathered force in the 1820s and

---

[92] Act of March 3, 1839, ch. 88, 5 Stat. 353, 354–55, §11.   [93] Id., 354, §10.

[94] Oscar Handlin and Mary Flug Handlin, *Commonwealth: A Study of the Role of Government in the American Economy: Massachusetts 1774–1861* (New York: New York University Press, 1947), 53–54; Harry N. Scheiber, "Government and the Economy: Studies of the Commonwealth Policy in Nineteenth Century America," 3 *J. of Interdisciplinary Hist.* 136 (1972).

[95] On the commonwealth tradition in America, see Oscar Handlin and Mary Flug Handlin, *Commonwealth: A Study of the Role of Government; Louis Hartz, Economic Policy and Democratic Thought: Pennsylvania 1776–1860* (Cambridge, Mass.: Harvard University Press, 1948); Carter Goodrich, *Government Promotion of American Canals and Railroads 1800–1890* (New York: Columbia University Press, 1960); L. Ray Gunn, *The Decline of Authority: Public Economic Policy and Political Development in New York 1800–1860* (Ithaca, N.Y.: Cornell University Press, 1988). For a general survey, see Robert A. Lively, "The American System: A Review Article," 29 *Bus. Hist. Rev.* 81 (1955); Scheiber, "Government and the Economy."

[96] On corporate charters, see Ronald E. Seavoy, *Origins of the American Business Corporation 1784–1855: Broadening the Concept of Public Service during Industrialization* (Westport, Conn.: Greenwood Press, 1982); E. Merrick Dodd Jr., *American Business Corporations until 1860* (Cambridge, Mass.: Harvard University Press, 1954); John W. Cadman Jr., *The Corporation in New Jersey: Business and Politics 1791–1875* (Cambridge, Mass.: Harvard University Press, 1949); Oscar Handlin and Mary Handlin, "Origins of the American Business Corporation," 5 *J. Econ. Hist.* 1 (1945).

1830s. At the heart of the Jacksonian outlook was a deep commitment to equal opportunity in the distribution of wealth and power.[97] Concerned by the growing inequalities of emerging American capitalism, Jacksonians saw the role of government as ensuring that the conditions for economic and social prosperity are available on an equal basis to all members of society (which at the time meant white males). As Jackson put it in his bank veto speech, government must "as Heaven does its rains, shower its favors alike on the high and the low, the rich and the poor" and not "grant titles, gratuities, and exclusive privileges, to make the rich richer and the potent more powerful."[98] Fearing the creation of an entrenched oligarchy of the "monied aristocracy," Jacksonians opposed "special class" legislation of any kind. They condemned special corporate charters, tax exemptions, subsidies, monopoly privileges, and protectionist tariffs as unequal laws based on corrupt favoritism that were bound to entrench the dominance of the wealthy few.[99] Underlying the opposition to such measures was also a declining belief that a clear, cohesive interest common to all segments of society existed or could be identified by government.[100] From this perspective, the role of government was not to encourage the few best suited to promote the public weal, but rather to foster the ability of all to prosper and pursue their own welfare on an equal basis. To reflect these ideals patents had to be handled in a way very different from the traditional privilege approach.

John Ruggles, a Jacksonian senator from Maine, a future patentee, and the moving force behind the legislation of the 1836 Patent Act, was deeply committed to these new ideals. The report he wrote and distributed widely as chair of the Senate committee for examining the patent laws was a perfect reflection of the Jacksonian creed in the universe of patents.

[97] Arthur M. Schlesinger Jr., *The Age of Jackson* (Boston: Little, Brown, 1946), 306–7; Joseph Fishkin and William E. Forbath, "The Anti-oligarchy Constitution," 94 *Boston U. L. Rev.* 671, 674 (2014). To be sure, the Jacksonian equal opportunity vision often intertwined with concerns over states' rights and the sheltering of the Southern slavery system. See Richard E. Ellis, *The Union at Risk: Jacksonian Democracy, States' Rights, and the Nullification Crisis* (New York: Oxford University Press, 1987), 198.

[98] Andrew Jackson, Veto Message (July 10, 1832), reprinted in James D. Richardson, ed., *A Compilation of the Messages and Papers of the Presidents, 1789–1897* (Washington, D.C.: G.P.O., 1896), vol. 2, 590.

[99] Lawrence Frederick Kohl, *The Politics of Individualism: Parties and the American Character in the Jacksonian Era* (New York: Oxford University Press, 1989), 215; Harry L. Watson, *Liberty and Power: The Politics of Jacksonian America* (New York: Hill and Wang 1990), 34–35; Schlesinger, *The Age of Jackson*, 334–39.

[100] Schieber, "Government and the Economy," 136; Handlin and Handlin, *Commonwealth*, 182–202.

It opened by attributing the technological advancement of England, France, and Germany to their encouragement of genius, observing that in these countries "patronage by wealthy associations" has done much "to supply whatever was wanting in the liberality of Government." It went on to observe, however, that "such patronage is necessarily partial in its operation" because "[i]t is limited to particular objects, if not to particular individuals." The superior alternative was a universal, standardized regime open to all:

There appears to be no better way of measuring out appropriate rewards for useful inventions than, by a general law, to secure to all descriptions of persons, without discrimination, the exclusive use and sale, of the thing invented.[101]

The 1836 act with its standardized, bureaucratic examination was meant to do just that. The report still referred to patents through the traditional terminology of tolerable monopolies justified by their contribution to the public good. But there was a deeper conceptual transformation here: from the Jacksonian point of view, standardized patents stopped being objectionable, special monopolies conferred on the privileged few and became universal property rights formally open to all. Just as with the later shift from special corporate charters to general incorporation statutes, it was this new feature of patents that changed their status from suspect privileges to palatable rights.[102] Arthur Schlesinger Jr. pointed out the irony of Jacksonian general incorporation statutes that ended up promoting the very ends they intended to defeat, since they "sprinkled holy water on corporations, cleansing them of the legal status of monopoly and sending them forth as the benevolent agencies of free competition."[103] The same applied to the Jacksonian attack on the traditional framework of patents. Except that here there was no gap: Jacksonians never seriously contemplated eliminating patents.

There was no greater public defender of this view of patents than the *Scientific American*. The science and technology magazine that was launched in 1845 was owned by the Munn & Co. patent agency.

---

[101] Ruggles, "1836 Senate Committee Report," 855.

[102] On the shift to general incorporation statutes, see Seavoy, *Origins of the American Business Corporation*, 191–224. Willard Hurst's observation that with the move to general incorporation the legitimacy of corporations shifted from being rooted in a specific public service performed by each to the general utility of the regime as a whole is equally applicable to patents. See Willard Hurst, *The Legitimacy of the Business Corporation in the Law of the United States 1780–1970* (Charlottesville: University Press of Virginia, 1970).

[103] Schlesinger Jr., *The Age of Jackson*, 337.

In 1850 it accused the patent examiners of being "each a feudal baron on his domain" and declared: "We like impartiality, system and fair dealing in every respect ... We care not who the applicant is, let him be Jew or Gentile." The occasion for these pronouncements was a demand for "uniform rules and regulations for all cases in the Office."[104] The magazine was particularly alarmed by proposals to subject legal rights to a substantive examination of the value of inventions. Such proposals were circulating for decades. In 1834, for example, one published essay entitled "Useless Patents" complained of the proliferation of "nonsensical machines" that find their way to the patent office. The author suggested "a jury of twelve mechanics" with "the discretionary power of denying letters patent" when the invention is "improper or useless."[105] In the early 1850s such proposals resurfaced, often suggesting to replace patents altogether with monetary rewards administered by an expert panel that would evaluate the invention. In 1850 one reader of the *Scientific American* proposed that a "corps of scientific and practical examiners at Washington" would examine each submitted invention, "decide upon its utility and pay the inventor or his representative for the same, out of a fund created for that purpose, and make the same public at once." The writer promised that such a system "would be thoroughly republican, free from both aristocracy and monopoly."[106] But the magazine was consistently outraged by such proposals. It argued that those who make them "know not what they talk about" and warned that they "may deceive the people by their sophistry."[107] The source of this adamant objection was that any proposal of this kind, no matter the promise of technocratic impartiality by experts, seemed to be a return to discretionary decisions based on substantive evaluations of social value. This was the antithesis of the Jacksonian line of standardized, universal rights. The *Scientific American* framed this objection using the classic terms of opposition to special privileges and favoritism:

This system of committee caballing and maneuvering, to lighten the pockets of Uncle Sam, and to get special monopoly privileges we do detest. Give us broad just and workable laws, and let them be carried out faithfully – none of your special systems, where favors are sought for and obtained by particular parties in a particular manner.[108]

---

[104] "Patent Office and Reform of the Patent Laws," 5 *Sci. Am.* 317 (1850).
[105] "Useless Patents," *The Mechanic* (November 1834), 344, 345.
[106] H. Baker, "Parker's Reaction Water Wheels," 5 *Sci. Am.* 315 (1850).
[107] "The Benefits of Patents," 7 *Sci. Am.* 293 (1852).
[108] "Government Rewards for Discoveries," 7 *Sci. Am.* 221 (1852).

If neither government officials nor experts could be trusted to measure the social value of inventions and reward them accordingly, who would do it? Jacksonians had a readymade answer to this question: in a universal regime of rights the market is the proper arbiter of social value and reward. The 1836 committee report on patents recommended a standardized examination system on the grounds of its superiority in measuring appropriate reward for invention. In such a system, it promised, inventors would "derive a just and appropriate encouragement proportioned to the value of their respective inventions."[109] Just as in copyright, the shift in economic and legal thought away from an objective concept of value spawned resistance to conditioning patents on any substantive evaluations of inventions.[110] Willard Phillips, who in his 1837 patent treatise prematurely declared the triumph of Justice Story's minimalist approach to utility, was also one of the writers who in the field of economics attacked the idea that goods could have inherent value detached from the subjective market demand for them. In his treatise on political economy he argued that a thing "can hardly be said to have an intrinsic value" apart from the market demand for it."[111] The two ideas, underscoring the shift toward patent rights, were intertwined: in a world that reduced all value to market demand it was only natural to restrict government's legitimate role to the administration of universal property rights seen as instruments for extracting market value. An anonymous article published in the *Atlantic Magazine* in 1825 and indexed under the subject of "intellectual economy" expressly made this connection between economic conceptions and political ideals. It preached that the principle "now acknowledged to be true, with regard to the relative value of the various branches of mere material industry" must be "extended to the finer and less palpable fabrics of the intellect." In such a system where no "branch of human industry is stimulated into more activity and growth than then natural demand would have created and sustained," the result is that "[t]he supply of literature and science will be in proportion to their demand; and their demand in proportion to their usefulness."[112]

The Jacksonian attack was thus targeted not at patents but at the old framework of patents as privileges. Patents as universal property rights

---

[109] Ruggles, "1836 Senate Committee Report," 855.   [110] See Chapter 2.
[111] Willard Phillips, *A Manual of Political Economy with Reference to the Institutions, Resources and Conditions of the United States* (Boston: Hilliard, Gray, Little, and Wilkins, 1828), 29.
[112] *Atlantic Mag.* (February 1, 1825), 272, 273.

seemed to promise both equal opportunity free of special class favoritism and proportional reward through the market. The traditional privilege framework, however, was not eliminated in one fell swoop. Under the 1836 examination regime courts still maintained the power to scrutinize patents for satisfaction of the utility requirement. For several decades many courts persisted in applying a rigorous version of the requirement under the dual assumption that to be patentable inventions had to have real demonstrable social value and that value could be judged objectively and independently from market demand. In 1846 one law journal note could still reject Story's attack on the traditional understanding of utility and make the case for this understanding in terms explicitly grounded in the privilege framework. Considering "the paternal character of the government" and the general purpose of the constitution of "progressive improvements," the writer argued, it is clear that the purpose of the intellectual property clause was to promote in the fields of science and the useful arts "progressive and successive improvement." It followed that utility in patent law meant "useful in comparison with that which it is designed to fill the sphere of, useful in the aggregate beyond it, or the inventor gives no consideration to society, and is entitled to nothing for his useless and futile labor." Requiring any less, the note concluded, "would be a legalized humbug, with the seal of the United States to give it credit and capacity for imposition."[113]

It was only around the time of the Civil War that the traditional understanding of utility and together with it the remnants of the privilege framework had gradually declined in patent law.[114] It became rare for courts to demand specific evidence of the positive social value of patented inventions. Many courts explicitly cited Story's approach and refused to invalidate patents on the basis of evaluating the social value of inventions, except in an ever-shrinking zone of extreme immorality.[115] This reflected a growing judicial reluctance to play the role of discretionary granters of privileges as opposed to that of enforcers of universal rights.

---

[113] "Thoughts upon the Rights of Patentees," 3 *Western L. J.* 471, 472–73 (1846).

[114] On the decline of the traditional view of utility and its connection to the new concept of market value, see Armstrong, "From the Fetishism of Commodities to the Regulated Market," 93–96; Bracha, "The Commodification of Patents," 234–35.

[115] See e.g. *Roberts v. Ward*, 20 F. Cas. 936 (C.C.D. Mich. 1849); *Wintermute v. Redington*, 30 F. Cas. 367, 370 (C.C.N.D. Ohio 1856); *Lee v. Blandy*, 15 F. Cas. 142, 145 (C.C.S.D. Ohio 1860); *Tilghman v. Werk*, 23 F. Cas. 1260 (C.C.S.D. Ohio 1862); *Seymour v. Osborne*, 78 U.S. 516, 549 (1870); *Crouch v. Speer*, 6 F. Cas. 897, 898 (C.C.D. N.J. 1874); *Gibbs v. Hoefner*, 19 F. 323, 324 (C.C.N.D. N.Y. 1884).

The reasoning of courts taking such attitudes was often laced with the concept of market value. Sales of the invention to the public, a factor whose relevance Justice Livingstone could dismiss offhandedly in 1822, came to be frequently accepted as evidence of utility.[116] Another argument that had become popular in this context was that an infringer could never argue lack of utility in the invention, because the very fact that he or she used it proved that there was some demand and thus some value to it.[117] One court succinctly summarized the new approach in 1886: "any element which increases the salability of an article may be said to contain the elements of utility."[118]

The utility doctrine had never disappeared altogether, but it had ceased being a central defining feature of patents. By the end of the nineteenth century the utility requirement had become the exotic periphery of patent law, composed of exceptional cases of gambling devices,[119] snake-oil medicine,[120] and exploding machines.[121] The discussion of utility in Albert Walker's 1889 patent treatise demonstrates the radical transformation of the requirement. More than seventy years earlier Justice Story gave the example of an invention whose entire purpose is to poison others as one of the extreme cases falling within the zone of immorality where a patent must be denied on utility grounds. But what about an invention whose purpose is to shoot others? Walker used Colt's revolver as an example of an invention that has both social benefits and injurious effects on the morals, health, and good order of society. "By what test . . . is utility to be determined in such cases?" he asked. His answer was unequivocal: "everything [is] useful within the meaning of the law if it can be used to accomplish a good result, though in fact it is oftener to accomplish a bad one." Firmly rejecting the possibility of "balancing the good functions with the evil functions," Walker explained that this criterion "cannot stand, because if it could it would make the validity of the patents to depend on a question of fact, to which it would often be

[116] See *Lorillard v. McDowell*, 15 F. Cas. 893, 894 (C.C.E.D. Pa. 1877); *Magowan v. New York Belting & Packing Co.*, 141 U.S. 332, 343 (1891); *Gandy v. Main Belting Co.*, 143 U.S. 587, 593 (1892). See also William C. Robinson, *Law of Patents for Useful Inventions* (Boston: Little, Brown, 1890), vol. 1, 467.
[117] See *Lehnbeuter v. Holthaus*, 105 U.S. 94, 97 (1882); *Vance v. Campbell*, 28 F. Cas. 956, 958 (C.C.S.D. Ohio 1859); *Smith v. Prior*, 22 F. Cas. 629 (C.C.D. Cal. 1873).
[118] *Nebury v. Fowler*, 28 F. 454, 460 (C.C.D. Ill. 1886).
[119] See e.g. *Schultz v. Holtz*, 82 F. 448 (N.D. Cal. 1897); *National Automatic Device Co. v. Lloyd*, 40 F. 89 (C.C.D. Ill. 1889).
[120] See *Richard v. Du Bon*, 103 F. 868, 873 (2nd Cir. 1900).
[121] See *Mitchell v. Tilghman*, 86 U.S. 287 (1874).

impossible to give a reliable answer."[122] The hypothetical underscores how far patents had come. The activity that previously had been the most fundamental duty of the sovereign when granting patents – the balancing of "good and evil" to establish whether the invention serves the public good – now became a forbidden zone. A previous conviction that patents are based on an ad hoc calculus of social cost and benefit now gave way before the axiom that reliable answers to such questions are impossible. By the end of the nineteenth century the last vestiges of the privilege framework dissolved and patents became rights. This process redefined the relationship between the sovereign and the patent owner. Who, however, could qualify as a patent owner?

PRODUCTS OF GENIUS

In 1793 Joseph Barnes wrote that "[o]f property there are two species, viz. *local* and *mental*." While the former meant personal and real property, the latter included "the *products* of *genius*, which consists in discoveries in science, and in the useful arts; by means of which agriculture, navigation, manufactures, and manual labor are, not only facilitated, but much promoted."[123] Barnes had written the short pamphlet, which he ambitiously called "Treatise on the Justice, Policy, and Utility of Establishing an Effectual System for Promoting the Progress of Useful Arts, by Assuring Property in the Products of Genius," for a specific purpose. Congress was in the process of revising the patent laws, and Barnes, deeply involved in early patent practice, had some strong opinions on how to do it. Self-interest notwithstanding, Barnes captured the time's understanding of patents and its strong association with a new image of the inventor.

For most of the colonial period technological innovation was not strongly associated with community welfare or progress.[124] Inventions and inventors did not hold their later heroic status and they only seldom caught the public eye, usually as curiosities.[125] These attitudes were reflected in colonial quasi-patents. These individual legislative privileges did not single out technological innovation as a separate sphere meriting a

---

[122] Albert H. Walker, *Text Book of the Patent Laws of the United States of America*, 2nd ed. (New York: L.K. Strouse, 1889), 64–65.

[123] Barnes, *Treatise on the Justice, Policy, and Utility*, 4.

[124] Neil Longley York, *Mechanical Metamorphosis: Technological Change in Revolutionary America* (Westport, Conn.: Greenwood Press, 1985), 6; Hugo A. Meier, "American Technology and the Nineteenth-Century World," 10 *American Quarterly* 117 (1958).

[125] York, *Mechanical Metamorphosis*, 44–46.

targeted policy. The grants were given to entrepreneurs or craftsmen in return for putting into practice a publicly beneficial economic activity. Technological innovation was an occasional background element, rather than an essential feature of these grants.[126] Nor did colonial grants envision technological innovation in intellectual or informational terms. Skilled craftsmen who were often in demand were not defined by intellectual capacities or by an ability to make discoveries. Although often innovative, the positive defining features of craftsmen were their technical skills and actual useful activities.[127]

Around the time of the Revolution these attitudes began to change. Technology gradually captured the minds of Americans and came to be seen as a key for national prosperity and power. Conflicts with Britain over technological transfer and the proliferation of manufacturing and useful arts societies fueled this process.[128] As technology emerged as a distinct important sphere, technological innovation became the defining feature of the increasingly differentiated category of the inventor. The figure of the inventor, marked by his intellectual capacities for creating new technological developments, gradually achieved recognition and even fame.[129] These developments were reflected in state patent privileges, many of which came to emphasize technological innovation, treat invention as a special category, and occasionally exhibit some concerns about originality or priority.[130] The practice of state patents also gave rise to new justifications for legal rights focused on the figure of the inventor. These justifications comprised an uneasy mix of utilitarian and natural rights arguments. The earlier emphasis on encouraging a useful economic activity by entrepreneurs or craftsmen was supplanted by two kinds of arguments. One relied on the justice of protecting the natural property rights of inventors in the product of their intellectual labor. The other celebrated the social utility of encouraging inventors to engage in their creative mental activity and bestow its beneficial fruits on society.[131]

---

[126] See Oren Bracha, "Geniuses and Owners: The Construction of Inventors and the Emergence of American Intellectual Property," in Daniel W. Hamilton and Alfred L. Brophy, eds., *Transformations in American Legal History: Essays in Honor of Professor Morton J. Horwitz* (Cambridge, Mass.: Harvard Law School, 2009), 372.

[127] Id., 372–73.

[128] On technology transfer, see Ben-Atar, *Trade Secrets*, 34–43; John F. Kasson, *Civilizing the Machine: Technology and Republican Values in America, 1776–1900* (New York: Grossman, 1976), 8–11. On manufacturing and useful art societies, see Ben-Atar, *Trade Secrets*, 93–103; York, *Mechanical Metamorphosis*, 163–71.

[129] See York, *Mechanical Metamorphosis*, 183–206.

[130] Bracha, "Geniuses and Owners," 373–74.   [131] Id., 374–75.

Common to both was the new centrality of the inventor. By the time of the first federal patent regime, patents were already firmly grounded within this new ideological framework. The constitutional clause and the 1790 act demarcated a special sphere of the "useful arts" and defined the focus of patents as the rights of "inventors."[132] Patents were now the unique and exclusive domain of inventors, defined as innovators in the realm of technological ideas.

In the first decades of the patent regime the new figure of the inventor made many rhetorical appearances and was often explicitly tied to exclusive legal rights. This attested to the importance of the concept, but also to the fragility of the new status claimed for it. Thus, midway through his pamphlet on the mental property of inventors, Barnes lapsed into a long discussion of Archimedes and his services to the king of Syracuse.[133] Thomas Fessenden spent long pages in the introduction of the first American patent treatise published by him in 1810 describing the technological achievements of inventors of many cultures in history ranging from those of ancient Egypt to the Medicis.[134] The short-lived magazine the *Useful Cabinet* featured a lengthy series of pseudo-historical essays entitled "Origin of Arts." The series supplied "a brief chronological history of the various inventions and discoveries in the sciences and mechanic arts, to which mankind are indebted for civilization, and all the valuable enjoyments of wealth, power, equal laws, and civil governments."[135] The declared purpose of the series was to correct a historiographical wrong: "we are struck with astonishment at the genius and labor the historian has exhibited, in raising monuments of lasting fame to the memory of ambitious adventurers, whose lives were spent in the destruction of their fellow creatures, while scarcely any mention is made of those benefactors, who by their inventions and discoveries have conferred upon mankind real and permanent benefit."[136] The hoped-for effect of this correction was "to create a sense of gratitude toward those, who have multiplied the blessings of life, and a spirit of patronage."[137] The editor of the *Useful Cabinet* was Benjamin Dearborn, who in 1806 founded the New England Association of Inventors and Patrons of Useful Arts. One of the main goals of the association, listed in its

[132] U.S. Const. art. I, sec. 8, cl. 8; 1 Stat. 109, §1.
[133] Barnes, *Treatise on the Justice, Policy, and Utility*, 6–7.
[134] Thomas G. Fessenden, *An Essay on the Law of Patents for New Inventions* (Boston: D. Mallory, 1810).
[135] "Origin of Arts," Useful Cabinet, January 1808, 21.   [136] Id., 21–22.   [137] Id., 22.

constitution, was to cultivate a "liberal disposition to protect and patronize the production of genius."[138]

The genius inventor was to American patents what the romantic author was to copyright. It was a powerful ideological concept that took its place at the heart of patent thought at the moment that the American patent system was created. Just as in copyright, however, there was a gap between the unqualified embrace of the new abstract concept of inventorship and its instantiation within the actual institutional details of patent law. In some respects, early American patent law did express the ideology of inventorship on which it was based. One example was the question of patents of importation. These were patents in technology not invented in the modern sense, but rather imported into the country. Under old English law, the importer of new technology was just as much an inventor as the developer.[139] But this was hardly compatible with the new ideological status of the genius creator. Britain would follow the traditional rule recognizing patents of importation well into the nineteenth century. By contrast the American 1790 act and its successors did not mention the importer of technology as a potential patentee, apparently due to a conscious intention by the drafters to exclude such patents.[140] Despite some ambiguity and debate that persisted for decades,[141] the dominant view that appeared early on was that the only beneficiary of the patent regime was the "true inventor" and not the mere importer.[142] It is possible that in practice early federal patents were given to importers of technology, but the break of the formal rule with the British tradition was a clear expression of the new importance of inventorship.

A similar if somewhat murkier pattern appeared in the context of priority of invention. One would expect a patent system that takes seriously the concept of the inventor to care about priority of invention and prefer the original first inventor. Despite some engagement with the

---

[138] *Rules and Regulations Adopted October 22nd, 1807 by the Association of Inventors and Patrons of Useful Arts* (1807), section 15.

[139] *Edgeberry v. Stephens*, 91 Eng. Rep. 387 (K.B. 1691).

[140] During the legislative process of the 1790 Patent Act, language that expressly mandated patents of importation was added to the statute's draft and later was struck out. See Walterscheid, *To Promote the Progress*, 121, 125–28, 137. This legislative history suggests that the possibility of importation patents was contemplated and rejected.

[141] See also id., 379–82.

[142] See *Reutgen v. Kanowrs*, 20 F. Cas. 555, 556 (C.C.D. Pa. 1804); *Dawson v. Follen*, 7 F. Cas. 216 (C.C. Pa. 1808); *Evans v. Eaton*, 8 F. Cas. 846, 853 (C.C.D. Pa. 1816). It is possible that at least some of the earliest patents granted in the United States were importation patents. See id., 379.

question during the legislative process, the 1790 statutory regime remained completely silent on the issue.[143] It seems that the Patent Board did its best to avoid deciding priority disputes.[144] By contrast, the 1793 regime included a detailed arbitration system for determining priority of invention in cases of disputes.[145] The arrangement was toothless and probably ineffective and the statute was still completely silent regarding the substantive rule of priority.[146] It was only in 1836 that an effective system of "interferences" was put into place, and the rule that favored the first to invent that would become the hallmark of American patents was clearly legislated.[147] Nevertheless the early engagement with the question of priority and the creation of a detailed institutional mechanism for dealing with it is indicative of the rising importance of the modern notion of the inventor. The contrast with Britain is telling. Although the 1624 Statute of Monopolies mandated that patents could be granted only to the "true and first inventor,"[148] by the late eighteenth century there were not yet in Britain clear rules and procedures for determining priority.[149] When such rules consolidated there during the nineteenth century, they gave priority to the first person to file a patent application rather than to the first to invent.[150]

Yet another doctrinal reflection of the new concept of the inventor followed the British example rather than broke with it. The traditional English rule going back to the seventeenth century was that lawful patents

[143] During the legislation process several suggestions pertaining to the procedure of determining priority of invention were considered, but the final act remained silent on both procedure and substantive standard. See E.C. Walterscheid, "Priority of Invention: How the United States Came to Have a 'First to Invent' Patent System," 23 *AIPLA Q.J.* 263, 283–91 (1996).

[144] When the Patent Board was faced with the question of priority in the high-profile struggle over the steamboat patent involving no less than four claimants – John Fitch, James Rumsey, Nathan Read, and John Stevens – the board most probably avoided making a priority determination and simply issued four patents, presumably not overlapping in coverage. Walterscheid, *To Promote the Progress*, 184–94; Walterscheid, "Priority of Invention," 296–97.

[145] 1 Stat. 319, §9.

[146] Walterscheid, "Priority of Invention," 309–13. In 1816 Justice Story ruled that a refusal to participate in the priority arbitration process was not a ground for voiding a patent. *Stearns v. Barret*, 22 F. Cas. 1175 (C.C.D. Mass. 1816).

[147] 5 Stat. 119–21, §§7–8.   [148] 21 James I cap. 3., §6.

[149] See Walterscheid, "Priority of Invention," 265–69.

[150] See Richard Godson, *A Practical Treatise on the Law of Patents for Inventions and of Copyright* (London: J. Butterworth and Son, 1823), 54–55; W.A. Hindmarch, *A Treatise on the Law Relative to Patent Privileges for the Sole Use of Inventions* (Harrisburg, Pa.: I.G. M'Kinley and J.M.G. Lescure, printers 1847), 19–20.

could be granted only to new manufactures and not to improvements of existing ones.[151] The reason for the rule was that an improvement was "but to put a new button on an old coat."[152] In the early seventeenth century when the concept of patents was dominated by the idea of introducing new industries or trades and technological innovation played only a minor background role, the rule made perfect sense to contemporaries. By the late eighteenth century, when technological innovation took over patent thought, it had become unintelligible. English cases from this time simply dismissed the rule against improvements, describing it as an empty scholastic distinction that if taken seriously would invalidate any patent ever granted.[153] In the United States there was no question. The 1790 act and its successors explicitly included any "improvement" as patentable subject matter.[154] At this point in time English law had just come around to rejecting the centuries-old distinction between introducing a new trade and mere improvements. In the American patent system, born wrapped in the ideology of inventorship, this distinction could never take root.

THE GENIUS AND THE MECHANIC

Some aspects of early American patent law reflected its official ideal of inventorship. But the heart of the ideal found no expression in the law. The image of the genius inventor, as it was deployed rhetorically countless times, meant much more than someone who independently developed some minor technological tinkering. Joel Barlow's 1787 lines, "While rising clouds, with genius unconfined/Through deep inventions lead the astonish'd mind," for example, promised ingenuity, intellectual prowess, and value.[155] In another version from an 1807 pamphlet, the inventor

---

[151] The sources of the rule were the unreported Mathey and Bricot cases. Bricot's case was decided in Exchequer Chamber and is known mainly from Edward Coke's reference to it his *Institutes*. See Edward Coke, *The Third Part of the Institutes of the Laws of England* (London: E. and R. Brooke, 1797), 183. Mathey's case was decided in the Privy Council and is known from a reference in one of the reports of *Darcy v. Allen*. See *Allen v. Darcy*, 74 Eng. Rep. 1131 (K.B. 1603). See also abridgment of the case in Charles Viner, *A General Abridgment of Law and Equity*, 2nd ed. (London: G.G.J. and J. Robinson, 1793), 201–11.

[152] Coke, *Institutes*, 183.

[153] The watershed moment was the 1776 unreported decision in *Morris v. Bramson*. The case is known mainly from a reference to it in *Boulton & Watt v. Bull*, 126 Eng. Rep. 651, 664 (C.P. 1795).

[154] See 1 Stat. 109, §1; 1 Stat. 318, §§1–2.

[155] Joel Barlow, *The Vision of Columbus* (Hartford, Conn.: Hudson and Goodwin, 1787), 203.

ranks "highest in the scale of useful beings," while "[n]ext to him rank the farmer and mechanic, and to this trio are the world indebted for all artificial enjoyments."[156] Of course, during this time most technological innovators *were* "mechanics," meaning skilled machinists working in small workshops and occasionally engaging in tinkering.[157] The new sharp distinction between the inventor and the mechanic on the basis of mental capacity and output was predominantly an ideological move. For the entire nineteenth century the rich ideological image of the genius inventor, its expression in the law, and the gap between the two would preoccupy jurists and provide a store of rhetorical and legal strategies for interested parties.

Occasional attempts to adjust patent doctrine to reflect a more robust standard of inventorship started early on. In 1791, for example, a bill that would eventually become the Patent Act of 1793 denied patent protection to an invention that "is so unimportant and obvious that it ought not to be the subject of an exclusive right."[158] This text never made it into the final version of the act. It was only in 1825, however, that the genius inventor received his chance to fight for recognition in patent doctrine. It was a complete failure. The defendant in *Earle v. Sawyer* faced a difficult situation. He had to admit that the plaintiff's patented shingle-making machine was new.[159] Arguing the case in Joseph Story's circuit, his attorneys probably also realized that trying to challenge the utility of the machine was not a promising strategy. The alternative was to attack the patent by denying that the patentee was an inventor. In essence, the defense argument was that being an inventor required much more than simply creating something new. The patentee's only contribution was replacing the perpendicular saw in existing designs with a circular saw. That, the argument went, was the tinkering of the ordinary mechanic rather than the ingenuity of the inventor; something that "deserves not the name of an invention."[160] And thus "[t]here was considerable conflict of testimony in the cause (which was left to the jury), as to the question whether the application of

[156] *Remarks on the Rights of Inventors and the Influence of Their Studies in Promoting the Enjoyments of Life and Public Prosperity* (Boston: E. Lincoln 1807), 8.
[157] See Paul Israel, *From Machine Shop to Industrial Laboratory: Telegraphy and the Changing Context of American Invention, 1830–1920* (Baltimore, Md.: Johns Hopkins University Press, 1992), 18; Nathan Rosenberg, "Technological Change in the Machine Tool Industry, 1840–1910," 23 *J. Econ. Hist.* 414–43 (1963).
[158] H.R. 121. Reprinted in Walterscheid, *To Promote the Progress*, 470.
[159] *Earle v. Sawyer*, 8 F. Cas. 254 (C.C.D. Mass.1825).   [160] Id., 255.

the circular saw to the old machine was an invention or not, scientific witnesses differing in opinion on the subject."[161]

In his decision, Justice Story restated the argument, clearly capturing the underlying distinction between an ordinary tinkerer and an inventor:

It is not sufficient, that a thing is new and useful, to entitle the author of it to a patent. He must do more. He must find it out by mental labor and intellectual creation. If the result of accident, it must be what would not occur to all persons skilled in the art, who wished to produce the same result. There must be some addition to the common stock of knowledge, and not merely the first use of what was known before ... An invention is the finding out by some effort of the understanding. The mere putting of two things together, although never done before, is no invention.[162]

Then he flatly rejected it. "It is of no consequence," he wrote, "whether the thing be simple or complicated; whether it be by accident, or by long, laborious thought, or by an instantaneous flash of mind, that it is first done." Instead, the law "gives the first inventor, or discoverer of the thing, the exclusive right, and asks nothing as to the mode or extent of the application of his genius to conceive or execute it."[163] The dry legal reasoning was that the statutory language required only that the patented subject matter be new and useful. As the statute also had ample references to inventing and inventors, this textual reasoning hardly was inescapable. What actually motivated the rejection of a separate inventorship requirement in *Earle* remains unknown. It does not seem far-fetched, however, to assume that the inventive quality argument seemed to be a threat to the framework of patent law as free from all substantive judgments of value that Story had painstakingly toiled to develop since 1817. Determining whether a developer of technology was a genuine inventor seemed to tread dangerously close to making substantive judgments about the quality of the invention or the mental process that produced it. Story preferred to limit the statutory requirements to the seemingly neutral parameters of novelty and his eviscerated version of utility, leaving all value determinations to the market.

Earle's approach dominated the first half of the century. In the rare occasion when an argument was made that patents were limited to cases where a special inventive quality was present, the response was that "[n]ovelty and utility in the improvement seem to be all that the law requires."[164] The question of inventorship was swept under the rug

---

[161] Id., 254.　　[162] Id., 255.　　[163] Id., 256.
[164] *McCormick v. Seymour*, 15 F. Cas. 1322 (C.C.D. N.Y. 1853). See also *Adams v. Edwards*, 1 F. Cas. 112, 113 (C.C.D. Mass. 1848).

during this period, but it did not disappear. The rug was the novelty requirement. Unlike its later incarnation, the requirement that a patentable invention must be new was not read narrowly as limiting anticipation to cases of complete or nearly complete identity between a patented invention and preexisting technology. The question of identity was common to the context of novelty and infringement. During this period courts applied the same tests to determine whether there was anticipation of the invention by an earlier machine or art and whether it was infringed by subsequent ones. Both were governed by the concept of substantial identity. The original grounding of the concept was the statutory language in the 1793 act that "simply changing the form or the proportions of any machine, or composition of matter, in any degree shall not be deemed a discovery."[165] The text probably found its way into the American enactment from a 1791 French statute, but in the United States it assumed a life of its own.[166] Courts built on it the rule that legal identity of technologies did not require full identity. It was enough that the two devices were the same in principle and no exact duplication of form was required.[167]

The metaphysics of substantial identity opened up room for maneuver, and this space was often filled up with discussions of the nature of invention. Speakers naturally moved back and forth between the question of whether a patented device was different in principle and not just in form from earlier devices and the inquiry of whether it was a creation of an inventor rather than a mere adaptation of an existing device. Phillips' 1837 discussion of substantial novelty was typical of this tendency. The rule that "simply changing the form or the proportions of any machine, or composition of matter in any degree, shall not be deemed a discovery," he explained, is "but the branch of a more general rule in giving a construction to the law, namely, that any change or modification of a machine or other patentable subject, which would be obvious to every person acquainted with the use of it, and which makes no material

---

[165] 1 Stat. 321, §2.

[166] See John Duffy, "Inventing Invention: A Case Study of Legal Innovation," 86 *Tex. L. Rev.* 1, 36 (2007); Phillips, *The Law of Patents for Inventions*, 135.

[167] *Evans v. Eaton*, 8 F. Cas. 846, 852 (C.C.D. Pa. 1816); *Gray v. James*, 10 F. Cas. 1019, 1020 (C.C.D. Pen. 1817); *Evans v. Eaton*, 20 U.S. 356, 431 (1822); *Davis v. Palmer*, 7 F. Cas. 154, 159 (C.C.D. Vir. 1827); *Whitney v. Emmett*, 29 F. Cas. 1078. See generally Kenneth J. Burchfiel, "Revising the 'Original' Patent Clause," 2 *Harv. J. L. Tech.* 155, 191–202 (1989).

alterations in the mode and principle of its operation, and by which no material addition is made, is not a ground for claiming a patent."[168]

Philips, however, also observed that "the sufficiency of the invention depends not upon the labor, skill, study or expense applied or bestowed upon it."[169] If skill and labor were irrelevant, what was the quality that distinguished real invention? Some courts and commentators simply equated this quality with substantial differences in the mechanical operation or design of the invention.[170] Thus an inventive quality was what defined substantial difference, and substantial difference defined, in turn, the inventive quality. Others who tried to fill this formula with more content usually ended up turning to the substantive value of the invention. George Ticknor Curtis' treatment of the subject in his 1854 treatise is a classic example of how substantial identity, inventive quality, and value were fused together. Curtis started his discussion with the *Earle* orthodoxy under which "it is of no consequence whether a great or small amount of thought, ingenuity, skill, labor or experiment has been expended."[171] Next, however, there came an important qualification: "It may not be necessary that there should be positive evidence of design, thought or ingenuity, but it is necessary that the possibility of these qualities having been exercised should not be excluded by the character of the supposed invention."[172] What was the meaning of this odd potential-ingenuity criterion? It quickly became apparent that Curtis equated inventorship with material improvement:

... the utility of the change, and the consequences resulting therefrom may be such, as to show that the inventive faculty may have been at work; and in such cases though in point of fact, the change was the result of accident its utility and importance will afford the requisite test of the amount of invention involved in the change.[173]

In many cases, Curtis explained, "the materiality and novelty of the change can be judged of only by the effect on the result; and this effect is tested by the actual improvement."[174] For Curtis novelty became

[168] Phillips, *The Law of Patents for Inventions*, 125–26. See also *Hovey v. Stevens*, 12 F. Cas. 609, 612 (C.C.D. Mass. 1846).

[169] Phillips, *The Law of Patents for Inventions*, 127.

[170] See e.g. *Whittemore v. Cutter*, 29 F. Cas. 1123, 1124 (C.C.D. Mass. 1813); *Gray v. James*, 10 F. Cas. 1020; *Davis v. Palmer*, 7 F. Cas. 159; Phillips, *The Law of Patents for Inventions*, 126.

[171] Curtis, *A Treatise on the Law of Patents*, 27.   [172] Id., 28.   [173] Id., 29.

[174] Id., 30.

synonymous with "beneficial results, superior to what had been before attained" or with "the utility of the change."[175] Many antebellum court decisions exhibited similar reasoning. Substantial novelty occurred, the argument went, when the change of an existing form produced new substantial or more than trivial value. This was not the only test, but courts frequently identified novelty with "new and greater advantage"[176] or with "a "better, cheaper, or quicker method."[177] The question of identity and the degree of added value tended to merge in this way, or as one court put it: "An improvement upon an old contrivance, in order to be of sufficient importance to be the subject of a patent, must embody some originality, and something substantial in the change producing a more useful effect and operation."[178] Ironically, the rule that Story devised in *Earle* to avoid substantive value judgments only too often led courts exactly to such inquiries.

THE INVENTIVE FACULTY

The 1851 Supreme Court decision in *Hotchkiss v. Greenwood* is commonly considered the moment when an independent requirement of inventorship was introduced into American patent law.[179] The invention at issue was a doorknob whose only improvement over existing designs was the substitution of clay or porcelain for the wood or metal previously used. The trial court had instructed the jury that if "no more ingenuity or skill required to construct the knob in this way than that possessed by an ordinary mechanic acquainted with the business, the patent was invalid."[180] On appeal, Justice Samuel Nelson, writing for the majority, upheld this instruction and the lower's court judgment that found the patent void. His opinion shifted the focus of the analysis from added value to the intellectual skill that he saw as the hallmark of true invention. The analysis was premised on the assumption that the new doorknob was a substantial improvement since "by connecting the clay or porcelain knob with the metallic shank in this well-known mode, an article is produced better and cheaper than in the case of the metallic or wood knob."[181] Nelson concluded, however, that "this, of itself, can never be

---

[175] Id., 31, 36.   [176] *Hovey v. Stevens*, 12 F. Cas. 612.
[177] *Whitney v. Emmet*, 29 F. Cas. 1078. See also *Treadwell v. Bladen*, 24 F. Cas. 144, 146 (C.C.E.D. Pa. 1831).
[178] *Hall v. Wiles*, 11 F. Cas. 280, 283 (S.D. N.Y. 1851).   [179] 52 U.S. 248 (1851).
[180] Id., 265.   [181] Id., 266.

the subject of a patent," because "the difference is formal, and destitute of ingenuity or invention."[182] The material point was not whether the new doorknob was better, but whether it could be said to be the product of an inventor. To convey this point Nelson drew on the familiar distinction between the ingenious inventor and the mere mechanic: "more ingenuity and skill ... were required ... than were possessed by an ordinary mechanic acquainted with the business, there was an absence of that degree of skill and ingenuity which constitute essential elements of every invention. In other words, the improvement is the work of the skilful mechanic, not that of the inventor."[183]

Justice Levi Woodbury wrote a strong dissent. He appealed to *Earle* and its progeny as authority for the proposition that "the skill necessary to construct it, on which both the court below and the court here rely, is an immaterial inquiry."[184] It is likely that Woodbury, an avid Jacksonian, saw an inventive ingenuity requirement as a suspiciously elitist threat to the democratized patent system that he favored. Ironically, in rejecting such a requirement he turned to the concrete meaning of substantial novelty that had developed in the courts in the decades following *Earle*, one that was based on assessing the substantive social value of the claimed invention. The crucial fact to which Woodbury's opinion appealed repeatedly was that the new doorknob was doubtless "better and cheaper." The "true test of its being patentable," Woodbury said, was not whether "an ordinary mechanic could have made or devised it," but rather "if the invention was new, and better and cheaper than what preceded it."[185] Inventions made "without the exercise of great skill, which are still in themselves both novel and useful," he wrote, "are entitled to protection by a patent, because they improve or increase the power, convenience, and wealth of the community."[186]

Fearing that the distinction between the inventor and the mechanic was an elitist barrier on access to patents, Woodbury was pushed to embrace instead judgments of substantive social value usually frowned on by Jacksonians. Nelson, by contrast, was swayed by other considerations. His distinction between the inventor and the mechanic appears to have been motivated by a genuine belief in an inherent meaning of inventorship. He saw intellectual ingenuity as the defining feature of the inventor. Three years later Nelson would write an opinion that was a copyright twin of *Hotchkiss*. He premised it on the proposition that copyright could

---

[182] Id.   [183] Id., 267.   [184] Id., 269.   [185] Id., 268.   [186] Id., 269.

apply only to the work of a true author exhibiting mental ingenuity as opposed to that of the mere mechanic of ordinary skill in the relevant expressive art.[187]

Hotchkiss was not immediately seen as a cosmic event in American patent law. In later cases courts adhered to traditional substantial novelty analysis and did not seem to assume that the decision created a new inventiveness requirement.[188] Even when *Hotchkiss* began to take root it was at first understood as applicable only to a limited category of substitution of material cases, and its incompatibility with the *Earle* rule was often overlooked.[189] It was only after the Civil War that the new standard was generally recognized. In the last quarter of the century the general rule became that "[n]ovelty and utility must indeed characterize the subject of a patent; but they alone are not enough to make anything patentable ... things to be patented must be invented things, as well as new and useful things."[190] As originality in copyright, inventorship came to be seen as a fundamental element of patents inherent in the concept of an inventor. Some courts even suggested that the invention requirement was grounded on the constitutional level. In the 1885 *Thompson v. Boisselier*, for example, Justice Samuel Blatchford remarked that "[t]he provision of the Constitution, Art. 1, sec. 8, subdivision 8, is, that the Congress shall have power 'to promote the progress of science and useful arts, by securing for limited times to authors and inventors the exclusive right to their respective writings and discoveries.' The beneficiary must be an inventor and he must have made a discovery."[191]

What triggered this belated blooming of the inventorship principle in patent law? The 1870s saw a wave of discontent over the proliferation of patents and their alleged deleterious effect on legitimate business. Such waves occurred before, but this time the attack on patents was backed by a heavyweight contender: railroad companies. In the 1860s, stirred by a wave of infringement lawsuits and increasingly sophisticated strategies by patentees targeting their technological systems, railroads began to see

---

[187] *Jollie v. Jaques*, 13 F. Cas. 910 (S.D. N.Y. 1850).
[188] See Burchfiel, "Revising the 'Original' Patent Clause," 204–8.
[189] Id., 204. This helps to explain why in a reported decision following *Hotchkiss* Justice Nelson held that only novelty and utility were required to sustain patentability. See *McCormick v. Seymour*, 15 F. Cas. 1323.
[190] Walker, *Text Book of the Patent Laws*, 21.
[191] *Thompson v. Boisselier*, 114 U.S. 1, 11 (1884). See also *Gardner v. Herz*, 118 U.S. 180, 191–92 (1886); *Johnston v. Woodbury*, 96 F. 421, 434 (C.C.N.D. Cal. 1899).

patents as a major threat.[192] To protect themselves the railroads launched a two-pronged attack on patents in Congress and in the courts. One of the main arguments employed by the antipatent advocates was a critique of the harmful economic effects of fragmented property rights in numerous trifle innovations. As one railroad attorney put it in an 1878 congressional hearing, there were "fifteen times as many patents as ought to issue."[193] In terms remarkably similar to modern-day critique of patent thickets, he argued that this proliferation of patents interferes with the "progress and steady improvement" of "lines" of innovation.[194] Describing how a single technological innovation can be subject to numerous crisscrossing patents, he observed that patents "for the most insignificant things in the world" lead to "constantly and uniformly arising" infringement claims that are "difficult and embarrassing."[195]

In making their case against the proliferation of trivial patents, the advocates of railroads turned the traditional argument on its head: patents, they said, were becoming a drag on economic innovation and progress rather than a motivating force. Perhaps, as suggested by Herbert Hovenkamp, these arguments were also implicitly drawing on emerging marginalist economic thought. From this perspective, as the number of patents increased significantly, their marginal beneficial contribution decreased and their potential negative effects multiplied.[196]

The vehicle chosen for making all of these arguments about the economic effects of patents was the figure of the inventor. Given patents' firm grounding in the ideology of inventorship, alluding to an absence of the inventive quality was a natural and effective way of framing the issue. When courts started enforcing a meaningful inventiveness requirement, they turned exactly to this fusion of arguments about economic effects and inventive qualities. The Supreme Court's opinion in the 1882 *Atlantic Works v. Brady* was a classic example:

> To grant to a single party a monopoly of every slight advance made, except where the exercise of invention, somewhat above ordinary mechanical or engineering skill, is distinctly shown, is unjust in principle and injurious in its consequences ... The design of the patent laws is to reward those who make some substantial

[192] Steven W. Usselman, "Patent Politics: Intellectual Property, the Railroad Industry, and the Problem of Monopoly," 18 *J. Policy Hist.* 96, 107–9 (2006).
[193] *Arguments before the Committee on Patents of the Senate and the House*, 45 Cong., 3rd Sess. (1878), 110.
[194] Id.   [195] Id., 111.
[196] Herbert Hovenkamp, *The Opening of American Law: Neoclassical Legal Thought, 1870–1970* (New York: Oxford University Press, 2015), 189–91.

discovery or invention, which adds to our knowledge and makes a step in advance in the useful arts. Such inventors are worthy of all favor. It was never the object of those laws to grant a monopoly for every trifling device, every shadow of a shade of an idea, which would naturally and spontaneously occur to any skilled mechanic or operator in the ordinary progress of manufactures. Such an indiscriminate creation of exclusive privileges tends rather to obstruct than to stimulate invention. It creates a class of speculative schemers who make it their business to watch the advancing wave of improvement, and gather its foam in the form of patented monopolies, which enable them to lay a heavy tax upon the industry of the country, without contributing anything to the real advancement of the arts.[197]

This prose reflected, almost in the exact same words, the antipatent arguments of the railroads. Its author was Justice Joseph P. Bradley, the Court's patent expert, who wrote several of its decisive, new inventorship opinions. Prior to being appointed to the Court, Bradley served for many years as the general counsel of the Camden and Amboy Railroad.[198] Bradley's patent jurisprudence was complex and far from uniformly hostile to patents.[199] Here, however, he was clearly stating the wisdom he internalized or cultivated during his years in practice.

The late revival of the genius inventor was thus not accidental. While the concept carried its own ideological weight, it was also a convenient vehicle for framing and incorporating into legal doctrine the economic concerns of the day and the worries of powerful interests. Whatever the reason, at last, so it seemed, patent law was taking seriously the ideological image of the inventor on which it was based for a century. Treatises would now have long sections devoted to "invention." The new fundamental element of patentability was described as requiring that to merit a patent "a thing must be the product of some exercise of the inventive faculties."[200] "An invention," William Robinson explained, "in that it is an invention, possesses certain attributes without which it could not be an invention – attributes which the law cannot alter, and which it cannot ignore."[201]

When it came to applying and explaining the invention requirement, however, there was neither a consensus nor much clarity. In 1891 Justice Henry Brown admitted that "the word cannot be defined in such manner as to afford any substantial aid in determining whether a particular

---

[197] 107 U.S. 192, 200 (1882).   [198] See Usselman, "Patent Politics," 116–17.
[199] Id., 117–18; Christopher Beauchamp, *Invented by Law: Alexander Graham Bell and the Patent That Changed America* (Cambridge, Mass.: Harvard University Press, 2015), 83.
[200] Walker, *Text Book of the Patent Laws*, 21.
[201] Robinson, *Law of Patents*, vol. 1, 114.

device involves an exercise of the inventive faculty or not." That "impalpable something which distinguishes invention from simple mechanical skill," he wrote, could be identified only in an ad hoc manner.[202] In an address delivered at the 1893 World's Fair in Chicago, one dismayed commentator lamented the uncertainty of the inventiveness requirement under which "great injustice is done to an inventor" and called for a return to the "simple rule of law laid down in 1825 by Mr. Justice Story in *Earle v. Sawyer*."[203] This was a pipe dream. At a time when courts were developing the idea that the distinction between the inventor and the mechanic was one of the most basic conceptual and constitutional foundations of patents as inventors' rights, there was no return to *Earle*.

Amid the confusion about the meaning of the new requirement some patterns could be detected. The most important trend was a retreat from the explicit embrace of judgments about the added value of the invention. On occasion a court opinion would still explicitly associate inventiveness with value.[204] But the dominant new attitude was to separate the "inventive faculty" from questions of substantial value or utility. In the 1885 *Hollister v. Benedict*, for example, the Supreme Court found that the patented system was very effectual in preventing fraud "in connection with the collection of the tax on distilled spirits." Nevertheless, the Court concluded that the patented system was not a true invention because it did not "spring from that intuitive faculty of the mind put forth in the search for new results, or new methods, creating what had not before existed, or bringing to light what lay hidden from vision." The invention, it concluded, despite its value "is but the display of the expected skill of the calling, and involves only the exercise of the ordinary faculties of reasoning upon the materials supplied by a special knowledge, and the facility of manipulation which results from its habitual and intelligent practice; and is in no sense the creative work of that inventive faculty which it is the purpose of the Constitution and the patent laws to encourage and reward."[205] Another court summed up this idea succinctly: "It is invention of what is new, and not comparative superiority, or greater excellence, in what was before known, which the law protects, as

---

[202] *McClain v. Ortmayer*, 141 U.S. 419, 427 (1891).
[203] Benjamin F. Lee, "What Constitutes a Patentable Subject Matter," 3 *Counsellor* 191, 199 (1894).
[204] See e.g. *Atlantic Works*, 107 U.S. 192.
[205] *Hollister v. Benedict*, 113 U.S. 59, 72, (1885).

exclusive property; and it is that alone which is secured by patent."[206] The new aphorism governing this area was: "not all improvement is invention."[207] Robinson agreed. "The magnitude of the result which flows from the inventive act," he wrote in 1890, "furnishes no test by which its merits are determined."[208] Thus "[t]he advance made by the inventor may be slight, the benefit conferred upon the public may be small, but though these considerations influence the recompense which he eventually receives, they do not affect the intrinsic character of the creative act." What mattered was only the "exercise of the inventive faculties."[209]

The test of the "exercise of the inventive faculties" was thus an escape from the need to base the validity of patents on examining the social value of the inventions they protected. The inventive faculty was supposedly a trait of the invention and its creator that could be observed in the world without reference to its value. As Robinson put it: "the word 'inventors' in our law ... is confined to those by whom creative skill and genius have been exercised. It is the exercise of this creative skill alone which is here recognized as an inventive act, and only the result of such an act ... is an invention."[210] Following *Hotchkiss*, the common trope used in legal discourse to convey this idea was the distinction between the mechanic and the inventor. The essential difference between the two was the employment of intellectual creativity rather than mere technical skill.[211] In Robinson's words, "the mental faculties employed in the inventive act are the *creative* not the *imitative* ones."[212]

As soon as substantive value judgments were thrown out through the front door, however, they crept back through the back one. A long series of cases established the principle that an invention's utility may create an evidentiary presumption of inventorship. In 1882, for example, the Supreme Court ruled that "[i]t may be laid down as a general rule, though

---

[206] *Smith v. Elliott*, 22 F. Cas. 529, 530 (S.D. N.Y. 1872). See also *Klein v. Seattle*, 77 F. 200, 204 (9th Cir. 1896); *Grant v. Walter*, 148 U.S. 547, 556 (1893); *Christy v. Hygeia Pneumatic Bicycle Saddle Co.*, 93 F. 965, 969 (4th Cir. 1899); *Lettelier v. Mann*, 91 F. 909, 915 (C.C.S.D. Cal. 1899).

[207] Walker, *Text Book of the Patent Laws*, 21. See also *Pearce v. Mulford*, 102 U.S. 112, 118 (1880); *Slawson v. Railroad Co.*, 107 U.S. 649, 653 (1882); *Rosenwasser v. Berry*, 22 F. 841, 843 (C.C.D. Maine 1885).

[208] Robinson, *Law of Patents*, vol. 1, 130.   [209] Id., 130–31.   [210] Id., 105.

[211] See e.g. *Pickering v. McCullough*, 104 U.S. 310 (1881); *Vinton v. Hamilton*, 104 U.S. 485, 492 (1881); *Morris v. McMillin*, 112 U.S. 247 (1884); *Pearl v. Ocean Mills*, 19 F. Cas. 56, 59 (C.C.D. Mass. 1877).

[212] Robinson, *Law of Patents*, vol. 1, 116.

perhaps not an invariable one, that if a new combination and arrangement of known elements produce a new and beneficial result, never
attained before, it is evidence of invention."[213] It went on to find that
"[i]t was certainly a new and useful result to make a loom produce fifty
yards a day when it never before had produced more than forty."[214]
Many other cases declared the same principle.[215] In some instances the
speed of the movement from denying utility as the measure of invention to
admitting it as an evidentiary presumption was dazzling. Thus in 1898 the
Court of Appeals for the Seventh Circuit ruled: "It is not enough that a
thing shall be new, in the sense that in the shape or form in which it is
produced it shall not have been before known, and that it shall be useful,
but it must, under the constitution and statute, amount to an invention or
discovery." In the very next sentence it explained that "[i]n determining
whether a new combination of old elements constitutes invention, the
most important and controlling considerations are the intrinsic novelty
and utility of the concrete invention."[216]

Unlike under the substantive novelty rule, however, utility was pushed
to the periphery. Begrudgingly accepting the frequent need to examine
invention through the prism of added value, courts treated it with suspicion and caution.[217] In 1891 the Supreme Court remarked that "[w]hile
this court has held in a number of cases ... that in a doubtful case the fact
that a patented article had gone into general use is evidence of its utility, it
is not conclusive even of that – much less of its patentable novelty."[218]
Another court pointed out in 1896 that a patented invention "may, in fact,
embrace utility and novelty in a high degree, and still be only the result of
mechanical skill, as distinguished from invention."[219] Yet another court
cautioned that "the test of invention is mental conception not larger sales,
or improved results, or benefits conferred on mankind."[220] Walker argued

---

[213] *Loom Co. v. Higgins*, 105 U.S. 580, 591 (1882).   [214] Id., 591–92.

[215] See e.g. *Smith v. Goodyear Dental Vulcanite Co.*, 93 U.S. 486, 495 (1877); *Washburn & Moen Mfg. Co. v. Haish*, 4 F. 900, 909 (C.C.N.D. Ill. 1880); *Hill v. Biddle*, 27 F. 560 (C.C.E.D. Pa. 1886).

[216] *Kelly v. Clow*, 89 F. 297, 303 (7th Cir. 1898).

[217] See e.g. *Stanley Works v. Sargent*, 22 F. Cas. 1054, 1055 (C.C.D. Conn. 1871); *Smith v. Goodyear Dental Vulcanite Co.*, 93 U.S., 495–96; *Christy v. Hygeia Pneumatic Bicycle Saddle Co.*, 93 F. 965, 969–70 (4th Cir. 1899); *Lovell Mfg. Co. v. Cary*, 147 U.S. 623, 636 (1893); *Grant v. Walter*, 148 U.S. 547, 557 (1893).

[218] *McClain v. Ortmayer*, 141 U.S.429.

[219] *Klein v. Seattle*, 77 F. 200, 204 (9th Cir. 1896).

[220] *American Laundry Machinery Mfg. Co. v. Adams Laundry Mach. Co.*, 161 F. 556, 563 (N.D. N.Y 1908).

in his treatise that the utility of the invention should be considered only in cases when "the mind remains in uncertainty" and "the other facts in a case leave the question of invention in doubt."[221]

Importantly, when utility was used as a measure of invention, it was almost always defined in subjective terms of market demand. Courts no longer tried to assess whether the patented subject matter offered sufficient intrinsic value to be considered an invention. Instead, the question became whether the invention enjoyed "general public demand"[222] or "large sales."[223] In this respect, the use of market demand as an indicator of invention was harmonious with the late-nineteenth-century trend of purging patent law of questions of substantive social value. From this perspective, social value was strong evidence of the presence of true inventorship, and social value meant, in turn, subjective market demand.

As it emerged in the late nineteenth century, the doctrinal requirement of invention, later to be known as nonobviousness, uneasily contained all of these various elements and tensions. The new explicit requirement expressed an ideological commitment to the constitutive myth of the field, that of the genius inventor. Thus the inventive faculty – the supposed defining feature of the inventor – was often described as creating observable traces in the world. Ideally these traces could be used to delimit patents within their proper realm of inventors and inventions without having to resort to substantive value judgments. The inventive faculty, however, quickly turned out to be an elusive and slippery criterion. Such difficulties often pushed courts back, however reluctantly, to assessing the value of innovations in determining their inventive status. The concept of the inventive faculty contained these tensions. Constant assertions to the contrary notwithstanding, the inventive faculty only too often turned out to be synonymous with considerable market demand for the innovation.

---

[221] Walker, *Text Book of the Patent Laws*, 38. [222] *Hill v. Biddle*, 27 F. 560.

[223] *Eppinger v. Richey*, 8 F. Cas. 741, 744 (S.D. N.Y. 1877). See also *Washburn & Moen Mfg. Co. v. Haish*, 4 F. 900, 909 (C.C.N.D. Ill. 1880); *Magowan v. Packing Co.*, 141 U.S. 332, 343 (1891). Some decisions questioned the credibility of market success as an indicator of utility. See *McClain v. Ortmayer*, 141 U.S. 428; *Duer v. Corbin Lock Co.*, 149 U.S. 216, 223 (1893); *Fox v. Perkins*, 52 F. 205, 213 (6th Cir. 1892); *Billings & S Co. v. Van Wagoner & W Hardware Co.*, 98 F. 732, 734 (C.C.N.D. Ohio 1899). The conclusion that courts drew from such doubts, however, was not that they needed to make direct judgments of social value, but rather that they should give utility a smaller weight or ignore it altogether within the inventiveness analysis.

By the turn of the twentieth century there emerged in patent law specific institutional structures that concretized in elaborate and sometimes convoluted ways each of the two elements of the abstract concept of inventors' rights. What did it mean, however, for the rights of inventors in their inventions to be property rights? We turn next to the gradual evolution in American patent law of the notions of ownership of intangibles and of such intangibles as objects of property.

5

Owning Inventions

The cover page of the January 1808 issue of the *Useful Cabinet* featured the seal of the recently founded New England Association of Inventors and Patrons of the Useful Art. The seal showed a figure watering a tree laden with fruits growing within a walled garden. It bore the motto: "IN ITS OWN SOIL, PROTECT AND NOURISH IT." For slow readers who might have missed the less than subtle metaphor, the magazine provided an explanation:

The Fruitful Tree represents the Benefits which Society may derive from the Labours of the Inventor, if properly secured by a Wall of Protection. The nourishment received from the hand of TIME, is emblematical of the long and arduous attention necessary for bringing to maturity a Useful Improvement.[1]

As shown by Mark Rose, images of property and especially ownership of land played a crucial role in eighteenth-century England by helping to connect a new understanding of authorship with claims for legal rights.[2] The same rhetorical strategy was used in the United States in regard to both authors and inventors. Alongside depictions of patents as governmental grants justified by the social utility of promoting technological innovation, there was also a wide circulation of accounts describing patents as natural property rights of inventors in the product of their intellectual labor.[3] It was a patent case in which Justice Levi Woodbury

---

[1] Useful Cabinet, January 1808, 1.
[2] Mark Rose, *Authors and Owners: The Invention of Copyright* (Cambridge, Mass.: Harvard University Press, 1993).
[3] Oren Bracha "Geniuses and Owners: The Construction of Inventors and the Emergence of American Intellectual Property," in Daniel W. Hamilton and Alfred L. Brophy, eds.,

wrote in 1845 about the need to protect "intellectual property, the labors of the mind, productions and interests as much a man's own, and as much the fruit of his honest industry, as the wheat he cultivates, or the flocks he rears."[4]

Unlike the copyright context where arguments about the natural rights of authors in the product of their mind gave rise to claims of common law entitlements, assertions of inventors' rights usually fell short of claiming absolutist property. An 1806 petition to Congress was typical of this disconnect between an ambitious theoretical account of inventors as owners of natural property rights and the actual claims for legal protection made on their behalf. The "Address of the Advocate of the Patentees" makes the bold claim that "mental property . . . is as justly and bona fide the property of those who thus acquire it as any real or personal property can be."[5] Immediately after arguing that the necessary implication of this proposition is perpetual duration of patents, however, the pamphlet concedes that this may be practically impossible. Thus it goes on to argue that "the aggrieved" might be satisfied with a shorter patent term "say for and during the life of the inventor, and his heirs and assigns, to the third generation; or for fifty years certain."[6]

There were deep reasons for this gap between the abstract image of property rights in inventions and its translation into practical terms. For centuries patents were seen in the English tradition as state-created monopolies. A common narrative celebrated the curbing by the Statute of Monopolies of the abusive royal prerogative to grant "odious monopolies."[7] The common law was strongly associated in this context with restricting unchecked monarchical power and protecting the rights of Englishmen to freely pursue their trades, not with protecting the property rights of inventors. Some justifications of patents as natural

---

Transformations in American Legal History: Essays in Honor of Professor Morton J. Horwitz (Cambridge, Mass.: Harvard Law School, 2009).

[4] *Davoll v. Brown*, 7 F. Cas. 197, 199 (C.C.D. Mass. 1845).

[5] *Address of the Advocate of the Patentees Inventors of Useful Improvements in the Arts and Sciences* (Washington, D.C.: Duane & Son, 1806), 11. The petition was most probably written by Oliver Evans. On December 13, 1806, a week prior to the date of the petition's submission, Evans wrote Jefferson and mentioned that he was in Washington to represent the "patentees petitioners" to Congress. See Oliver Evans to Thomas Jefferson, December 13, 1806, in Founders Online, National Archives, http://founders.archives.gov/documents/Jefferson/99-01-02-4674.

[6] *Address of the Advocate of the Patentees*, 10.

[7] See Oren Bracha, "The Commodification of Patents 1600–1836: How Patents Became Rights and Why We Should Care," 38 *Loy. L.A. L. Rev.* 192–200 (2004).

property rights appeared in Britain, but there was no patent equivalent there of the struggle to assert common law copyright or the literary property debate it spawned.[8] In fact, British advocates of common law copyright desperately tried to distinguish patents and copyright, since the former were so indisputably state-created privileges.[9] In the United States it became more common to depict both fields as based on the common principle of natural property rights in mental labor. But the lack of legal precedents or a mythical narrative of immemorial common law rights predating the statute – both of which existed in the copyright context – was a formidable obstacle to fully following through the implications of such claims. There appeared no serious patent equivalent of accounts of common law copyright based on natural rights.

Common law rights aside, the general property framework adopted by early American patent thought contained an even more important gap. Patents were commonly seen as property in the sense of inventors' ownership rights in intangible objects of property. But at the dawn of the nineteenth century the concrete meaning and specific institutional expression of the elements of property in inventions were either missing or in their infancy. In colonial times patents could cover any useful economic activity, but what exactly could be owned under patents newly conceived as a form of property and what lay beyond the reach of private exclusive control? At the end of the eighteenth century the answers to these questions were only beginning to emerge in Britain and were sketchy at most. Similarly, it was not clear how to understand the new intangible object of property. What are the boundaries of this elusive entity? What is the scope of powers given to its owner and what does it mean to trespass on it? American patent law would only gradually develop a conceptual framework within which to answer and debate these questions about the concrete meaning of ownership of inventions. As with authorship in copyright, the emerging framework was not the result of an unfolding of a predetermined logic of inventors' property. The early, abstract ideology of inventorship was converted into concrete legal concepts through the prism of economic pressures, the pull of interests, and a set of other ideological influences. The result

---

[8] For the different views in Britain during the nineteenth-century debates, see H.I. Dutton, *The Patent System and Inventive Activity during the Industrial Revolution, 1750–1852* (Manchester: Manchester University Press, 1984), 17–33.

[9] See Oren Bracha, "Owning Ideas: A History of Anglo-American Intellectual Property," S.J.D. diss., Harvard University (2005), 235–40.

that emerged by the beginning of the twentieth century was often riddled with inconsistencies and unresolved tensions.

THE FUEL OF INTEREST

Nowhere was the tension between the abstract ideology of inventors' property and the economic pressures that shaped patent doctrine more apparent than in the area of employee ownership of inventions. Early patent law reflected the most fundamental principle of ownership of inventions. Inventors – those who actually created the mental object of property – were the only original owners of patents. This principle of inventor's ownership was buttressed by American law's emphasis on restricting patents only to "the first and true inventor" and rejecting importation patents.[10] In the second half of the nineteenth century, however, this principle came under mounting pressure by employers' claims to the inventions of their employees. By the early twentieth century, employee–inventors were still nominally recognized as original owners, but as a substantive matter, in a broad swath of cases they no longer owned the patents in their inventions, not even ab initio. Catherine Fisk referred to this process, paraphrasing Abraham Lincoln, as "removing the 'fuel of interest' from the 'fire of genius.'"[11] The story of how employee–inventors lost their patent rights reflects, however, the real fuel of interest that shaped much of modern patent law: the interest of big business in a changing social context where the bulk of technological innovation shifted to the setting of large, hierarchical business organizations.

For half a century the norm of inventors' ownership was undisturbed. After all, what could be more indisputable in a system of inventors' rights than the principle that those who invented are the original owners? To be sure, like other property rights, patents could be voluntarily assigned and many were assigned.[12] But original ownership belonged to inventors.

---

[10] See Chapter 4.

[11] Catherine Fisk, "Removing the 'Fuel of Interest' from the 'Fire of Genius': Law and the Employee-Inventor, 1830–1930," 65 *U. Chi. L. Rev.* 1127 (1998).

[12] On patent assignments in the nineteenth century, see Naomi R. Lamoreaux and Kenneth L. Sokoloff, "Inventors, Firms, and the Market for Technology in the Late Nineteenth and Early Twentieth Centuries," in Naomi R. Lamoreaux et al., eds., *Learning by Doing in Markets, Firms, and Countries*, (Chicago, Ill.: University of Chicago Press, 1999); Naomi R. Lamoreaux and Kenneth L. Sokoloff, "Market Trade in Patents and the Rise of a Class of Specialized Inventors in the Nineteenth-Century United States," 91 *American Economic Review, Papers and Proceedings*, 39 (2001); Naomi Lamoreaux et al., "Patent Alchemy: The Market for Technology in US History," 87 *Bus. Hist. Rev.* 3 (2013).

The first signs of pressure on this universal principle began to appear a few decades into the nineteenth century. At first the typical cases involved not direct disputes between employees and employers, but third parties who defended against infringement lawsuits by arguing that patents owned by employers were invalid because they were obtained surreptitiously for inventions actually made by their employees. Courts analyzed such claims using the familiar vocabulary of inventorship.[13] The true inventor, they reasoned, was the person who "suggested the principle of the invention," whether he was master or servant.[14] In employment cases, just as in cases involving input by nonemployee parties, one did not cease being an inventor merely because he received "a hint"[15] from another or availed himself "of the mechanical skill of others, to carry out practically his contrivance."[16] In short, the inventor and therefore the owner of the patent was the mastermind whose intellect generated the inventive idea. This was completely in line with the ideological framework of inventorship.

Soon, however, the first cracks began to appear in the adherence to the inventors' ownership principle in the form of what came to be known as the "shop right." The shop right conferred on employers the privilege of using inventions made and patented by their employees. The 1843 Supreme Court decision in *McClurg v. Kingsland* in which the doctrine originated was not based on a special treatment of employee inventions.[17] The case was not decided in equity and the decision relied in part on interpreting some sections of the Patent Act, but the logic of the decision was that of the equitable doctrine of estoppel.[18] Under this doctrine one who knowingly allows certain conduct by another who relies on this acquiescence cannot later object to the conduct as a violation of his rights. Based on this rationale the Court decided in *McClurg* that a patent assignee did not have an infringement claim against the former employer of the inventor. The reason was that during the employment period the inventor had allowed the employer to use the invention.

[13] See *Dixon v. Moyer*, 7 F. Cas. 758,759 (C.C.D. Pa. 1821); *Sparkman v. Higgins*, 22 F. Cas. 878, 879 (C.C.S.D. N.Y. 1846); *Goodyear v. Day*, 10 F. Cas. 677 (C.C.D. N.J. 1852); *Dental Vulcanite Co. v. Wetherbee*, 7 F. Cas. 498, 502 (C.C.D. Mass. 1866).
[14] George Ticknor Curtis, *A Treatise on the Law of Patents for Useful Inventions in the United States of America*, 2nd ed. (Boston: Little, Brown, 1854), 42–43.
[15] *Alden v. Dewey*, 1 F. Cas. 329, 330 (C.C.D. Mass. 1840).
[16] *Sparkman v. Higgins*, 22 F. Cas. 879.　[17] 43 U.S. 202 (1843).
[18] See *Gill v. U.S.*, 160 U.S. 426, 430 (1896). See generally Fisk, "Removing the 'Fuel of Interest,'" 1144.

For decades this rationale that applied with equal force within and outside the employment context was followed.[19] In the late 1880s, however, courts gradually shifted their reasoning and created the modern shop right. The new decisions relied on the supposed inherent logic of the employment relationship instead of the permission given by the inventor. Employers were now seen as entitled to use inventions made by their employees on the job irrespective of initial permission because they owned the materials, tools, and facilities used to invent.[20] Thus when the Supreme Court summarized the doctrine almost half a century later, it attributed it to "equitable principles" quite different from the estoppel idea: "Since the servant uses his master's time, facilities, and materials to attain a concrete result, the latter is in equity entitled to use that which embodies his own property and to duplicate it as often as he may find occasion to employ similar appliances in his business."[21]

The early incarnation of the shop right gave some recognition to the interest of employers, but it was completely harmonious with the principle that inventors owned their inventions and ultimately retained the power to authorize their use. By contrast, the new shop right that based the employer's entitlement on the furnishing of the facilities and finance for the invention directly chipped away at the principle of inventors' ownership. If she happened to invent on the job, the person who originated the invention through her mental labor no longer enjoyed complete dominion over her invention. To be sure, the new shop right did not completely deprive employees of their inventions. But it created a form of truncated ownership that included no power to exclude the employer. This was a way of mediating the tension between the traditional principle of inventors' ownership and the mounting claims by employers for an interest in the intellectual product of their employees. In some contexts this Solomonic solution worked. Railroads, for example, were often content to allow much leeway to some of their employees to invent on the job and exploit the invention as long as they were immunized from the risk of being excluded. In some cases such employee innovation was encouraged, and occasionally modest sums were paid for the right to use it.[22]

---

[19] Fisk, "Removing the 'Fuel of Interest'," 1148–50.   [20] Id., 1151–59.

[21] *U.S. v. Dubilier Condenser Corporation*, 289 U.S. 178, 188–89 (1933).

[22] See Catherine Fisk, *Working Knowledge: Employee Innovation and the Rise of Corporate Intellectual Property 1800–1930* (Chapel Hill: University of North Carolina Press, 2009), 119–26.; Steven W. Usselman, *Regulating Railroad Innovation: Business, Technology, and Politics in America, 1840–1920* (New York: Cambridge University Press 2002), 104–5.

As invention in the employment setting was becoming more significant, other employers started demanding a bigger share of the ownership in the product of their employees' mental labor.

Direct conflicts over the full ownership in employee invention were handled through the legal concept of "hired to invent" that quickly proved to be highly unstable. The basic rule was that an employee who was hired to develop a specific innovation could not claim title to the patent in it. Sometimes courts treated "hired to invent" as a placeholder for the traditional analysis of who was the actual originator of the inventive idea or for an express agreement assigning the ownership.[23] But in its core the "hired to invent" rule was based on the construct of implied intent. Implied intent was a way of alleviating the tension between the competing claims of ownership. The concept obscured the difference between actual consent by employee inventors and a default ownership rule imposed on them.[24] Thus the Supreme Court explained in *Solomons v. U.S.* that when "one is employed to devise or perfect an instrument ... [t]hat which he has been employed and paid to accomplish becomes, when accomplished, the property of his employer. Whatever rights as an individual he may have had in and to his inventive powers, and that which they are able to accomplish, he has sold in advance to his employer."[25] This appears to be just an application of the principle of inventors' ownership accompanied by a voluntary assignment of the right. But the whole point of "hired to invent" was that it could shift ownership to employers when no actual agreement to assign existed. Courts treated the inferred "intent" of the parties as somehow inherent in the character of the specific employment relationship between them. The government's argument in *Solomons* is illustrative. The case involved a dispute over a patent for a "self-canceling" stamp developed by the head of the Bureau of Engraving and Printing in the Treasury Department during his employment. The government conceded in its brief that "the ordinary relation of master and servant does not require that the latter should tender to the former the fruits of his ingenuity." Nonetheless, it contended that "the nature and the object of the Bureau were such that a different implication arises, as between the Government and

---

[23] See *Agawam Woolen Co. v. Jordan*, 74 U.S. 583, 602–3 (1868); *Orcutt v. McDonald*, 27 App. D.C. 228, 233–34 (D.C. Cir. 1906); *Kreag v. Geen*, 28 App. D.C. 437, 440 (D.C. Cir. 1906); *Dalzell v. Dueber Watch-Case Mfg. Co.*, 149 U.S. 315 (1893).

[24] On the function of implied intent more generally, see Duncan Kennedy, *The Rise and Fall of Classical Legal Thought* (Washington, D.C.: Beard Books, 2006), 157.

[25] *Solomons v. U.S.*, 137 U.S. 342, 346 (1890).

the bureau Chief." In short, the government's claim for ownership of
another's invention was based not on an actual assignment but on an
"implied contract" derived from the nature of the specific employment
relationship.[26]

"Hired to invent" suppressed for a while the tension between the
principle of inventors' ownership and the growing willingness to accommodate employers' claims, but it ultimately proved to be an unreliable
instrument. The early Supreme Court decisions that recognized full
employer's ownership under this doctrine did so in dicta.[27] Initially,
many courts applied the rule in ways that made it very hard to
shift ownership away from inventors.[28] Other courts especially in later
decisions were more willing to find that an employee was hired to invent
and therefore forfeited his or her patent rights.[29] The doctrine was
unstable because courts could focus on different aspects of the employment relationship and apply them differently in their quest for the
implied intent.[30] By the early twentieth century the hired-to-invent
construct was buckling under the pressure of conflicting ownership
claims of employee–inventors and their employers. Unlike copyright
where a similar process led to an explicit flip in ownership rules under
the work-made-for-hire doctrine, in patent law employers' interests
prevailed through contract.

The shift of ownership of employee inventions to the hands of employers in the early twentieth century happened through express assignment
clauses in employment contracts and courts' growing tolerance of such
arrangements. On a strictly formal level contractual assignments appear
perfectly consistent with the principle of inventors' ownership. The freedom to assign was a corollary of allocating ownership to the inventor

---

[26] *Solomons v. the U.S., Brief for the United States*, 8–9.
[27] See *Solomons v. the U.S.*, 137 U.S. 346; *McAleer v. U.S.*, 150 U.S. 424, 429–31 (1893);
Gill v. U.S., 160 U.S. 435.
[28] See e.g. *Hapgood v. Hewitt*, 119 U.S. 226, 233 (1886); *Fuller & Johnson Manufacturing
Co v. Bartlett*, 31 NW 747, 752 (1887); *Connelly Manufacturing Co. v. Wattles*, 49 NJ
Eq 92 (1891); *Niagara Radiator Co. v. Meyers*, 40 NYS 572 (S. Ct. 1896); *Barber v.
National Carbon Co.*, 129 F 370, 372 (6th Cir. 1904); *American Circular Loom Co v.
Wilson*, 84 NE 133, 135 (1908); *Johnson Furnace & Engineering Co v. Western Furnace
Co.*, 178 F. 819, 823 (8th Cir. 1910).
[29] See e.g. *Silver Spring Bleaching & Dyeing Co. v. Woolworth*, 19 A. 528, 529 (1890);
Ingle v. Landis Tool Co., 262 F. 150, 153 (M.D. Penn 1919); *Wireless Specialty
Apparatus Co. v. Mica Condenser Co.*, 131 NE 307 (1921).
[30] See generally Fisk, "Removing the 'Fuel of Interest,'" 1170–79.

from the start. A closer glimpse at how assignment agreements came to be used and at the change in their legal treatment tells a different story.

By the late nineteenth century the validity of patent assignments including assignments of future inventions was well established.[31] And yet when courts encountered sweeping future assignments in the employment context they usually treated them with suspicion and hostility. An 1887 dictum from Justice Joseph Bradley captured this attitude:

A naked assignment or agreement to assign, in gross, a man's future labors as an author or inventor, – in other words, a mortgage on a man's brain, to bind all its future products, – does not address itself favorably to our consideration.[32]

Late-nineteenth-century courts understood well the difference between an assignment of a concrete existing or future invention and a blanket waiver of any future innovation as a fixed feature of the employment relationship. The latter was tantamount to alienation of one's inventive faculty – what Bradley called a "mortgage on a man's brain" – and as such it was at odds with the ideology of the owner–inventor. This was the source of the early judicial resistance to the emerging contractual strategies of employers. Despite Bradley's dictum, there was no general rule that sweeping future assignments were unenforceable.[33] Courts expressed their hostility to such contractual arrangements through more subtle means. The two main strategies they deployed were declining to find a binding contract in the absence of clear, ironclad evidence[34] and an exceedingly narrow interpretation of the agreement when a contract was found.[35]

Meanwhile, practices on the ground were beginning to change. As corporate research and development (R&D) laboratories started to appear, corporations such as Du Pont, Westinghouse, General Electric, and American Bell grew increasingly concerned about tightening their control over the mental products of their employees. Employee innovation was becoming a central corporate resource that had to be managed rationally. The means for achieving this were new sweeping assignment clauses that started to appear in the employment contracts of these firms.[36]

---

[31] See *Kinsman v. Parkhurst*, 59 U.S. 289, 293 (1855); *Littlefield v. Perry*, 88 U.S. 205, 226 (1874); *Westinghouse Air-Brake Co. v. Chicago Brake & Mfg. Co.*, 85 F. 786, 793–94 (C.C.N.D. Ill. 1898).

[32] *Aspinwall Mfg. Co. v. Gill*, 32 F. 697, 700 (C.C.D. N.J. 1887).

[33] See *Hulse v. Bonsack Mach. Co.*, 65 F. 864 (4th Cir. 1895).

[34] Fisk, "Removing the 'Fuel of Interest,'" 1186–89.   [35] Id., 1188–91.

[36] See David F. Noble, *America by Design: Science, Technology and the Rise of Corporate Capitalism* (New York: Knopf, 1977), 100–101. Fisk, *Working Knowledge*, 178–210.

As shown by Naomi Lamoreaux and Kenneth Sokoloff, the penetration of such policies was gradual. At the turn of the century most firms did not have strict policies in regard to employee inventions, and sweeping assignment clauses in employment contracts were the exception.[37] Nevertheless, at the dawn of the twentieth century some firms started to tighten their control over employee innovation, and after World War I this became the dominant trend.[38]

Edwin Prindle was at the forefront of this process. A mechanical engineer and a prominent patent lawyer, Prindle was one of the first members of the American Patent Law Association, founded in 1897. In his book *Patents as a Factor in Manufacturing*, published as part of a series by *Engineering Magazine*, Prindle included a chapter on "Patent Relations of Employer and Employee." In it he offered employers the following advice:

[I]t is evident that it is desirable to have a contract with every employee who is at all likely to make inventions which relate to the business of the employer, and as the courts will sustain such contracts, even though they contain no further provisions for return for the inventions than the payment of the ordinary salary, the employer should have such a contract with every such employee. There are manufacturing concerns where every man in the drafting room and in the sales department, and every skilled employee, is under such contract.[39]

To overcome resistance, Prindle suggested that company officers "will set the example by signing such a contract." He hastened to calm his readers though that "[t]his is often a mere matter of form," as the officer is usually "not inventive" or happy to take his share in the form of dividends.[40] In a more philosophical essay called "The Art of Inventing," Prindle remarked that "[m]any large concerns constantly employ a large corps of inventors."[41] The metaphor was not accidental. Though he recognized the existence of "freelancers," for Prindle the paradigmatic model of modern innovation was that of an army of employees whose creativity was organized, controlled, and owned hierarchically by the corporation. Being a man of action as well as words, Prindle was in

[37] See Lamoreaux and Sokoloff, "Inventors, Firms, and the Market for Technology," 44–48.

[38] Id., 49; see also B. Zorina Khan and Kenneth L. Sokoloff, "Institutions and Technological Innovation during Early Economic Growth: Evidence from the Great Inventors of the United States, 1790–1930," NBER Working Paper no. 10966 (December 2004), 26.

[39] Edwin J. Prindle, *Patents as a Factor in Manufacturing* (New York: The Engineering Magazine, 1908), 101.

[40] Id.   [41] Edwin J. Prindle, *The Art of Inventing* (1906), 4.

the thick of putting his theories into practice. As counsel for Du Pont he was deeply involved in the company's shift toward an aggressive policy of comprehensive contractual assignment of employee inventions.[42]

Changing realities and perceptions of corporate innovation gradually changed the courts' attitude. The appearance of centralized corporate innovation, methods of scientific management, and the bureaucratization of the employment relationship pushed toward standardization of sweeping contractual assignment of employee innovation.[43] Courts began to see the economic "need" for such arrangements. The changing focus of the perception of invention – from individual genius to a managed collective process – facilitated this shift. Gross assignment of the creative faculty ceased being a "mortgage on a man's brain" and came to be seen as an integral part of rationally managing invention through corporate supervision of a "corps of inventors." Gradually, courts became more hospitable to employers' claims of ownership in employee inventions. Early in the twentieth century the rule in cases of employer–employee disputes over inventorship became a rebuttable presumption in favor of the employer.[44] The crucial development, however, was a growing willingness of courts to enforce sweeping contractual assignments. As early as 1895 courts declared such clauses in employment agreements enforceable even in the absence of specific indefinable consideration.[45] In the first decades of the twentieth century the earlier judicial hostility dissolved and contractual assignment was gradually accepted and normalized.

The 1911 Seventh Circuit's decision in *National Wire Bound Box Co. v. Healy*, though not a standard employment case, was a resounding expression of this shift.[46] The court held that an oral agreement to assign future inventions by two of the corporation's directors and stockholders was enforceable on equity principles of fiduciary duties. The counsel for the inventors tried to portray inventive creativity as uniquely personal and therefore outside the scope of doctrines governing

[42] See Fisk, *Working Knowledge*, 203.
[43] Samuel Haber, *Efficiency and Uplift: Scientific Management in the Progressive Era: 1820–1920* (Chicago, Ill.: University of Chicago Press, 1964); Robert Kanigel, *The One Best Way: Frederick Winslow Taylor and the Enigma of Efficiency* (New York: Viking, 1997); Sanford M. Jacoby, *Employing Bureaucracy: Managers, Unions, and the Transformation of Work in the 20th Century* (Mahwah, N.J.: Lawrence Erlbaum, 2004).
[44] *Miller v. Kelley*, 18 App. D. C. 163, 171 (D.C. Cir. 1901).
[45] See *Hulse v. Bonsack Mach. Co.*, 65 F. 864; *Thibodeau v. Hildreth*, 124 F. 892, 893 (1st Cir. 1903); *Detroit Lubricator Co. v. Lavigne Mfg. Co.*, 115 N.W. 988, 991 (1998).
[46] 189 F. 49 (7th Cir. 1911).

ordinary commercial relations. "[F]uture inventions," he argued, "are not something that the principal himself could have acquired – are something that, but for the inventors' creative faculty, would not have existed at all – they are not within the possible subject-matter of this doctrine of trustee-ship through fiduciary relationship."[47] But the court had a radically different conception of inventions as yet another ordinary business asset:

> Commercially and industrially, the same principles apply to future inventions ... for the exploration of the laws of nature and mechanics, for something that will aid a specific commercial or business end, practically and commercially is not different from explorations for mineral or gas deposits to a like commercial end. Neither has any value until it is obtained. Both create a value that did not exist before they were obtained. One is the reclamation from the earth of something beneficial to commerce and industry; the other is the reclamation from the laws of mechanics or nature of something beneficial to commerce and industry. To both, once their boundaries are ascertained, the law gives the quality and protection of legal title. Both, equally, can be bought and sold and otherwise enter into business and commerce. Why should equity, dealing with them in the light of these commercial ends, run any distinction between them upon lines purely psycho-logical; for it must be remembered that it is with inventions, as a part of commerce and industry, that we are dealing, not with inventions as a part of historical science; and it is by putting inventions, and the patents that embody them, into this, their true commercial setting, that courts can best carry out the purpose of our constitution and laws in protecting them.[48]

Ironically, the real property metaphor now turned on inventors, reducing any claim for the unique personal dimension of creativity into an unreli-able "purely psychological" distinction.

The real emphasis, however, was on the "true commercial setting" of invention. At play here was a growing recognition of the function of patents as business tools for central control and strategic planning. For the court the crucial fact in the case was the purpose of the transaction between the parties, described by it as "to unify, throughout the United States, the business of making this kind of box." It was to this end that "the ownership and control of patents for this kind of box were to be unified; and corporations were to be organized, to which a common character of license should be granted; and to this end, all the inventions in that line, future as well as past, were to be kept together." Only by grasping the strategic role of patents within this business scheme, the court insisted, could the proper nature of the parties' relationship be understood. Once this broader context was kept in mind, it became

---

[47] Id., 55.   [48] Id., 56.

apparent that just as in the case of mineral exploitation, "unification here is an economic necessity" and so is "solidification of the holdings." The court made explicit what it saw as an economic necessity for centralized ownership and management of innovation:

A given lawful enterprise, to be successful, often depends upon its power to obtain the benefit of every improvement introduced. Protection for the future requires that inventions already controlled be not undermined and diverted by other inventions along the same line ... And where, in the development of business enterprise, it is necessary that there should be a look forward, as well as a look just around them, inventions in the future can be made the subject-matter of a fiduciary relationship, just as much so as the future discoveries of deposits of natural gas.[49]

The upshot of all of this was depersonalization of invention: "An invention is not something that, but for the particular inventor or inventors, would not have been. Inventions come along as the discovery of gas deposits come along – the contribution of some particular person to the world's knowledge – but if not by that person, then, in the course of time, and usually in a very short time, by some one else."[50] This was a complete reversal of the classic ideology of inventors' property. Invention was no longer the unique mental product of a heroic genius. It became just another impersonal, alienated input to a planned industrial scheme, much like the physical labor of factory workers. The individual genius inventor was caught in the net of corporate liberalism.

Thirteen years later in *Standard Parts Co. v. Peck* the Supreme Court gave its blessing to the trend of accommodating blanket assignment of employee innovation.[51] Reversing the court of appeals, the Court read an employee contractual obligation to "devote his time to the development of a process and machinery" for the employer as creating an assignment of patents in future inventions. Doctrinally, the decision combined an approach of a thumb on the scale in favor of employers in regard to the "hired to invent" analysis with endorsement of express assignments. *Standard Parts* was the kind of case where earlier courts could have easily found that there was no intent to assign implied in the relationship and that in the absence of clear, explicit written obligation there was no express contractual assignment. The Supreme Court brushed aside such reasoning, finding that the ambiguous agreement created an enforceable assignment of future inventions.

[49] Id., 55.   [50] Id.   [51] 264 U.S. 52 (1924).

The Court's background assumptions about the role of patents in the modern business context were, however, far more important than its exact legal ruling. The Court found the answer to the question of who owned the inventions to be "inevitable and resistless." It was the employer "who engaged the services and paid for them." It was significant that the inventions were "not for temporary use, but perpetual use, a provision for a business, a facility in it, and an asset of it." Justice Joseph McKenna found particularly egregious the employee's intention to license the patent to others and thereby "subject the company to the rivalry of competitors."[52] The employee, he wrote, "seems somewhat absorbing in his assertion of rights" because he "virtually asserts ... doing nothing more than he was engaged to do and paid for doing, that the product of the services was so entirely his property that he might give as great a right to any member of the mechanical world as to the one who engaged him and paid him – a right to be used in competition with the one who engaged him and paid him."[53] Once it came to be seen as an interference by a wage-earner with the firm's ability to protect itself from market competition, a formerly common-sense assertion of the inventor's property rights became an outrage.

The changing landscape of patent ownership in the employment context was similar to that of the parallel area in copyright. Both fields moved from early strict adherence to a principle of creators' ownership to a period of instability under an implied intent framework and finally to an outright embrace of employer ownership. There was one glaring difference, however. Copyright shifted to an explicit rule of initial employer's ownership under the work-made-for-hire doctrine. By contrast, patent law never formally abandoned the idea that inventions and the original ownership in them must be traced back to the actual creator. This was clearly reflected in the fact that in all cases, even when the patent was assigned ab initio, patent applications and patents had to name a specific individual as the actual inventor. In the field of patents, employer's ownership was embraced through various contractual constructs, the most important of which was acceptance of sweeping, standardized assignments. Why the difference? The main reason was that in copyright firms had an urgent interest in obtaining full initial ownership rather than mere assignment. Copyright's period of protection was divided into two terms, the second of which required renewal

[52] Id., 60.   [53] Id.

by authors or their statutory successors in title. These technical rules of copyright renewal meant that employers seeking assignment of the second term had to locate and enter into contracts with a large number of potential successors of the author's interest. Even then, they would get only partial security against the renewal interest reverting to some unaccounted-for widow or orphan. The only way around these difficulties was to make sure that employers got original ownership. Patents involved no such complications. An assignment gave the employer a full and certain ownership for the entire patent term. Thus a sweeping contractual assignment was just as serviceable as original ownership, especially for the most powerful firms with the highest stakes, which implemented blanket assignment of employee inventions as a standard feature of their employment contracts.

As a bonus, relying on contractual assignment reduced the tension with the fundamental principle of inventors' ownership. Standardized, sweeping assignment made employers the original owners de facto. But such arrangements could be portrayed as arm's-length transactions, thus preserving the appearance of the traditional framework of awarding the inventor the property right in his mental product together with the power to assign it. In 1909 Fredrick Fish, a prominent patent lawyer and the former president of the American Telephone & Telegraph Co. (AT&T), explained to listeners in the annual meeting of the American Institute of Electrical Engineers that "[n]o one except the true inventor can obtain a valid patent." He further explained: "In so far as there is any foundation to the contention that under modern conditions, the inventor himself does not get all that he should for his work, the basis for the contention is not the patent system or the law, but the social and industrial conditions which prevail."[54] In this narrative employee–inventors were still patent owners. The fact that it was their employers who owned the product of their creativity was not the doing of a coercive law, but rather the upshot of free contractual choices mandated by the economic necessity of "social and industrial conditions."

Early in the twentieth century rules governing patent ownership in the employment context crystallized into a curious pattern. While formally adhering to inventors' ownership, the doctrine facilitated a massive shift of ownership to employers via contractual and semi-contractual arrangements. This pattern was the result of the heavy friction in this area

---

[54] Quoted in Noble, *America by Design*, 101.

between the individualist ideology of inventors' ownership underlying patent law and the economic interests produced by technological innovation in the settings of bureaucratized, collective, business organizations. Fitting the genius inventor into the new machine of corporate liberalism produced some strange noises.

FROM FRAUD TO MECHANICAL EQUIVALENTS

The late-eighteenth-century paradigm of patents as inventors' property rights produced a host of unresolved questions not just about the owner, but also about the owned object of property. A novel concept of the invention as an intangible object of property started to appear in the English case law of the period. In the traditional privilege framework of the seventeenth century, patents were not seen as legal control over an owned "object." Patent grants were understood in more dynamic terms as the exclusive economic entitlement to exercise a certain economic "trade" or "art."[55] In the 1770s, led by several decisions by Lord Mansfield, English courts developed a very different theory of patent as ownership of an informational object.[56] They built this theory on the established administrative practice of requiring patentees to deposit a specification, namely, a detailed written description of their invention.[57] Seizing on this

[55] Brad Sherman and Lionel Bently, *The Making of Modern Intellectual Property Law: The British Experience, 1760–1911* (New York: Cambridge University Press, 1999), 48.

[56] See John N. Adams and Gwen Averley, "The Patent Specification: The Role of *Liardet v. Johnson*," 7 *J. Legal Hist.* 156, 162–65 (1986); Edward C. Walterscheid, "The Early Evolution of the United States Patent Law: Antecedents" (pt. 3), 77 *J. Pat. Off. Soc'y.* 771, 793–97. The relevant cases are unreported. The most important case in this vein is *Liardet v. Johnson* (1778), which involved two separate trials. Reports of the first trial were published in the *Morning Post* and *Daily Advertiser* on February 23, 1778, and in the *London Chronicle* and *Daily Advertiser* on February 24, 1778. Reports of the second trial were published in the *Morning Post Gazeteer* and the *New Daily Advertiser* on July 20, 1778. Other relevant cases were summarized in Mansfield's notebooks, discovered in 1967 in an attic at Scone Palace – the family home of the Earls of Mansfield. They are *Yerbury v. Wallace* (1768), *Taylor v. Suckett* (1770), and *Horton v. Harvey* (1781). For references to the cases, see John Adams, "Intellectual Property Cases in Lord Mansfield's Court Notebooks," 8 *J. Legal Hist.* 18 (1987).

[57] Historians disagree on the exact reasons for the introduction of the specification. Some argue that the specification was introduced on the initiative of patentees seeking to make their grants more predictable. Others emphasize the role of the specification in enabling postgrant review of patents and speculate that it was introduced by the law officers handling patents. See E. Wyndham Hulme, "On the Consideration of the Patent Grant Past and Present," 13 *L.Q.R.* 313, 317 (1897); D. Seaborne Davies, "Early History of the Patent Specification" (pt. 1), 50 *L.Q.R.* 88, 90 (1934); Christine MacLeod, *Inventing the*

practice, English courts declared a new version of the "patent deal" between the patentee and the public. In this new version the consideration given by the patentee in exchange for the patent's legal exclusivity was no longer the introduction in practice of a useful economic activity, but the disclosure of information.[58] By 1795 it became standard to observe that "the specification is the price which the patentee is to pay for the monopoly."[59]

The new image of the patent deal had important implications for understanding patent ownership. The information that was given to the public as consideration was now also what the patentee enjoyed exclusive rights in for the duration of the patent. Patents came to be seen as control over an informational object "detached from all physical existence whatever," namely, the invention.[60] This moment when patents became *intellectual* property was just the starting point of a long struggle to come to terms with the exact meaning, nature, and scope of the owned informational object. The debate that would stretch over the next century was often framed in intensely metaphysical terms. Its implications, however, were anything but metaphysical. Wrapped in the abstract questions about the boundaries of an intangible invention were commercial struggles about the extent of the economic power created by patents.

Brad Sherman and Alain Pottage described the nineteenth-century image of invention as one embedded in the context of the industrial revolution. An invention, they argue, was conceptualized as an intellectual template from which numerous, identical, physical embodiments of a device could be replicated.[61] But this left enormous room for maneuver. Within this framework patentable invention could be defined on very different levels of abstraction. The case that would define the conceptual terrain in this area for the following several decades in both Britain and the United States was the 1795 *Boulton and Watt v. Bull*.[62] It involved an attempt by James Watt to obtain a broad scope for his steam engine

Industrial Revolution: The English Patent System 1660–1800 (New York: Cambridge University Press, 1988), 51.

[58] E. Wyndham Hulme, "On the History of Patent Law in the Seventeenth and Eighteenth Centuries," 18 *L.Q.R.* 280, 285 (1902).

[59] *Boulton and Watt v. Bull*, 126 Eng. Rep. 651, 656 (C.P. 1795). See generally Walterscheid, "The Early Evolution" (pt. 3), 801.

[60] *Boulton and Watt v. Bull*, 126 Eng. Rep. 667.

[61] Alain Pottage and Brad Sherman, *Figures of Invention: A History of Modern Patent Law* (New York: Oxford University Press, 2010).

[62] 126 Eng. Rep. 651 (C.P. 1795). A considerable part of the first American patent treatise written by Thomas Fessenden was devoted to summarizing and discussing this case. See

patent by claiming the general principles of his method for "lessening
the consumption of steam and fuel in fire engines" and not describing in
detail any specific engine design.[63] The opinions of the four judges in the
case were equally divided.[64] The split defined two competing attitudes
to the scope of patent ownership that would dominate this area during
the early nineteenth century. An old-fashioned wing strove to define
patentable invention in narrow terms. While grudgingly accepting
the notion of entitlements in intangibles, this view described patentable
invention as confined to a narrow set of variations on a concrete physical
embodiment, referred to by one judge as the "organization of a
machine."[65] The other camp advocated a broader concept of the invention as "the mechanical improvement, and not the form."[66]

   Early in the nineteenth century the views of the most influential English
commentators tended toward the conservative camp. Richard Godson,
the leading treatise writer in the field, offered a narrow interpretation of
what he called patentable "manufacture" as a "substance or a thing
made." He elaborated a slew of patentability requirements such as
"materiality" and "vendibility" that, taken together, created a semi-
materialist concept of the invention and limited its scope.[67] To avoid
trivializing patents, those taking this position explained that reproducing
the invention with minor changes constituted a fraudulent attempt
to evade the patent and therefore was considered an infringement.
As Godson put it, "[t]he law cannot be evaded by fraud or deceit of any
kind."[68] Thus when someone created an article "with slight and immaterial additions or by substitution of things somewhat different … Yet if
the manufactures are really the same and substantially the same," the
patent would be infringed.[69] One English court writing in this spirit
defined infringement as encompassing "a slight departure from the specification for the purpose of invasion only" that "would of course be a

---

Thomas G. Fessenden, *An Essay on the Law of Patents for New Inventions* (Boston:
   D. Mallory, 1810).

[63] 16 Eng. Rep. 652. On Watt's attempts to push the limits of patent protection, see Erick
   Robinson, "James Watt and the Law of Patents," 13 *Technology and Culture* 115
   (1972).

[64] Because the opinions of the judges were equally divided, no judgment was issued. The
   validity of Watt's patent was finally upheld four years later in *Hornblower & Maberly v.
   Boulton*, 101 Eng. Rep. 1285 (K.B. 1799).

[65] 126 Eng. Rep. 661.   [66] Id., 659.

[67] Richard Godson, *Law of Patents for Inventions and Copyrights* (London: J. Butterworth
   and Son, 1823), 58, 84.

[68] Id., 173.   [69] Id., 174.

fraud upon the patent."[70] Similarly, when Hindmarch discussed infringement in his 1847 treatise he wrote of "means only colourably different." He went on to state the rule that "[t]o be an infringement of a patent privilege, the defendant's act must be either a use of the art invented by the patentee, or a fraudulent imitation of it, made for the purpose of evading the privilege."[71]

Although it was unencumbered by some of the older relics of British patent jurisprudence, early American patent law inherited this basic framework for conceptualizing inventions. When faced with competing claims about the scope of patents, American courts initially used concepts taken from the vocabulary of the more conservative British view of invention. In this approach invention was identified with a concrete design, the paradigmatic case being that of a machine. Predictably, this raised the problem that others might copy a patented invention with impunity by introducing minor variations. To avoid this problem courts followed the queue of English commentators and defined the area of patent protection as encompassing an additional penumbra of versions of the protected design with only colorable differences intended to evade the patent. In an 1814 decision Justice Joseph Story spoke of "[m]ere colorable differences, or slight improvements" that "cannot shake the right of the original inventor."[72] Six years later, Justice Bushrod Washington analyzed the question of identity between the invention and an allegedly infringing embodiment by explaining that "if the difference between them be only in form, or proportions, they are the same in legal contemplation; since to permit the defendant to shelter himself under a mere formal difference, would be to sanction a fraudulent evasion of the plaintiff's right."[73] Story and Washington decided the majority of patent cases in the early decades of the century.[74] In *Davis v. Palmer* Chief Justice John Marshall instructed the jury in the same spirit: "The patent, undoubtedly, covers only the improvement precisely described. But if the imitation be

[70] *Hill v. Thomson*, 129 Eng. Rep. 427 (1818).
[71] W.A. Hindmarch, *Treatise Relating to the Law of Patent Privileges for the Sole Use of Inventions* (London: V. & R. Stevens & G.S. Norton and W. Benning, 1847), 258.
[72] *Odiorne v. Winkley*, 18 F. Cas. 581 (C.C.D. Mass. 1814). See also *Barrett v. Hall*, 2 F. Cas. 914, 924 (C.C.D. Mass 1818); *Earle v. Sawyer*, 8 F. Cas. 254 (C.C.D. Mass. 1825).
[73] *Dixon v. Moyer*, 7 F. Cas. 758 (C.C.D. Pa. 1821).
[74] Together Story and Washington decided forty of fifty-eight reported cases until 1835. See Edward C. Walterscheid, *To Promote the Progress of Science and Useful Arts: American Patent Law and Administration, 1798–1836* (Littleton, Colo.: F.B. Rothman, 1998), 359.

so nearly exact as to satisfy the jury that the imitator attempted to copy the model, and to make some almost imperceptible variation, for the purpose of evading the right of the patentee, this may be considered as a fraud on the law, and such slight variation be disregarded."[75]

Within this mode of thinking an invention was seen as the intangible equivalent of a physical template, having a concrete design and used to produce many specimens in its exact image. The penumbra of colorable variations was a prudential measure added to prevent rendering patents meaningless through fraud. This was exactly the description offered by the editor of the *Journal of the Franklin Institute* in 1830:

The modification of the mechanical powers are numerous; one may frequently as readily be substituted for another, without affording the slightest claim for invention. If after a man has devised a machine his neighbour may in this way rob him of his just dues with impunity, the patent law becomes a mere false light, to allure man to their destruction ... A custom house oath has been long a by-word, but really when persons who have only crooked a lever, or substituted a screw for a wedge, will swear that they have invented a machine, the sacredness of the averment must be as little felt, and its fallacy as palpable as testifying to false invoice.[76]

In the 1830s the emphasis began to change. The terminology of evasion or fraud did not completely disappear later in the century. Such concepts were sometimes infused into inquiries about coverage of patents and identity of inventions for many decades to come.[77] But evasion and fraud lost their defining role and sunk into the background. Courts began to explicitly instruct juries that motive or knowledge were irrelevant for purposes of determining infringement.[78] Discussions of the nature of invention gradually shifted to a metaphysical construct

---

[75] 7 F. Cas. 154, 159 (C.C.D. Va. 1827).

[76] "Specification of a patent for a machine, denominated the 'Facilitator,' for the Napping of Hats," *J. Franklin Inst.* 93 (August 6, 1830).

[77] See e.g. *Many v. Sizer*, 16 F. Cas. 684 (C.C.D. Mass. 1849); *Blanchard v. Reeves*, 3 F. Cas. 638, 639 (C.C.E.D. Pa. 1850); *McCormick v. Seymour*, 15 F. Cas. 1322, 1324 (N.D. N.Y. 1851); *Rich v. Lippincott*, 20 F. Cas. 672, 674 (C.C.W.D. Pa. 1853); *Byam v. Eddy*, 4 F. Cas. 935, 936 (C.C.D. Vt. 1853); *Sickles v. Gloucester Mfg. Co.*, 22 F. Cas. 94, 99 (C.C.D. N.J. 1856); *Page v. Ferry*, 18 F. Cas. 979, 984 (C.C.E.D. Mich. 1857).

[78] See *Parker v. Hulme*, 18 F. Cas. 1138, 1143 (C.C.E.D. Pa. 1849); *Parker v. Haworth*, 18 F. Cas. 1135, 1136 (C.C.D. Ill. 1848); *Matthews v. Skates*, 16 F. Cas. 1133, 1135 (C.C.S.D. Ala. 1860). There never existed an explicit requirement of intention or knowledge as an element of patent infringement. Nevertheless, the early formulas that discussed infringement in terms of fraud and evasion infused the infringement inquiry with notions of bad motives. The rejection of intention and knowledge was thus related to the decline of the notions of fraud and evasion.

of invention as an intellectual essence capable of manifestation in a multitude of concrete material forms.

As in other contexts, Story was at the forefront of redefining the terms of the field. While emphasizing that a patent can be only for "a theory reduced to practice in a particular structure or combination of parts," Story also insisted that a patent protects not one concrete structure but rather "the principles of a machine."[79] Relying in part on statutory language, he explained that "a mere change of the form or proportions of any machine cannot, per se, be deemed a new invention."[80] But what exactly was this "principle of the machine"? There were two intertwined notions throughout Story's opinions. One described the protected invention as a set of insubstantial variations on a physical structure. Thus Story referred to "a particular structure or combination of parts" or "mere changes of form, without any material alteration in real structure" and concluded that a "patent must be for a specific machine."[81] The second notion of invention was more abstract. It described invention as "the modus operandi, the peculiar device or manner of producing any given effect.[82]" The test of identity here was "whether the given effect is produced substantially by the same mode of operation, and the same combination of powers, in both machines."[83] The modus operandi was the ghost in the machine. It was a postulated intellectual essence that remained constant despite changes of physical structure. Decades later a counsel arguing before the Supreme Court would suggest a "thought experiment" to "prove" the following proposition: "It is obvious that, where the invention is in machinery, the mode of operation embodied in such machinery must constitute the essence of the means of producing the result. If any one think [*sic*] otherwise, let him test it by supposing the mode of operation to be taken away from the machine, and see what will remain. To enforce this truth, imagine, if possible, a machine without any mode of operation, and what is it? Clearly nothing but the wood and metal composing it."[84] By breaking the ties to any particular physical structure, the idea of the modus operandi laid the foundation for a dramatic expansion of the concept of invention.

---

[79] *Lowell v. Lewis*, 15 F. Cas. 1018, 1019 (C.C.D. Mass. 1817). See also *Odiorne*, 18 F. Cas. 582; *Treadwell v. Bladen*, 24 F. Cas. 144 (C.C.E.D. Pa. 1831).

[80] *Lowell v. Lewis*, 15 F. Cas. 1021.

[81] *Id.*, 1019, 1021. See also *Wyeth v. Stone*, 30 F. Cas. 723, 727 (C.C.D. Mass. 1840).

[82] *Whittemore v. Cutter*, 29 F. Cas. 1120, 1124 (C.C.D. Mass. 1813).

[83] *Odiorne v. Winkley*, 18 F. Cas. 582.   [84] *Burr v. Duryee*, 68 U.S. 531 (1863).

Story's opinions, which were joined by others, marked a move beyond the narrow concepts of fraud and evasion. The new approach would soon be formalized into what became known as the doctrine of mechanical equivalents. The term "mechanical equivalents" first appeared in American patent law in the 1840s. At first it was used in the context of novelty. Machines that were mere "mechanical equivalents" of existing devices, courts explained, could not be considered new inventions and hence were ineligible for a patent.[85] Soon the same terminology was being used in the context of infringement. By the 1850s the "mechanical equivalents" test had taken over judicial analysis of patent infringement. The question of identity came to be consistently defined as whether the defendant's machine, despite changes in exact design, was the "mechanical equivalent" of the patented invention.[86]

There was considerable flexibility built into the concept of mechanical equivalents. In 1868 an essay published in the *American Law Register* declared: "Thus far, it is only as the defendant has been found to have employed mechanical equivalents for the construction specified by the patentee, that he has been held guilty of infringement." Yet continuing pressures by patentees to expand protection also brought the author to remark that "[i]t is very possible that the courts may give a larger range to the doctrine of equivalents, in order to secure to the discoverer of a new physical property an adequate reward for his ingenuity."[87] The open-ended nature of the equivalence test allowed interpretation and application on different levels of abstraction. One bewildered reader of the *Scientific American* pleaded for help:

What is a "mechanical equivalent?" I know what an equivalent is and I have some idea of the terms as applied to mechanics, but what I desire to know is – what construction would be given to it by a court? I find among inventors a wide difference of opinion on this point, and a great anxiety to have it settled.[88]

---

[85] See *Cochrane v. Waterman*, 5 F. Cas. 1145 (C.C. D.C. 1844); *Allen v. Blunt*, 1 F. Cas. 448 (C.C.D. Mass. 1845); *Woodworth v. Rogers*, 30 F. Cas. 581 (C.C.D. Mass. 1847). These decisions developed earlier precedents that dealt with the question of identity in the context of invention without using the concept of mechanical equivalents. See *Evans v. Eaton*, 20 U.S. 356 (1822).

[86] The first reported case to use the term in the context of infringement is *Parker v. Stiles*, 18 F. Cas. 1163 (C.C.D. Ohio 1849). In the years 1850–1860 thirty reported federal cases used the term "mechanical equivalents."

[87] S.H.H., "Patenting a Principle," 16 *Am. L. Reg.* 129, 140 (1868).

[88] "Mechanical Equivalents in Law," 11 *Sci. Am.* 203 (1856).

The editor's answer to this query was far from satisfactory. Courts applying the mechanical equivalents test interpreted it on different levels of abstraction. *Morgan v. Seaward*, the 1836 English case that was sometimes cited by Americans in support of the doctrine of equivalents, stated it in terms that were close to earlier, narrower notions of protected invention. It described the test as "whether the defendant's machine was only colourably different, that is whether it differed merely in the substitution of what are called mechanical equivalents for the contrivances which are resorted to by the patentee."[89] When later American courts applied the doctrine of equivalents they tended to change the emphasis and move beyond the narrow notion of colorable differences. The specific articulations of the test were not uniform. Looking backward from 1889, Albert Walker observed that "[t]o define an equivalent is at present a weighty and difficult undertaking. It is weighty because many rights of property now depend, and always will depend upon the definition. It is difficult because the deliverances of the Supreme Court upon the subject are inharmonious, and because none of those deliverances are accompanied by elementary reasoning on the merits of the question."[90] Still the general trend was abstraction and expansion.

An important 1854 Supreme Court decision, *Winans v. Denmead*, nicely demonstrates the dynamics of flexibility and abstraction characteristic of the doctrine of equivalents.[91] Formally, the question in the case was about the correct construction of a patent claim. But the discussion was quickly extended to questions of identity of inventions and equivalence. The patent at issue was for a conical cargo railroad car, a shape that proved to be safer and more efficient than existing designs. The defendants made octagonal and pyramidal cars with similar advantages. Was the patentee's invention a conical car or a car of any shape that supplied similar advantages? Relying on a long string of English cases including *Morgan v. Seaward*, the plaintiff's counsel argued that the defendants' designs were clearly equivalents of the patented one. The defendants' side argued, by contrast: "It may be admitted, without hesitation, that the substitution of mechanical or chemical equivalents, as they are called, will not affect the rights of a patentee, but the cases in which this principle holds are where the modus operandi embraces more than a single way to

[89] 1 Web. Pat. Cas. 170, 171 (1836).
[90] Albert H. Walker, *Text Book of the Patent Laws of the United States of America*, 2nd ed. (New York: L.K. Strouse, 1889), 272.
[91] 56 U.S. 330 (1854).

reach the desired end. Where the invention consists of a principle embodied in a single form, the form is the principle and the principle the form, and there can be no violation of the principle without the use of the form."[92]

A slim majority of five Justices found equivalence. The court divided five to four on this question. Justice Benjamin R. Curtis, the brother of the patent treatise writer George Ticknor Curtis and an ardent Whig, wrote for the majority. According to a later treatise writer, his opinion mentioned the phrase "mode of operation" no less than twenty times. Curtis found that the "substance is a new mode of operation, by means of which a new result is obtained. It is this new mode of operation which gives it the character of an invention, and entitles the inventor to a patent; and this new mode of operation is, in view of the patent law, the thing entitled to protection." In the case at hand, "by means of this change of form, the patentee has introduced a mode of operation not before employed in burden cars, that is to say, nearly equal pressure in all directions by the entire load."[93] Having defined the invention on this high level of abstraction, Curtis naturally went on to conclude that it covered a variety of shapes and that the inventor did not limit himself to only one geometrical form. Curtis explicitly stated his motivation in choosing this high level of abstraction: "the property of inventors would be valueless, if it were enough for the defendant to say, your improvement consisted in a change of form; you describe and claim but one form."[94] For Curtis the fundamental concern was protecting the invention's market value. This led him to expand the scope of invention through the convenient device of equivalence.

Justice John Campbell produced a spirited dissent. Campbell was a Jacksonian suspicious of government patronage of industrialist and corporate interests, and his dissent was joined by three other southerners. The patentee, he wrote, "professes to have discovered the precise form most fitted for the objects in view. He describes this form, as the matter of his invention, and the principle he develops applies to no other form."[95] Campbell defined the essence of the invention on a much more concrete level, compared with Curtis: "The principle stated in the patent applies only to circular forms. The modes of operation in coal transportation have experienced no change from the skill of the plaintiff, except by the change from the rectilineal figure to the circular."[96] Campbell too was

[92] Id., 337.   [93] Id., 339.   [94] Id., 343.   [95] Id., 345.   [96] Id., 346.

explicit about his motivation. He saw the potential endless flexibility of a broad notion of equivalence as a danger to competition and innovation:

Will this be the limit to that claim? Who can tell the bounds within which the mechanical industry of the country may freely exert itself? What restraints does this patent impose in this branch of mechanic art? To escape the incessant and intense competition which exists in every department of industry, it is not strange that persons should seek the cover of the patent act, for any happy effort of contrivance or construction; nor that patents should be very frequently employed to obstruct invention, and to deter from legitimate operations of skill and ingenuity.[97]

Metaphysical debates about intangible essences and physical forms were thus fused with practical policy concerns. The absence of any naturally defined borders to the new objects of property made the connection between the malleable boundaries of the property right and the conflicting policy concerns only too obvious. Mechanical equivalence, as *Winans v. Denmead* demonstrated, was a battleground for competing views on the proper scope of invention. Gradually, broader and more abstract views of the invention, motivated by the concern of protecting market value, won this battle.

A MATTER OF PRINCIPLE

In American patent law before the Civil War, the central debate was over the patentability of principles. In 1835 a writer in the *Westminster Review* wrote: "There is another word which in patent causes, is used as a rival to the forgoing word 'manufacture,' but still more ambiguous in its meaning and which, recommended by such ambiguity, is in very frequent requisition. The word is 'principle.'" He went on to observe: "To make this law-phantom, the witchcraft used by the lawyers consists in mingling three different meanings together, and, by the aid of certain professional solemnities, producing a mystical word, capable of harlequinizing an idea into many various forms."[98] The same "law-phantom" haunted American patent law. Every now and then a judge or a commentator remarked that the debate over the patentability of principles is rooted in semantic confusion, that the opposing views are perfectly reconcilable because they

---

[97] Id., 347.
[98] "Unreasonableness of Judge-made Law in Setting Aside Patent," 22 *Westminster Review*, 242, 249 (American ed. 1835).

use the term "principle" to denote different things.[99] And then the debate
would rage on. The patentability of principles debate had a magnetic
power because it was a meeting point of three major forces shaping
nineteenth-century patent law: an economic pressure to expand patent
protection, a countervailing anxiety over the monopolization of
knowledge, and an emerging concept of the invention as an intellectual
essence encompassing many concrete forms.

The debate revolved around two dovetailing legal questions: What
kind of subject matter can be owned by a patent? and What constitutes
an infringement? Going all the way back at least to *Boulton and Watt v.
Bull,* there were two universally accepted propositions. One was that
patent ownership encompasses more than exact reproduction of a specific
design. The other was that knowledge of nature cannot be owned and
must remain free for use by all. The two propositions were on a clear
collision course. In his 1854 treatise Curtis stated the first proposition
as follows: "an infringement is a copy made after and agreeing with the
principle laid down in the specification."[100] This claim was sometimes
presented as a mere elaboration of the doctrine of mechanical equivalents.
An 1850 essay in the *Scientific American* about the "Nature of the Patent
Right" explained that "the *essence,* the *spirit*" of the invention is the
"mode of applying the natural law in question, and also all merely
equivalent means," and concluded that an invention is "*a principle
embodied in practice.*"[101] But frequently claiming protection to principles
was an argument for expanding the patent scope beyond the zone of
structural variations covered by the doctrine of equivalents. An 1868
American Law Register note outlined the disagreement on the question.
It described the "diversity of sentiment . . . as to the extent of the right" in
terms of two conflicting camps. One camp argued that a patentee
"is entitled to the exclusive use of the principle, when employed for the
same purpose by whatever instrumentalities the purpose is effected; and
that a patent should expressly claim not only the instrumentalities
adopted by the patentee, but also the use of the principle for the purpose
however applied."[102] The other camp believed that a patentee "is entitled
to a patent for the method, or process or mechanism which he has

---

[99] See e.g. Willard Phillips, *The Law of Patents for Inventions* (Boston: American Stationers' Co., 1837), 96, 101 n. 37; *Barrett v. Hall,* 2 F. Cas. 923.
[100] Curtis, *A Treatise on the Law of Patents,* 306.
[101] 6 *Sci. Am.* 101 (1850). See also *Blanchard v. Reeves,* 3 F. Cas. 639.
[102] "Patenting a Principle," 129.

contrived, and that he can set up no claim to anything more, nor vindicate a right to anything more."[103]

In 1831 the *Journal of the Franklin Institute* published an article proposing "Patents for Principles" on the theory that "[n]ew principles may be discovered by persons who do not see any useful application of them; yet as soon as they are made known, such application is quickly made by others." The author speculated that "[i]f the first person who discovered that steam is capable of exerting great expansive force had obtained a patent for that discovery, and thereby given publicity to the fact, it is probable that ... the steam engine and many other inventions with which the force of steam is connected, would have been employed beneficially some centuries earlier."[104] Such direct calls for ownership of natural principles by the first to discover them were rare. It was much more common to argue for ownership of principles while affirming the orthodox view that laws of nature and fundamental truths must not be propertized. But how could one distinguish between patenting a "principle" irrespective of "instrumentalities" and patenting an abstract truth? Much ink was spilled by American jurists wrestling with this question.

One typical strategy devised to deal with the problem was the distinction between a principle and the application of a principle. It was Curtis who in his 1854 treatise supplied one of the earliest versions of this distinction. Curtis started his discussion of patentability by reciting the familiar axiom that "the subject of a valid patent ... cannot be a mere elementary principle, or intellectual discovery." This rule, he assured the readers, addressed concerns about the monopolization of knowledge: "The consequences of allowing a patent for an abstract art or principle ... are apparent, when it is considered that principles are the elements of science; and if a patent could be taken for a newly discovered principle in science; it would cover every object to which that principle could be applied, and the whole field of the arts would thus at once be occupied by a few monopolists."[105] At the same time, Curtis insisted that "[a]ny definition or description ... of the act of invention which excludes the application of the natural law, or power, or property of matter, on which the inventor has relied for the production of a new effect, and the object of such application, and confines it to the precise arrangement of the particles of matter which he may have brought together, must be erroneous."[106] Instead, the scope of protection covered many concrete forms. As Curtis

[103] Id., 130.   [104] *Journal of the Franklin Institute* 276 (October 1831).
[105] Curtis, *A Treatise on the Law of Patents*, 91.   [106] Id., 8.

explained: "If the patentee has invented some mode of carrying the principle into effect, he is entitled, it is said, to protect himself from all other modes of carrying the same principle into effect."[107] The implications of this move became clear in the discussion of infringement:

[W]hen a party has invented some mode of carrying into effect a law of natural science, or a rule of practice, it is the application of that law or rule which constitutes the peculiar feature of this invention … he is entitled to protect himself from all other modes of making the same application … The substantial identity, therefore, that is to be looked to in cases of this kind, respects that which constitutes the essence of the invention, namely, the application of the principle. If the mode of carrying the same principle into effect, adopted by the defendant, still shows only that the principle admits of the same application in a variety of forms, or by a variety of apparatuses, the jury will be authorized to treat such mode as a piracy of the original invention.[108]

Protection for the "application of a principle," thus construed, meant the expansion of the patent's scope beyond the boundaries of minor structural variations.

Curtis was walking a thin line. He took pains to abstract the patent scope while simultaneously insisting that no fundamental truths of science were appropriated. As he put it: "It is in truth, wholly incorrect to say that the inventor, in such cases, because his patent is held to embrace such a general claim, monopolizes the law, property or quality of matter which he has applied by a particular means to the accomplishment of a certain end. His patent leaves the law, property, or quality of matter, precisely where it found it, as common property, to be used by any one, in the production of a new end, by a new adaptation, of a different character. It appropriates the law, property, or quality of matter, only so far as it is involved in the subject with which, the means by which, and the end for which the inventor has applied it; and this application constitutes the essence and substance of the invention."[109] Woven into these arguments was a concept of the invention as an intellectual essence that persisted despite changes of mere "form." "[I]t is obvious," Curtis wrote, "that there is a characteristic, an essence, or purpose of every invention, which, in our law has been termed by jurists its *principle*; and that this can ordinarily be perceived and apprehended by the mind."[110] It was this elusive "essence," rather than the ephemeral "form" that was owned, or, in the words of Curtis, "[I]nventions are independent of form."[111] The upshot of such arguments was unmooring

---

[107] Id., 93.   [108] Id., 337–38.   [109] Id., 15–16.   [110] Id., 10.   [111] Id., 17.

invention from any concrete design and expanding its scope beyond the notion of mechanical equivalents.

The debate unfolded in the case law in only slightly less metaphysical terms. Views similar to those advocated by Curtis began to gather force among courts with real implications for the scope of patent rights. Judge John Kintizing Kane at the Eastern District of Pennsylvania was a vocal advocate of patents for principles. In 1849 he upheld the validity of the Zebulon and Austin Parker reaction water wheel patent, which claimed "the propulsive effect of vortical motion of water in a reaction wheel, operating by its centrifugal force." In his opinion Kane wrote the following manifesto:

All machines may be regarded as merely devices, by the instrumentality of which the laws of nature are made applicable and operative to the production of a particular result. He who first discovers that a law of nature can be so applied, and having devised machinery to make it operative, introduces it in a practical form, to the knowledge of his fellow-men, is a discoverer and inventor of the highest grade – not merely of the mechanism, the combination of iron, brass, and wood, in the form of levers, screws or pulleys – but the force which operates through the mechanical medium – the principle ... and this title as a discoverer he may lawfully assert, and secure to himself by letters patent; thus establishing his property, not only in the formal device for which mechanical ingenuity can at once, as soon as the principle is known, imagine a thousand substitutes – some as good, others better, perhaps all dissimilar, yet all illustrative of the same principle, and depending on it – but in the essential principle which his machine was the first to embody, to exemplify, to illustrate, to make operative, and to announce to mankind.[112]

Kane denied that such protection to principles was "to patent an abstraction." It is rather, he wrote, "to patent the invention as the inventor has given it to the world, in its full dimensions and extent; nothing less, but nothing more."[113]

In 1853 it was revealed that the Supreme Court was bitterly divided on the question of patenting principles. At issue in *Le Roy v. Tatham* was a patent for a pipe-making machine.[114] It was doubtful that the design of the machine was new. The innovation consisted in applying the new discovery that solid lead could be made to cohere under conditions of high heat and pressure. The patented machine used solid lead under such conditions instead of molten lead. Sitting as a Circuit Court judge,

---

[112] *Parker v. Hulme*, 18 F. Cas. 1138, 1141 (C.C.E.D. Pa. 1849).
[113] Id. See also *Detmold v. Reeves*, 7 F. Cas. 547 (C.C.E.D. Pa. 1851).
[114] 55 U.S. 156 (1853).

Justice Samuel Nelson instructed the jury not to consider the novelty of the machine's structural design because it was sufficient that the machine was "used and applied in connection with the practical development of a principle, newly discovered, producing a new and useful result."[115] This, the defendant objected, amounted to a patent in the newly discovered principle. Justice John McLean, writing for the majority of the Supreme Court, agreed. "The word principle," he complained, "is used by elementary writers on patent subjects, and sometimes in adjudications of courts, with such a want of precision in its application, as to mislead."[116] Trying his own hand at a definition, McLean described a principle as "a fundamental truth; an original cause; a motive" and made it clear that "these cannot be patented, as no one can claim in either of them an exclusive right." Nor could anyone, including the first discoverer, claim an exclusive right in a natural abstract "power" such as steam power, electricity, or "any other power in nature, which is alike open to all."[117] For the majority, avoiding the unacceptable result of private ownership of natural principles required defining patentable invention as the concrete design of some physical apparatus. To prevent a patent in a principle the court construed the plaintiff's patent as claiming the structural design of a specific machine and therefore reversed the lower's court instruction that the novelty of this design was immaterial.

Writing for the three dissenters was none other than Justice Nelson, who formulated the challenged jury instruction at the court below. His dissent was a vigorous defense of patenting principles. Nelson insisted that the thing invented and patented was not any aspect of the structural design of the machine, but rather the application of the newly discovered trait of lead for the making of pipes irrespective of the apparatus used. "[T]he leading feature of the invention," he explained, "consists in the discovery of a new property in the article of lead."[118] Nelson distinguished between the essence of the invention and incidental aspects of applying it: "The discovery of this new element or property led naturally to the apparatus, by which a new and most useful result is produced. The apparatus was but incidental, and subsidiary to the new and leading idea of the invention."[119] This naturally led to the conclusion that the thing invented and patented was "not simply ... the apparatus employed by the patentees, but ... the embodiment or employment of the newly-discovered property in the metal, and the practical adaption

---

[115] Id., 174.   [116] Id.   [117] Id., 175.   [118] Id., 180.   [119] Id., 182.

[*sic*] of it, by these means, to the production of a new result, namely, the manufacture of wrought pipe out of solid lead."[120]

His reasoning positioned Nelson face to face with the inevitable question: "[I]s this the proper subject matter of a patent?" Nelson responded with his own rhetorical question: "And why should not this be the law?" To limit the patent to the "mode or means of the new application," he said, would be perverse, "as no one can but see, that the original conception reaches far beyond these."[121] For him the structural design of the machine was "but incidental, and flowing naturally from the original conception; and hence of inconsiderable merit."[122] The majority's approach, Nelson said, would have limited Benjamin Franklin to patenting his kite, thread, and key. Nelson must have been aware that his anachronistic suggestion that Franklin could have patented "his great original conception" was setting off all the majority's alarm bells. Wasn't he advocating a patent in an "element of nature"? Nelson said no. The patentee, he wrote, "is protected only in the enjoyment of the application for the special purpose and object to which it has been newly applied by his genius and skill. For every other purpose and end, the principle is free for all mankind to use."[123]

The Supreme Court's decision in *Tatham* was read as standing for the firm proposition that abstract "principles" could not be patented.[124] Natural principles could not be owned even by the person who was the first to discover them and had to stay open to all. In reality, *Tatham* demonstrated the considerable flexibility built into the terms of the debate. All agreed that natural principles and scientific truths could not be owned. Within this joint framework, however, radically different positions could be maintained. The majority articulated a narrow concept of invention as a set of close variations on a concrete structural design and described broader concepts as propertizing natural principles. The dissent insisted that the true nature of invention encompassed a much broader scope, which nevertheless left the elements of nature untouched. The narrow concept won for now, but the terms of the discourse proved to be extremely malleable.

The climax of the debate over patenting principles was what came to be known as the Great Telegraph Case. This was, in fact, a series of different cases litigated in various federal courts and involving a variety of devices. The motivating force was an attempt by firms associated with

---

[120] Id., 183.   [121] Id., 187.   [122] Id.   [123] Id.
[124] See "Principles of Patents: Important Decision," 8 *Sci. Am.* 238 (1853).

Samuel Morse's nascent telegraph empire to quash competition through patent infringement lawsuits. The cases involved a complex array of business relationships and legal arguments, but the patentability question looming large over all of them was the same. At the heart of the issue was Morse's attempt, much like James Watt more than half a century earlier, to define his invention as broadly as possible. Morse was preoccupied with both capturing his technological contribution and fending off rivals and their various devices. In his writings he formulated and reformulated the essence of his invention. He tried such formulas as "Telegraphic Speech by Electricity" or even the "possibility of marking or printing intelligible characters at any distance by means of any power whatever." According to his biographer Morse was preoccupied with this issue until the end of his life.[125] In litigation it was the broad eighth claim in Morse's 1848 reissued patent that gave lawyers headaches. The claim that, if valid, would ensnare telegraph designs significantly different from Morse's read:

I do not propose to limit myself to the specific machinery, or parts of machinery, described in the foregoing specifications and claims; the essence of my invention being the use of the motive power of the electric or galvanic current, which I call electro-magnetism, however developed, for making or printing intelligible characters, letters, or signs, at any distances, being a new application of that power, of which I claim to be the first inventor or discoverer.[126]

Here was an attempt to patent a "principle," if there ever was one.

The litigation campaign produced uneven results. The first decision issued involved the "Columbian" telegraph, a device invented by Samuel Zook and Edward Barnes and used by Henry O'Reilly, a former Morse associate turned a bitter rival. A Kentucky federal court upheld Morse's broad claim and found it was infringed.[127] Two years later in a Massachusetts case involving the House telegraph, Justice Levi Woodbury strongly rejected the argument that one could have a valid patent for "a mere principle." "The patent," he wrote, "must be in order to possess validity, not for the principle, but for the mode, machine or manufacture, to carry out the principle and to reduce it to practice." Patents for principles, he warned, would "render the first improver a monopolist and "petrify everything as it stood, to the great loss of mankind, and in derogation of both private and public rights to advance human

---

[125] Kenneth Silverman, *Lightening Man: The Accursed Life of Samuel F.B. Morse* (New York: Knopf, 2003), 302.

[126] *O'Reilly v. Morse*, 56 U.S. 62, 112 (1854).

[127] *Morse v. O'Reilly*, 17 F. Cas. 871 (C.C.D. Ky. 1848).

improvement and human power."[128] It took another year before Judge Kane in Pennsylvania produced an equally forceful opinion that upheld Morse's broad claim and emphatically justified patenting general principles.[129] This time it was Baine's automatic telegraph that was accused of infringement. In his opinion Kane developed the notion of inventing and patenting an "art." An art was one of the statutory categories of patentable subject matter, but Kane used the term loosely as a basis for a qualitative hierarchy of inventions. He distinguished between ordinary inventions limited to a specific machine or process and foundational innovations establishing a whole new art. The inventor of an art, he argued, deserved as much protection as that of an ordinary invention. "Why should the type, or the ink, or the press itself," he asked, "be dignified beyond the art, to which they minister in such humble subordination, and without which they are rubbish?"[130] Kane's hierarchy was clear. In his narrative makers of ordinary improvements were no doubt inventors who "toiled ingeniously and well, to advance or embellish a preexisting art." But such inventors "had no share in the discovery of the art itself, and can no more claim to share the property, which its discovery may have conferred on another, than he who has devised some appropriate setting for a gem can assert an interest in the gem itself."[131] Morse, by contrast, was obviously a maker of a gem. Morse, Kane wrote, "declared the existence of a new art, asserted his right in it as its inventor and owner, and announcing fully its nature and merits, invoked in return the continued protection of the laws. From this time his title was vested as patentee of the art."[132]

By 1853 Morse's patent had produced a wide range of judicial opinions on the nature and scope of patentable invention. The same was true of public debate The *Scientific American* took a strong position against patenting principles. The journal called Kane's opinion "an extraordinary document" and praised Woodbury. "There can be no such a thing as an art apart from a process," it declared, and concluded that "[r]ecording messages without any reference to the means of doing so, is a mere abstraction."[133] In another article in the *Scientific American* the writer turned the argument of inventors' just reward on its head. Decisions such as that of Judge Kane, he said, lead to "the miserable conclusion" of "placing the barbaric Chinese mode of printing over the splendid

---

[128] *Smith v. Downing*, 22 F. Cas. 511, 519 (C.C.D. Mass. 1850).
[129] *French v. Rogers*, 9 F. Cas. 790 (C.C.E.D. Pa. 1851).   [130] Id., 794.   [131] Id.
[132] Id., 793.   [133] "Great Telegraph Case: Uncertainties of Law," 7 *Sci. Am.* 67 (1851).

discoveries of Gutenberg." It is, he concluded, "a daring presumption against the general rights of inventors," and "many poor and honest inventors have been deprived unjustly of their rights by such decisions."[134] The magazine allowed Amos Kendall – Morse's close business associate and a former Postmaster General – to present his views on the subject. Kendall argued that a person who discovered a new principle and reduced it to practice should "secure the principle," including "every mode of applying the principle or agent as to produce the specified result." He appealed to the by now familiar arguments: "[H]e who discovers a principle, and renders it valuable to society" is "the most useful and meritorious of all inventors," and any other rule would "permit another, who would have never thought of the subject but for my discovery (which may be used in a thousand modes), to come in and take it from me by a new mode".[135] The *Scientific American* replied that "[t]he policy of an inventor, is to ask for a patent for what he has invented and not to fence himself with wide claims."[136]

The question finally arrived at the Supreme Court on appeal from the Kentucky decision.[137] By now the arguments were well rehearsed. R.H. Gillet, who represented O'Reilly, presented the patentability question dramatically: "This is the most important question raised in this case. Its decision will determine whether our patent laws really promote the progress of the useful arts ... whether the principle of nature not invented by man can be monopolized by one to the exclusion of others." Gillet argued that Morse tried to claim "that a power provided by the Ruler of the universe can be patented to or monopolized by other man" and called it "bold intrusion upon the common property of man."[138]

The Supreme Court was divided again. Chief Justice Roger Taney, writing for the majority, found that Morse's claim was overbroad and invalid. His opinion blended indistinguishably two reasons for this finding. One was that Morse tried to claim the kind of subject matter that could not be owned by a patent not a specific design but an abstract natural principle. The other reason was that the broad claim failed the statutory requirement of submitting a written description of the invention

[134] "Telegraph – Principles of Patents – Judge Kane's Decision," 7 *Sci. Am.* 181 (1852).
[135] "Principles of Patents," 8 *Sci. Am.* 170 (1853).   [136] Id.
[137] *O'Reilly v. Morse*, 56 U.S. 62.
[138] Ransom H. Gillet, *First Telegraph Case before the United States Supreme Court: Henry O'Reilly and others, appellants, versus S.F.B. Morse and others, appellees. Sketch of the Opening Argument of R.H. Gillet on the Appeal of O'Reilly from the Decision of Judge Monroe in Kentucky* (New York: John A. Gray, 1853), 19.

detailed enough to enable others to make and use it. Morse's claim encompassed numerous ways of communicating by using electromagnetism, possibly including many that were not yet known. But his description taught the public how to use only his specific design, not all the other potential ways covered by his claim. While Taney was vague on the exact legal reasoning, his conclusion was clear: abstract principles, detached from a concrete design, could not be protected by a patent. "No one," he wrote, "will maintain that Fulton could have taken out a patent for his invention of propelling vessels by steam, describing the process and machinery he used, and claimed under it the exclusive right to use the motive power of steam, however developed, for the purpose of propelling vessels ... Neither could the man who first discovered that steam might, by a proper arrangement of machinery, be used as a motive power to grind corn or spin cotton, claim the right to the exclusive use of steam as a motive power for the purpose of producing such effects."[139]

Justice Robert Grier, writing for the three dissenters, insisted that Morse's claim was valid. He based this conclusion on a broad concept of invention as an intellectual essence that could take many forms. Echoing Kane's notion of inventing an art, Grier argued that in some cases the "application of a principle is the most important part of the invention, and where the machinery, apparatus, or other means, by which the principle is applied, are incidental only and not of the essence of his invention." In such cases, "the essential agent in the invention" is not the "application of the mechanical devices" but rather "the new application of the operative element." Grier did not deny that abstract laws of nature could not be patented. But he insisted that Morse's case was different because "he who takes this new element or power, as yet useless, from the laboratory of the philosopher, and makes it the servant of man; who applies it to the perfecting of a new and useful art, or to the improvement of one already known, is the benefactor to whom the patent law tenders its protection." Restricting such an inventor to patenting a specific design, Grier said, is "viewing a statue or a monument through a microscope."[140]

O'Reilly won the battle but lost his war. Although he invalidated Morse's broad claim, Taney found that the Columbian telegraph was similar enough under the conventional doctrine of mechanical equivalents to infringe the other more narrowly drawn claims in the patent.[141] Regardless of the outcome, the legacy of *O'Reilly v. Morse* was that

---

[139] 56 U.S. 113.   [140] Id., 133.   [141] Id., 123–24.

natural principles could not be patented.[142] Arguments for patenting principles did not disappear altogether following the decision, but they found little judicial sympathy. In the 1864 case *Burr v. Duryee* Justice Grier, the writer of the dissent in *O'Reilly*, condemned in the name of a unanimous Court a patentee's attempt to claim broadly, which he described as a "first experiment in the art of expansion by an equivocal claim which may be construed as a claim for the result or product of the machine, or for its principle."[143] He also described the claim as an "attempt to convert an improved machine into an abstraction, a principle or mode of operation, or a still more vague and indefinite entity often resorted to in argument, an 'idea'" that "may be used as successfully to mystify a plain matter as the words used in the specification."[144] Grier did not formally recant his former views. He distinguished between foundational innovations that "consist in a new application of certain natural forces to produce a certain result to which they had never before been applied" and more modest inventions in the form of a "labor-saving machine, which is a mere combination of certain mechanical devices."[145] Presumably, patenting principles was permissible only in the former case. The enduring aspect of the decision, however, was not Grier's rationalization but his strongly professed aversion to mystification through abstraction. Decades later, one commentator remarked on *Burr* that "the Supreme Court has ever since had a positive tendency to disregard whatever is abstract and intangible in questions of infringement and to base its conclusions upon the concrete features of the issues at bar."[146] Other courts responded to direct attempts of claiming principles in the same spirit.[147]

Thus the debate on patenting principles was concluded in a triumph for the view that rejected such patents as too abstract and as an attempt to monopolize knowledge. But this was far from the end of the story. After the Civil War the prolific minds of patent lawyers would devise new ways of drafting patents as broadly as Morse's eighth claim without explicitly claiming principles. In the following decades, these maneuvers

[142] See "The Late Telegraph Decision," 9 *Sci. Am.* 189 (1854); "The Great Telegraph Case," 9 *Sci. Am.* 22 (1854).
[143] *Burr v. Duryee*, 68 U.S. 531, 568 (1864).   [144] Id., 577.   [145] Id., 568.
[146] Walker, *Text Book of the Patent Laws*, 268.
[147] See e.g. *Corning v. Burden*, 56 U.S. 252, 268 (1854); *Singer v. Walmsley*, 22 F. Cas. 207, 210 (C.C.D. Md. 1860); *Steam Gauge & Lantern Co. v. St. Louis Railway Supplies Mfg. Co.*, 25 F. 491, 492 (C.C.E.D. Missouri 1885); *Excelsior Needle Co. v. Union Needle Co.*, 32 F. 221, 224 (1885); *Reay v. Raynor*, 19 F. 308, 310 (S.D. N.Y. 1884).

gradually won approval. Through solicitation for such practices courts expanded the permissible scope of patents, while insisting all along that knowledge remained free as the air. Underlying this process were important developments in how patents were used and conceived of by important economic actors.

WITHIN HIS DOMAIN THE PATENTEE IS CZAR

The most important driving force in shaping patent ownership in the late nineteenth and early twentieth centuries was a pressure from big business to expand and abstract the scope of patents. An important preliminary question pertains to the source of this drive. Business firms were as likely to find themselves subjected to the exclusionary power of patents as they were to wield it. For every Morse there was an O'Reilly. In fact, some dominant economic interests – the prime example being railroad companies – were much more concerned with the risk of being excluded from access to essential technology than they were interested in excluding others from their own technological innovation through patents. The source of the economic pull toward broad patents was thus not simply a disproportionate expectation of reaping rewards for innovation relative to bearing patents' cost on access to it. The crucial factor was, rather, the rise of patents as important tools for stabilization, coordination, and management of the uncertainty of unbridled competition. The single most important development in the late-nineteenth-century American economy was the rise of what Alfred Chandler called "the visible hand."[148] Large, bureaucratized, and integrated corporations gradually came to dominance in various sectors. Production and distribution were brought under the control of centralized management instead of the invisible hand of the market. Within this context there were several interlocking forces pulling in the direction of stability and predictability as major economic goals. The interest of established corporations in maintaining their position combined with an emerging distrust of the vagaries of competition fueled by the shocks of business cycles.[149] The shift of power to a professional managerial class

[148] Alfred Chandler Jr., *The Visible Hand: The Managerial Revolution in American Business* (Cambridge, Mass.: Belknap Press, 1977).

[149] See Gabriel Kollko, *Railroads and Regulation, 1877–1916* (Princeton, N.J.: Princeton University Press 1965), 7–29; Martin J. Sklar, *The Corporate Reconstruction of American Capitalism, 1890–1916: The Market, the Law, and Politics* (New York: Cambridge University Press 1988), 53; Morton J. Horwitz, *The Transformation of American Law*

tended to encourage policies that prioritized long-term stability and growth over short-term profits.[150] These trends were buttressed by a new rising culture of "scientific management" designed to bring rationality and order to economic life.[151] Patents were not the central plank of the new trend toward economic stabilization and control. But they became one important tool in the arsenal of business leaders pursuing this goal, especially in technology-intensive industries.

The telegraph industry was one of the earliest examples of the new form of business organization. As shown by Paul Israel, it was also pioneering in the use of patents as industrial strategy instruments.[152] Morse's mid-century attempt to patent principles was part of a strategy of building an industrial empire on the foundation of a patent. The main goal of asserting the broad scope of Morse's patent was not to expand the sources of income of Morse the inventor from his invention. It was designed to allow the various enterprises based on the Morse telegraph to control the national and local markets by dominating rivals who used a variety of competing technologies. The strategy was thwarted by the Supreme Court, and when Western Union became the unchallenged dominant player in the field after the Civil War, patents did not play a major role in helping it gain this position. As the telegraphy industry matured, however, it rediscovered the value of patents and perfected their use.

Strategic uses of patents first appeared in smaller, niche telegraphy markets. John Gamewell, the founder of the Gamewell Fire Alarm Telegraph Company, pursued a policy designed "to have every patent issued on Fire Telegraph examined as soon as issued and if found to contain any point of value at once to purchase the same and incorporate it into [the] system."[153] The Gold and Stock Telegraph Company, which specialized in business news, was another early innovator. In 1870 its president established a policy "to control all improvements which may present themselves and by the possession of which we can more surely

1870–1960: The Crisis of Legal Orthodoxy (New York: Oxford University Press, 1992), 81–83.

[150] Chandler, *The Visible Hand*, 10.

[151] Samuel Haber, *Efficiency and Uplift: Scientific Management in the Progressive Era, 1890–1920* (Chicago, Ill.: University of Chicago Press, 1964); Robert Kanigel, *The One Best Way: Frederick Winslow Taylor and the Enigma of Efficiency* (New York: Viking, 1997).

[152] Paul Israel, *From Machine Shop to Industrial Laboratory: Telegraphy and the Emerging Context of American Invention, 1830–1920* (Baltimore, Md.: Johns Hopkins University Press, 1992), 121–51.

[153] Quoted in id., 124.

control our business."[154] Under the leadership of William Orton, Western Union started taking notice of such strategies. In 1871, motivated by fear that a competitor might gain control of technology essential for its system, Western Union purchased the Charles Grafton Page patent for the induction coil. Obtaining and enforcing the patent was costly, but it brought home the point of the importance of patent control over key technologies.[155] In the same year Orton allowed Joseph B. Stearns to experiment on the company system with "duplexing" – a method for simultaneously sending two messages in opposite directions over a single line. Orton came to see this technology as extremely valuable. Western Union purchased all duplexing patent rights and began to aggressively enforce them against competitors.[156] Gradually, more subtle strategies began to emerge. In 1872 Western Union hired Thomas Edison, who had established a reputation for developing variations on existing technologies. In a letter to Stearns, Orton explained that he hired Edison because he became apprehensive that "processes for working Duplex would be devised which would successfully evade your patents" and because the attorneys "had not done their work in shutting out competitors." Edison, he said, was hired to invent as many related processes as possible for the following purpose: "to anticipate other inventors in new modes and also to patent as many combinations as possible."[157]

George Westinghouse was one of the first inventors to attune his patent strategy to the new world of corporate stability. Westinghouse made his commercial break with the air brake, an invention that ensured him a tough clientele. Railroads' technology policy prioritized stability and standardization over innovation. Concerned about being excluded from essential technology, railroads often used their power and high level of technical expertise to gain control over it. Westinghouse neutralized the railroads' technological conservatism by targeting the one area most susceptible to public and political pressures for innovation, namely, safety.[158] He outmaneuvered the railroad companies in the race for controlling the technology by shrewdly using patents. To prevent his clients from acquiring a strong position in the market for the technology or improvements to it, Westinghouse insisted on selling the final product and adamantly refused persistent demands for licensing.[159] When the

[154] Quoted in id., 125.   [155] Id., 136.   [156] Id., 138.   [157] Quoted in id.
[158] Steven W. Usselmlman, "From Novelty to Utility: George Westinghouse and the Business of Innovation during the Age of Edison," 66 *Bus. Hist. Rev.* 251, 283 (1992).
[159] Id., 286–87.

hegemonic position of the air brake was at risk of being undermined by the vacuum brake, he went on the attack with a broad interpretation and aggressive enforcement of his carefully built patent portfolio.[160] And when this strategy was exhausted, he ended up buying the manufacturer of the vacuum brake along with its patents, only to shut down this technology after announcing that an impartial evaluation showed the air brake to be superior.[161] Threats from other upstart technologies were neutralized by preventing interoperability. This last maneuver relied heavily on enforcing Westinghouse's patent on a hose coupling essential for connecting brakes manufactured by others to systems employing his own.[162]

When his earlier patents expired, Westinghouse managed to capture the freight train market by patenting some improvements on key technologies necessary for the safe operation of the air brake on such trains.[163] In the 1880s and 1890s Westinghouse employed a similar strategy to dominate the emerging train-signaling market. This time, however, he relied mainly on purchasing the key patents. In 1881 Westinghouse bought a fundamental patent on electrical circuits activated by train and started working on adding and patenting improvements. By carefully buying patents on many innovations in the field, he managed to stay ahead of the competition and maintain a dominant position in yet another lucrative railroad supply market.[164] When Westinghouse and his enterprise entered the field of electricity, they replicated the same patent strategies that served them so well in the railroad area.

Strategic uses of patents for stabilization became significant in the late nineteenth century. For companies using technology, this usually meant planned efforts for locating and purchasing from external inventors patents essential for their business strategy.[165] The major development of the early twentieth century was the rise of corporate R&D. Internalizing invention achieved a more perfect union of bureaucratized management and its typical interest in stability with the use of patents as means for corporate security. Rather than being dependent on external development, firms could now direct and shape the inventive process ab initio in accordance with their corporate security goals. In the words of

[160] Id., 289–90. [161] Id., 290. [162] Id., 291. [163] Id., 293–95.
[164] Id., 293–98.
[165] In the 1870s under Orton's leadership Western Union made some efforts to support and nurture innovation. This strategy was abandoned, however, after Orton's death. Israel, *From Machine Shop to Industrial Laboratory*, 141–42.

Willis R. Whitney, the first director of research at General Electric: "Our research laboratory was a development of the idea that large industrial organizations have both an opportunity and a responsibility for their own life insurance."[166]

AT&T was one of the earliest and strongest examples of this trend. In its first decades telephony followed in the footsteps of the telegraph industry. AT&T did what the original Morse enterprises could not. With the help of a favorable court decision it built a hegemonic empire in telephony on the foundation of the broad Bell patent. As the original patent approached its end toward the end of the century, the company's "life insurance" strategy followed the familiar pattern of acquiring control of externally developed inventions essential for securing its supremacy. The earliest move in this direction was acquiring telephone exchange patents. Theodore Vail, AT&T's president, described it as follows:

One of the first things that was fully developed in our minds was the necessity of occupying the field; not only that but of surrounding ourselves with everything that would protect the business ... Just as soon as we started into the district exchange system we found that it would develop a thousand and one little patents and inventions with which to do the business which was necessary, and that is what we wanted to control and get possession of.[167]

The next target was dominating long-distance telephony by controlling the key technology in this area – the amplifier, or as AT&T called it, a "repeater." For that purpose the company acquired Michael Pupin's loading coil patent and then Lee DeForest's audion patent.[168]

Things took a new turn in 1907 with the reorientation of the research department under J.J. Carty toward in-house technological innovation. As the company began to control and direct the innovation process, a new variety of subtle strategies for using patents as a means of corporate security had emerged. Patents in fundamental technologies used to exclude others from markets based on them or obtain a competitive edge remained important. But now there were other strategies as well. As Vail's "thousand and one patents" reference implied, one concern was coverage. Control over an area often required patenting numerous alternative ways

---

[166] Quoted in Leonard S. Reich, *The Making of American Industrial Research: Science and Business at GE and Bell, 1876–1926* (New York: Cambridge University Press, 1985), 37.

[167] Quoted in Federal Communications Committee, *Investigation of the Telephone Industry in the United States* (Washington, D.C.: G.P.O., 1939), 181, n. 6.

[168] Leonard S. Reich, "Research, Patents, and the Struggle to Control Radio: A Study of Big Business and the Uses of Industrial Research," 51 *Bus. Hist. Rev.* 208, 211–13 (1977).

for achieving the same end, sometimes at the expense of further innovation. In 1912 Carty, by then the vice president of AT&T, instructed its research subsidiary Western Electric that "the patenting of the alternatives is a very important feature of our work ... the idea being that as far as possible on all new developments of substantial importance, we patent the alternative methods."[169] Another important strategy was safeguarding one's position in its main market by obtaining a strong hold on technology in another. In 1920 AT&T's chief engineer, Frank Jewett, remarked on his company's research and patenting in the field of radio: "[I]f we never derive any other benefit from our work than that which follows the safe-guarding of our wire interests we can look upon the time and money as having been returned to us many times over."[170] Jewett meant that although AT&T had no interest in the radio market, its strong technological position there allowed it to make sure through agreements and trade of rights that the other dominant players in radio would not encroach on its primary market of wired public communication. One of the company's lawyers similarly observed that "though we have weathered the storm, to a large extent, there may be other storms where we will need our patent protection." Leaving no room for doubt, he explained that what he had in mind was "various companies throughout the country becoming familiarized with wireless apparatus, and attempting to use such apparatus in wire broadcasting or in leased-wire telegraphy or telephony."[171] In the earlier days of its foray into radio, AT&T's policy was aimed at achieving enough innovation to dominate the field but not too much as to run the risk of making radio an alternative to wired public communication.[172] By the early twentieth century corporate security through patents grew into an array of strategies, anything from excluding competition from one's market through holding leverage in existing and potential markets to hoarding bargaining chips for negotiating access to necessary technology controlled by others. Major corporations such as AT&T, GE Westinghouse, Eastman Kodak, Du Pont, and others established their own R&D divisions and adopted such strategies.

In 1908 Edwin Prindle, who as a patent lawyer for some of the emerging R&D giants spent most of his time hammering patents into

---

[169] *Investigation of the Telephone Industry*, 192, n. 29. See Reich, "Research, Patents, and the Struggle to Control Radio," 231–32.

[170] Quoted in *Investigation of the Telephone Industry*, 209.   [171] Quoted in id.

[172] Leonard S. Reich, "Industrial Research and the Pursuit of Corporate Security: The Early Years of Bell Labs," 54 *Bus. Hist. Rev.* 504, 521–22 (1980).

tools for corporate stability, wrote a book about the subject. Unlike other patent treatises or guides, his book was primarily addressed not to lawyers or inventors but to the manufacturer. His aim, Prindle wrote, was not "to make the manufacturer his own lawyer" but "to open his eyes to what it was possible to do in connection with patents."[173] When he came to explain these possibilities, he did not mince words:

Patents are the best and most effective means of controlling competition. They occasionally give absolute command of the market, enabling their owner to name the price without regard to the cost of production ... There are a number of great companies whose position commercially is, or has been, almost only due to the possession of controlling patents.[174]

It is too easy to read these remarks as limited to recommending patents as an end run around antitrust restrictions on monopolization. No doubt, this is exactly what Prindle meant when he wrote that "[p]atents are the only legal form of absolute monopoly."[175] But when he echoed a recent court decision declaring that "[w]ithin his domain the patentee is Czar," he meant more than that.[176] Prindle was advocating the entire panoply of strategies of patents as corporate life insurance. His examples included patenting an invention even when a manufacturer did not intend to exclude others as a guarantee against being excluded by someone else, making money "by permitting others to use the invention in other non-competing arts," using patents "to prevent a manufacturer's product from being used in a way not intended," and "how a counter advantage may be gained" against a competitor in possession of patents.[177] Prindle's book was thus a brochure exhibiting to the "manufacturer" the patent strategies for corporate stability that he, together with others, was busy developing.

Some of the early strategic uses of patents, as in telegraphy or telephony, leveraged a single or a handful of broad, pioneering patents to control an entire industry. In 1932 Jewett explained that such opportunities continued to crop up, and therefore the "possession of a strong and un-mortgaged patent position on the part of an industry needing rights" was critical. But he also mentioned the leverage enjoyed by an owner of a necessary secondary patent over the owner of a patent in a fundamental invention.[178] This highlighted the fact that many of the strategic uses of

---

[173] Prindle, *Patents as a Factor in Manufacturing*, 18.   [174] Id. 14.   [175] Id., 16.
[176] Id.   [177] Id., 17–18.
[178] Quoted in Reich, "Research, Patents, and the Struggle to Control Radio," 233.

patents depended on controlling and employing them in groups. When corporate players realized the strategic value of patents, they grasped this aspect as well and worked to develop patent portfolios. The ultimate form of the en masse strategic use of patents was the patent pool. As the name implies, it consisted of several firms joining forces and pooling their patents together. Scholars disagree as to whether patent pools were means for oligopolistic control of markets or beneficial devices for licensing property rights and reducing transaction cost.[179] Most likely they were both, sometimes in the very same case. Either way, the patent pool in its variety of forms was a definitive specimen of using patents for stabilization and coordination.

The creation of the 1856 sewing machine combination, generally recognized as the first patent pool, followed a full-scale patent warfare in which numerous manufacturers were "suing each other out of existence."[180] This situation was attributable in large part to the existence of multiple patents necessary for the manufacture of a sewing machine held by different owners. The solution was for the four owners of the major patents to combine them into one pool. Licenses were granted for agreed-on royalties to all members. Outside manufacturers were also given licenses, although there were recurring complaints of monopolization and exorbitant fees.[181] A percentage of the licensing fees was set aside as a litigation fund for enforcing the patents. The sewing machine patent pool was, in short, a classic case of industry-wide coordination designed to overcome ruinous competition fueled by fragmented patent rights.

Toward the end of the century patent pools became more numerous and grew in ambition and scope. Some, such as the National Harrow Company, established in 1890, or the United Shoe Machinery Company, were clear attempts to monopolize an industry by pooling together essential patents, limiting licensing, dictating prices, and other

---

[179] Cf. Robert P. Merges, "Institutions for Intellectual Property Transactions: The Case of Patent Pools," in Rochelle C. Dreyfuss et al., eds., *Expanding the Boundaries of Intellectual Property: Innovation Policy for the Knowledge Society* (New York: Oxford University Press, 2001); Adam Mossoff, "The Rise and Fall of the First American Patent Thicket: The Sewing Machine Wars of the 1850s," 53 *Ariz. L. Rev.* 165 (2011); and William Greenleaf, *Monopoly on Wheels: Henry Ford and the Selden Automobile Patent* (Detroit: Wayne State University Press, 1961), 87–89; Noble, *America by Design*, 87–88.

[180] Ruth Brandon, *A Capitalist Romance: Singer and the Sewing Machine* (Philadelphia: Lippincott, 1977), 95.

[181] Cf. Mossoff, "The Rise and Fall," 196–98, and Greenleaf, *Monopoly on Wheels*, 87.

restrictive policies.[182] The 1896 Westinghouse–GE patent cooperation known as the "Board of Patent Control" was a particularly significant example that served as a model for others. GE – which already constituted a consolidation of major players in the field and their patent rights – and Westinghouse had an abundance of patents in the emerging electrical industry. By 1896 they had more than three hundred patent lawsuits pending against each other. The two giants decided to cross-license all their patents, except those for electric lighting, for agreed-on royalties. The agreement not only freed the companies from their mutual gridlock, but also secured them against challenges from smaller competitors who were not included in the licensing agreement.[183] The Motion Pictures Patent Company, established in 1908 and inspired by the GE–Westinghouse pool, was an even more ambitious design for central control of an entire field. The trust agreement, based on pooling patents for the industry's essential technology, contained a detailed blueprint for the operation of the film industry and was appropriately designated "A Plan to Reorganize the Motion Pictures Business of the United States."[184]

There is probably no better example of the patent pool as an instrument of corporate security than the radio patent pool. This pool was created after World War I by the four major players in the field: GE, its subsidiary RCA, AT&T, and Westinghouse. The pool that contained more than 1200 patents converted an industry that one historian described as "competitive and chaotic" into a well-coordinated structure.[185] It did not simply cross-license the patents to participants but carefully defined permissible zones of operation for each of them. Each of the giants removed substantial threats and uncertainties it was facing and safeguarded its main strategic interests. AT&T, which had little interest in wireless communication as such, maintained exclusive control of public communication including radio equipment integrated

[182] Floyd L. Vaughan, *The United States Patent System: Legal and Economic Conflicts in American Patent History* (Westport, Conn.: Greenwood Press, 1972), 41–43, 84–88.
[183] Noble, *America by Design*, 10; Reich, *The Making of American Industrial Research*, 52–53.
[184] Robert Anderson, "The Motion Pictures Patent Company: A Reevaluation," in Tino Balio, ed., *The American Film Industry* (Madison: University of Wisconsin Press, 1985), 140.
[185] Reich, *The Making of American Industrial Research*, 222. See also Louis Galambos, "The American Economy and the Reorganization of the Sources of Knowledge," in Alexandra Oleson and John Voss, eds., *The Organization of Knowledge in Modern America 1860–1920* (Baltimore, Md.: Johns Hopkins University Press, 1979), 277.

into this network. The other three divided between them the market of radio communication, both international and for amateurs. The companies involved judged that a stable division of the growing market was more profitable than a bloody contest based on excluding each other from essential technology. The agreement was the epitome of corporate security through patent management.

Shortly after it was launched, the arrangement was destabilized because of its failure to anticipate the rise of broadcast as a lucrative market. By 1926, however, a new arrangement had been reached that divided in an even more stable way the domains of each party. A year later a top official of the AT&T subsidiary, Western Electric, attempted to capture the benefits of the patent pool and produced a manifesto of patents as corporate security:

The regulation of the relationship between two such large interests as the American Telephone & Telegraph Co. and the General Electric Co. and the prevention of invasion of their respective fields is accomplished by mutual adjustment within "no man's land" where the offensive of the parties as related to these competitive activities is recognized as a natural defense against the invasion of the major fields. Licenses, rights, opportunities, and privileges in connection with these competitive activities are traded off against each other and interchanged in such manner as to create a proper balance...[186]

The new nature of patents as strategic tools for corporate stability created a constant push toward expansive and strong patent protection. Some of the battles were fought on the borderline of patents and antitrust. Beginning in the second decade of the twentieth century, courts became gradually more suspicious of patent pools and started scrutinizing them more closely.[187] By the 1940s this trend would lead to the temporary demise of patent pools. But the effect of the new industrial uses of patents was just as important internally within patent law. Using patents as tools for corporate security meant a "need" for broad and secure patents. Firms had conflicting interests in regard to specific patents, but patents in general became the currency with which new corporate strategies of cooperation, trade, control, and exclusion were pursued by most dominant players.

There was some resistance, of course. Grangers had a strong agenda of opposing patents, which they saw as means for oppressing and robbing

---

[186] Quoted in *Investigation of the Telephone Industry*, 210.
[187] Vaughan, *The United States Patent System*, 43.

farmers in the service of Eastern industrialists and speculators.[188] For a while they found support for this cause from strange bedfellows: the railroads. Railroads became increasingly concerned over patents after the Civil War when the potential implications for their vast systems often dependent on key technologies became apparent.[189] By 1879, however, the political effort to legislatively reform patent law was defeated.[190] Railroads shifted their energies to other defensive tactics against the patent menace. Partly, they learned how to play the litigation game scoring occasional victories. But their main strategy relied on pooling not patents but other resources. Beginning in the 1860s railroads created industry-wide associations that shared technological information and coordinated legal action. The sharing of information empowered railroads to avoid patents, innovate around them using their own technological capabilities, or defeat them on grounds of preexisting prior-art. The coordinated defense and settlement policy gave the railroads a much better strategic position when litigation happened or in preventing it.[191] By the late 1880s the number of patent lawsuits against railroads had declined dramatically, and the former patent threat became mostly irrelevant for these companies.[192]

The early incarnation of the strong business interest in broad patents was the mid-century struggle for recognition of patents in principles. In the decades following the 1854 *O'Reilly v. Morse* decision, however, it became clear that this was a lost cause. The claim for patents in natural principles collided head on not just with fears of monopolies, but also with an entrenched ideological resistance to allowing private ownership of scientific knowledge. The second wave of asserting broad patents that coincided with the rise of patents as a means for corporate security was more subtle. Abandoning direct claims for patenting natural principles, it consisted of a myriad of techniques for drafting patents, interpreting them, and making legal arguments about their scope. Such technical methods neutralized the ideological pitfalls of explicitly claiming ownership in

---

[188] Steven W. Usselman, "Patent Politics: Intellectual Property, the Railroad Industry, and the Problem of Monopoly," 18 *J. Policy Hist.* 96, 110 (2006); Usselman, *Regulating Railroad Innovation*, 146–50;

[189] Usselman, "Patent Politics," 105–9.

[190] Usselman, *Regulating Railroad Innovation*, 169.

[191] Id., 171–76; Steven W. Usselman, "Patents Purloined: Railroads, Inventors, and the Diffusion of Innovation in 19th-Century America," 32 *Technology and Culture* 1047, 1064–74 (1991).

[192] Usselman, "Patents Purloined," 1070.

knowledge, and yet they often proved effective in achieving the goal of broad patent protection. In the last decades of the nineteenth century the focus of defining and abstracting the meaning of patent ownership shifted to these more refined forms of legal reasoning and practices.

USEFUL ARTS

The opening section of Albert H. Walker's 1889 patent treatise resolutely denied the patentability of "laws of nature" that "can never be invented by man, though they may be discovered by him."[193] Walker had, however, to wrestle with a tough question. Discussing four Supreme Court decisions that upheld broad patent claims, three of which were from the preceding two decades, Walker found the upheld claims strangely hard to distinguish from Morse's condemned attempt to claim natural principles.[194] With dismay Walker asked what could explain the disparate treatment of "the claims of Morse on the one hand, and the claims of Harley, Whitney, Tilghman and Bell on the other." He acknowledged that the difference did not "consist in anything outside of the use of laws of nature, because all five claims extended to accomplishing results by means of such law or laws, regardless of the particular apparatus used in the respective processes." Indeed "the apparatus described by Harley, Whitney, Tilghman and Bell" was not "claimed as their sole respective inventions, any more than the particular telegraph described by Morse was made essential to his eighth claim." Eventually, Walker could find only one "radical difference" between Morse's invalidated claim and those upheld by the Supreme Court. In the four cases each of the patentees "produced a process which utilized several laws of nature," and each claimed "the use of all those laws in the order and method described." Morse, on the other hand, "also made an invention which utilized several laws of nature, but instead of claiming his combined and methodical use of all of those laws, his eighth claim was construed as confined to one of them alone."[195] The celebrated *Morse* decision, the epitome of the great maxim of unpatentability of natural principles, was reduced to a hair-splitting distinction. It hinged, according to Walker, on the fact that

---

[193] Walker, *Text Book of the Patent Laws*, 3.
[194] The cases were *McClurg v. Kingsland*, 42 U.S. 202 (1842); *Mowry v. Whitney*, 81 U.S. 14 (1871); *Tilghman v. Proctor*, 102 U.S. 707 (1880); the *Telephone Cases*, 126 U.S. 531 (1888).
[195] Walker, *Text Book of the Patent Laws*, 13–15.

Morse claimed only the use of the electric current for purposes of communication, instead of the use of both the electric current and electromagnetism. It was no coincidence that the four decisions that precipitated Walker's desperate intellectual efforts all involved process patents. After it became clear that direct attempts to assert patents in natural principles were doomed, process patents emerged as a common strategy for bypassing this obstacle. In skillful hands, claims for methods could be drafted in a way that unmoored the invention from any particular apparatus or design. Such claims captured a broad zone, sometimes as broad as any patent for a "principle," but studiously avoided directly claiming natural principles.

Method patents had been long entwined with the gradual development of the idea of intellectual property in Anglo-American jurisprudence. In England patenting methods had been a hotly contested question, beginning with the first major judicial attempt to come to terms with patents as ownership of intangibles in the 1795 case of *Boulton & Watt v. Bull*.[196] Claiming methods was problematic because it inescapably confronted jurists with a case where the patent right had no physical object to attach to. For this reason, method patents were rejected by many who still refused to fully accept the idea of intellectual property and conceptualized patents in semi-materialist terms. For decades English commentators continued to reject pure method patents as too uncertain or as failing to meet various requirements such as "materiality" or "vendibility."[197] It was only in the 1842 decision in *Crane v. Price* that the question was finally settled in England.[198] Ostensibly, the situation was very different in the United States. The first Patent Act of 1790 listed "Useful Art" as an independent category of patentable subject matter, and a similar statutory category continued to exist throughout the century.[199] American patent law was also free of most of the archaic doctrinal requirements that inhibited the acceptance of process patents in England. This led a later commentator to observe that in the United States processes were always recognized "as having the same title for protection as a machine or an article of manufacture."[200]

---

[196] 126 Eng. Rep. 651 (C.P. 1795).
[197] See William Hands, *The Law and Practice of Patents for Invention* (London: W. Clarke, 1806), 6; Godson, *Law of Patents for Inventions*, 84.
[198] 134 Eng. Rep. 239 (K.B. 1842).   [199] Act of April 10, 1790, ch. 7, 1 Stat. 109, §1.
[200] William C. Robinson, *Law of Patents for Useful Inventions* (Boston: Little, Brown, 1890), vol. 1, 238.

In reality things were murkier. Early-nineteenth-century American courts sometimes recognized patents in subject matter that decades later would be identified as "processes," but such decisions neither used the terms "process" or "method" nor identified a clear, distinct category of subject matter.[201] There was also much ambiguity around the meaning of the statutory category of an "art." Phillips, for example, followed in his 1837 treatise the English tradition and discussed methods and processes under the rubric of "manufacture," while providing a separate cursory discussion of the American statutory category of an "art."[202] In the 1840s and 1850s supporters of patentability of principles latched on to the statutory term "art" and interpreted it as designating not methods in the technical sense but a pioneering discovery foundational of an entire field.[203] Even in 1853 Justice Grier still explained: "A process, eo nomine, is not made the subject of a patent in our act of Congress. It is included under the general term 'useful art.' An art may require one or more processes or machines in order to produce a certain result or manufacture."[204]

In the second half of the nineteenth century the concept of a method patent began to stabilize. The category of a "process" gradually received a more technical meaning, and with time the statutory category of an "art" came to be regarded as synonymous with it. Process patents remained, however, a contested battleground where competing visions of the patent scope were deployed. Process claims often offered clever patent drafters an attractive means for expanding and abstracting the scope of patents. A section of Robinson's 1890 treatise entitled "An Art the Most Comprehensive of Inventions" explained why. An art, he wrote, "can be patented as such without reference to the specific instruments engaged or the specific objects in which its effects may be produced," and so "its outer limits are less easily discernable than those of any other class of operative means."[205] Patent lawyers were quick to test these outer limits by drafting claims drawn to abstract "methods" not restricted by any particular structural design.

Initially, many courts were suspicious of attempts to expand patents through method claims. In the 1854 *Corning v. Burden* the Supreme

[201] See e.g. *Kneass v. Schuylkill*, 14 F. Cas. 746 (C.C.D. Pa. 1820); *McClurg v. Kingsland*, 42 U.S. 202.
[202] Phillips, *The Law of Patents for Inventions*, 82–95, 109–13.
[203] *French v. Rogers*, 9 F. Cas. 790, 793 (C.C.E.D. Pa. 1851).
[204] *Corning v. Burden*, 56 U.S. 252, 267 (1853).
[205] Robinson, *Law of Patents for Useful Inventions*, 243–44, 246–47.

Court was faced with a classic attempt of this kind. The original patentee, who invented a machine for rolling "puddle balls" (i.e. wrought iron), included in his patent a broad method claim. Justice Grier, writing for the court, specified the main question in the case: "Is the plaintiff's patent for a process or a machine?"[206] The critical move in answering this question was the premise that "where the result or effect is produced by chemical action, by the operation or application of some element or power of nature, or of one substance to another, such modes, methods, or operations, are called processes."[207] This definition envisioned two completely distinct categories of patentable inventions. The one included machines and other devices, the other extended to nonmechanical methods such as chemical reactions. According to Grier, the statutory category of a process was limited to "all methods or means which are not effected by mechanism or mechanical combinations."[208] This definition blocked the most common attempts to expand the patent scope through process claims because it restricted drafters' ability to smuggle in mechanical devices as methods. This was apparent in *Corning* where it was found that "the agent which effects the pressure is a machine or combination of mechanical devices." A patentee, the court said, "cannot describe a machine which will perform a certain function, and then claim the function itself, and all other machines that may be invented to perform the same function."[209] A string of decisions adopted *Corning*s definition of a process and applied its logic to hold process patents at bay.[210]

Other decisions went further and kept displaying the traditional suspicion toward process claims detached from a clear material embodiment even after the category was well established. The most conspicuous example was the 1862 decision in *Morton v. New York Eye Infirmary*, also known as the Ether Case.[211] The patentee in this case discovered the anesthetic effect of ether and tried to claim the use for surgical purposes of "the process of rendering the system insensible to pain by the inhalation of ether" in certain quantities.[212] This was certainly a process and not an attempt to disguise a structural design. The court, however, was deeply troubled. "What is the process which is here set forth?" it asked, and answered: "The process of inhalation of the vapor, and nothing else.

[206] 56 U.S. 267.   [207] Id.   [208] Id., 268.   [209] Id., 269.
[210] See e.g. *Mackay v. Jackman*, 12 F. 615, 619 (S.D. N.Y. 1882); *Brainard v. Cramme*, 12 F. 621, 622 (C.C.N.D.N.Y. 1882); *Goss v. Cameron*, 14 F. 576, 578 (C.C.N.D. Ill. 1882); *Hatch v. Moffitt*, 15 F. 252, 253 (C.C.D. Mass. 1883). See also Walker, *Text Book of the Patent Laws*, 7.
[211] 17 F. Cas. 879 (S.D. N.Y. 1862).   [212] Id., 883.

To couple with it the effect produced by calling it a process of rendering the system insensible to pain, is merely to connect the results with the means ... The means, that is the process of inhalation of vapors, existed among the animals of the geologic ages preceding the creation of our race. That process, in connection with these vapors, is as old as the vapors themselves ... We have, after all, only a new or more perfect effect of a well-known chemical agent, operating through one of the ordinary functions of animal life." Mingling subject matter with novelty reasoning in a typical nineteenth-century fashion, the court found the patent invalid because it claimed "the application of a well-known agent, by well-known means."[213] The court's concern with lack of materiality became apparent when it waxed poetic about a "naked discovery" that "may be the soul of an invention, but it can not be the subject of the exclusive control of the patentee, or the patent law, until it inhabits a body, no more than can a disembodied spirit be subjected to the control of human laws."[214]

The so-called double-use doctrine reflected the same suspicion toward immaterial processes. The doctrine that was applied vigorously around the middle of the century prohibited patenting a new use of a known invention, as in the hypothetical case of a known coffee-grinder newly used to grind peas.[215]. Such patents usually tried to claim a known machine as a product on the basis of a newly developed use for the machine. Neither lawyers nor courts, however, considered the possibility of patenting the new use as a process. Despite the formal existence of process patents, it simply did not occur to courts that a new use of a known apparatus was itself a patentable invention even if no new mechanical variation was developed.[216]

Beginning in the 1870s the treatment of process patents started to change. Within two decades the double-use doctrine became so riddled with exceptions that little coherence was left in it. In 1890 Robinson identified the source of this incoherence as "the failure to distinguish properly between inventions and their uses." Fully abstracting the use from any mechanical design, he realized that a new invention could consist not in "the art or instrument itself" but in "the manner of its

---

[213] Id.   [214] Id., 882.   [215] *Ames v. Howard*, 1 F. Cas. 755, 757 (C.C.D. Mass. 1833).
[216] See *Whittemore v. Cutter*, 29 F. Cas. 1123, 1124 (C.C.D. Mass. 1813); *Howe v. Abbott*, 12 F. Cas. 656 (C.C.D. Mass. 1842); *Bean v. Smallwood*, 2 F. Cas. 1142 (C.C.D. Mass. 1843); *Conover v. Roach* (1857); *Bray v. Hartshorn* (1860); Curtis, *A Treatise on the Law of Patents*, 119–24.

use" that was patentable as a process.[217] The general definition of a process subtly changed in the same direction. *Corning v. Burden* was still cited, but the insistence at its heart on a clear distinction between processes and machines was gradually abandoned. In the 1876 *Cochrane v. Deener* Justice Bradley defined a process as "a mode of treatment of certain materials to produce a given result" or "an act, or a series of acts, performed upon the subject-matter to be transformed and reduced to a different state or thing."[218] In the course of performing the process, Bradley said, different tools or devices may be employed, but that "a process may be patentable, irrespective of the particular form of the instrumentalities used, cannot be disputed."[219]

The growing acceptance that a process is "so far abstract that it is capable of contemplation by the mind apart from any one of the specific instruments by which it is performed"[220] opened the door for the lawyerly strategy of claiming broadly through process claims. Two Supreme Court decisions involving a patent by Robert Tilghman (the brother of the more famous inventor Benjamin Tilghman) were a dramatic illustration of this trend. In the 1874 *Mitchell v. Tilghman* a majority of the Court found that the patented invention was a "process of manufacturing fat-acids and glycerin from fatty or oily substances by the action of water at a high temperature and pressure."[221] The Court construed the patent narrowly and found a series of concrete elements, such as not allowing air or steam into the heating vessel, to be "material and indispensable conditions of the patented method."[222] Because the defendant used a somewhat different apparatus that did not contain these elements, he was allowed to escape under the rule that "one who afterwards discovers a method of accomplishing the same object, substantially and essentially differing from the one described, has a right to use it."[223] Six years later in *Tilghman v. Proctor*, involving the very same patent, the Supreme Court reversed course. Justice Bradley, writing for a unanimous court, explained that "[u]pon the renewed consideration which has been given to the subject, the court is unanimously of opinion, contrary to the decision in the Mitchell case, that the patent of Tilghman must be sustained as a patent for a process, and not merely for the particular mode of applying and using the process pointed out in the specification."[224]

---

[217] Robinson, *Law of Patents for Useful Inventions*, vol. 1, 364.
[218] 94 U.S. 780, 788 (1876).   [219] Id., 787.
[220] Robinson, *Law of Patents for Useful Inventions*, vol. 1, 230–31.
[221] 86 U.S. 287, 379–80 (1874).   [222] Id., 388.   [223] Id., 392.   [224] 102 U.S. 708.

The fatal flaw of *Mitchell* was that "sufficient consideration was not given to the fact that the patent is for a process, and not for any specific mechanism for carrying such process into effect."[225] The significance of the new orthodoxy under which the essence of a process did not depend on specific instrumentalities became clear when Bradley wrote that "[t]he apparatus for performing the process was not patented, and was not material," and hence "surely the identity of the process was not changed by thus changing the form of apparatus."[226] The rest of the opinion analyzed a long list of differences between the devices used by the patentee and the defendant and dismissed each of them as "immaterial" to the process.

Tilghman v. Proctor was a powerful example of the opportunities for broad claiming presented by the new judicial approach to process patents. At this point nobody was willing to support the mid-century argument for the patentability of principles. The decisive advantage of broad process claims was that they often allowed a patent scope as broad as any "principles" patent while still denouncing the patentability of principles. Some wondered whether the ghost of patents for principles was being revived through recognition of process patents as unlimited by specific "instrumentalities." In 1884, after surveying the recent process cases, Judge Drummond commented bewilderedly on the distinction between principles and processes:

It is to be regretted that the difficulty inherent in the subject is so great that a more intelligible distinction has not been made, for it must be admitted that the application of the rule which has been established by the supreme court to other cases, as they hereafter arise, may cause embarrassment, for there must be a method by which the principle or law which has been discovered is applied; and, if that method is immaterial, then it is difficult to understand why it does not become substantially a patent for the discovery of the principle or the law of nature.[227]

Denial was, however, a much more common strategy. The Supreme Court in *Tilghman v. Proctor* religiously cited *O'Reilly v. Morse* and embraced its rejection of patenting principles. It also found *Morse* irrelevant for the case at hand. The opposite assumption, it said, was a mistake that had "undoubtedly arisen from confounding a patent for a process with a patent for a mere principle."[228] In 1890 Robinson used a similar reasoning when discussing in his treatise *Le Roy v. Tatham*, one of the

[225] Id., 710.   [226] Id., 720, 722.
[227] *New Process Fermentation Co. v. Maus*, U.S. 20 F. 725 (C.C.N.D. Ind. 1884).
[228] 102 U.S. 726.

important mid-century principle patent cases. Robinson utterly rejected Justice Nelson's dissenting opinion, which was based on embracing the patenting of principles. He found, however, that the broad claim in that case was, in fact, valid as an ordinary process claim. "Where the discovery relates to new susceptibilities in the object, and consists in the perception that it may be affected in a new way by the application to it of a force not hitherto known as capable of producing this effect upon it," Robinson wrote, "the direction of such force upon this object is a new and substantive invention and may be patented as a process ... without reference to the particular instruments employed."[229] This was a rather complicated way of saying that a "principle" was patentable after all, as long as it was called a "process."

RAISING WHEAT BY THE GERMINATION OF THE SEED

The increasingly accommodating approach toward broad method patents was not part of a one-dimensional, pro-patent policy by late-nineteenth-century courts. Some aspects of patent law exploited by patentees to expand the number and breadth of patents were reined in during this period. One important example was reissues. The procedure, which allowed canceling a grant based on inadvertent mistakes and replacing it with a new one, was widely used and abused by patentees to broaden the scope of their patents, often capturing unanticipated new terrain developed by the competition. Charles Goodyear's 1848 reissue of his vulcanized rubber patent was a prime example, but there were many others.[230] Reissues attracted vocal opposition and complaints of abuse. Beginning in the 1870s both Congress and the courts clamped down on the practice of reissue, thereby significantly limiting patentees' ability to use it for smuggling new subject matter into their patents.[231] The post–Civil War rise of the nonobviousness requirement followed a similar pattern. It is unclear whether nonobviousness blocked more patents than the older substantial novelty approach. Yet in the new doctrinal landscape of the late nineteenth century, courts consciously wielded this

[229] Robinson, *Law of Patents for Useful Inventions*, vol. 1, 193.
[230] Christopher Beauchamp, *Invented by Law: Alexander Graham Bell and the Patent That Changed America* (Cambridge, Mass.: Harvard University Press, 2015), 25–26; Kendall J. Dood, "Pursuing the Essence of Inventions: Reissuing Patents in the 19th Century," 32 *Technology and Culture* 999, 1004–8 (1991).
[231] Dood, "Pursuing the Essence of Inventions," 1015–16. See *Miller v. Bridgeport Brass Co.*, 104 U.S. 350 (1881).

requirement as a shield against the proliferation of patents in trivial inventions.[232] Late-nineteenth-century developments in patent law were thus not indiscriminately patent friendly. Nevertheless, the changing approach to method patents unequivocally facilitated a broader patent scope grounded in a capacious and flexible understanding of invention. This new concept of the owned invention became entrenched. It survived even in later periods of patent skepticism.

Method patents came to play a significant ideological role because they were instruments for mediating conflicting pressures on late-nineteenth-century patent law. Offering a way for claiming inventions broadly irrespective of specific instrumentalities, these patents created an effective channel for the demand of broad and certain private control of innovation on which to build corporate security. At the same time method patents seemed to accommodate the traditional fear of broad monopolies and the widespread resistance to ownership of scientific knowledge. Unlike the defunct patents in principles, method patents disavowed any claim for owning natural knowledge. The ideological effect was twofold. Construed broadly enough, method patents allowed private control as broad as previously claimed under patents for principles accompanied by the soothing assertion that knowledge of natural principles remained unowned. Furthermore, the very assertion inherent in the doctrine of a clear line dividing the proper object of private ownership from subject matter that had to stay open to the public was misleading. Far from creating such a bright line, the doctrine in this area offered an assortment of techniques that a skillful lawyer could use to negotiate the flexible and shifting boundary between property and that which could not be owned. On a strictly logical level method patents were not unique. Like other patents the subject matter potentially covered by them could be interpreted on different levels of abstraction. It was the ideological function of these patents in this particular moment of the emerging thought about patents as intellectual ownership coupled with their practical potential that made them an attractive instrument for clever drafters and litigators.

There was no more powerful demonstration of the practical and ideological role of method patents than the mammoth patent litigation campaign of the 1880s known as the *Telephone Cases*. Involving hundreds of lawsuits, several reported circuit court cases, a split decision by

---

[232] See Chapter 4; Beauchamp, *Invented by Law*, 71.

the Supreme Court, and a designated volume of the *U.S. Reports*, the *Telephone Cases* were the epitome of the new landscape of corporate security through patents. At the heart of the campaign was the struggle of the Bell Telephone Company to build a national empire on the foundation of a broad patent. The company's strategy for consolidating its monopoly over telephony was based on suing under the original Bell patent any potential competitor, including those who used devices very different from Bell's original design.[233] The parallel to Morse's doomed strategy three decades earlier was obvious. And this parallel presented Bell's lawyers with a dilemma. Their task was to capture in the patent's net the broadest possible area in order to suppress all possible competition from rival devices. At the same time, keeping in mind Morse's legal failure, they had to avoid the forbidden zone of claiming principles. For a skillful patent lawyer the answer to the dilemma was clear: a broad method claim. And the fifth claim of the Bell patent offered exactly that. It read:

the method of, and apparatus for, transmitting vocal or other sounds telegraphic-ally, as herein described, by causing electrical undulations, similar in form to the vibrations of the air accompanying the said vocal or other sounds, substantially as set forth.[234]

It is doubtful that this claim was originally drafted with the intention that it would serve as the foundation for broad control of the telephone market.[235] But it is clear that once litigation started, the lawyers seized on it. Chauncey Smith, the first general council of the Bell Company, insisted early in the litigation that the focus would be on the fifth method claim.[236]

This was a dangerous gambit. The broad claim stretched the outer limits of protection and came dangerously close to claiming natural prin-ciples. There were, however, two substantial advantages to the strategy. Most important, the method claim swept in a broad array of competing devices that bore little resemblance to Bell's original design. Focusing on a broad method for speech transmission also allowed the invocation of a line of precedents about pioneer patents. Under this rule the scope of patent protection varied according to the nature of the invention. Pioneer inven-tions that embodied broad technological breakthroughs enjoyed a broader scope of protection compared with ordinary inventions that represented

[233] Beauchamp, *Invented by Law*, 49.   [234] The *Telephone Cases*, 126 U.S. 531.
[235] Beauchamp, *Invented by Law*, 46.   [236] Id., 66.

more modest improvements on existing technological designs.[237] This rule foreshadowed the modern scholarly distinction between macroinventions and microinventions.[238] More important, the "liberal" treatment of pioneer inventions was yet another reincarnation of the ghost of patenting principles. Many of the mid-century supporters of patents in principles grounded their argument in a distinction between the true inventor who through a great discovery created an entirely new "art" and the ordinary technological improver working within the confines of an existing art. By the 1880s patents for principles were dead, but their spirit lived on in the more technical legal rule that a pioneer inventor enjoys a broader property right. Focusing on the claim for the fundamental method of transmitting voice allowed Bell to be cast in the role of a pioneer inventor responsible for founding a new art with the attendant consequences.

The gamble paid off. The lower courts accepted both the premise that Bell's invention was a pioneer one and that his method claim was not limited to any concrete structural design.[239] One of the more influential decisions was written by U.S. Supreme Court Justice Horace Gray, sitting as a circuit judge in Massachusetts.[240] Gray would later have to recuse himself from the Supreme Court deliberations after it was revealed that his relatives held Bell stock.[241] In his Massachusetts opinion he explained that "[t]here can be no patent for a mere principle, . . . natural force or a scientific fact," but the inventor of "a process by which a certain effect of one of the forces of nature is made useful to mankind . . . is entitled to a patent for the process of which he is the first inventor, and is not restricted to the particular form of mechanism or apparatus by which he carries out that process."[242] Since Bell's patent was "clearly not intended to be limited to a form of apparatus, but embraces a method or process," the conclusion followed that "the essence of his invention consists not merely in the form of

---

[237] See *McCormick v. Talcott*, 61 U.S. 402 (1857); *Railway Company v. Sayles*, 97 U.S. 554, 556–57 (1878); Walker, *Text Book of the Patent Laws*, 263–65.

[238] Joel Mokyr, *The Lever of Riches: Technological Creativity and Economic Progress* (New York: Oxford University Press, 1990), 13.

[239] See *American Bell Tel. Co. v. Spencer* (C.C.D. Mass. 1881); *American Bell Tel. Co. v Dolbear*, 15 F. 448 (C.C.D. Mass. 1883); *American Bell Tel. Co. v Dolbear*, 17 F. 604 (C.C.D. Mass. 1883); *American Bell Tel. Co. v. People's Tel. Co.*, 22 F. 309 (S.D. N.Y. 1884); *American Bell Tel. Co. v Molecular Tel. Co.*, 32 F. 214 (S.D. N.Y. 1885); *American Bell Tel. Co. v Globe Tel. Co.*, 31 F. 729 (S.D. N.Y 1887).

[240] *American Bell Tel. Co. v. Dolbear*, 15 F. 448.

[241] Beauchamp, *Invented by Law*, 79.

[242] *American Bell Tel. Co. v. Dolbear*, 15 F. 449.

apparatus which he uses, but in the general process or method of which that apparatus is the embodiment." As a result the protected invention extended to any device that used "undulatory vibrations of electricity to correspond with those of the air, and transmitting them to a receiving instrument capable of echoing them."[243]

This was broad indeed. Arguing before the Supreme Court, the counsel for one of the appellants called Gray's reasoning a "dangerous – I was going to say wild – theory of patentable invention."[244] The court was not impressed. Chief Justice Morrison Waite, writing for the majority, sustained the broad interpretation of the claim and refused to limit Bell's patent to a concrete structural design. Combining the pioneer patent rule with a liberal approach to method patents, he reasoned that Bell was both an inventor and a discoverer. His discovery of an art consisted in "changing the intensity of a continuous electric current, so as to make it correspond exactly to the changes in the density of the air caused by the sound of the voice." His invention was the specific means of "making it useful." This entitled Bell to two sorts of protection, "as discoverer, for the useful art, process, method of doing a thing he has found; and as inventor; for the means he had devised." The patent for the art was not limited to "the particular means employed for using it." "Surely a patent for such a discovery," Waite wrote, "is not to be confined to the mere means he improvised." This reasoning was a return to mid-century arguments of patenting a discovery or an art under a very thin cover of a "process." Yet this type of argument was supposed to be long dead after *O'Reilly v. Morse*. The Court religiously cited *Morse* and the rule against patenting principles. But what was the difference between the broad claim of Morse and that of Bell? The difference, Waite said, was that Morse's eighth claim was for "the use of magnetism as a motive power, without regard to the particular process with which it was connected." In contrast, Bell's claim was "not for the use of the current of electricity in its natural state as it comes from the battery, but for putting a continuous current in a closed circuit into a certain speci-fied condition suited to the transmission of vocal and other sounds." Thus Bell claimed the use of electricity only "in that condition," namely, "the art of creating changes in intensity in a continuous current of electricity, exactly corresponding to the changes of density in the air caused by the vibrations which accompany vocal or other sounds, and of

[243] Id., 454.   [244] The *Telephone Cases*, 126 U.S. 497.

using that electrical condition thus created for sending and receiving articulate speech telegraphically."[245]

The distinction was very thin. Reacting to it in their briefs, counsels for the appellants frantically oscillated between amusement and horror. Grosvenor Lowrey argued that Bell's broad claim was "a Monopoly of a Scientific Fact or a Law of Nature." What Bell discovered "was not that electrical undulations *can* (as if there were some choice on the part of the inventor), but that they *do*, transmit sound by conforming themselves to the characteristics of the energy which creates the sound." The claim, he argued, was one for a principle dressed up as a method. It amounted to claiming "the electrical transmission of speech under the form of a pretended description of how nature does it!"[246] Causten Browne similarly commented on Justice Gray's decision in Massachusetts: "The learned Justice misunderstood. It is not a question of *the only way* to transmit speech by electricity. Producing electrical changes upon the line corresponding to the sonorous air changes is not *a way* of transmitting speech by electricity. *It is doing it.* It is that in which the electrical transmission of speech consists. It is the alternative form of word for the same thing." The fifth claim, Browne argued, "while denying Mr. Bell a patent *in terms* for the use of electricity to transmit speech, gives it to him *in substance* by giving him a patent for that which is done necessarily, in the nature of things, *ex vi termini*, whenever speech is transmitted by electricity ... He has changed the words of his claim but not the thing claimed."[247] Lowery summed it up sarcastically: "To allow a patent claim for such discovery might be likened to a claim for raising wheat by the germination of the seed: *leaving mankind free to produce wheat by all other methods!*"[248] All of this was to no avail. Chief Justice Waite, echoing Gray's circuit court opinion, simply repeated his observation that the patent was for a process and not a principle. "It may be that electricity cannot be used at all for the transmission of speech except in the way Bell has discovered," he said, "but that does not make his claim one for the use of electricity distinct from the particular process."[249]

The *Telephone Cases* were a dramatic demonstration of how resourceful lawyers, working to shape patents as broad property rights in the service of corporate security, found ways around the rejection of patents in principles. Professing their allegiance to the orthodoxy that knowledge

[245] Id., 533–34.   [246] Id., 208.   [247] Id., 498.   [248] Id., 210.   [249] Id., 535.

could not be owned, they perfected other techniques for obtaining and defending patents every bit as broad as those previously characterized as patents for principles. These techniques included an adept use of method claims and invocation of the rule of pioneer inventions. At the heart of all of these techniques stood a common development: the rise of patents as a textual form of property. Texts that had been part of patent practice for centuries came to play an increasingly dominant role. Lawyers, the masters of textual strategies, were playing here on their home turf. The textualization of patents was thus the fulcrum supporting the new lawyerly strategies for constructing patents' intangible object of property.

THEY HAVE PLUCKED OUT THE HEART OF THE INVENTION: TEXTUAL OBJECTS OF PROPERTY

Every intellectual property right requires translation. The law works through texts. It has no unmediated access to the intellectual objects it purports to regulate. To bring an intangible subject matter into the domain of the law is to textualize it. This representation in text is constitutive: it constructs rather than simply reflects the object of property. Copyright and patent developed over the centuries different modes of textualizing the intangible. In copyright this happened through judicial reasoning, lawyers' arguments, master in chancery reports that dissected the works, and later expert testimony. Patent law developed its own distinct modes of textualization marked by more formal separation of the text from its referent. In the second half of the nineteenth century this textual intermediation between technology and legal reasoning increased. In 1920 one Court of Appeals confidently observed that "infringement of a patent is an erroneous phrase; what is infringed is a claim, which is the definition of invention."[250] The text was no longer seen as an imperfect but necessary representation of a technological reality known as the invention. The text was now officially the object of property.

Patents came to the United States with an established historical tradition of textualization. The written description of the invention that came to be known as the "specification" emerged out of the seventeenth-century English patent grant practices. By the late eighteenth century English courts had built a theoretical construct on this practice. The written disclosure submitted by the inventor, they said, was the transfer of the

---

[250] *Fulton Co. v. Powers Regulator Co.*, 263 F. 578, 580 (2nd Cir. 1920).

invention to the public and the consideration for the legal monopoly conferred on him by a patent. Americans embraced both the practice and the theory. Instances of requiring a written description of the invention go back to colonial patents. Submitting a specification became a staple of American patent law beginning with the first Patent Act of 1790, and the requirement was perpetuated and deepened in subsequent statutory revisions. For much of the nineteenth century, however, the notion that the deposited specification effectively gave the knowledge embodied in the invention to the public had little to do with reality. Patentees often submitted obscure and evasive specifications; the patent office did little to facilitate and for a period actively restricted public access to the written disclosure; and innovators rarely relied on these written texts as an effective source of technological information.[251] For many decades the main significance of the specification was ideological. The practice of the specification introduced a formal text as an intermediary between technological reality and legal conception. Textualizing the invention made patents intellectual property in the sense of rights in intangibles by eclipsing older, semi-materialist conceptions of invention. The text made the abstract invention detached from any physical embodiment, a "thing," a definite object in the world.[252] In 1846 one court observed that the "invention may be said to be reduced to practice" when a machine is "described in such a manner that it may be made and used."[253] That it was possible to say that to make the invention was to describe it in a text marked the fact that increasingly the text was taken to be the invention.

The text came to be seen as the invention, yet for most of the century this textual level was understood to be porous – an imperfect embodiment of a richer technological reality lurking just beneath it. Courts reflected this duality in their attitude toward the respective roles of technological and legal knowledge in the field of patents. Judges often insisted that questions of the scope of the invention or identity between inventions were ultimately legal ones. Mechanics could offer useful technological clarifications, but "professors or mechanics cannot be received to prove to the court or jury what is the proper or legal construction of any instrument of writing."[254] An invention was unabashedly understood as a legal

---

[251] Pottage and Sherman, *Figures of Invention*, 55–59.
[252] Id., 51; Mario Biagioli, "Patent Republic: Representing Inventions, Constructing Rights and Authors," 73 *Soc. Res.* 1129, 1143 (2006).
[253] *Heath v. Hildreth*, 11 Fed. Cas. 1003, 1006 (C.C. D.C. 1841).
[254] *Winans v. New York & E.R. Co.*, 62 U.S. 88, 100 (1858). See also *Barrett v. Hall*, 2 F. Cas. 914, 923 (C.C.D. Mass. 1818).

construct embodied in a text to be discerned by legal methods. But the textual legal construct was only a thin layer over the technological reality of the invention. And it was this technological reality that judges and juries working through texts were ultimately after. In 1869 Justice Bradley explained why despite the textuality of inventions it was juries aided by input from expert testimony who decided questions of novelty of inventions. Wasn't the judge the competent interpreter of texts? Not when it comes to patent specifications, said Bradley, which are "documents of a peculiar kind." Specifications capture technologies that "have their existence in pais, outside of the documents themselves." Moreover "the whole subject-matter of a patent is an embodied conception outside of the patent itself, which, to the mind of those expert in the art, stands out in clear and distinct relief." This "outward embodiment of the terms contained in the patent is the thing invented, and is to be properly sought, like the explanation of all latent ambiguities arising from the description of external things, by evidence in pais."[255] Bradley used as a metaphor the old law of real property where certain transactions considered to be in the knowledge of the country (i.e. "in pais") were established by evidence external to the written deed.[256] He did not deny the textuality of inventions but insisted that the purpose of the legal construct was to make accessible technological reality. His point applied more generally to the patent jurisprudence of the time. The search for the modus operandi of inventions and the free-flowing doctrine of equivalents typical of the period's patent litigation was built on this principle of reaching for the technological reality of invention through textual gateways. The specification made the invention the province of lawyers by textualizing it, but for much of the nineteenth century the text was never too far from the technology.

The gradual process of insulating the text from technological reality began with the shift to an examination system in 1836. Prior examination by the patent office entailed bureaucratization and standardization. It also entailed the rise of patent prosecution and litigation as a "field" of professionals.[257] The patent application, previously handled mostly by inventors directly, turned into a bureaucratic process and was quickly taken over by a new class of professionals.[258] Patent agents, or "patent

---

[255] *Bischoff v. Wethered*, 76 U.S. 812, 815 (1869).
[256] Pottage and Sherman, *Figures of Invention*, 63.
[257] See Pierre Bourdieu, *Practical Reason: On the Theory of Action* (Cambridge: Polity, 1998), 31–34.
[258] See Kara W. Swanson, "The Emergence of the Professional Patent Practitioner," 50 *Technology and Culture* 519 (2009); Kara W. Swanson, "Authoring an Invention:

attorneys," as they were commonly referred to, were mostly nonlawyers. Their expertise typically consisted of some combination of background in the mechanical arts and experience with the emerging federal government machinery. Shortly after it emerged, this new professional class started warning inventors of the foolish presumption that they could handle their own patent applications, "an erroneous impression" that "has led many applicants into great trouble and expense."[259] The Patent Office clung for a bit longer to the notion that in America unlike under the Byzantine English patent procedure inventors could secure their rights by themselves. Eventually, however, it too would recommend inventors to use the services of professionals.[260] An application for a patent became an elaborate bureaucratic process known as patent prosecution. It consisted of Patent Office bureaucrats communicating with professionals in increasingly standardized and formalized modes. The process took the form of a contest over a text that constituted the patented invention. The fact that "to *invent* and to *secure a patent*" became two different things further insulated this text from technological reality.[261] In the new bureaucratized world of patents the mechanic concluded his useful contribution at the gates of the legal realm where he was expected to cede control over the meaning of his invention to professionals employing standardized textual strategies in a contest over a text.

Patent litigation experienced similar developments. One side effect of the mid-nineteenth-century patent enforcement campaigns that accounted for a substantial part of the federal courts' dockets was the early emergence of legal specialization.[262] Patent cases were often litigated by generalist elite members of the legal profession; an organized patent bar would be established only at the end of the century. Yet in the 1840s and 1850s – considerably earlier than in other fields of law – there started to emerge lawyers who built successful practices specializing in patent litigation.[263] Similar to patent agents, these lawyers developed specialized skills for dealing with patents as texts. This was reflected in the changing patterns of litigation. Pottage and Sherman described the increased focus on the text in patent litigation as a transition from "a relation between

Patent Protection in the Nineteenth Century United States," in Martha Woodmansee et al., eds., *Making and Unmaking Intellectual Property: Creative Production in Legal and Cultural Perspective* (Chicago, Ill.: University of Chicago Press, 2011).
[259] *Hints to Inventors Concerning the Procuring of Patents* (New York: Munn & Co., 1861), 24.
[260] Swanson, "Authoring an Invention," 49.   [261] *Hints to Inventors*, 34.
[262] Beauchamp, *Invented by Law*, 30–31.   [263] Id., 31–32.

world and word" to "a relation between word and word."[264] Court reviews of patent reissues by the Patent Office that revolved around comparing two patent texts, the declining role of the patent model in litigation, and the general jurisprudence of the patent scope all embodied the growing focus on textual strategies.[265] These strategies that fused together technological and legal skills were the domain of the specialized patent lawyer.

In 1879 Alexander Graham Bell bitterly complained about what the Bell team of lawyers led by Chauncey Smith had done to his patent: "They have hacked it to pieces – They have torn it limb from limb – They have plucked out the *heart* of the invention and have thrown it away – They have cast aside as useless all that I thought most valuable. They have subjected my invention to hydraulic pressure from legal minds and have squeezed out *into the gutter* – the very life-blood of the idea. All that remains of my poor specification is – a *little dry dust* – which they blow in my face as the essence of the speaking Telephone!"[266] But Bell was wrong. The lawyers' strategy of focusing on the broad method claim of the Bell patent proved itself. By presenting Bell's invention as creating a whole new field they managed to detach it from the area of telegraphy and portray it as a pioneer one deserving a broad scope of protection. By walking a thin line between claiming natural principles and limiting the claim to a concrete structure, they obtained the corporate security goals of the Bell Company based on dominating a large variety of innovations by competitors. Those were the kinds of benefits that the new breed of specialized patent lawyers wielding their textual weapons were uniquely situated to obtain. The implication, as Bell was told, was that "[a]n inventor is the worst judge of his own case."[267] The age when lawyers tell inventors what they invented had arrived.

In 1907 a distinguished alumnus addressed the graduating class of Lehigh University in Bethlehem, Pennsylvania. The prominent patent lawyer Edwin Prindle titled his address "Patents as Affecting the Young Engineer."[268] Tellingly, he opened its discussion of modern patents with a long description of the art of drafting patent claims. Prindle demonstrated drafting techniques, praised "skillfully drawn" claims, and

[264] Pottage and Sherman, *Figures of Invention*, 125.   [265] Id., 107–25.
[266] Cited in Beauchamp, *Invented by Law*, 65–66.   [267] Id., 66.
[268] Edwin J. Prindle, *Patents as Affecting the Young Engineer: An Address by Edwin J. Prindle M.E. & L.L.M. of the Class of 1890* (1907).

warned against "unfortunately limited" ones.[269] This was hardly a traditional opening for a popular exposition of patents. But the prominent discussion of claims was a sign of the times as well as a manifestation of the speaker's professional identity. In the last quarter of the nineteenth century the textualization of patents entered a new phase marked by a growing strict distinction between the claims and the specification. This shift unfolded gradually in a process that lasted well into the twentieth century, but the fundamental elements were put in place by the 1880s.

Claims – a distinct part of the patent's text, defining the scope of the protected invention – had been used informally since the early nineteenth century and were officially required starting with the 1836 Patent Act.[270] Yet courts did not impute special importance to this text and often reached to the more detailed description in the specification and beyond it to try to capture what they saw as the true invention. The 1876 Supreme Court Decision in *Merrill v. Yeoman* marked the rise of a very different approach to the claims.[271] The patent in the case was for an "improved manufacture" of certain industrial oils. Because the defendant – a dealer who sold the relevant oils – never engaged in manufacture, he could infringe only if the patent was for the product and not for the process of making it. In these circumstances it was in the patentee's interest to argue that the patent was not for the process of manufacture but for the oil itself. It was none other than Chauncey Smith who represented the patentee. Ironically, in a reversal of what would be his successful strategy a few years later in the *Telephone Cases*, he passionately argued that the patent was for a product rather than a process. The argument had a fair chance of success. At the time it was common for courts to reach beyond the exact text of the patent to find "that which was really invented."[272] But Justice Samuel Miller refused to interpret the vague language in the patent in favor of the patentee. He insisted that the claims were of "primary importance" in ascertaining the patented invention and found that the language of the claims in the patent at issue was "far from possessing that precision and clearness of statement with which one who proposes to secure a monopoly at the expense of the public ought

---

[269] Id., 7.
[270] Act of July 4, 1836, ch. 357, 5 Stat. 117, 119, §6. See Karl B. Lutz, "Evolution of the Claims of U.S. Patents" (pt. 1), 20 *J. Pat. Off. Soc'y.* 134, 134–42 (1938); John M. Golden, "Constructing Patents According to Their 'Interpretive Community': A Call for an Attorney-plus-Artisan Perspective," 21 *Harv. J. L. Tech.* 321, 350–51 (2008).
[271] 94 U.S. 568 (1876).   [272] Id., 573.

to describe the thing which no one but himself can use or enjoy."[273]
Although Miller's interpretation of the claims relied in part on the
patent's specification, the decision marked a growing formalization of
the claims. Under the new approach, what mattered was not what a
patentee invented or even what he described in writing. The invention
was to be determined primarily by the stylized textual demarcation of its
boundaries in the claims.

A year later Justice Bradley ruled that patentees "cannot expect the
courts to wade through the history of the art, and spell out what they
might have claimed." Nor could they "show that their invention is
broader than the terms of their claim."[274] This was the foundation of
what would come to be known as "peripheral claiming" – the modern
approach to patents under which the text of the claims is seen as demarcating the outer limits of the invention rather than forming a starting
point for a freewheeling search by courts. Strict adherence to peripheral
claiming would take root only gradually, and the announcements by
some later commentators of the death of the doctrine of equivalents were
premature.[275] Yet it is clear that beginning in the 1870s courts came to
put increasing emphasis on the patent's text. They identified the formalized claim as a textual gravitational center around which any attempt to
identify the invention must revolve. The change is apparent in the practical patent literature. Prior to 1880 one finds only scant and cursory
discussion of claims in such sources, whereas later publications contain
long elaborations of the growing labyrinth of rules pertaining to
constructing and drafting claims.[276]

The rise of claims was rooted in the legalization of patent prosecution.
In the late nineteenth century the Patent Office was increasingly staffed
by personnel with legal backgrounds.[277] Patent agents experienced a
similar process of legalization. While nonlawyers were never banished
from the profession, lawyers increasingly entered the area of patent

---

[273] Id., 570.
[274] *Keystone Bridge Company v. Phoenix Iron Company*, 95 U.S. 274, 279 (1877).
[275] John A. Dienner, "Claims of Patents," 18 *J. Pat. Off. Soc'y.* 389, 403 (1936).
[276] Compare the cursory discussion of claims in Charles Sidney Whitman, *Patent Laws and
Practice of Obtaining Letters Patent for Inventions in the United States and Foreign
Countries*, 2nd ed. (Washington, D.C.: W.H. & O.H. Morrison, 1875), 303–4, with the
much more extensive discussion in George H. Knight, *Patent-Office Manual: Including
the Law and Practice of Cases in the United States Patent Office and the Courts Holding
a Revisory Relation Thereto* (Boston: Little, Brown, 1894), 83–129.
[277] Swanson, "The Emergence of the Professional Patent Practitioner," 542.

prosecution.[278] In *Merrill* Justice Miller wove the legalization of patents into a story of modernization. "The growth of the patent system in the last quarter of a century in this country," he said, "has reached a stage in its progress where the variety and magnitude of the interests involved require accuracy, precision, and care in the preparation of all the papers on which the patent is founded."[279] Miller's account was one of Weberian legal-bureaucratic rationality achieved through formal texts.[280] The patent system had grown into "an organized system, with well-settled rules, supporting itself at once by its utility, and by the wealth which it creates and commands." In this "developed and improved condition" there was no room for "ambiguous language or vague descriptions."[281] In *Keystone Bridge Co.* Justice Bradley similarly described patent prosecution as a bureaucratic process that imposed ordered formal rationality on unruly technological reality. Through this process an inventor's assertion of a technological innovation was converted into a formalized claim that was "examined, scrutinized, limited, and made to conform" to legal rules.[282] This bureaucratic process produced a formal, textual artifact with which subsequent courts and lawyers could work with little direct resort to the realm of technology. This account meshed with a more general judicial ideology of legal formality as an engine of economic growth. Formal legal texts with stable meanings discernible by professional lawyers were seen as the basis for the predictability required for business to thrive.[283] Identifying the invention with the increasingly distinct and formalized text of claims drafted and managed by professionals was the manifestation in the realm of patents of this belief in the symbiosis between bureaucratic rationality and economic prosperity.

Judges tended to combine their new ideology of patent's bureaucratic rationality with the centuries-old theme of wariness of monopolies. The demand for clear and exhaustive claims, Justice Miller said, ensured that "the public should not be deprived of rights supposed to belong to it, without being clearly told what it is that limits these rights."[284]

---

[278] Id., 530–37.   [279] 94 U.S. 573.

[280] Max Weber, *Economy and Society: An Outline of Interpretive Sociology* (New York: Bedminster Press, 1968), 955–58. See also David M. Trubeck, "Max Weber and the Rise of Capitalism," 1972 *Wis. L. Rev.* 720, 739–45 (1972).

[281] 94 U.S. 573.   [282] 95 U.S. 278.

[283] See Morton J. Horwitz, *The Transformation of American Law 1780–1860* (Cambridge, Mass.: Harvard University Press, 1977), 263.

[284] 94 U.S. 573.

Yet the new emphasis on formal textuality did not necessarily limit the scope of patents. Its main effect was to empower the new class of patent professionals. One could obtain patent protection at least as broad as in earlier times as long as skilled professionals correctly used their skills in drafting the claims, prosecuting the patent, and squeezing the most out of its text in subsequent litigation. For most of the nineteenth century patents typically contained one to five claims. By the early twentieth century it was not uncommon to find patents containing hundreds of claims, leading one later commentator to observe that "[w]e are claim ridden in this country."[285]

This climate consolidated the ranks of patent professionals as a separate trade. Its members became the masters of a powerful mystery in the old guild sense: the art of textual creation and manipulation of patent texts. These unique set of skills differentiated patent professionals from both the technological and legal communities in the interface between which they worked. Practical patent literature that started to grow at the end of the nineteenth century taught the mystery to professionals: drafting techniques, construction conventions, bureaucratic maneuvers, and magic words.[286] In 1922 one practical patent manual referred to this new essential body of knowledge as "claimology."[287] The self-flattering image by its author portrayed claim drafting as a "science in itself" subject to "definite and prescribable principles" that could produce identical claims for identical inventions even if drafted by different lawyers.[288] Claimology in this account was a bureaucratized version of Bacon's *Novum Organum*, a set of professional techniques developed and refined in order to bridge the gap between language and nature and accurately capture technological reality. Yet claimology was undeniably a science for hire. The point of the sharpened skills of patent professionals was to navigate the patent system in a way that best served their clients' interests. One drafted or constructed claims not to capture the true heart of an invention, but rather to maximize the scope of

---

[285] Melville Church, "Comments on Recent Articles," 13 *J. Pat. Off. Soc'y.* 459 (1931).
[286] See e.g. Knight, *Patent-Office Manual; Paul Synnestvedt, Notes on Patents and Patent Practice* (Pittsburgh, Pa.: Federal Publishing, 1906); James Love Hopkins, *The Law of Patents and Patent Practice in the Patent Office and the Federal Courts* (Chicago, Ill.: Callaghan, 1911); John Franklin Robe, *Patent Essentials for the Executive, Engineer, Lawyer and Inventor: A Rudimentary and Practical Treatise on the Nature of Patents, the Mechanism of Their Procurement, Scientific Drafting of Patent Claims, Conduct of Cases and Special Proceedings, Including Forms* (New York: Funk & Wagnalls, 1922)
[287] Robe, *Patent Essentials*, 201.   [288] Id., 145.

patent protection or strategically avoid it. All of this was true of patents in general and of all patentees, big or small. But the new formalized rationality of patents fitted the dominant goal of patents as corporate security like a glove. Formalized texts produced through a rationalized bureaucratic process were the tools of large business organizations – themselves increasingly bureaucratized – for seeking predictability and security in the face of economic and technological uncertainty. Professional patent lawyers emerged as a new class of mandarins wielding their specialized textual techniques in the service of these goals. Formally textualized inventions thus became the ultimate form of ownership of intangibles in the age of corporate security.

Conclusion

In February 1888 the Presbyterian clergyman Henry Van Dyke delivered a sermon in Washington, D.C. In the audience were First Lady Frances Cleveland Preston, several congressmen, and Alexander Graham Bell.[1] The topic was "The National Sin of Literary Piracy."[2] The sermon was part of a campaign for international copyright orchestrated by the American Copyright League. Unprecedented in scale and intensity, the campaign included extensive lobbying of congressmen, public readings by prominent authors throughout the nation, a blizzard of pamphlets, and coordinated newspaper articles, as well as a White House reception for authors taking place two months after Van Dyke's sermon.[3] Three years later, in April 1891 President Benjamin Harrison delivered a short address to an impressive group of dignitaries assembled in Washington to launch the three-day-long Patent Centennial Celebration. According to the *Scientific American*, "The notable group of prominent men assembled on the stage of the Lincoln Music Hall Washington, on the afternoon of April 8, at the opening ceremonies of the centennial celebration of the American patent system formed a picture which will live while memory lasts in the minds of all who were fortunate enough to be present, and one to which the brush or pencil of the

---

[1] "International Copyright," *Washington Post*, February 13, 1888, 1.
[2] The sermon was later published as a pamphlet. See Henry Van Dyke, *The National Sin of Literary Piracy* (New York: C. Scribner's Sons, 1888).
[3] Catherine Seville, *The Internationalisation of Copyright Law: Books, Buccaneers and the Black Flag in the Nineteenth Century* (New York: Cambridge University Press, 2006), 228–32.

artist or delineator can do but feeble justice."[4] Intellectual property had attained a prominent place on the national agenda.

When Americans discussed the fundamentals of their intellectual property regime they often harked back to the wisdom and foresight of the Founding Fathers, who laid its foundation in the Constitution. So it was no surprise that when the head of the Patent Office, Charles Elliot Mitchell, followed President Harrison and spoke of the "The Birth and Growth of the American Patent System" he too invoked the framers. But then, breaking with orthodoxy, he went on to say that the "[w]ise and illustrious" framers "had no conception of the importance of what they did." "They thought they were applying the finishing strokes and touches to an edifice which was otherwise completed," Mitchell said, "when they were really at work upon its broad foundations."[5] Mitchell was right. It was not just the scale of the system that had changed unrecognizably since the humble beginnings of 1789. By the end of the nineteenth century Americans had created a conceptual scheme for understanding ownership of intangibles that would have bewildered the founders even as they spoke of literary property or the natural property rights of inventors. This modern idea of intellectual property pervaded and gave meaning to the copyright and patent regimes. The two areas shared many fundamental elements of the modern concept of ownership of intangibles, but they also differed in some important respects.

Most fundamentally, patents and copyrights became rights. Eighteenth-century colonial and state grants of patents and copyrights were discretionary privileges. They were political acts by the sovereign granting tailored privileges to named individuals in return for a specified consideration and justified by their concrete public utility. By contrast, modern patents and copyrights came to be universal rights: a standard bundle of entitlements conferred on anyone who satisfies a set of general criteria as a matter of right and justified on the basis of the public utility of the system as a whole.

The other patterns of the new framework of intellectual property shared by patent and copyright related to the identity and character of the owner, the owned intellectual object, and the nature of ownership. By the late eighteenth century, the new truism of both fields was that intellectual property rights are rooted in the act of individual intellectual creation and therefore belong to the creator – the author or the inventor.

---

[4] "The Patent Centennial Celebration," 64 *Sci. Am.*, 243 (1891).   [5] Id.

Formally, this fundamental principle remained constant. At the dawn of the twentieth century, however, actual legal rules departed markedly from the official principle of authorial ownership in a broad set of cases. Authors and inventors were still the iconic figures of intellectual property owners, but in the ever more pervasive context of employment they were no longer owners. A similar tension characterized the criteria for identifying authorship developed by the law. In copyright originality acquired a prominent status as a fundamental principle of the field even as its substantive content was systemically whittled down until at the turn of the century the bar set by it sometimes approached triviality. The rise of nonobviousness as a fundamental patentability requirement in the last third of the nineteenth century exhibited an attenuated version of the same pattern. Nonobviousness embodied the premise that patents applied only to the handiwork of true inventors who exhibited genius distinct from the skill of the ordinary mechanic. Unlike originality, nonobviousness was not reduced to a triviality and came to play a more central role in the actual demarcation of valid property rights. At the same time, however, the application of nonobviousness was marked by a growing reluctance of courts to engage in substantive evaluations of inventions, resulting in a complex and confusing doctrine.

During the nineteenth century, copyright and patents, originally understood in semi-materialist terms as the ownership of a copy or a machine, developed a concept of a postulated intangible object of ownership. The two fields operationalized this idea in different ways, with patent eventually emphasizing formalized textualized forms of constructing invention. But the basic underlying idea was the same: the work and the invention were conceptualized as an intellectual essence that could take an endless variety of concrete forms. This understanding of the object of property correlated with a new understanding of ownership. Abandoning the older notion of patents and copyrights as limited economic privileges to engage in certain economic activities, intellectual property came to be seen as a general control of the economic exploitation of the intangible owned object. Inventions and works could take many different forms, each representing a stream of market revenue, and ownership meant the right to control this market value, regardless of form or medium. The inevitable expansion and abstraction of private ownership built into this notion of owning intangibles clashed with another fundamental ideological commitment: that knowledge must remain free for all. As a result copyright and patent developed doctrinal and conceptual mechanisms such as the idea/expression dichotomy, the fair use doctrine, or the rule against patenting of natural principles. These mechanisms were used as tools for imposing some boundaries on what otherwise seemed a boundless logic of expansion. Ideologically, they cultivated the assertion that all knowledge remained publicly free even as private exclusionary power expanded in scope and intensity.

What accounts for this elaborate framework of ownership of ideas? As I argue throughout this book, various influences – ideological, economic, intellectual, and political – helped shape different parts of this framework. Zooming out, however, the bigger picture reveals two fundamental elements at work. The modern framework of intellectual property emerged from a clash between eighteenth-century possessive individualism and late-nineteenth-century corporate liberalism over the appropriate modes of understanding and regulating creative innovation as well as allocating power over it. By the end of the eighteenth century, patent and copyright were dominated by a new ideology that combined a vision of romantic authorship and heroic invention with an individualistic conception of property. The institutional forms inherited from the past, however, were forged in another age and were not replaced overnight. The process of giving the abstract ideology of authorial ownership of the product of the mind concrete meaning was gradual and was necessarily mediated by preexisting institutions and new contingencies. As this process unfolded, the material and ideological context changed. Beginning in the second half of the nineteenth century and increasingly so in its last third, a new economic, cultural, and political system had emerged. Big business was the dominant factor in this new climate. Intellectual property thought became increasingly influenced by the interests of big business, by its perceived economic "needs," and by the changed context of producing and exploiting intellectual works. In this new context intellectual innovation was typically seen as a coordinated and hierarchically controlled process. Intellectual works were both inputs necessary for this coordinated process of production and an increasingly commodified output that had to be rationally exploited in any possible market. Intellectual property rights became first and foremost instruments of firms' security – tools for achieving stability and control in the face of the unpredictability of the market. All of this stood in considerable tension with the earlier vision of intellectual property as a thoroughly individualistic right rooted in an idiosyncratic and personal creative act. Yet possessive individualism was not simply supplanted by corporate liberalism in the area of intellectual property. The two continued to coexist uneasily. The individual heroic inventor or romantic author continued to be the official icons of a regime that became increasingly geared toward the interests and needs of a corporate behemoth. The result was a variety of curious syntheses, uneasy compromises, and often outright ideological contradictions.

The basic framework of ownership of ideas that consolidated at the end of the nineteenth century survived throughout the twentieth century, although copyright and patent law experienced many important changes. The pattern of the later development of American copyright is best described as universal particularism. Copyright that started its life as the unique regulation of the book trade had been transformed into a general field based on an abstract principle of ownership of creative expression. The conceptual change went hand in hand with the changing political economy landscape. As new information industries such as photography, recorded music, and motion pictures developed, they identified the potential of copyright and lobbied for inclusion. This trend that started in the late nineteenth century intensified in the following one. Yet the same process that pushed toward universal copyright also generated a constant pull for fragmentation. The official insistence on universalism notwithstanding, each time a new area was brought in, copyright's regulation power was extended to a different set of economic, technological, and social circumstances. Each diverse context came with its own tapestry of groups with crisscrossing interests and ready to take part in the struggle for shaping the law.

Copyright had always been shaped by interest group politics, but in the late nineteenth century a new pattern emerged. The early roots of intellectual property's "industrial pluralism," which Steven Wilf identified with the New Deal, were in this era.[6] In numerous battles, including the late incarnation of the international copyright debate, the news copyright struggle, scuffles over new music markets, and the process leading to the 1909 act, a new pattern of interest group politics solidified.[7] It was characterized by a clear division of interests along industry lines; coordinated and concentrated action on the legislative,

---

[6] Steven Willf, "The Making of the Post-War Paradigm in American Intellectual Property Law," 31 *Colum. J. L. Arts* 139, 175 (2008).

[7] See Seville, *Internationalisation of Copyright Law*, 196–246; Robert Brauneis, "The Transformation of Originality in the Progressive-Era Debate over Copyright in News," 27 *Cardozo Arts Ent. L. J.* 321 (2009–10); Stuart Banner, *American Property: A History of How, Why and What We Own* (Cambridge, Mass.: Harvard University Press, 2011), 109–20.

adjudicative, and public sphere fronts; and a major role played by trade associations. Copyright had officially become both the battleground and the product of industrial society's interest group politics. Lawmakers gradually came to accept, as a political necessity as well as a normative conviction, an image of copyright as a mosaic of compromises between relevant interest groups. New mechanisms were developed to embody these complex compromises through a combination of increasingly intricate statutory provisions, administrative procedures, and private-ordering industry associations. The specific patterns of these arrangements varied greatly because of the contingencies and divisions of power unique to each of the different fields brought under copyright's umbrella. Copyright's twentieth-century development, including the central reform of 1976, was characterized by this dialectics of universal particularism.[8] Ironically, copyright's very presumption of being a unified gigantic empire ever-colonizing new lands resulted in it becoming an archipelago of loosely connected islands.

For a long period, the logic of fragmentation through inclusion was much milder in the area of patent. New industries were absorbed into the field in ways that allowed patent law to maintain at least a semblance of cohesion. Subject matter from the rising chemical industries was handled within patent law through legal concepts of general applicability, such as the prohibition on patents in the "product of nature" and its various exceptions.[9] Living-organism subject matter posed a continuing challenge to fundamental precepts of patentability.[10] For a long time, however, the challenge was kept at bay, partly by the internal doctrines

---

[8] Jessica D. Litman, "Copyright, Compromise, and Legislative History," 72 *Cornell L. Rev.* 857 (1987); Robert P. Merges, "One Hundred Years of Solicitude: Intellectual Property Law, 1900–2000," 88 *Cal. L. Rev.* 2187, 2192–200 (2000); Banner, *American Property*, 120–29; Graeme Austin, "Radio: Early Battles over the Public Performance Right," in Brad Sherman and Leanne Wiseman, eds., *Copyright and the Challenge of the New* (Alphen aan den Rijn: Kluwer Law International, 2012), 115–39.

[9] Christopher Beauchamp, "Patenting Nature: A Problem of History," 16 *Stan. Tech. L. Rev.* 257 (2013); Daniel J. Kelves, "Inventions, Yes; Nature, No: The Products-of-Nature Doctrine from the American Colonies to the U.S. Courts," 23 *Perspectives on Science* 13, 18–20 (2015).

[10] See Banner, *American Property*, 248–51; Alain Pottage and Brad Sherman, *Figures of Invention: A History of Modern Patent Law* (New York: Oxford University Press, 2010), 153–82; Daniel J. Kevles "New Blood, New Fruits: Protection for Breeders and Originators, 1789–1930," in Martha Woodmansee et al., eds., *Making and Unmaking Intellectual Property: Creative Production in Legal and Cultural Perspective* (Chicago, Ill.: University of Chicago Press, 2011), 254.

of patentability and partly by creating a sui generis regime external to general utility patents in the form of the 1930 Plant Protection Act.[11]

The major force shaping the development of twentieth-century patent law was the ebb and flow of the antimonopoly sentiment against patents. In principle, patents were no more or less monopolies than copyrights. Occasionally copyright too was caught in the fire of anti-monopoly as in the early struggle over rights in recorded music at the dawn of the twentieth century or in the later debate over collective licensing in the radio industry.[12] But generally the fear of monopolies cast a much darker and more persistent shadow on patents. Perhaps this was due to a strong ideological legacy of identifying patents with monopolies going back all the way to the 1624 Statute of Monopolies and seventeenth-century English common law. Or maybe it was the fact that patents were perfected into industry-wide tools of control and coordination earlier and on a much more systemic scale compared with copyrights. Whatever the cause, by the late Progressive era courts that were previously unambiguously friendly to uses of patents as tools for industrial control started to change their tune. Patents were now seen as the new frontier of antitrust.[13] A series of court decisions treated patent pooling schemes and other tying arrangements based on patents with suspicion and subjected them to various limitations.[14] The New Deal brought a host of more fundamental challenges to the estab-lished framework of patents. In principle, the intellectual climate of the New Deal was ambivalent about large-scale business, but for many observers patents – or what was seen as abuses of patent power – came to embody the dark side of economic concentration. Thurman Arnold, the head of the Antitrust Division of the Justice Department between 1938 and 1943, decried what he called the "abuse of patents" and marked it as a major target of his agency.[15] This attitude brought about a storm of commissions and reports that criticized various antic-ompetitive uses of patents and recommended taking measures for

[11] Act of May 23, 1930, ch. 312, 46 Stat. 376. See Cary Fowler, "The Plant Patent Act of 1930: A Sociological History of Its Creation," 82 *J. Pat. Trademark Off. Soc'y.* 621 (2000).
[12] Banner, *American Property*, 113–20; Willf, "The Making of the Post-War Paradigm," 176–83.
[13] Willf, "The Making of the Post-War Paradigm," 193–96.
[14] See e.g. *Standard Sanitary Manufacturing Co. v. United States*, 226 U.S. 20 (1912); *Motion Picture Patents Co. v. Universal Film Manufacturing Co.*, 243 U.S. 502 (1917).
[15] Thurman Arnold, "The Abuse of Patents," *Atlantic Monthly*, July 1942, 14.

preventing them.[16] There was a flurry of suggested reforms. Some threatened to upend the basic framework of patents and to alter the concept of property rights it embodied through measures such as restrictions of the owner's licensing power, limitations on patent pooling, extensive compulsory licensing, forfeiture of patents, regulation of prices, and other administrative oversight.[17]

At the end patents weathered the storm with little fundamental change. Aggressive antitrust enforcement forced a hiatus in pooling and tying patent arrangements until new winds started blowing in the area of antitrust thought in the 1970s.[18] But little came out of the far-reaching proposals for legislative reform. Judicial hostility for patents continued to be fairly common into the 1950s and 1960s, especially by New Deal appointees such as Supreme Court Justices William O. Douglas and Hugo Black. This attitude of his brethren provoked Justice Robert H. Jackson to comment in 1949 that "the only patent that is valid is one which this Court has not been able to get its hands on."[19] Yet even patent skeptics relied heavily on the concepts and tools offered by the familiar scheme of patents as intellectual property rights: tightening of the novelty standard, a demanding application of the nonobviousness bar of invention, or textual strategies for narrow claim construction. The basic framework of patents that emerged in the late nineteenth century survived mostly unscathed. Despite remaining hostility, the long process of gradual rehabilitation of patents started with the return to normalcy in the 1950s. The 1952 Patent Act was mostly a restatement and consolidation of existing patent jurisprudence and contained hardly any traces of the more radical reform proposals from the previous decades.[20] Ironically, when one of the measures originally proposed by New Deal reformers as a remedy for patent abuses was implemented in 1982 with the establishment of a specialized federal court for patent appeals, the result was a reinvigorated friendly and accommodating judicial approach to patents.

Patents and copyrights followed their separate paths of development, but both remained largely within the basic conceptual framework of owning intangibles forged by the dawn of the twentieth century. Gradual destabilization brought about by more fundamental challenges started

---

[16] Willf, "The Making of the Post-War Paradigm," 200–202; Larry Owens, "Patents, the 'Frontiers' of American Invention and the Monopoly Committee of 1939: Anatomy of a Discourse," 32 *Technol. Cul.* 1076 (1991).

[17] Willf, "The Making of the Post-War Paradigm," 200–203.   [18] Id., 203.

[19] *Jungerson v. Ostby & Barton Co.*, 335 U.S. 560, 572 (1949).

[20] Act of July 19, 1952, ch. 950, 66 Stat. 792.

to appear toward the end of the century. In copyright the main catalyst was digital information technology and the digital economy as well as political economy built around it. The technology created avenues for massive evasion of copyright laws, unprecedented opportunities for decentralized expressive creativity, and disruptive business models that challenged established industry patterns and exposed latent ambiguities in copyright law. At the same time the new digital technologies spawned new forms of dissemination and consumption of information goods, brought about the rise of new powerful intermediaries in media markets, and created the possibility of unprecedented control through restrictive technology over individual interaction with and consumption of information. Much of the legal response to these challenges – a mix of increasingly draconian protective measures and attempts to balance the interest in the spirit of "industrial pluralism" – has been within the traditional framework of copyright. Yet some actual and proposed legal responses to the challenges of the digital age seem to push copyright beyond its traditional patterns.

In patent law it has been mainly the rise of computer technology and biotechnology that exerted pressure on traditional concepts. Struggles around many different technologies in these areas have reopened forcefully fundamental questions such as what is the appropriate subject matter of private property rights and what are the essential features of the inventive act. The resurgence of various industrial strategies for the use of patents gave rise to new discontent over "patent thickets" and "patent trolls," not unlike the older ones. Since we are in the very midst of these events, it would be too risky to predict whether they will lead to a fundamental change in our intellectual framework of owning ideas. It is safer to observe, however, that whatever changes are in store for this framework, they are taking place through the same process of intellectual bricolage that created it in the past. As we struggle to redefine the appropriate legal infrastructure to govern the production and use of ideas in the information society, our starting points are still the fundamental concepts that were forged over a century ago when eighteenth-century possessive individualism met late-nineteenth-century corporate liberalism.

Index

Index

CPSIA information can be obtained
at www.ICGtesting.com
Printed in the USA
LVHW020323240720
661392LV00013B/303